A·N·N·U·A·L E·D·I·T·I·O·N·S

American Foreign Policy

07/08

Policy

Thirteenth Edition

EDITOR

Glenn P. Hastedt

James Madison University

Glenn Hastedt received his Ph.D. from Indiana University. He is professor of political science at James Madison University, where he teaches courses on U.S. foreign policy, national security policy, and international relations. His special area of interest is on the workings of the intelligence community and the problems of strategic surprise and learning from intelligence failures. In addition to having published articles on these topics, he is the author of *American Foreign Policy: Past, Present, Future*; coauthor of *Dimensions of World Politics*; and editor and contributor to *Controlling Intelligence*. He has also published two volumes of readings, *Toward the Twenty-First Century* and *One World, Many Voices*.

Contemporary Learning Series

2460 Kerper Blvd., Dubuque, IA 52001

Visit us on the Internet
http://www.mhcls.com

Credits

1. **The United States and the World: Strategic Choices**
   Unit photo—Department of Defense photo by Master Sgt. James Bowman, U.S. Air Force
2. **The United States and the World: Regional and Bilateral Relations**
   Unit photo—John Wang/Getty Images
3. **The Domestic Side of American Foreign Policy**
   Unit photo—The McGraw-Hill Companies, Inc./John Flournoy, photographer
4. **The Institutional Context of American Foreign Policy**
   Unit photo—Department of Defense Department photo by PH3 Aaron Burden, USN
5. **The Foreign Policy-Making Process**
   Unit photo—John Hollingsworth/Getty Images
6. **U.S. International Economic Strategy**
   Unit photo—Photo courtesy of Department of State by Basil Shahin
7. **U.S. Military Strategy**
   Unit photo—Public Domain
8. **The Iraq War and Beyond**
   Unit photo—Dept. of Defense photo by Airman 1st Class Kurt Gibbons III, U.S. Air Force

Copyright

Cataloging in Publication Data
Main entry under title: Annual Editions: American Foreign Policy. 2007/2008.
1. U.S. Foreign Relations—Periodicals. I. Hastedt, Glenn P., *comp.* II. Title: American Foreign Policy.
ISBN-13: 978–0–07–339735–1   ISBN-10: 0–07–339735–0   658'.05   ISSN 1075–5225

Thirteenth Edition

Cover image © Department of Defense photo by Helene C. Stikkel and Photos.com
Printed in the United States of America   1234567890QPDQPD987654   Printed on Recycled Paper

Editors/Advisory Board

Members of the Advisory Board are instrumental in the final selection of articles for each edition of ANNUAL EDITIONS. Their review of articles for content, level, currentness, and appropriateness provides critical direction to the editor and staff. We think that you will find their careful consideration well reflected in this volume.

Staff

Preface

This thirteenth edition of *Annual Editions: American Foreign Policy* presents an overview of American foreign policy. Prior to September 11, 2001, the debate over the future of American foreign policy proceeded at a measured pace since few pressing threats to American national security seemed to exist. The foreign policy debate centered on selection strategies and tactics that could guide the United States in the transition period between the end of the cold war and the emergence of a post–cold war era. It was a debate largely conducted in the language of academics and it was one that did not engage large numbers of the American public. All of that has changed. After September 11, the conduct and content of American foreign policy is seen as important by virtually all Americans.

The immediate issue was combating and eradicating terrorism and the geographic focal point was Afghanistan and the target was the Taliban government and Osama bin Laden's al Qaeda terrorist organization. Few quarreled with the merits of this military undertaking either in the United States or abroad. This was not true for the Bush administration's next major foreign policy initiative when the war against terrorism was expanded to Iraq with the objective of removing Saddam Hussein from power. This successful military action was followed by an occupation marked by violence and political turmoil. Additional international challenges surfaced in short order; the most noteworthy being revelations concerning the North Korean and Iranian nuclear programs, and growing conflict over trade and monetary matters with China. As a consequence we are now witnessing a wide ranging debate over the strategic and tactical choices open to the United States in an era when it is the dominant (and some would say unchallenged) world power. To date this debate has produced far more questions than it has answers and it extends beyond questions of responding to terrorism and Iraq.

Annual Editions: American Foreign Policy 07/08 is divided into eight units. The first unit addresses questions of grand strategy. The second unit focuses on selected regional and bilateral relations. In the third unit, our attention shifts inward to the ways in which domestic forces affect the content of American foreign policy. The fourth unit looks at the institutions that make American foreign policy. In the fifth unit, the process by which American foreign policy is made is illustrated through accounts of recent foreign policy decisions. The sixth and seventh units provide an overview of the economic and military issues confronting the United States today. The final unit looks in depth at the issues surrounding the war in Iraq and its aftermath from a variety of different perspectives.

Together the readings in these eight units provide students with an up-to-date overview of key events in American foreign policy, the forces that shape it, and the policy problems on the agenda. The essays were chosen for their ability to inform students and spark debate. They are not designed to advance any particular interpretation of American foreign policy.

I would like to thank Ian Nielsen for supporting the concept of *Annual Editions: American Foreign Policy* many years ago. Also deserving of thanks are the many people at McGraw-Hill/Contemporary Learning Series who worked to make the project a success and those faculty on the Advisory Board who provided input on the selection of articles. In the end, the success of *Annual Editions: American Foreign Policy* depends upon the views of the faculty and students who use it. I encourage you to let me know what worked and what did not so that each successive volume will be better than its predecessor. Please complete and return the postage-paid *article rating form* at the end of this book.

Glenn Hastedt

Glenn Hastedt
Editor

Contents

UNIT 1
The United States and the World: Strategic Choices

The concepts in bold italics are developed in the article. For further expansion, please refer to the Topic Guide and the Index.

UNIT 2
The United States and the World: Regional and Bilateral Relations

The concepts in bold italics are developed in the article. For further expansion, please refer to the Topic Guide and the Index.

UNIT 3
The Domestic Side of American Foreign Policy

UNIT 4
The Institutional Context of American Foreign Policy

The concepts in bold italics are developed in the article. For further expansion, please refer to the Topic Guide and the Index.

UNIT 5
The Foreign Policy Making Process

The concepts in bold italics are developed in the article. For further expansion, please refer to the Topic Guide and the Index.

UNIT 6
U.S. International Economic Strategy

UNIT 7
U.S. Military Strategy

The concepts in bold italics are developed in the article. For further expansion, please refer to the Topic Guide and the Index.

UNIT 8
The Iraq War and Beyond

The concepts in bold italics are developed in the article. For further expansion, please refer to the Topic Guide and the Index.

The concepts in bold italics are developed in the article. For further expansion, please refer to the Topic Guide and the Index.

Topic Guide

This topic guide suggests how the selections in this book relate to the subjects covered in your course. You may want to use the topics listed on these pages to search the Web more easily.

On the following pages a number of Web sites have been gathered specifically for this book. They are arranged to reflect the units of this *Annual Edition*. You can link to these sites by going to the student online support site at *http://www.mhcls.com/online/*.

ALL THE ARTICLES THAT RELATE TO EACH TOPIC ARE LISTED BELOW THE BOLD-FACED TERM.

Afghanistan
3. The Dilemma of the Last Sovereign
7. The United States and Russia in Central Asia: Uzbekistan, Tajikistan, Afghanistan, Pakistan, and Iran

Africa
13. China's Africa Strategy

Alliances
2. Hegemony on the Cheap
3. The Dilemma of the Last Sovereign
5. Strategic Fatigue
29. Base Politics
31. A Nuclear Posture for Today

American values
2. Hegemony on the Cheap
14. The Author of Liberty: Religion and U.S. Foreign Policy
15. The Tipping Points
21. The Need for a Military Draft: Protecting Superpower Status
22. Checks, Balances, and Wartime Detainees
23. Law, Liberty and War

Arab-Israeli conflict
1. Grand Strategy in the Second Term

Arms control
9. The Fallout of a Nuclear North Korea
31. A Nuclear Posture for Today
32. A Modest Proposal
33. Apocalypse Soon
34. When Could Iran Get the Bomb?

Asia
3. The Dilemma of the Last Sovereign
8. China's Response to the Bush Doctrine
9. The Fallout of a Nuclear North Korea
10. America's New Strategic Partner
13. China's Africa Strategy
26. America's Sticky Power

Bush, George W.
1. Grand Strategy in the Second Term
2. Hegemony on the Cheap
3. The Dilemma of the Last Sovereign
4. The Eagle Has Crash Landed
5. Strategic Fatigue
8. China's Response to the Bush Doctrine
11. The U.S. and Latin America Through the Lens of Empire
14. The Author of Liberty: Religion and U.S. Foreign Policy
17. The Return of the Imperial Presidency?
18. The Truman Standard
23. Law, Liberty and War
24. Words vs. Deeds: President George W. Bush and Polling
25. The Pros from Dover
31. A Nuclear Posture for Today
33. Apocalypse Soon

Central Asia
7. The United States and Russia in Central Asia: Uzbekistan, Tajikistan, Afghanistan, Pakistan, and Iran
8. China's Response to the Bush Doctrine
29. Base Politics

Central Intelligence Agency
4. The Eagle Has Crash Landed
19. In Defense of Striped Pants
20. Great Expectations: Intelligence as Savior
30. The Terrorism Index

China
3. The Dilemma of the Last Sovereign
6. Exploiting Rivalries: Putin's Foreign Policy
8. China's Response to the Bush Doctrine
9. The Fallout of a Nuclear North Korea
13. China's Africa Strategy
16. Trade Talk
26. America's Sticky Power
27. The New Axis of Oil
31. A Nuclear Posture for Today
32. A Modest Proposal
40. Contemplating the Ifs

Clinton, Bill
1. Grand Strategy in the Second Term
2. Hegemony on the Cheap
14. The Author of Liberty: Religion and U.S. Foreign Policy
24. Words vs. Deeds: President George W. Bush and Polling
31. A Nuclear Posture for Today

Cold war
1. Grand Strategy in the Second Term
2. Hegemony on the Cheap
18. The Truman Standard
23. Law, Liberty and War
31. A Nuclear Posture for Today

Congress
15. The Tipping Points
17. The Return of the Imperial Presidency?
19. In Defense of Striped Pants
22. Checks, Balances, and Wartime Detainees
23. Law, Liberty and War

Defense department
19. In Defense of Striped Pants
21. The Need for a Military Draft: Protecting Superpower Status
28. Requiem for the Bush Doctrine

Democratization
1. Grand Strategy in the Second Term
2. Hegemony on the Cheap
3. The Dilemma of the Last Sovereign
5. Strategic Fatigue
13. China's Africa Strategy

Internet References

The following Internet sites have been carefully researched and selected to support the articles found in this reader. The easiest way to access these selected sites is to go to our student online support site at *http://www.mhcls.com/online/*.

AE: American Foreign Policy 07/08

The following sites were available at the time of publication. Visit our Web site—we update our student online support site regularly to reflect any changes.

General Sources

Avalon Project at Yale Law School
http://www.yale.edu/lawweb/avalon/terrorism/terror.htm

The Avalon Project website feaures documents in the fields of law, history, economics, diplomacy, politics, government, and terrorism.

Center for Strategic and International Studies (CSIS)
http://www.csis.org

The Center for Strategic and International Studies (CSIS), which is a nonpatisan organization, has been dedicated to providing world leaders with strategic insights on, and policy solutions to, current and emerging global issues for 40 years. Currently, CSIS has responded to global terrorism threats by developing a variety of well-defined projects and responses that are available at this site.

The Federal Web Locator
http://www.lib.auburn.edu/madd/docs/fedloc.html

Use this handy site as a launching pad for the Web sites of federal U.S. agencies, departments, and organizations. It is well organized and easy to use for informational and research purposes.

Foreign Affairs
http://www.foreignaffairs.org

The *Foreign Affairs* site allows users to search the magazine's archives and provides access to the field's leading journals, documents, online resources, and so on. Links to dozens of other related Web sites are possible from here.

International Information Programs
http://usinfo.state.gov

This wide-ranging page offered by the State Department provides definitions, related documentation, and a discussion of topics of concern to students of foreign policy and foreign affairs. It addresses today's hot topics as well as ongoing issues that form the foundation of the field. Many Web links are provided.

Oneworld.net
http://www.oneworld.net/section/partners/

Search this site for information and news about issues related to human sustainable development throughout the world. Information is available by topic or by country.

United Nations Home Page
http://www.un.org

Here is the gateway to information about the United Nations.

U.S. International Affairs
http://www.state.gov/www/regions/internat.html

Data on U.S. foreign policy around the world are available here. Some of the areas covered are arms control, economics and trade, international organizations, environmental issues, terrorism, current treaties, and international women's issues.

UNIT 1: The United States and the World: Strategic Choices

The Bulletin of the Atomic Scientists
http://www.bullatomsci.org

This site allows you to read more about the Doomsday Clock and other issues as well as topics related to nuclear weaponry, arms control, and disarmament.

The Henry L. Stimson Center
http://www.stimson.org

The Stimson Center, a nonprofit and (self-described) nonpartisan organization, focuses on issues where policy, technology, and politics intersect. Use this site to find assessments of U.S. foreign policy in the post-cold war world and to research many other topics.

International Network Information Center at University of Texas
http://inic.utexas.edu

This gateway has many pointers to international sites, organized into African, Asian, Latin American, Middle East, and Russian and East European subsections.

ISN International Relations and Security Network
http://www.isn.ethz.ch

Maintained by the Center for Security Studies and Conflict Research, this site is a clearinghouse for information on international relations and security policy. The many topics are listed by category (Traditional Dimensions of Security and New Dimensions of Security) and by major world regions.

UNIT 2: The United States and the World: Regional and Bilateral Relations

Inter-American Dialogue (IAD)
http://www.iadialog.org

This IAD Web site provides data on U.S. policy analysis, communication, and exchange in Western Hemisphere affairs. The organization has helped to shape the agenda of issues and choices in hemispheric relations.

Political Science RESOURCES
http://www.psr.keele.ac.uk/psr.htm

This is a link to sources available via European addresses. Listed by country name, it includes official government pages, official documents, speeches, elections, and political events.

Russian and East European Network Information Center
http://reenic.utexas.edu/reenic/index.html

Information ranging from women's issues to foreign relations and coverage of more than two dozen countries in Central and Eastern Europe and western Asia may be found here. Also check out University of Texas/Austin's site on Broader Asia (*http://asnic.utexas.edu/asnic/index.html*) for more insight into bilateral/regional relations.

World Wide Web Virtual Library: International Affairs Resources

http://www.etown.edu/vl/

Extensive links are available here to help you learn about specific countries and regions, to research for various think tanks, and to study such vital topics as international law, development, the international economy, human rights, and peacekeeping.

UNIT 3: The Domestic Side of American Foreign Policy

American Diplomacy

http://www.unc.edu/depts/diplomat/

American Diplomacy is an online journal of commentary, analysis, and research on U.S. foreign policy and its results around the world. It provides discussion and information on current news, such topics as Life in the Foreign Service, and A Look Back.

Carnegie Endowment for International Peace (CEIP)

http://www.ceip.org

One of the most important goals of CEIP is to stimulate discussion and learning among both experts and the public on a range of international issues. This site provides links to the magazine *Foreign Policy,* to the Carnegie Moscow Center, and to descriptions of various programs.

RAND

http://www.rand.org

RAND, a nonprofit institution that works to improve public policy through research and analysis, offers links to certain topics and descriptions of RAND activities as well as major research areas (such as international relations and strategic defense policy).

UNIT 4: The Institutional Context of American Foreign Policy

Central Intelligence Agency (CIA)

http://www.cia.gov

Use this official CIA page to learn about many facets of the agency and to connect to other sites and resources.

The NATO Integrated Data Service (NIDS)

http://www.nato.int/structur/nids/nids.htm

NIDS was created to bring information on security-related matters within easy reach of the widest possible audience. Check out this Web site to review North Atlantic Treaty Organization documentation of all kinds, to read *NATO Review* magazine, and to explore key issues in the field of European security and transatlantic cooperation.

U.S. Department of State

http://www.state.gov/index.html

This State Department page is a must for any student of foreign affairs. Explore this site to find out what the department does, what services it provides, what it says about U.S. interests around the world, and much more.

United States Institute of Peace (USIP)

http://www.usip.org

The USIP, which was created by Congress to promote peaceful resolution of international conflicts, seeks to educate people and disseminate information on how to achieve peace.

U.S. White House

http://www.whitehouse.gov

This official Web page for the White House includes information on the President and Vice President and What's New. See especially The Virtual Library and Briefing Room for Hot Topics and latest Federal Statistics.

UNIT 5: The Foreign Policy Making Process

Belfer Center for Science and International Affairs (BCSIA)

http://ksgwww.harvard.edu/csia/

BCSIA is the hub of the John F. Kennedy School of Government's research, teaching, and training in international affairs and is related to security, environment, and technology. This site provides insight into the development of leadership in policy making.

The Heritage Foundation

http://www.heritage.org

This page offers discussion about and links to many sites of the Heritage Foundation and other organizations having to do with foreign policy and foreign affairs.

National Archives and Records Administration (NARA)

http://www.archives.gov/index.html

This official site, which oversees the management of all federal records, offers easy access to background information for students interested in the policy-making process, including a search of federal documents and speeches, and much more.

U.S. Department of State: The Network of Terrorism

http://usinfo.state.gov/products/pubs/

This Web site offers complete coverage from the American government's viewpoint regarding the war against terrorism. It provides a wealth of first-hand documentation and evidence.

UNIT 6: U.S. International Economic Strategy

International Monetary Fund (IMF)

http://www.imf.org

This Web site is essential reading for anyone wishing to learn more about this important body's effects on foreign policy and the global economy. It provides information about the IMF, directs readers to various publications and current issues, and suggests links to other organizations.

United States Agency for International Development

http://www.usaid.gov/

Information is available here about broad and overlapping issues such as agriculture, democracy and governance, health, economic growth, and the environment in many regions and countries around the world.

United States Trade Representative

http://www.ustr.gov

The mission of the U.S. Trade Representative is presented on this site. Background information on international trade agreements and links to other sites may be accessed.

World Bank

http://www.worldbank.org

News (including press releases, summaries of new projects, and speeches), publications, and coverage of numerous topics regarding development, countries, and regions are provided at this Web site. It also contains links to other important global financial organizations.

UNIT 7: U.S. Military Strategy

Arms Control and Disarmament Agency (ACDA)

http://dosfan.lib.uic.edu/acda/

This archival ACDA page provides links to information on arms control and disarmament. Researchers can examine texts of various speeches, treaties, and historical documents. For further current information, go to the Bureau of Arms Control page at *http://state.gov/t/ac/*.

Counterterrorism Page

http://counterterrorism.com

A summary of worldwide terrorism events, groups, and terrorism strategies and tactics, including articles from 1989 to the present of American and international origin, plus links to related Web sites and graphs are available on this site.

DefenseLINK

http://www.defenselink.mil/news/

Learn about the Department of Defense at this site. News, publications, photos, and other related sites of interest are noted.

Federation of American Scientists (FAS)

http://www.fas.org

FAS, a nonprofit policy organization, maintains this site to provide coverage of such topics as terrorism and weapons of mass destruction.

Human Rights Web

http://www.hrweb.org

The history of the human rights movement, text on seminal figures, landmark legal and political documents, and ideas on how individuals can get involved in helping to protect human rights around the world can be found here.

UNIT 8: The Iraq War and Beyond

White House: Renewal in Iraq

http://www.whitehouse.gov/infocus/iraq/

View official White House reports, including presidential remarks, on this site.

We highly recommend that you review our Web site for expanded information and our other product lines. We are continually updating and adding links to our Web site in order to offer you the most usable and useful information that will support and expand the value of your Annual Editions. You can reach us at: *http://www.mhcls.com/annualeditions/*.

UNIT 1

The United States and the World: Strategic Choices

Unit Selections

1. **Grand Strategy in the Second Term**, John Lewis Gaddis
2. **Hegemony on the Cheap**, Colin Dueck
3. **The Dilemma of the Last Sovereign**, Zbigniew Brzezinski
4. **The Eagle Has Crash Landed**, Immanuel Wallerstein
5. **Strategic Fatigue**, Graham E. Fuller

Key Points to Consider

• Make a scorecard of the successes and failures of the Bush administration's foreign policy to date. Defend your choices and explain why these policies turned out as they did.

• How powerful is the United States today? How should it use this power?

• Make a list of the five most important foreign policy problems facing the United States today. Defend your choices and explain why you ranked them in this order.

• Has the United States become a rogue superpower? Defend your answer.

• What principles do you think should guide American foreign policy in the future?

• How much and what type of responsibility does the United States have for maintaining world order?

• How helpful is the past as a guide to the future in constructing foreign policy strategies?

Student Web Site

www.mhcls.com/online

Internet References

Further information regarding these Web sites may be found in this book's preface or online.

The Bulletin of the Atomic Scientists
http://www.bullatomsci.org

The Henry L. Stimson Center
http://www.stimson.org

International Network Information Center at University of Texas
http://inic.utexas.edu

ISN International Relations and Security Network
http://www.isn.ethz.ch

Choice in foreign policy is always present. The September 11, 2001, terrorist attacks on the World Trade Center and the Pentagon did not change this reality. The strong sense of national unity that followed these attacks momentarily quieted the debate on the proper conduct and content of American foreign policy but it did not end it. This debate was renewed as the George W. Bush administration moved toward war with Iraq and it emerged with new force as the United States entered into a period of occupation and reconstruction in Iraq. While much of the current debate is highly politicized we also see the outlines of a more far-reaching conceptual discussion about the shape of the future world that the United States wishes to see come into existence and how to bring it about.

The strategic debate today is different from the debate that long dominated the scene. For much of the cold war, the foreign policy debate focused on tactics. A consensus had formed around the policy of containment. But there were still choices. Rolling back the iron curtain was a minority view during the 1950s and cooperation with the Soviet Union was advocated by some during the immediate post-World War II period. In the late 1960s, détente emerged as a serious competitor to containment and succeeded in supplanting it for a brief period of time.

No single vision of American foreign policy emerged as dominant in the first decade of the post-cold war era. For some, the 1990s provided the United States with the long-awaited opportunity to walk away from the distracting and corrupting influence of international affairs and focus instead on domestic concerns and embrace traditional American values. For others, the 1990s represented a moment to be seized. Adherents to this perspective were divided over how to proceed. One group advocated replacing the strategies of conflict and confrontation of the cold war with ones designed to foster cooperation among states and to lift the human condition. A second group saw it as an opportunity to reorder the world in America's image–for it had won the cold war.

When he entered office, George W. Bush's administration's early initiatives suggested it would pursue a foreign policy based on unilateralist principles and favoring disengagement from global problem-solving efforts. This was evidenced in its withdrawal from the Kyoto protocol, and its stated desire to extract the United States from involvement in the Balkans, negotiations with North Korea, and brokering a Middle East peace accord. Pursuit of a national ballistic missile defense system in face of global opposition further reinforced this perception.

The terrorist attacks of September 11 forced the Bush administration to reexamine its approach to foreign policy. Still pragmatic, there now is also present a strong sense of missionary zeal. Still unilateralist at heart, the administration now confronts demands that it work with the broader international community in order to achieve its foreign policy goals. Still reluctant to play the role of global policeman, it finds itself drawn much more deeply into regional and global disputes. The result has been a foreign policy that often seems at war with itself. At the same time it is

self-confident, if not defiant, yet often appears to stumble as it moves forward.

The essays in this unit introduce us to the scope of the contemporary debate over the strategic choices open to the United States. The first article, "Grand Strategy in the Second Term" by John Lewis Gaddis asserts that the fundamental outlines of the Bush administration's first term foreign policy will be and should be continued. What is needed are modest midcourse corrections. The other essays in this section provide critiques of the administration's strategy. In "Hegemony on the Cheap," Colin Dueck criticizes Bush's pursuit of an ambitious Wilsonian agenda without adequate resources. Bush is not the first Wilsonian to error in this regard argues Dueck. "The Dilemma of the Last Sovereign" by former national security advisor Zbigniew Brzezinski contends that for most states sovereignty today is little more than a legal fiction. He identifies the United States as the last remaining sovereign state but fears that American efforts to perpetuate its sovereignty may end up threatening American security and undermining civil liberties at home. The next article, "The Eagle Has Crash Landed," raises the possibility that the United States has become a powerless superpower. The final essay, "Strategic Fatigue," argues that a universal problem has befallen the Bush administration. As a result the United States is moving toward imperial overreach and in the process threatens to tarnish the very values it seeks to promote.

Grand Strategy in the Second Term

John Lewis Gaddis

Reconsiderations

Second terms in the White House open the way for second thoughts. They provide the least awkward moment at which to replace or reshuffle key advisers. They lessen, although nothing can remove, the influence of domestic political considerations, since re-elected presidents have no next election to worry about. They enhance authority, as allies and adversaries learn—whether with hope or despair—with whom they will have to deal for the next four years. If there is ever a time for an administration to evaluate its own performance, this is it.

George W. Bush has much to evaluate: he has presided over the most sweeping redesign of U.S. grand strategy since the presidency of Franklin D. Roosevelt. The basis for Bush's grand strategy, like Roosevelt's, comes from the shock of surprise attack and will not change. None of F.D.R.'s successors, Democrat or Republican, could escape the lesson he drew from the events of December 7, 1941: that distance alone no longer protected Americans from assaults at the hands of hostile states. Neither Bush nor his successors, whatever their party, can ignore what the events of September 11, 2001, made clear: that deterrence against states affords insufficient protection from attacks by gangs, which can now inflict the kind of damage only states fighting wars used to be able to achieve. In that sense, the course for Bush's second term remains that of his first one: the restoration of security in a suddenly more dangerous world.

Setting a course, however, is only a starting point for strategies: experience always reshapes them as they evolve. Bush has been rethinking his strategy for some time now, despite his reluctance during the campaign to admit mistakes. With a renewed and strengthened electoral mandate, he will find it easier to make midcourse corrections. The best way to predict their extent is to compare what his administration intended with what it has so far accomplished. The differences suggest where changes will—or at least should—take place.

Pre-Emption and Prevention

The narrowest gap between Bush's intentions and his accomplishments has to do with preventing another major attack on the United States. Of course, one could occur at any moment, even between the completion of this article and its publication. But the fact that more than three years have passed without such an attack is significant. Few Americans would have thought it likely in the immediate aftermath of September 11. The prevailing view then was that a terrorist offensive was underway, and that the nation would be fortunate to get through the next three months without a similar or more serious blow being struck.

Connecting causes with consequences is always difficult—all the more so when we know so little of Osama bin Laden's intentions or those of his followers. Perhaps al Qaeda planned no further attacks. Perhaps it anticipated that the United States would retaliate by invading Afghanistan and deposing the Taliban. Perhaps it foresaw U.S. military redeployments from Saudi Arabia to Afghanistan, Uzbekistan, Kyrgyzstan, and Iraq. Perhaps it expected a worldwide counterterrorist campaign to roll up substantial portions of its network. Perhaps it predicted that the Bush administration would abandon its aversion to nation building and set out to democratize the Middle East. Perhaps bin Laden's strategy allowed for all of this, but that seems unlikely. If it did not, then the first and most fundamental feature of the Bush strategy—taking the offensive against the terrorists and thereby surprising them—has so far accomplished its purposes.

A less obvious point follows concerning pre-emption and prevention, a distinction that arose from hypothetical hot-war planning during the Cold War. "Pre-emption" meant taking military action against a state that was about to launch an attack; international law and practice had long allowed such actions to forestall clear and immediately present dangers. "Prevention" meant starting a war against a state that might, at some future point, pose such risks. In mounting its post–September 11 offensive, the Bush administration conflated these terms, using the word "pre-emption" to justify what turned out to be a preventive" war against Saddam Hussein's Iraq.

It did so on the grounds that, in a post–September 11 world, both terrorists and tyrants threatened the security of the United States. Al Qaeda could not have acted without the support and sanctuary the Taliban provided. But the traditional warnings governments had used to justify pre-emption—the massing of armed forces in such a way as to confirm aggressive intent—would not have detected the September 11 attacks before they took place. Decisions made, or at least circumstances tolerated, by a shadowy regime in a remote country halfway around the world produced an act of war that killed more Americans than the one committed six decades earlier by Japan, a state known at the time to pose the clearest and most present of dangers.

Pre-emption in its older and narrower sense might have worked against the Japanese fleet as it approached Pearl Harbor—had it been detected in time. Pre-emptive arrests would have stopped Mohammed Atta and his 18 co-conspirators as they approached their respective airports if it had been possible to read their minds. No nation's safety, however, can depend on such improbable intelligence breakthroughs: as the Pearl Harbor historian Roberta Wohlstetter pointed out years ago and as the *9/11 Commission Report* has now confirmed, detecting telltale signals in a world full of noise requires not just skill, but also extraordinary luck.

That is why the Bush administration's strategists broadened "pre-emption" to include the Cold War meaning of "prevention." To wait for terrorist threats to become clear and present was to leave the nation vulnerable to surprise attacks. Instead, the United States would go after states that had harbored, or that might be harboring, terrorist gangs. It would at first seek to contain or deter such regimes the familiar means by which the Cold War had been fought—but if those methods failed, it reserved the right to pre-empt perceived dangers by starting a preventive war.

The old distinction between pre-emption and prevention, therefore, was one of the many casualties of September 11. That event revealed a category of threats so difficult to detect and yet so devastating if carried out that the United States had little choice but to use preemptive means to prevent their emergence. John Kerry made it clear during the 2004 campaign that he would not have relinquished that option had he won the presidency. His successful opponent certainly will not do so, nor are his successors likely to. This feature of the Bush grand strategy is here to stay.

Speaking More Softly—and More Clearly

Pre-emption defined as prevention, however, runs the risk amply demonstrated over the past two years—that the United States itself will appear to much of the world as a clear and present danger. Sovereignty has long been a sacrosanct principle in the international system. For the world's most powerful state suddenly to announce that its security requires violating the sovereignty of certain other states whenever it chooses cannot help but make all other states nervous. As the political scientist G. John Ikenberry has pointed out, Washington's policy of pre-emption has created the image of a global policeman who reports to no higher authority and no longer allows locks on citizens' doors. However shocking the September 11 attacks may have been, the international community has not found it easy to endorse the Bush administration's plan for regaining security.

Bush and his advisers anticipated this problem. After brushing aside offers of help in Afghanistan from NATO allies, the administration worked hard to win multilateral support for its first act of pre-emption for preventive purposes: the invasion of Iraq. It expected success. After all, who, apart from the United States, could organize the overthrow of Saddam Hussein, a dictator who had abused his people, started wars, flouted UN resolutions, supported terrorists, and, in the view of intelligence agencies everywhere, probably possessed weapons of mass destruction (WMD)? The use of U.S. power to depose such a monster, Bush's strategists assumed, would be welcomed, not feared.

They were wrong. The war in Iraq gained far less international support than the administration had anticipated. One can debate at length the reasons why: the outdated structure of the UN Security Council, which better reflected the power balance of 1945 than 2003; the appearance Bush gave of having decided to go to war with or without that body's consent; the difficulty of establishing a credible connection between Saddam Hussein and al Qaeda; the absence of incontrovertible evidence that the Iraqi dictator really did have WMD; the distrust that lingered from Bush's unnecessarily harsh rejections of the Kyoto Protocol, the International Criminal Court, and the Anti-Ballistic Missile Treaty. Whatever the

explanation, his strategy of pre-emption by consent did not get consent, and this was a major failure.

President Bush's decision to invade Iraq anyway provoked complaints that great power was being wielded without great responsibility, followed by an unprecedented collapse of support for the United States abroad. From nearly universal sympathy in the weeks after September 11, Americans within a year and a half found their country widely regarded as an international pariah.

It is easy to say that this does not matter—that a nation as strong as the United States need not worry about what others think of it. But that simply is not true. To see why, compare the American and Soviet spheres of influence in Europe during the Cold War. The first operated with the consent of those within it. The second did not, and that made an enormous difference quite unrelated to the military strength each side could bring to bear in the region. The lesson here is clear: influence, to be sustained, requires not just power but also the absence of resistance, or, to use Clausewitz's term, "friction." Anyone who has ever operated a vehicle knows the need for lubrication, without which the vehicle will sooner or later grind to a halt. This is what was missing during the first Bush administration: a proper amount of attention to the equivalent of lubrication in strategy, which is persuasion.

The American claim of a broadly conceived right to pre-empt danger is not going to disappear, because no other nation or international organization will be prepared anytime soon to assume that responsibility. But the need to legitimize that strategy is not going to go away, either; otherwise, the friction it generates will ultimately defeat it, even if its enemies do not. What this means is that the second Bush administration will have to try again to gain multilateral support for the pre-emptive use of U.S. military power.

Doing so will not involve giving anyone else a veto over what the United States does to ensure its security and to advance its interests. It will, however, require persuading as large a group of states as possible that these actions will also enhance, or at least not degrade, their own interests. The United States did that regularly—and highly successfully—during World War II and the Cold War. It also obtained international consent for the use of predominantly American military force in the 1991 Persian Gulf War, in Bosnia in 1995, in Kosovo in 1999, and in Afghanistan in 2001. Iraq has been the exception, not the rule, and there are lessons to be learned from the anomaly.

One is the need for better manners. It is always a bad idea to confuse power with wisdom: muscles are not brains. It is never a good idea to insult potential allies, however outrageous their behavior may have been. Nor is it wise to regard consultation as the endorsement of a course already set. The Bush administration was hardly the first to commit these errors. It was the first, however, to commit so many so often in a situation in which help from friends could have been so useful.

Another lesson relates to language. The president and his advisers preferred flaunting U.S. power to explaining its purpose. To boast that one possesses and plans to maintain "strengths beyond challenge" may well be accurate, but it mixes arrogance with vagueness, an unsettling combination. Strengths for what purpose? Challenges from what source? Cold War presidents were careful to answer such questions. Bush, during his first term, too often left it to others to guess the answers. In his second, he will have to provide them.

A final and related lesson concerns vision. The terrorists of September 11 exposed vulnerabilities in the defenses of all states. Unless these are repaired, and unless those who would exploit them are killed, captured, or dissuaded, the survival of the state system itself could be at stake. Here lies common ground, for unless that multinational interest is secured, few other national interests—convergent or divergent can be. Securing the state will not be possible without the option of pre-emptive military action to prevent terrorism from taking root. It is a failure of both language and vision that the United States has yet to make its case for pre-emption in these terms.

Iraq is Not Vietnam

The Bush administration believed that it could invade Iraq without widespread consent because it expected a replay of the Afghanistan experience: military resistance would quickly evaporate, Iraqis would welcome the Americans and their allies, and the victorious coalition would quickly install an Iraqi regime capable of controlling and rebuilding the country. Success on the ground, together with confirmation that Saddam Hussein did indeed have WMD, would yield the consensus that diplomacy had failed to produce. The occupation of Iraq would become a broadly supported international effort, even if the invasion had not been.

The military campaign proceeded as anticipated, but nothing else did. Enough troops were deployed to defeat the Iraqi army, but not to restore order, suppress looting, and protect critical infrastructure. Iraqis did not step forward to form a new government, however grateful they may have been to have their old one removed. Pentagon planners misjudged how quickly many Iraqis would begin to see their liberators as oppressors. They even hastened that process through a laissez-faire attitude toward the rights of prisoners that produced sickening abuses. WMD were not found. And the expanded multilateral assistance Bush had hoped for in running the occupation never arrived. To note gaps between intentions and accomplishments in Iraq is to understate: they littered the landscape.

The Bush administration has been scrambling ever since to close those gaps. It has done so with an indecisiveness that is quite at odds with its normal method of operation: it has seemed, far too often, simply not to know what to do. As a consequence, it has come close, more than once, to losing the initiative in Iraq. Visions of a Vietnam-like quagmire have begun to loom.

Such visions are, however, premature. After a year and a half of fighting, U.S. casualties in Iraq have yet to exceed what the monthly total in the Vietnam War frequently was. Iraqi losses, although much greater, are nowhere near what the Vietnamese suffered. The insurgents receive far less external aid than the Soviet Union and China provided to the North Vietnamese and the Viet Cong. There is no Iraqi equivalent to Ho Chi Minh: Iraq's division among Sunnis, Shia, and Kurds has created a balance of antagonisms, not a unified resistance.

It is also the case that the U.S. military tends to learn from its mistakes. Historians now acknowledge that American counterinsurgency operations in Vietnam were succeeding during the final years of that conflict; the problem was that support for the war had long since crumbled at home. Military learning is also taking place in Iraq, but the domestic opposition is not even approaching Vietnam-era proportions: 2004 was nothing like 1968. There is still time, then, to defeat the insurgency—even though the insurgents are no doubt also learning from their own mistakes.

Victory, in the end, will go to the side that can rally the "silent majority" of Iraqis who have so far not taken sides. Here an advantage lies with the Americans and their allies, for they can offer elections. The insurgents cannot. Opportunities to vote in equally dangerous circumstances—in El Salvador, Cambodia, and most recently Afghanistan—have punctured the pretensions of terrorists by diminishing the fears on which they depend. There are, to be sure, no guarantees. Elections could produce governments that are weak, incompetent, unrepresentative, brutal, or even fanatically opposed to the occupiers themselves. The risks of holding them, however, are preferable to the alternatives of swamping Iraq with U.S. troops or abandoning it altogether.

And what if the United States, despite its best efforts, ultimately fails in Iraq? It is only prudent to have plans in place in case that happens. The best one will be to keep Iraq in perspective. It seems to be the issue on which everything depends right now, just as Vietnam was in 1968. Over the next several years, however, President Richard Nixon and National Security Adviser Henry Kissinger showed that it was possible to "lose" Vietnam while "gaining" China. What takes place during the second Bush term in Afghanistan, Egypt, Iran, Libya, Morocco, Pakistan, Saudi Arabia, Syria, Turkey, and especially the Israeli-Palestinian relationship may well be as significant for the future of the Middle East as what occurs in Iraq. And what happens in China, India, Russia, Europe, and Africa may well be as important for the future of the international system as what transpires in the Middle East. All of which is only to say that Iraq must not become, as Vietnam once was, the single lens through which the United States views the region or the world.

Winning the War on Terrorism

Grand strategy is as much about psychology as it is facts on the ground. The Bush administration intended that a demonstrated capacity for retaliation, pre-emption, and/or prevention in Afghanistan and Iraq would convince al Qaeda that the United States could not be run out of the Middle East. "Shock and awe" would dry up recruiting for that organization. And it would deter other states in the region and elsewhere from supporting terrorism in the future. The record of accomplishments here is mixed.

Not even bin Laden can now expect a diminished U.S. presence in the Middle East: in political, economic, and certainly military terms, the United States is more firmly entrenched there than it was prior to September 11. It is less clear, though, that the Bush strategy has impeded al Qaeda's recruiting. The toppling of Saddam Hussein humiliated at least as many Arabs as it pleased. The occupation of Iraq revealed irresolution and inefficiency as often as the firmness it was meant to convey. The Israeli-Palestinian conflict remains a festering grievance: military victory in Iraq removed a threat to Israel, but it has yet to speed a settlement. On balance, U.S. power has become more respected in the Middle East. But respect for U.S. culture, institutions, and leadership has significantly declined.

Efforts to deter dangerous states have also produced mixed results. Whatever Colonel Muammar al-Qaddafi's reasons for abandoning Libya's quest for WMD, his decision was just what the Bush strategists hoped would happen on a wider scale. They can also claim, as a success, Pakistan's dismantling of Abdul Qadeer Khan's network for marketing nuclear weapons components. In Iran and North Korea, however, the picture is bleaker: the invasion of Iraq appears to have convinced leaders in those countries that they must have a nuclear capability of their own. Far from deterring them, the United States may have pushed them into finding ways to deter it.

Grand strategies always have multiple audiences: actions aimed at particular adversaries can (and usually do) make unintended impressions on others. A major priority for the second Bush administration, then, will be to determine the extent to which its aggressive use of U.S. military power in Afghanistan and Iraq has produced results it did not want elsewhere, and to adjust strategy accordingly.

It will be necessary, in doing this, to avoid extremes of pessimism and optimism. The Bush team made the worst of Saddam Hussein's alleged WMD, while making the best of the more credible capabilities Iran and North Korea have been developing. Whatever the reasons behind this disparity, it is not sustainable. For even if the United States should succeed in Iraq, its larger strategy will have failed if it produces a nuclear-capable Iran or North Korea, and those countries behave in an irresponsible way.

This is not to predict that they will. States that have acquired nuclear weapons have so far handled them carefully. To take comfort in this pattern, however, is like trying to find reassurance in an extended game of Russian roulette: sooner or later the odds will turn against you. The same is true of the risk that nuclear, chemical, and biological weapons could make the leap, like some lethal virus, from potentially deterrable states to undeterrable terrorists. It may take the use of such weapons to awaken the world to this danger. That too, however, is a Russian roulette solution, which makes it not worth waiting for.

There are opportunities, then, for a renewed U.S. commitment to the task of keeping WMD out of the hands of tyrants and terrorists by multilateral means. The prospects for such an effort, like those for the Iraqi occupation, are better than they might at first seem. UN sanctions do appear to have prevented the rebuilding of Saddam Hussein's WMD after the Gulf War. That organization has shown itself effective as well in publicizing, if not resolving, the crisis over Iran's nuclear program. Cooperative initiatives elsewhere have also shown promise: examples include the Nunn-Lugar program to dismantle nuclear stockpiles, the Proliferation Security Initiative to intercept illegal weapons shipments, and the tacit agreement North Korea's neighbors have reached that none has an interest in seeing Pyongyang develop the capacity for mass destruction.

The Bush administration has been proceeding in this direction. Its multilateralism outside of Afghanistan and Iraq is insufficiently acknowledged—probably because it has been inadequately explained. What is needed now is a clear and comprehensive statement of which international organizations and initiatives the United States can cooperate with, which it cannot, and why. It is as bad to promise too much, as the Clinton administration did, as to propose too little, as happened during Bush's first term. But with tact, flexibility, and a willingness to listen—as well as the power to pre-empt if such strategies fail—Americans could by these means regain what they have recently lost: the ability to inspire others to want to follow them.

Sowing the Seeds of Change

President Bush has insisted that the world will not be safe from terrorists until the Middle East is safe for democracy. It should be clear by now that he is serious about this claim: it is neither rhetorical nor a cloak for hidden motives. Democratization, however, is a long-term objective, so it is too early to assess accomplishments. What one can evaluate is the extent to which the Bush strategists have succeeded in a more immediate task they set for themselves: to clear the way for democratization by shattering a status quo in the Middle East that they believed had victimized the people of the region and had become a threat to the rest of the world.

The regimes responsible for this situation had three characteristics. They were authoritarian: liberation from colonialism and its equivalents had left the region in a new kind of bondage to tyrannical or at least unrepresentative rule. Most of them benefited from the geological accident of where oil lay beneath the surface of the earth, so that the need to remain competitive within a global economy did not produce the political liberalization that it did almost everywhere else. And several of these regimes had cut deals with an Islamist religious establishment that had its own reasons for resisting change, thereby reinforcing a long-standing trend toward literal readings of the Koran that left little room for alternative interpretations. This unhealthy combination of authoritarianism, wealth, and religious literalism, the Bush administration maintained, fed frustrations for many and fueled rage in a few: that was enough to bring about September 11. Breaking this status quo would make the world safer in the short run and facilitate democratization in the long run.

The shock and awe that accompanied the invasions of Afghanistan and Iraq were meant to begin this process, but Bush and his advisers did not rely solely on military means to sustain its momentum. They expected that September 11 and other terrorist excesses would cause a majority of Muslims to recoil from the extremists among them. They anticipated that the United States would be able to plant the seeds of democracy in the countries where it had deposed dictators, and that these would spread. They also assumed that the Middle East could not indefinitely insulate itself from the democratization that had already taken hold in much of the rest of the world.

Divisions have indeed surfaced among Muslims over the morality and effectiveness of terrorism. Saudis have seen the terrorists they financed strike back at them. Well before Yasir Arafat's death, Palestinians were questioning what suicide bombing and a perpetual intifada had accomplished; now there is even more room for second thoughts. Iraqis have begun to speak out, if cautiously, against the hostage-taking and televised beheadings that have afflicted their country. And the Beslan massacre—the taking of a school in southern Russia, with the subsequent slaughter of more than 300 children and teachers has raised doubts throughout the Middle East that terror directed against innocents can ever be justified when decoupled from any apparent political objective.

Whether democracy can be "planted" through military occupation in that part of the world is not yet clear, however, and may not be for some time. Three years after the invasion of Afghanistan, that country still is not secure. Taliban and al Qaeda elements remain, economic recovery is spotty, warlords rule, opium cultivation thrives, and Westerners cannot travel safely much beyond Kabul. And yet, on October 9, 2004, millions of Afghans lined up to vote in an election that had no precedent in their nation's long history. Had anyone predicted this three years ago, the response would have been incredulity—if not doubts about sanity.

What this suggests is that forces of disruption and construction coexist in Afghanistan: their shifting balance is beyond precise measurement. If that is true there, then it is all the more so in Iraq, where the contradictions are greater, the stakes are higher, and the standards for making optimistic or pessimistic judgments are even more opaque. The best one can say at the moment, of both countries, is that they defy generalization. That is less than the Bush administration hoped for. It is far more, however, than any previous American administration has achieved in the Middle East. For better or for worse, the status quo exists no longer.

And what of the region's insulation from the wave of democratization that has swept the globe? According to Freedom House statistics, no countries allowed universal suffrage in 1900. By 1950, 22 did, and by 2000, the number had reached 120, a figure that encompassed 62.5 percent of the world's population. Nor, as the examples of Bangladesh, India, Indonesia, and Turkey suggest, is there reason to think that representative government and Islam are incompatible. Democratization has indeed been delayed in the Arab world, as Arabs themselves have begun to acknowledge. To conclude that it can never take hold there, however, is to neglect the direction in which the historical winds have been blowing. And the best grand strategies, like the most efficient navigators, keep the winds behind them.

The second Bush administration will now have the opportunity to reinforce the movement—the shift in the status quo—that the first Bush administration started in the Middle East. A Kerry administration would probably have done the same. What September 11 showed was that the United States can no longer insulate itself from what happens in that part of the world: to do so would be to ignore clear and present danger. A conservative Republican administration responded by embracing a liberal Democratic ideal—making the world safe for democracy—as a national security imperative. If that does not provide the basis for a renewed grand strategic bipartisanship, similar to the one that followed Pearl Harbor so long ago, then one has to wonder what ever would.

What Would Bismarck Do?

Finally, one apparent assumption that runs through the Bush grand strategy deserves careful scrutiny. It has to do with what follows shock and awe. The president and his advisers seem to have concluded that the shock the United States suffered on September n required that shocks be administered in return, not just to the part of the world from which the attack came, but to the international system as a whole. Old ways of doing things no longer worked. The status quo everywhere needed shaking up. Once that

had happened, the pieces would realign themselves in patterns favorable to U.S. interests.

It was free-market thinking applied to geopolitics: that just as the removal of economic constraints allows the pursuit of self-interest automatically to advance a collective interest, so the breaking up of an old international order would encourage a new one to emerge, more or less spontaneously, based on a universal desire for security, prosperity, and liberty. Shock therapy would produce a safer, saner world.

Some such therapy was probably necessary in the aftermath of September 11, but the assumption that things would fall neatly into place after the shock was administered was the single greatest misjudgment of the first Bush administration. It explains the failure to anticipate multilateral resistance to pre-emption. It accounts for the absence of planning for the occupation of Iraq. It has produced an overstretched military for which no "revolution in military affairs" can compensate. It has left official obligations dangerously unfunded. And it has allowed an inexcusable laxity about legal procedures—at Guantánamo, Abu Ghraib, and elsewhere—to squander the moral advantage the United States possessed after September 11 and should have retained.

The most skillful practitioner ever of shock and awe, Otto von Bismarck, shattered the post-1815 European settlement in order to unify Germany in 1871. Having done so, however, he did not assume that the pieces would simply fall into place as he wished them to: he made sure that they did through the careful, patient construction of a new European order that offered benefits to all who were included within it. Bismarck's system survived for almost half a century.

The most important question George W. Bush will face in his second term is whether he can follow Bismarck's example. If he can shift from shock and awe to the reassurance—and the attention to detail—that is necessary to sustain any new system, then the prospects for his post–September 11 grand strategy could compare favorably m Bismarck's accomplishments, as well as to those of U.S. presidents from Roosevelt through Clinton. For their post–Pearl Harbor grand strategy, over more than half a century, persuaded the world that it was better off with the United States as its dominant power than with anyone else. Bush must now do the same.

JOHN LEWIS GADDIS is Robert A. Lovett Professor of History at Yale.

Reprinted by permission of *Foreign Affairs*, January/February 2005, pp. 2-15. Copyright © 2005 by the Council on Foreign Relations, Inc.

Hegemony on the Cheap

Liberal Internationalism from Wilson to Bush

COLIN DUECK

One of the conventional criticisms of the Bush administration's foreign policy is that it is excessively and even disastrously unilateralist in approach. According to the critics, the administration has turned its back on a long-standing and admirable American tradition of liberal internationalism in foreign affairs, and in doing so has provoked resentment worldwide.[1] But these criticisms misinterpret both the foreign policy of George W. Bush, as well as America's liberal internationalist tradition. In reality, Bush's foreign policy since 9/11 has been heavily influenced by traditional liberal internationalist assumptions—assumptions that all along have had a troubling impact on U.S. foreign policy behavior and fed into the current situation in Iraq.

The conduct of America's foreign relations has—for more than a hundred years, going back at least to the days of John Hay's "Open Door" Notes and McKinley's hand wringing over the annexation of the Philip-pines—been shaped, to a greater or lesser extent, by a set of beliefs that can only be called liberal. These assumptions specify that the United States should promote, wherever practical and possible, an international system characterized by democratic governments and open markets.[2] President Bush reiterated these classical liberal assumptions recently, in his speech last November to the National Endowment for Democracy, when he outlined what he called "a forward strategy of freedom in the Middle East." In that speech, Bush argued that "as long as the Middle East remains a place where freedom does not flourish, it will remain a place of stagnation, resentment, and violence ready for export." In this sense, he suggested, the United States has a vital strategic interest in the democratization of the region. But Bush also added that "the advance of freedom leads to peace," and that democracy is "the only path to national success and dignity," providing as it does certain "essential principles common to every successful society, in every culture."[3] These words could just as easily have been spoken by Woodrow Wilson, Franklin Roosevelt—or Bill Clinton. They are well within the mainstream American tradition of liberal internationalism. Of course, U.S. foreign policy officials have never promoted a liberal world order simply out of altruism. They have done so out of the belief that such a system would serve American interests, by making the United States more prosperous, influential, and secure. Americans have also frequently disagreed over how to best promote liberal goals overseas.[4] Nevertheless, it is fair to say that liberal goals and assumptions, broadly conceived, have had a powerful impact on American foreign policy, especially since the presidency of Woodrow Wilson.

The problem with the liberal or Wilsonian approach, however, has been that it tends to encourage very ambitious foreign policy goals and commitments, while assuming that these goals can be met without commensurate cost or expenditure on the part of the United States. Liberal internationalists, that is, tend to define American interests in broad, expansive, and idealistic terms, without always admitting the necessary costs and risks of such an expansive vision. The result is that sweeping and ambitious goals are announced, but then pursued by disproportionately limited means, thus creating an outright invitation to failure. Indeed, this disjuncture between ends and means has been so common in the history of American diplomacy over the past century that it seems to be a direct consequence of the nation's distinctly liberal approach to international relations.

The Bush administration's current difficulties in Iraq are therefore not an isolated event. Nor are they really the result of the president's supposed preference for unilateralism. On the contrary, the administration's difficulties in Iraq are actually the result of an excessive reliance on classically liberal or Wilsonian assumptions regarding foreign affairs. The administration has willed the end in Iraq—and a very ambitious end—but it has not fully willed the means. In this sense, the Bush administration is heir to a long liberal internationalist tradition that runs from Woodrow Wilson, through FDR and Harry Truman, to Bill Clinton. And Bush inherits not only the strengths of that tradition, but also its weaknesses and flaws.

The Lost Alliance

The liberal internationalist pattern of disjuncture between ends and means really begins in earnest with Woodrow Wilson. Wilson, of course, traveled to Europe at the end of 1918, in the wake of the First World War, intending to "make the world safe for democracy" while insisting that a universal League of Nations serve as the linchpin for a new international order. Wilson intended the League to function as a promoter of collective security arrangements, by guaranteeing the territorial integrity and political independence of all member states. But Wilson also intended the League to function, more broadly, as the embodiment of a nascent liberal international order where war would be outlawed and self-determination would remain supreme. The other great powers were to be asked to abandon their imperialistic spheres of influence, their protectionist tariff barriers, their secretive military alliances, and their swollen armories.[5]

Needless to say, in practice, such concessions were hard to extract. The actual outcome at the Paris Peace Conference, contrary to Wilson's desire, was a series of compromises: Japan maintained its sphere of influence in the Chinese province of Shantung; Britain maintained its great navy, as well as its colonial conquests from Germany and Turkey; many of the arrangements negotiated in secret by the Allied powers during the war were in fact observed, though running contrary to Wilson's own pronouncements (including the famous Fourteen Points); and in blatant disregard of Wilson's alleged aversion to "old diplomacy" horse trading, France and Britain had their way vis-à-vis the peace terms imposed on Germany at Versailles while obtaining an explicit security guarantee from the United States.[6] To be sure, Wilson did succeed in winning the assent of the other victorious powers toward common membership in a new League of Nations. Furthermore, it is clear that he took the League's collective security obligations quite seriously. He certainly hoped that future acts of territorial aggression could be prevented through such peaceful means as deterrence, arbitration, and the use of economic sanctions. But in the final analysis, he understood perfectly well that collective security would at times have to be enforced militarily, through the use of armed force on the part of member states. Indeed, Wilson said quite explicitly that the League was meant to function as "a single overwhelming, powerful group of nations who shall be the trustee of the peace of the world."[7] And the United States was to be the leading member of this group.

Still, at the same time that Wilson laid out this extremely ambitious vision, he refused to draw the logical implications for the United States. Obviously, under any sort of meaningful commitment to a worldwide collective security system, the United States would henceforth be obliged to help enforce the peace in areas outside its traditional sphere of influence as proclaimed in the Monroe Doctrine (and subsequent "corollaries")—that is to say, in Europe and Asia. This would necessarily require maintaining a large standing army. Yet Wilson refused to admit that any such requirement existed, just as he disingenuously maintained that the League's covenant would not impinge on America's sovereignty, by insisting that said article carried only a "moral" obligation. In fact, he argued that the League would render a large standing army unnecessary.

Some of Wilson's Republican critics, especially in Congress, far from being isolationist know-nothings, saw through the contradictions in the president's vision, and advocated a pragmatic alternative. Led by Sen. Henry Cabot Lodge, these conservative internationalists called for a straightforward security pact with France and Great Britain as the key to their and America's own postwar security. Lodge and his supporters were willing to enter into the new League of Nations, but not into any global collective security arrangement. These Republican internationalists favored clear but restricted U.S. strategic commitments within Western Europe as the best guarantee of future peace.[8]

Lodge's alternative of a limited, Western alliance actually made perfect sense, strategically speaking. It avoided the impossible implication that America would come to the aid of any state, worldwide, whose territory or integrity was threatened. At the same time, it specified that the United States would defend France from any future attack by Germany while encouraging Britain to do the same. In this way, America's strategic commitments would be based upon concrete, vital national interests, rather than upon vague universalities; and upon real military capabilities, rather than utopian aspirations. The one problem with this alternative vision is that it seems to have been incompatible with domestic liberal pieties. Even Lodge admitted in 1919—at the time of the battle in the Senate over the League—that the idea of a League of Nations was quite popular in America. As Wilson himself suggested, the only way to preserve America's sense of moral superiority, while at the same time bringing its weight to bear in favor of international stability, was through membership in a universal organization, rather than through any particular and "entangling alliances."[9] Lodge and his supporters managed to defeat Wilson's League in the Senate, but they did not succeed in replacing it with a more realistic alternative.

Containment

During the Second World War, Franklin Roosevelt attempted to learn from Wilson's mistakes by carefully building domestic support for American membership in a postwar United Nations. Roosevelt was much more flexible in his approach than Wilson had been. But in terms of his substantive vision for the postwar order, Roosevelt was hardly any less idealistic than Wilson. Roosevelt's "grand design" was that the five major powers fighting the Axis would cooperate in policing the postwar system, each power (more or less) within its own regional sphere of influence. At the same time, however, each great power was to respect such liberal norms as nonaggression, democratic institutions, and free trade within its own sphere.[10] FDR was strikingly successful in nudging the American public toward a new internationalist consensus. His administration laid the groundwork for U.S. postwar leadership of a more liberal international political and economic order. The one great stumbling block to Roosevelt's plans was the Soviet Union. Roosevelt recognized that Moscow would end the war with disproportionate influence over Eastern Europe, but he insisted that such influence be exercised in a benign, democratic, and non-coercive fashion. Stalin, of course, would not accept such conditions, whatever his rhetorical commitments to the contrary. Once this basic clash of interests between Washington and Moscow became visible for all to see, by the end of 1945, American officials were faced with the inevitable dilemma of how to respond to Soviet behavior. To allow the Soviet Union to construct, with impunity, an autarchic, militarized sphere of influence within Eastern Europe—and beyond—would have flown in the face of America's wartime objectives. The United

States, under Truman, therefore settled on a strategy of containment in order to curb Soviet power and at the same time preserve FDR's hope for a more liberal world order.

Containment was a pragmatic strategy, but it was also very much influenced by Wilsonian assumptions regarding the nature of international relations. The purpose of containment, after all, was not simply to check or balance the Soviet Union, but also to nurture the long-term vitality and interdependence of an American-led, liberal international order outside of the Communist bloc.[11] The strategists of containment refused to accept permanent Soviet control over Eastern Europe, or to negotiate in earnest with Moscow over the outlines of a general postwar settlement that did not accord with Wilsonian principles. Instead, they hoped to achieve an eventual geopolitical, economic, and ideological victory over the Soviet Union by using every means short of war.[12] The goal was not to learn to coexist with the enemy, but gradually to convert and/or help him destroy himself. It was precisely this ideological, uncompromising tone that gave containment its political viability at home.

During the late 1940s, under the strategy of containment, the United States embarked upon a series of dramatic and unprecedented commitments abroad. Military and economic aid was extended to friendly governments worldwide; anticommunist alliances were formed around the globe; and U.S. troops were deployed in large numbers to Europe and Asia. The Truman Doctrine, the Marshall Plan, and NATO all embodied this new commitment to a forward strategic presence overseas. The problem, however, was that the Truman administration hoped to implement this very ambitious strategy without sacrificing the traditional American preference for limited liability abroad. Defense expenditures, in particular, were at first kept at a level that was exceedingly low, given the diverse and worldwide military commitments the United States had actually undertaken. In effect, the administration gambled that the Soviet Union and its clients would not test America's willingness or ability to contain military aggression by conventional means.[13] With the outbreak of the Korean War in 1950, this gamble proved to be a failure. As a result, in the early 1950s, the United States finally raised defense expenditures to a level commensurate with its strategic commitments overseas. Inevitably, the Wilsonian preference for low-cost internationalism reasserted itself: high levels of defense spending turned out to be politically unsustainable at home, leading the Eisenhower administration to return to a potentially risky reliance on nuclear deterrence. Americans wanted to contain the Soviet Union—an ambitious and in many ways a remarkably idealistic strategy—but they did not necessarily want to bear the full costs of such a strategy. In this sense, even at the height of the Cold War, U.S. foreign policy operated very much within the Wilsonian tradition.

The implementation of containment continued to be characterized by a persistent gap between ambitious liberal ends, and somewhat limited capabilities. In the early 1960s, John F. Kennedy made a concerted effort to close this gap through a strategy of "flexible response," emphasizing conventional and counterinsurgent, as well as nuclear, capabilities. Yet at the same time, Kennedy escalated America's military involvement in Vietnam, without providing any clear idea of how that conflict could be won. The decision to stand by Saigon, on the part of both Kennedy and, later, Lyndon Johnson, was driven primarily by concerns over the credibility of America's worldwide alliance commitments. But this decision was also very much informed by the Wilsonian belief that developing countries such as Vietnam could be reformed, liberalized, and won over to America's side through a vigorous, U.S.-assisted program of nation building.[14] In the words of Walt Rostow, one of Kennedy's leading foreign policy advisors, "Modern societies must be built, and we are prepared to help build them."

In Vietnam, America's willingness to sustain serious costs on behalf of a liberal strategy of containment and nation building was tested to the breaking point. Within the United States, domestic political support for a protracted, expensive, and bloody engagement in Southeast Asia proved to have definite limits. The Johnson administration itself was unwilling to call for maximum effort on behalf of its goals in the region; instead, it tried to achieve them through a process of limited and gradual escalation. The Nixon administration, having inherited this immense commitment, attempted to square the circle through a policy of "Vietnamization." The United States would slowly withdraw its forces from the conflict, relying upon air power and increased military aid to bolster the regime in Saigon. But Nixon's approach was no more able to achieve its stated aims than Johnson's. If Communist forces in Vietnam could not be defeated by half a million American troops, a lower level of American engagement was not going to do the trick. In the end, the United States proved neither willing nor able to bear the costs of meeting its commitments to Saigon—commitments that had been deeply informed by liberal internationalist assumptions.

Even as they experimented with Vietnamization, the Nixon-Kissinger team attempted to place the United States in a more sustainable strategic position by toning down the Wilsonian rhetoric. The new emphasis was on great power relations, rather than on ideological crusades to liberalize or reform the internal politics of other states. As Henry Kissinger put it in 1969, "We will judge other countries, including Communist countries, on the basis of their actions and not on the basis of their domestic ideologies."[15] This more pragmatic approach bore considerable fruit through a relaxation of tensions with the Soviet Union, as well as a dramatic improvement in relations with China. Despite these successes, Nixon and Kissinger were attacked from both left and right for abandoning America's Wilsonian mission overseas. Both Jimmy Carter, who took office in 1977, and Ronald Reagan, who succeeded him in 1981, criticized the policy of détente from a Wilsonian perspective. Both Carter and Reagan, despite their many differences, insisted that U.S. foreign relations should be rebuilt upon the premise that the United States had a vital practical as well as moral interest in the promotion of a liberal world order. The collapse of the Soviet Union in 1989 seemed to many to have vindicated the Wilsonian approach. But it was the combined economic and military power of the United States and its allies, not Wilsonian idealism, that finally brought the Soviet Union to its knees. In the euphoria over the collapse of communism, the fact that for over 40 years the United States had often pursued a sweeping and ambitious foreign policy with inadequate means was forgotten.

The United States had been forced to pay for this strategic mismanagement in both Korea and Vietnam. In the end, the relative weakness of the Soviet Union gave U.S. policy makers considerable room for error. However, the upshot was that Americans misattributed their victory in the Cold War to the unique virtues of the Wilsonian tradition, which only led to a continuing gap between ends and means in the conduct of American foreign policy.

Democratic Enlargement

Following the end of the Cold War, the United States was faced with the choice of either expanding its military and political presence abroad, or retrenching strategically. The Clinton administration decided to do both. Thus it pursued a very ambitious strategy of "democratic enlargement," designed to promote the spread of market democracies worldwide. This included, notably, a new emphasis on humanitarian intervention in civil conflicts of seemingly peripheral interest to the United States. But it also tried to carry out this strategy at an extremely low cost in terms of blood and treasure. Defense expenditures, for example, were kept at a level that was unrealistically low, given the global range of America's military commitments. Just as significantly, Clinton also proved remarkably reluctant to use force in support of his Wilsonian agenda.

Clinton came into office having criticized the foreign policy of George H. W. Bush for being insufficiently true to America's democratic ideals. The new president promised to be more consistent than his immediate predecessor in promoting democracy and human rights in countries such as China, the former Yugoslavia, and Haiti. A leading test of the Clinton administration's rhetorical commitment to the liberal internationalist credo was on the question of humanitarian intervention. Clinton and his advisors repeatedly stated that the United States had a vital humanitarian interest in cases of civil war and disorder. The administration therefore placed a new emphasis on American-led peacekeeping, peacemaking, and nation-building operations.[16] More broadly, foreign policy officials articulated a doctrine of "enlargement," by which they meant that the United States would press for the expansion of free trade, open markets, democratic governments, and human rights worldwide.[17] Their assumption— building on the old Wilsonian gospel—was that such an expansion would encourage an upward cycle of global peace and prosperity, serving American interests and allowing the United States to deemphasize its own military strength.

Under the Clinton administration, the liberal internationalist assumptions of democratic enlargement informed U.S. policy in virtually every region of the globe. In Central Europe, three new members were brought into NATO. In Russia, democratic market reforms were the price demanded for improved bilateral relations with the United States. In China, U.S. diplomats pressed Beijing on human rights issues while working to bring the People's Republic into the international economic system. And in Bosnia, Haiti, Somalia, and Kosovo, Washington undertook to help create or recreate stable, democratic polities, through military intervention, amidst generally unfavorable conditions.[18]

Nevertheless, even as President Clinton laid out his extremely ambitious foreign policy goals, he proved unwilling to support them with the necessary means. In particular, he proved reluctant to support these initiatives with the requisite amount of military force. In one case after another of humanitarian intervention, a pattern emerged: the Clinton administration would stake out an assertive and idealistic public position, then refuse to act on its rhetoric in a meaningful way. Yet in every such case, whether in Somalia, Haiti, Bosnia, or Kosovo, the president was ultimately forced to act, if only to protect the credibility of the United States.[19] The result was a series of remarkably halfhearted, initially low-risk interventions, which only reinforced the impression that the United States was unwilling to suffer costs or casualties on behalf of its stated interests overseas.[20]

It might be argued that the nature of U.S. interventions during the Clinton years was a function of the low geopolitical stakes involved, rather than a reflection of the administration's naiveté. Certainly, the stakes were relatively low. But from a classical realist perspective, the answer would have been to avoid putting America's reputation on the line in the first place—to avoid defining American interests in such an expansive manner as to then call the nation's credibility into question. The fact is that the Clinton administration said, in each case, that the United States had a vital national interest in the pursuit of liberal or humanitarian goals. Then it refused to protect this stated interest with requisite seriousness until American credibility had already been undermined. This may have been partially the result of a presidency characterized by unusual fecklessness on matters of national security. But it was also a pattern of behavior very much in the liberal internationalist tradition: sweeping commitments, too often supported by inadequate means.

Wilson Redux

At first, the inauguration of George W. Bush seemed to indicate, if nothing else, that America's national security capabilities would be brought into line with the nation's strategic commitments. As a candidate for president, Governor Bush had called for significant increases in defense spending. At the same time, he criticized what he termed the "open-ended deployments and unclear military missions" of the Clinton era.[21] Bush was especially critical of employing armed force in nation-building operations overseas; indeed, he suggested that he would not have intervened in either Haiti or Somalia. As Bush phrased it during a debate with Al Gore in October 2000, while referring to the question of intervention, "I would be very guarded in my approach. I don't think we can be all things to all people in the world. I think we've got to be very careful when we commit our troops."[22]

To be sure, neoconservative visions of American primacy always had a certain influence on Bush's thinking, but for the most part, the dominant tone of Bush's foreign policy pre-9/11 was one of "realism." The new administration was determined to be more selective on questions of nation building and humanitarian intervention than its predecessor. American foreign policy was to be refocused on considerations of great power politics and more immediate national interests, and the United States was to play down its pretensions as an international social engineer. Key figures such as Colin Powell and Richard Haass in the State Department and Condoleezza Rice at the National Security Council were well within the tradition of Republican pragmatism on foreign affairs, and hawks such as Vice President Dick Cheney and Secretary of Defense Donald Rumsfeld were either unwilling or unable to press for a comprehensive strategy of primacy across the board.[23] Above all, Bush seemed uninterested in any new, sweepingly ambitious—i.e., Wilsonian—foreign policy departures.

The terrorist attacks of September 11, 2001, changed all of that, coming as a severe shock to the president, his advisors, and the American public at large. These attacks stimulated the search for a new national security strategy. Key advocates of a different approach—at first within the administration, and then including the president himself—took advantage of the opportunity to build support for a new foreign policy agenda. This new national security strategy would be considerably more assertive than before and, in important ways, considerably more idealistic.[24]

Within days of the September 11 attacks, and over the following months, the Bush administration began to outline and articulate a remarkable departure in American foreign policy. The clearest and most elaborate explanation of the new approach came in the National Security Strategy of September 2002. In that document, best known for its embrace of preventive military action against rogue states, the administration began by pointing out that "the United States possesses unprecedented—and unequaled—strength and influence in the world." It renounced any purely realpolitik approach to foreign policy, arguing instead that "the great strength of this nation must be used to promote a balance of power that favors freedom." The promotion of free trade and democratic institutions was held up as a central American interest. Democracy and human rights were described as "nonnegotiable demands." And, interestingly, the possibility of traditional great power competition was played down. Instead, other powers were urged to join with the United States in affirming the global trend toward democracy and open markets.[25]

Of course, this broad affirmation of classical liberal assumptions was no doubt employed, in part, for reasons of domestic political consumption. Liberal arguments have historically been used to bolster strategic arguments of any kind. But the United States had been no less liberal—broadly speaking—in the year 2000, when the nascent Bush team was stressing the need for realism in foreign affairs. So the new rhetoric does seem to have reflected a real shift on the part of the administration toward a more aggressive and, at the same time, more Wilsonian approach.

The implications of this new Wilsonianism were most visible in the decision for war against Iraq. The argument made by the pro-war camp was that a defeated Iraq could be democratized and would subsequently act as a kind of trigger for democratic change throughout the Middle East. As Bush put it in an address last February to members of the American Enterprise Institute, "a new regime in Iraq would serve as a dramatic and inspiring example of freedom for other nations in the region....

Success in Iraq could also begin a new stage for Middle Eastern peace, and set in motion progress toward a truly democratic Palestinian state."[26] From the perspective of many leading officials inside the Bush administration, this argument was probably secondary to more basic geopolitical and security concerns. But it did seem to have an effect on the president. And again, 9/11 was the crucial catalyst, since it appeared to demonstrate that U.S. support for authoritarian regimes in the region had only encouraged Islamic fundamentalism, along with such terrorist organizations as al-Qaeda.[27]

Here was a remarkably bold vision for American foreign policy, combining the argument for preventive war with Wilsonian visions of a liberalized or Americanized international system. The goals outlined were so ambitious as to invite intense domestic as well as international criticism. The most common objections to the Bush Doctrine, at least among foreign policy experts, were that the new national security strategy would lead America into "imperial overstretch"; that it would trigger antagonism and hostility toward the United States abroad; that it would set a precedent for aggression on the part of other countries; and that it would undermine sympathy and support for the United States overseas. These were the most frequently articulated criticisms, but in fact an even more likely danger was the opposite one: that the Bush team would fail to make good on its promise of a serious commitment to achieving peace, stability, and democratization in Iraq, let alone in the Middle East as a whole.

Certainly the precedent in Afghanistan was not encouraging. There, the United States relied upon proxy forces, supported by airstrikes, special forces operations, and financial aid, in order to overthrow the Taliban. The failure to send in American ground troops early on meant that many members of al-Qaeda were able to escape and reconstitute their terrorist camps along the Afghan-Pakistani border. Worse yet, the Bush administration proved unwilling to contribute substantially to the postwar political, military, or economic reconstruction of Afghanistan, leaving its central government without effective control over the countryside outside Kabul.[28]

Iraq's postwar reconstruction was even less well considered than Afghanistan's. Certainly, the Bush foreign policy team understood that Saddam Hussein would not be overthrown without a major commitment of American ground troops. But in terms of planning for a post-Saddam Iraq, the administration seems to have based its initial actions upon the most optimistic assumptions: ordinary Iraqis would rise up in support of U.S. forces; these same forces would rapidly transfer authority toward a friendly interim government; the oil would flow, paying for reconstruction efforts; and the great majority of American troops would come home quickly. These were never very likely prospects, and with all of the warnings that it received, the administration should have known better. As Bush himself said during the 2000 presidential campaign, nation building is difficult and expensive. The administration's preference has been to avoid nation-building operations—an understandable predilection in itself. But once the administration made the decision to go to war against Saddam Hussein, it was also obliged to prepare for the foreseeable likelihood of major, postwar nation-building operations—not only for humanitarian reasons, but in order to secure the political objectives for which it had gone to war in the first place.

The Bush administration's early reluctance to plan for Iraq's postwar reconstruction has had serious and deadly consequences. Once Saddam's government was overthrown, a power vacuum was created, and the United States did not initially step in to fill the void. Widespread looting, disorder, and insecurity were the inevitable result. This set the tone for the immediate postwar era. Moreover, because of these insecure conditions, many of Saddam's former loyalists were given the opportunity to develop and pursue a dangerous, low-level insurgency against American forces. The subsequent learning curve within the Bush administration has been steep. By necessity, the president has come a considerable distance toward recognizing how expensive this particular process of nation building is going to be. The approval by Congress of $87 billion for continuing operations in Iraq and Afghanistan is clearly a step in the right direction. Bush has indicated repeatedly that the United States cannot cut and run from its commitments. At the same time, there are disconcerting signs, with American casualties mounting, and the president's reelection looming, that the White House may in fact decide to withdraw American forces from Iraq. Indeed, the administration's latest adjustment seems to be toward a version of Vietnamization: handing over authority to a transitional government in Baghdad, while encouraging Iraq's own police and security forces to take up the greater burden with respect to counterinsurgency operations. In itself, this approach has certain virtues, but if it indicates a comprehensive withdrawal of U.S. resources and personnel from Iraq, then the results will not be benign, either for the United States, or for the Iraqi people. Nation-building operations sometimes fail, even under favorable conditions. But without robust involvement on the part of outside powers, such operations simply cannot succeed. It is an illusion to think that a stable, secure, and democratic Iraq can arise without a significant long-term U.S. investment of both blood and treasure.[29]

The administration responded to the challenge of 9/11 by devising a more assertive, Wilsonian foreign policy. The stated goals of this policy have been not only to initiate "rogue state rollback" but to promote a more open and democratic world order. By all accounts, Bush and his advisors really do believe that 9/11 has offered the United States, in the words of Secretary of Defense Donald Rumsfeld, an "opportunity to refashion the world."[30] The problem is not that the president is departing from a long tradition of liberal internationalism; it is that he is continuing some of the worst features of that tradition. Specifically, in Iraq, he is continuing the tradition of articulating and pursuing a set of extremely ambitious and idealistic foreign policy goals, without providing the full or proportionate means to achieve those goals. In this sense, it must be said, George W. Bush is very much a Wilsonian.

Whatever the immediate outcome in Iraq, America's foreign policy elites are not likely to abandon their longstanding ambition to create a liberal world order. What is more likely, and also more dangerous, is that they will continue to oscillate between various forms of liberal internationalism, and to press for a more open and democratic international system, without willing the means to sustain it.

Under the circumstances, the choice between unilateralism and multilateralism, which currently characterizes public debate over U.S. foreign policy, is almost beside the point. Neither a unilateral nor a multilateral foreign policy will succeed if Americans are unwilling to incur the full costs and risks that are implied in either case. It is impossible to promote the kind of international system that America's foreign policy elites say that they want without paying a heavy price for it. Iraq is simply the latest case in point. Americans can either take up the burden of acting on their liberal internationalist rhetoric and convictions, or they can keep costs and risks to a minimum by abandoning this ambitious interventionist agenda. They cannot do both. They cannot have hegemony on the cheap.

Notes

1. For representative criticisms in this vein, see David C. Hendrickson, "Toward Universal Empire: The Dangerous Quest for Absolute Security," *World Policy Journal,* vol. 19 (fall 2002), pp. 1-10; G. John Ikenberry, "America's Imperial Ambition," *Foreign Affairs,* vol. 81 (September/October 2002), pp. 44- 60; Robert S. Litwak, "The New Calculus of Preemption," *Survival*, vol. 44 (winter 2002), pp. 53-79; and Joseph S. Nye, Jr., *The Paradox of American Power: Why the World's Only Superpower Can't Go It Alone* (New York: Oxford University Press, 2002), pp. 15, 39, 141-63.

2. See Michael H. Hunt, *Ideology and US Foreign Policy* (New Haven: Yale University Press, 1988), pp. 17-18.

3. "Remarks by the President at the 20th Anniversary of the National Endowment for Democracy," Washington, D.C., November 6, 2003, available at www.whitehouse.gov/news/releases/2003/11/iraq/20031106-2.html.

4. For a discussion of various schools of thought in the American foreign policy tradition, see Henry R. Nau, *At Home Abroad: Identity and Power in American Foreign Policy* (Ithaca: Cornell University Press, 2002), pp. 43-59; and Walter Russell Mead, *Special Providence: American Foreign Policy and How It Changed the World* (New York: Knopf, 2001).

5. See Arthur S. Link, *Woodrow Wilson: Revolution, War and Peace* (Wheeling, Ill.: Harlan Davidson, 1979), pp. 72-103.

6. In the former Ottoman Empire, for example, Wilson's initial pronouncements in favor of self-determination had raised hopes for postwar national independence among Arabs, Armenians, Jews, and Turks. At Paris, Wilson even promised a U.S. protectorate over an independent Armenia. Yet the eventual settlement in the region, disguised through the creation of League "mandates," closely resembled a classic sphere-of-influence bargain among Europe's great powers. The one major exception was in Turkey itself, where Kemal Atatürk rallied nationalist forces and ejected foreign troops from the Anatolian heartland. In this way, American promises with regard to Armenia were rendered completely irrelevant, even before the Senate's rejection of the Versailles Treaty. For a lively discussion of the postwar settlement within the Middle East, see Margaret MacMillan, *Paris 1919: Six Months That Changed the World* (New York: Random House, 2002), pp. 347-455.

7. Ray Stannard Baker and William Dodd, eds., *Public Papers of Woodrow Wilson,* (New York: Harper and Brothers, 1925-1927), vol. 5, pp. 341-44.

8. William C. Widenor, *Henry Cabot Lodge and the Search for an American Foreign Policy* (Berkeley: University of California Press, 1980), pp. 298, 331.

9. Baker and Dodd, eds., *Public Papers of Woodrow Wilson,* vol. 5, pp. 352-56.

10. See Warren F. Kimball, *The Juggler: Franklin Roosevelt as Wartime Statesman* (Princeton: Princeton University Press, 1991), pp. 63-81, 107-57.

11. See Melvyn P. Leffler, *A Preponderance of Power: National Security, the Truman Administration, and the Cold War* (Stanford: Stanford University Press, 1992), pp. 8-9, 15-18.

12. As George Kennan put it, "Our first aim with respect to Russia in time of peace is to encourage and promote by means short of war the gradual retraction of undue Russian influence from the present satellite area." See George Kennan, NSC 20/1, "US Objectives with Respect to Russia," August 18, 1948, in Thomas H. Etzold and John Lewis Gaddis, eds., *Containment: Documents on American Policy and Strategy, 1945-1950* (New York: Columbia University Press, 1978), p. 184.

13. See Steven L. Rearden, *History of the Office of the Secretary of Defense: The Formative Years, 1947- 1950* (Washington, D.C.: United States Government Printing Office, 1984), pp. 532-36.

14. See John Lewis Gaddis, *Strategies of Containment* (New York: Oxford University Press, 1982), pp. 202-03, 217-18, 223-25.

15. Ibid., p. 284.

16. Stephen John Stedman, "The New Interventionists," *Foreign Affairs,* vol. 72 (spring 1993), pp. 4-5.

17. Anthony Lake, Assistant to the President for National Security Affairs, at Johns Hopkins University, September 21, 1993, in *Vital Speeches of the Day, 1993,* vol. 60, p. 15.

18. See Karin von Hippel, *Democracy by Force: U.S. Military Intervention in the Post-Cold War World* (New York: Cambridge University Press, 2000).

19. See, for example, in the case of Bosnia, James Gow, *Triumph of the Lack of Will: International Diplomacy and the Yugoslav War* (New York: Columbia University Press, 1997), pp. 208, 218.

20. Daniel L. Byman and Matthew C. Waxman, *The Dynamics of Coercion: American Foreign Policy and the Limits of Military Might* (New York: Cambridge University Press, 2002), p. 143.

21. Governor George W. Bush, "A Period of Consequences," September 23, 1999, The Citadel, South Carolina, available at www.citadel.edu/pao/addresses/pres_bush.html.

22. Presidential debates, October 3, 2000, at Boston, Massachussetts, and October 11, 2000, at Winston-Salem, North Carolina, available at www.foreignpolicy2000.org/debate/ candidate/candidate.html and www.foreignpolicy2000.org/debate/candidate/candidate2.html.

23. For a good exposition of the initially "realist" bent of one of Bush's leading foreign policy advisors, see Condoleezza Rice, "Campaign 2000: Promoting the National Interest," *Foreign Affairs,* vol. 79 (January/February 2000), pp. 45-62.

24. Nicholas Lemann, "Without a Doubt," *The New Yorker,* October 14 and 21, 2002, p. 177.

25. The National Security Strategy of the United States of America (Washington, D.C.: The White House, September 2002), pp. 1, 3-4, 26-28.

26. George W. Bush, "President Discusses the Future of Iraq," February 26, 2003, Washington Hilton Hotel, Washington, D.C., available at www.whitehouse.gov/news/releases/2003/02/iraq/20030226-11.html.

27. George Packer, "Dreaming of Democracy," *New York Times Magazine,* March 2, 2003, pp. 46-49.

28. Anja Manuel and Peter W. Singer, "A New Model Afghan Army," *Foreign Affairs,* vol. 81 (July/August 2002), pp. 44-59.

29. Frederick Kagan, "War and Aftermath," *Policy Review,* no. 120 (August/September 2003), pp. 3-27.

30. "Secretary Rumsfeld Interview," *New York Times,* October 12, 2001.

COLIN DUECK is assistant professor of political science at the University of Colorado, Boulder.

From *World Policy Journal,* Winter 2003/2004, pp. 1-11. Copyright © 2004 by MIT Press. Reprinted by permission.

The Dilemma of the Last Sovereign

ZBIGNIEW BRZEZINSKI

America today is the world's most sovereign state. To be sure, in our time the concept of sovereignty has been largely drained of content by the reality of increasing interdependence among states. For most states, sovereignty now verges on being a legal fiction. Even in the case of the more powerful few, practical rationality lessens the temptation to arbitrarily assert sovereignty. Ultimately, of course, any state (or rather, its leadership) can commit even a suicidal act of folly, but the scope for such self-assertion is increasingly constrained by the overlapping interests of some 200 states in a more politically congested and interwoven world.

In that context, America's military action against Iraq and its less dramatic but also largely solitary stance on the International Criminal Court and the Kyoto Treaty were striking assertions of the unique status of the United States as the last truly sovereign state. These steps and others like them reflect, especially after 9/11, the deep conviction of the Bush Administration that to protect America's national interest the United States must have a free hand: The sovereign Gulliver must not be tied down by feckless Lilliputians.

America's post-9/11 political rhetoric and the related strategic reorientation involve a sharp break with five decades of bipartisanship in the shaping of U.S. global policy. Though a few leading Democrats were outspoken in their criticisms of the Administration's formulations, the predominant inclination in the Democratic foreign policy establishment has been to tacitly accept the new strategic premises of the Bush worldview, and some Democratic leaders initially even acted as its cheerleaders. As a result, most Democratic foreign policy prescriptions acquired a "Bush lite" taste.

The issue for the longer run is not whether a revision of existing doctrines and national strategy was needed, for 9/11 clearly signaled that a rethinking was necessary. The key issue today is whether the diagnosis undertaken in the wake of 9/11, and particularly the concentration on terrorism, constitutes a wise response for America and for the world. After all, even the undeniable reality of America as the sovereign power of last resort still begs the question: Sovereignty for what? Doubtless many would answer: for the sake of America's national security. But that reply begs a deeper question: Might not efforts to perpetuate America's unique status as an unconstrained sovereign eventually come to *threaten* America's national security, and its civil liberty as well?

America needs to face squarely a centrally important new global reality: that the world's population is experiencing a political awakening unprecedented in scope and intensity, with the result that the politics of populism are transforming the politics of power. The need to respond to that massive phenomenon poses to the uniquely sovereign America an historic dilemma: What should be the central definition of America's global role? Serious discussion of this crucial issue has barely begun.

The Foreign Policy of 9/11: Political Triumph and Strategic Vulnerability

The Bush Administration had no foreign policy to speak of prior to September 2001, so it is no surprise that its policy since then largely has been shaped by the shock of 9/11. It is a policy derived from a single traumatic event, formulated in an atmosphere of public outrage, and that both rests on and exploits the anxieties that this event understandably unleashed. The Administration's immediate response was a campaign to imprint on the public mind its own definition of the new challenge faced by America, followed by the articulation of a more comprehensive global response to that challenge. Both focused on 9/11 as the defining moment and as the source of inspiration. The result has been a policy as narrow in its focus as it is far-reaching in its implications.

The intellectual core of the foreign policy of 9/11 is the notion of a fundamental strategic discontinuity in world affairs. The menace of terrorism, abetted by irresponsible "rogue" states and made more ominous by the proliferation of weapons of mass destruction, is said to have largely replaced the dangers posed by the more traditional rivalry among major powers. In that context, the emphasis on the "global war on terror" has been symbolically central, fostering patriotic mobilization and legitimating actions that otherwise could be viewed as extra-legal or even outright illegal. To the framers of the new strategy, 9/11 legitimated the *de facto* suspension of *habeas corpus* even for U.S. citizens, "stress interrogation" (a.k.a. torture) of detainees, and unilateral military action—just as Pearl Harbor eventually legitimated Hiroshima in the public mind. These are, it was felt, the inescapable, painful, but ultimately necessary attributes of waging a just war.

The focus on terrorism was also politically expedient because of its intrinsic vagueness. After 9/11, every American knew, without having to be told, what the word "terrorism" implied. As a consequence, there was no need to explain how a "global war on terror" had to be waged, or how one would know when such a novel war against an elusive foe had ended. There was no need to be more precise as to who the terrorists actually were, where they came from, or what historical motives, religious passions or political grievances had focused their hatred on America. Terrorism thus replaced Soviet nuclear weapons as the principal threat, and terrorists (potentially omnipresent and generally identified as Muslims) replaced communists as the ubiquitous menace.

The prompt articulation by the Bush Administration of a new worldview was pushed at the upper levels of the White House and the Department of Defense by an energetic group highly motivated by a shared strategic orientation. Internal cohesion fused with external public outrage, anxiety and thirst for action to preclude any lengthy or divisive political debate. Each of the now well-known three key components of the new strategy stressed historic discontinuity: 1) unilateralism, justified by the right to self-defense, replaced the notion of collective security based on the Atlantic Alliance and the need for legitimacy through UN sanction; 2) the right to forcibly prevent or even preempt a grave threat overshadowed deterrence as one of the key concepts of national defense (though the risk that poor intelligence might prompt a military intervention on mere *suspicion* was not initially recognized, and became the cause of major embarrassment subsequent to the invasion of Iraq); 3) reliance on *ad hoc* coalitions simultaneously downgraded the political centrality of existing alliance relationships (like NATO) and elevated the utility of expedient security arrangements with partners of tactical convenience (like Russia).

There is no gainsaying that the new strategy was responsive to both the *Zeitgeist* and the *Angst* of the moment, and in some measure also responded to the novel requirements of the post-Cold War era. The War on Terror made for an historically appealing formula. The most immediate demonstration of the new strategy was the prompt and effectively conducted military operation undertaken in the fall of 2001 to wipe out the hornets' nest in Afghanistan. It was an action applauded at home and largely supported abroad. The quick defeat of the Taliban and the dispersal of the al-Qaeda high command provided the public with welcome proof that the global war on terror was both real and winnable. Victory was in the air.

Alas, Afghanistan, which justifiably could have been viewed as a strategic triumph, was soon relegated to only a tactical success largely by the Administration's own doing. For motives widely debated though not yet clarified, those in charge of shaping U.S. strategy conflated the campaign against Osama bin Laden's al-Qaeda with a military operation to change the regime in Iraq, and did so regardless of international sanction. Iraq was thereby elevated into the central strategic theater of the global war on terror.

The public campaign alleging a grave terrorist threat continued even after the military successes in Afghanistan and Iraq, and lasted through the presidential election season of 2004.

Since the mass media are naturally drawn to compete in the business of fear, hardly a week passed without the public being treated— on television or in graphically-illustrated newspaper stories—to ever new potential horror scenarios. A legion of terror entrepreneurs (a.k.a. "experts on terrorism") also promptly sprouted. One can only speculate what would happen, for instance, if day after day both the mass media and the country's highest political authority admonished the public that everyone's health was rapidly deteriorating: that our hearts were weakening, our memories fading, our key organs wearing out, cancer spreading, and that a personal physical breakdown was inevitable. The result would surely be a nation of acute hypochondriacs.

No wonder then that—with frequent colorful official alerts of impending but otherwise unidentified danger triggering and sanctioning a widespread psychosis of fear—a self-confident America was being transformed into a fear-driven nation. Moreover, the term "war on terror" became a "heads-I-win, tails-you-lose" political formula. The absence since 9/11 of any terrorist attacks in America could be cited as evidence that the President was winning the war, while any reoccurrence of terrorism would be proof that the notion of continuing war was justified. Not surprisingly, and in keeping with historical precedents, the "wartime" re-election campaign of the incumbent "Commander-in- Chief " turned out to be successful.[1]

Political triumph for the Administration, however, has not brought strategic success for America. The war in Iraq, undertaken unilaterally in 2003 under false pretenses, proved in every respect to be much more costly than initially expected. Not only did many Americans continue to die even two years after the "end" of the war, with thousands more returning home maimed, but the aftermath of the war's major combat phase was badly mishandled, and its overall financial costs soon came to be measured in hundreds of billions of dollars. Internationally, the effect was the surfacing of historically unprecedented hostility toward America and a monumental loss of American (and especially presidential) credibility. Contributing to the decline of America's stature were the demagogy surrounding alleged weapons of mass destruction, the disgrace of America's honor (and of its top officials) in Abu Ghraib and Guantanamo, the dangerous over-stretching of U.S. military capabilities, and the concomitant decline in America's ability to prevent North Korea from acquiring nuclear weapons.

A self-confident America was being transformed into a fear-driven nation.

A special source of concern has to be the increased hostility toward America throughout the world of Islam. Though the Administration eschewed all anti-Islamic rhetoric, the thrust of its emphasis on the terrorist threat—abetted by TV serials, movies and homegrown anti-Arab vigilantes—has fostered the image of a lurking Muslim terrorist ready to strike at America. Coupled with Muslim resentment of the massive American support for Israel and of the U.S. invasion of Iraq,

15

the anti-Islamic undertones of America's public discourse played into the hands of Muslim fundamentalists propagating their hateful portrayal of America as "the Satan." The 9/11 Commission Report makes a powerful point to that effect. The ongoing civil war within Islam between fanatics and moderates was thereby being transformed into a conflict between Islam and America, to the disadvantage of Muslim moderates and of America itself.

Even more potentially dangerous to America's long-term interests has been the surfacing global trend toward regional coalitions with a thinly veiled anti-American orientation. Distancing oneself from the U.S. government and all things American has become politically popular in Asia, Europe and Latin America. That mood is facilitating China's efforts to quietly exclude the United States from its region by exploiting a rising pan-Asian identity in East and Southeast Asia; it gives a much less Atlanticist flavor to the continuing European effort to shape a more politically-minded European Union; and it encourages a cluster of new, democratically-elected but rather leftist Latin American presidents to cultivate closer relations with Europe and China. The emergence of strong pan-European and pan-Asian communities, rather than Transatlantic and Transpacific ones, would intensify America's global isolation.

By late 2004 and early 2005, recognition of these hazards started dawning even within the Administration, prompting a public redefinition of the central justification of its foreign policy. Henceforth its rhetoric was to be less about the war on terror and more about the global struggle for freedom. Concepts derived from Franklin D. Roosevelt's Atlantic Charter and Jimmy Carter's human rights campaign, not to mention Woodrow Wilson's Fourteen Points, were boldly incorporated into the January 2005 Inaugural rhetoric that grandly launched the crusade for freedom. Foreign skeptics could not fail to note, however, that the principal examples most frequently cited by the Administration of claimed success for the new democratic crusade were Afghanistan and Iraq, both subject to U.S. military occupation, and the Palestinian territories, still under Israeli occupation.

In brief, America's post-9/11 foreign policy is too short range in its focus, overly alarmist in its rhetoric, and has been too costly in its still early consequences. Its overall effect has been to increase America's national vulnerability while undermining the legitimacy of its international primacy. Even worse, the strategic diagnosis on which it rests does not provide an historically relevant, nationally unifying or internationally legitimating definition of America's long-term global role.

America and the Global Political Awakening

The policy diagnosis that follows accepts the proposition of historical discontinuity from 9/11 but argues that the central challenge of our time is posed not by global terrorism, but rather by the intensifying turbulence caused by the phenomenon of global political awakening. That awakening is socially massive and politically radicalizing. The challenge it poses to America's

sovereignty is not that Gulliver prevent the anti-American Lilliputians from tying him down, but that Gulliver muster the rapidly growing Lilliputians in a common effort to shape by stages an increasingly effective global community.

Though the global scope of today's political awakening is novel, the phenomenon itself has a considerable history. It was the French Revolution of 1789 that generated a contagious populist activism, first in France and then throughout Europe. Its intensity and social scope were unprecedented. An aroused mass political consciousness was stimulated by the spread of literacy— notably pamphleteering—and the country was galvanized by populist rallies, manifestos and flaming rhetoric on the public squares of urban centers, within numerous political clubs and even in remote villages. That burst of activism provoked not only the new bourgeoisie and the new urban lower classes (the *sans culottes*) but also the peasants, clergy and aristocrats.

The mythology of the French Revolution enshrined the noble concepts of *Liberté–Egalité–Fraternité* into the pantheon of political values. But the reality of the French Revolution was also the exaltation of orgiastic terror, revolutionary tribunals, nationalist passions and brutal class warfare—not to mention the exportation of revolution across Europe through wars of "liberation." Indeed, the notion of terror as a deliberate tool of political intimidation owes its origins to that revolution. Idealism and passion together made for a potent brew, transforming modern politics through the emergence of a socially powerful national consciousness.

During the subsequent 216 years, political awakening has spread gradually but inexorably like an ink blot. Europe of 1848, and more generally the nationalist movements of the late 19th and early 20th centuries, reflected the new politics of populist passions and growing mass commitment. In some places that combination embraced utopian Manichaeism for which the Bolshevik Revolution of 1917, the Fascist assumption of power in Italy in 1922, and the Nazi seizure of the German state in 1933 were the launch-pads. The political awakening also swept China, precipitating several decades of civil conflict. Anti-colonial sentiments galvanized India, where the tactic of passive resistance effectively disarmed imperial domination, and after World War II anti-colonial political stirrings elsewhere ended the remaining European empires. In the western hemisphere, Mexico experienced the first inklings of populist activism already in the 1860s, leading eventually to the Mexican Revolution of the early 20th century.

It is no overstatement to assert that now in the 21st century the population of much of the developing world is politically stirring and in many places seething with unrest. It is a population acutely conscious of social injustice to an unprecedented degree, and often resentful of its perceived lack of political dignity. The nearly universal access to radio, television and increasingly the Internet is creating a community of shared perceptions and envy that can be galvanized and channeled by demagogic political or religious passions. These energies transcend sovereign borders and pose a challenge both to existing states as well as to the existing global hierarchy, on top of which America still perches.

Today, one cannot analyze the future of China or India without considering the likely behavior of populations whose social and political aspirations are now shaped by impulses that are no longer exclusively local in origin. One cannot help but be struck by the political similarities of the recent turmoil in Kyrgyzstan, Egypt and Bolivia. The Muslims in the Middle East, Southeast Asia, North Africa, and a growing number of them in Europe—and Indians in Latin America, too—increasingly are defining what they desire in reaction to what they perceive to be the hostile impact on them of the outside world. In differing ways and degrees of intensity they dislike the status quo, and many of them are susceptible to being mobilized against the external power that they both envy and perceive as self-interestedly preoccupied with that status quo.

The youth of the Third World are particularly restless and resentful. The demographic revolution they embody is thus a political time-bomb, as well. With the exception of Europe, Japan and America, the rapidly expanding demographic bulge in the 25-year-old-and-under age bracket is creating a huge mass of impatient young people. Their minds have been stirred by sounds and images that emanate from afar and which intensify their disaffection with what is at hand. Their potential revolutionary spearhead is likely to emerge from among the scores of millions of students concentrated in the often intellectually dubious "tertiary level" educational institutions of developing countries.[2] Typically originating from the socially insecure lower middle class and inflamed by a sense of social outrage, these millions of students are revolutionaries-in-waiting, already semi-mobilized in large congregations, connected by the Internet and pre-positioned for a replay on a larger scale of what transpired years earlier in Mexico City or in Tiananmen Square. Their physical energy and emotional frustration is just waiting to be triggered by a cause, or a faith, or a hatred.

To sum up, the ongoing political awakening is now global in its geographic scope, with no continent or even region still largely politically passive; it is comprehensive in its social scale, with only very remote peasant communities still immune to political stimuli; it is strikingly youthful in its demographic profile and thus more receptive to rapid political mobilization; and much of its inspiration is transnational in origin because of the cumulative impact of literacy and mass communications. As a result, modern populist political passions can be aroused even against a distant target despite the absence of a unifying doctrine (such as Marxism), with America increasingly the conflicted focus of personal admiration, social envy, political resentment and religious abhorrence.

Terrorism is a destructive and extreme symptom of a widespread new reality of resentment, but terrorism as such—whether Islamist or otherwise—does not define the essence of international affairs in our time. It is undeniably a tactical threat to national security, and in the future a potential strategic one.[3] But to make terrorism the daily preoccupation of millions of anxious Americans would be as if American domestic politics in the late 1960s and early 1970s had focused mainly on reactions to the threat posed by the Black Panthers rather than on the need to redress the denial of full civil rights to African Americans. In today's world the elevation of terrorism to an almost apocalyptic threat can similarly result in an under-reaction to the wider global context that favors the rise of extremist violence. The majority of states existing today no longer rule relatively pliant populations, and many are vulnerable to being swamped by populist demands that transcend their capacity to respond effectively.

Recasting America's Global Mission

It will require increasingly supranational cooperation, actively promoted by the United States, to compensate for the weakness of nominally sovereign states that in fact are becoming ever less sovereign or even self-sustaining. The nation-state framework has become too narrow for the political solutions, economic remedies and social "depressurization" that a majority of populations urgently need. Globalization is intermingling domestic desires and grievances with a transnational awareness of "greener grass" being elsewhere, whether nearby (e.g., the European Union seen from Ukraine) or far away (e.g., the United States seen from Sri Lanka).

While no major international problem can be resolved without America, America cannot resolve any major international problem on its own: neither that posed by North Korean nukes nor the Iranian quest for them; the persistent absence of a fair settlement of the Palestinian issue; the slaughter in Darfur; the long-range issue of China's rising power; the brutal excesses in Chechnya by Russia's declining power; nor even the destructive regional consequences of America's preponderant power in Iraq.

To address these and other issues, America needs partners. Europe is America's historic ally, and hence the European Union's unity as well as its expansion is in America's interest. Japan is essential to a new Asian triangular balance of power involving the United States and China. But to have these friends and others, America must be prepared to address issues in common and seek a shared understanding of our historical era. A globally disliked America, which reduces world problems to slogans about terrorism and democracy, cannot do so. That case needs to be made explicitly if the American people are to have a genuine, not a "Bush lite", alternative to current policies.

The promotion of democracy is at best a partial response to the large and difficult challenge before us. Politically awakened mankind craves political dignity, which democracy can enhance, but political dignity also encompasses ethnic or national self-determination, religious self-definition, and human and social rights, all in a world now acutely aware of economic, racial and ethnic inequities. The quest for political dignity, especially through national self-determination and social transformation, is part of the pulse of self-assertion by the world's underprivileged.

It therefore follows that America needs to shore up its international legitimacy by a demonstrable commitment to shared political and social goals. Democracy per se is not an enduring solution, for without a socially developing and politically mature civil society, a hasty imposition of democratic processes—

for example, in the Middle East—is likely to be exploited by radically resentful populism, often with strong anti-American overtones cloaked in electoral legitimacy. Democracy for some without social justice for the many was possible in the aristocratic age, but it is no longer possible in the age of mass political awakening. Today, one without the other is self-defeating. The promotion of democracy must therefore be linked directly to efforts seeking the elimination of extreme poverty and a gradual diminution in global disparities.

The historic paradox of our time is that supranational cooperation toward these major goals is only possible if the lead is taken by the last sovereign state, and joined by the more resilient regional powers willing eventually to subsume their own sovereignty under more effective supranational arrangements. However, a comprehensive strategy for guiding the volatile and politically restless global mindset cannot be championed by a fear-driven country seeking refuge in a nation-wide gated community. An effective response can only come from a self-confident America genuinely committed to a new vision of global solidarity.

Let it be said right away that supranationality should not be confused with world government. Even if it were desirable, mankind is not remotely ready for world government, and the American people certainly do not want it. America must instead become the pacesetter in shaping a world that is defined less by the fiction of state sovereignty and more by the reality of expanding and politically regulated interdependence. With globalization no longer redefining just economic affairs but increasingly also transforming political relations, U.S. sovereignty harnessed in the service of the common good is likely to enjoy greater and longer global acceptance than America's current preoccupation with its own security.

Democracy for some without social justice for the many is no longer possible in the age of mass political awakening.

The promotion of socially responsive and politically stabilizing global solidarity in our increasingly restless world will have to move along both formal and informal tracks. Opportunities for formally institutionalized cooperation are greater currently in the socioeconomic and humanitarian areas than in the political-security domains. In the latter, for some time to come, informal arrangements among key power brokers will have to substitute for the inability of the some 200 nominally sovereign states to legitimate a decision-making process that reflects the realities of power. These informal arrangements will therefore have to be sought alongside existing UN structures.

Unfortunately, insofar as the global socioeconomic and humanitarian agenda is concerned, America's current global posture is sorely lacking. The U.S. position regarding the rising threat to the global environment has been perceived worldwide as essentially negativist. Whatever the merits of the official American reservations regarding the Kyoto Treaty, the decision not to ratify it was taken in a manner that conveyed to much of the international community a self-serving disregard for the common interest. The absence so far of any serious U.S. effort to develop an internationally acceptable alternative has reinforced that negative impression.

Though there has been some measurable progress during the last decade in meeting the Millennium Development Goals, the United States has been less than forthcoming in meeting the commitment made in Monterrey in 2002 to substantially increase the low level of its official development aid. The failure to do so stands in striking contrast to the massive rise in recent years in U.S. military and homeland security spending. The outcome of the ongoing WTO negotiations (the Doha Round) to resolve major disagreements with the developing countries regarding agricultural subsidies and access to markets is also quite uncertain. The privileged positions of the United States and the EU are being contested by a semi-organized bloc of developing countries led by China, India, Brazil and South Africa. Agreement is urgently needed because U.S. fast-track legislation will expire in 2007, thereafter making ratification by the U.S. Senate of any far-reaching compromise improbable at best.

Practical as well as moral reasons also dictate the desirability of enlarging the scope of supranational rules of conduct guiding interactions among states. The need for such rules is recognized and accepted in the commercial domain, and the rule-enforcement role of the WTO has been promoted by America. America remains more skeptical regarding supranational jurisdiction in the area of justice. However, despite official U.S. reticence, The Hague's ongoing war crimes prosecutions are gaining international support. In time, this should lead to a reconsideration of the increasingly isolated U.S. position against the International Criminal Court.

In the realm of international security, progress toward more inclusive political cooperation will have to move forward largely along an informal track. Although America's massive military power will continue to give credence to America's sovereign right to self-defense, and though deterrence still makes sense in relations among the major powers, major war as the highest form of absolute sovereignty is simply becoming old-fashioned. The new threats are fundamentally related to the rise in global restlessness. Nuclear proliferation is a persistent danger, in large measure because the desire for nuclear weapons is politically appealing. Moreover, percolating ethnic and religious violence in many parts of the world may at some point escalate to massively lethal levels, with the use of biological agents (inherently indiscriminate but more accessible than nuclear devices) probably posing the greatest long-range threat to international well-being.

Today's new threats are fundamentally related to the rise in global restlessness.

Because these threats are derived from a variety of local conditions and historical impulses, and especially because they are dispersed almost throughout the entire world, it follows that only deliberate international coordination can generate even a rudimentary global security policy. That coordination currently cannot be achieved either through the United Nations or through the existing major alliances. Neither the UN Security Council nor NATO provides the needed geographic universality, and neither truly reflects the actual distribution of global power. Moreover, the ongoing efforts to expand the UN Security Council are being checkmated by regional rivalries. Hence, a new mechanism for consultations among countries capable of making a serious contribution to global security has to be devised, though initially on an informal basis.

A semi-institutionalized even if still essentially consultative Global Security Summit, constituted with a membership designed to give it both universality in geographic scope as well as some reality in terms of power, would help to fill a persisting gap. A Global Security Summit could be reinforced by a standing secretariat to permit a more effective process of consultations. Its membership might include, in addition to the United States:

- Three European powers: Great Britain and France (since both of them are veto-wielding UN Security Council members as well as nuclear powers, and also have longer-range rapid reaction forces), and Germany (which has significant economic and military potential);
- Russia (a Eurasian power with a veto in the Security Council and a significant military power);
- Five Asian powers: China (with a veto in the Security Council), India (together with China accounting for a third of the world's population, and also nuclear-armed), Pakistan (a major nuclear-armed Muslim state), Indonesia (the most populous Muslim country), and Japan (a global economic power and worldwide lender);
- Two African states: Nigeria and South Africa (which have played leading roles in African peacekeeping missions);
- Two Latin American states: Brazil (which has played a role in peacekeeping in Haiti) and Mexico (a major force in the Central American and Caribbean regions).

An annual Global Security Summit among the proposed G-14 would not produce a global security policy overnight, but a mutually shaped perspective on proliferation or terrorism could further more genuine cooperation in dealing with such global dangers. A G-14 for global security would have the added advantage of engaging both China and India, each of which could become a disruptive force because of intensifying nationalism and growing muscle.[4] Indeed, it could even replace the increasingly anomalous G-8 in dealing both with security and socioeconomic issues. In any case, it would clearly benefit the United States to take the lead in convening such a club, though that process would also require a U.S. willingness to accept shared decisions in return for shared burdens.

A wide-ranging and ambitious redefinition of America's global role, in keeping with new historical realities, might help the United States to avoid some of the dire prospects foreseen in the influential writings of three major 20th-century political theorists: Oswald Spengler, Arnold Toynbee and Samuel Huntington. Each wrote at the cusp of a cataclysmic era: Spengler right after World War I and the collapse of his Imperial Germany; Toynbee in the aftermath of World War II, which exhausted his Great Britain; and Huntington in the wake of the disintegration of the Soviet Union and his America's emergence as the world's only superpower. Each approached the issue of the rise and fall of great powers from a different vantage point, but each reached conclusions that have an eerie relevance to America's contemporary global dilemmas.

Spengler saw the future of the West as the culmination of a process of political decay in which a vital national culture devolves into an overly ambitious and increasingly Caesarean civilization. In that civilization money rules the roost ("It is the money-spirit which penetrates unremarked the historical forms of the people's existence, often without destroying or even in the least disturbing these forms.") and creates conditions in which the manipulated people "clamour for weapons and force their leaders into a conflict to which they willed to be forced." In such conflicts, "the place of the permanent armies as we know them will gradually be taken by professional forces of volunteer war-keen soldiers. . . . In these wars of theirs for the heritage of the whole world, continents will be staked, India, China, South Africa, Russia, Islam, called out, new techniques and tactics played and counter-played." The result could even be "the slavery of an entire humanity under the regimen imposed by a few strong natures determined to rule."[5]

Toynbee takes a different tack but one no less ominous. He warns us to remember that "Militarism . . . has been by far the commonest cause of the breakdown of civilizations during the last four or five millennia." The reason for this, he argues, is that a dominant but also militant civilization, convinced of its own righteousness, unintentionally tends to replicate the barbaric evil that it has been contesting, with the result that "the alien universal state . . . becomes more and more unpopular. Its subjects are more and more offended by its alien qualities." Toynbee concludes that "the destruction which has overtaken a number of civilizations in the past . . . has always been in the nature of an act of suicide." He has a pithy phrase for it: "Suicidal statecraft."[6]

Huntington makes a compelling case that globalization, far from creating a common civilization, is spawning intensifying inter-civilizational clashes, of which the emerging collision between the West and Islam is the most threatening. He sums up by asserting that "European colonialism is over; American hegemony is receding. The erosion of Western culture follows, as indigenous, historically rooted mores, languages, beliefs, and institutions reassert themselves." He therefore warns that "democracy is inherently a parochializing not a cosmopolitanizing process" in which "the result is popular mobilization against Western-educated and Western-oriented elites." That mobilization is marked by a religious resurgence that, in the case of Asians and Muslims, involves also a strong sense of "the superiority of their cultures to Western culture."[7]

Spengler's notions of manipulated masses clamoring for a war willed by their leaders, Toynbee's of suicidal statecraft that undermines its own imperial power, and Huntington's of culturally antagonistic democratization have particular relevance to President Bush's foreign policy. For 250 years America's message to the world has been: "Give me your tired, your poor / Your huddled masses yearning to breathe free." Lately, it has been: "If you are not with us, you are against us." Today, after 9/11, the politically aroused world expects better from America: that it reach out with a serious commitment to uplift the human condition. Only with America's sovereignty dedicated in an historically relevant fashion to a cause larger than its own security will the American interest again coincide with the global interest.

Only with America's sovereignty dedicated to a cause larger than its own security will the American interest again coincide with the global interest.

Notes

1. A study by Robb Willer ("The Effects of Government-Issued Terror Warnings on Presidential Approval Ratings", *Current Research in Social Psychology*, vol. 10, no. 1, 2004), concludes that there is "consistent evidence supporting the hypothesis that government-issued warnings led to increases in President Bush's approval ratings." In a public discussion held after the 2004 elections former Secretary of Homeland Security Tom Ridge stated that he often disagreed with other senior officials who insisted on elevating the threat level to orange, noting, "There were times when some people were really aggressive about raising it." *USA Today*, May 11, 2005.

2. Depending on the definition of the tertiary educational level, there are currently worldwide between 80 and 130 million "college" students.

3. According to official World Health Organization and Department of State statistics, global deaths per year due to physical violence amounted to 1,600,000 (2002), traffic accidents 1,200,000 (2004), and terrorism 625 (2003).

4. A G-14 designed along the above lines would also provide a more responsible and inclusive response to the new global threats emanating from a politically-stirring world than the scheme quietly mooted by some Russian strategists to seduce the United States into a new "Holy Alliance", perhaps with Israel and India, ostensibly against global terrorism but in reality directed against the Muslim world and China, both of which Russia views as its principal long-range adversaries. Such an alliance could be fatal for America, for it would make it the central target of resulting resentments even while acting as a shield for Russian interests.

5. Spengler, *The Decline of the West: An Abridged Edition*, ed. Helmut Werner, trans. Charles F. Atkinson (New York: Oxford University Press, 1991), pp. 26–7, 376, 382, and 395–6.

6. Toynbee, *A Study of History: Abridgement of Volumes I-VI*, ed. D.C. Somervell, (New York: Oxford University Press, 1946), pp. 190, 419 and 422.

7. Huntington, *The Clash of Civilizations and the Remaking of World Order* (New York: Simon & Schuster, 2003), pp. 91, 94 and 102.

ZBIGNIEW BRZEZINSKI, a founding board member of the AI, is trustee and counselor at the Center for Strategic and International Studies, and served as National Security Advisor to President Carter.

The Eagle Has Crash Landed

Pax Americana is over. Challenges from Vietnam and the Balkans to the Middle East and September 11 have revealed the limits of American supremacy. Will the United States learn to fade quietly, or will U.S. conservatives resist and thereby transform a gradual decline into a rapid and dangerous fall?

IMMANUEL WALLERSTEIN

The United States in decline? Few people today would believe this assertion. The only ones who do are the U.S. hawks, who argue vociferously for policies to reverse the decline. This belief that the end of U.S. hegemony has already begun does not follow from the vulnerability that became apparent to all on September 11, 2001. In fact, the United States has been fading as a global power since the 1970s, and the U.S. response to the terrorist attacks has merely accelerated this decline. To understand why the so-called Pax Americana is on the wane requires examining the geopolitics of the 20th century, particularly of the century's final three decades. This exercise uncovers a simple and inescapable conclusion: The economic, political, and military factors that contributed to U.S. hegemony are the same factors that will inexorably produce the coming U.S. decline.

Intro To Hegemony

The rise of the United States to global hegemony was a long process that began in earnest with the world recession of 1873. At that time, the United States and Germany began to acquire an increasing share of global markets, mainly at the expense of the steadily receding British economy. Both nations had recently acquired a stable political base—the United States by successfully terminating the Civil War and Germany by achieving unification and defeating France in the Franco-Prussian War. From 1873 to 1914, the United States and Germany became the principal producers in certain leading sectors: steel and later automobiles for the United States and industrial chemicals for Germany.

The history books record that World War I broke out in 1914 and ended in 1918 and that World War II lasted from 1939 to 1945. However, it makes more sense to consider the two as a single, continuous "30 years' war" between the United States and Germany, with truces and local conflicts scattered in between. The competition for hegemonic succession took an ideological turn in 1933, when the Nazis came to power in Germany and began their quest to transcend the global system altogether, seeking not hegemony within the current system but rather a form of global empire. Recall the Nazi slogan *ein tausendjähriges Reich* (a thousand-year empire). In turn, the United States assumed the role of advocate of centrist world liberalism—recall former U.S. President Franklin D. Roosevelt's "four freedoms" (freedom of speech, of worship, from want, and from fear)—and entered into a strategic alliance with the Soviet Union, making possible the defeat of Germany and its allies.

World War II resulted in enormous destruction of infrastructure and populations throughout Eurasia, from the Atlantic to the Pacific oceans, with almost no country left unscathed. The only major industrial power in the world to emerge intact—and even greatly strengthened from an economic perspective—was the United States, which moved swiftly to consolidate its position.

But the aspiring hegemon faced some practical political obstacles. During the war, the Allied powers had agreed on the establishment of the United Nations, composed primarily of countries that had been in the coalition against the Axis powers. The organization's critical feature was the Security Council, the only structure that could authorize the use of force. Since the U.N. Charter gave the right of veto to five powers—including the United States and the Soviet Union—the council was rendered largely toothless in practice. So it was not the founding of the United Nations in April 1945 that determined the geopolitical constraints of the second half of the 20th century but rather the Yalta meeting between Roosevelt, British Prime Minister Winston Churchill, and Soviet leader Joseph Stalin two months earlier.

The formal accords at Yalta were less important than the informal, unspoken agreements, which one can only assess by observing the behavior of the United States and the Soviet Union in the years that followed. When the war ended in Europe on May 8, 1945, Soviet and Western (that is, U.S., British, and French) troops were located in particular places—essentially, along a line in the center of Europe that came to be called the Oder-Neisse Line. Aside from a few minor adjustments, they stayed there. In hindsight, Yalta signified the agreement of both sides that they could stay there and that neither side would use force to push the other out. This tacit accord applied to Asia as well, as evinced by U.S. occupation of Japan and the division of Korea. Politically, therefore, Yalta was an agreement on the status quo in which the

Soviet Union controlled about one third of the world and the United States the rest.

Washington also faced more serious military challenges. The Soviet Union had the world's largest land forces, while the U.S. government was under domestic pressure to downsize its army, particularly by ending the draft. The United States therefore decided to assert its military strength not via land forces but through a monopoly of nuclear weapons (plus an air force capable of deploying them). This monopoly soon disappeared: By 1949, the Soviet Union had developed nuclear weapons as well. Ever since, the United States has been reduced to trying to prevent the acquisition of nuclear weapons (and chemical and biological weapons) by additional powers, an effort that, in the 21st century, does not seem terribly successful.

Until 1991, the United States and the Soviet Union coexisted in the "balance of terror" of the Cold War. This status quo was tested seriously only three times: the Berlin blockade of 1948–49, the Korean War in 1950–53, and the Cuban missile crisis of 1962. The result in each case was restoration of the status quo. Moreover, note how each time the Soviet Union faced a political crisis among its satellite regimes—East Germany in 1953, Hungary in 1956, Czechoslovakia in 1968, and Poland in 1981—the United States engaged in little more than propaganda exercises, allowing the Soviet Union to proceed largely as it deemed fit.

Of course, this passivity did not extend to the economic arena. The United States capitalized on the Cold War ambiance to launch massive economic reconstruction efforts, first in Western Europe and then in Japan (as well as in South Korea and Taiwan). The rationale was obvious: What was the point of having such overwhelming productive superiority if the rest of the world could not muster effective demand? Furthermore, economic reconstruction helped create clientelistic obligations on the part of the nations receiving U.S. aid; this sense of obligation fostered willingness to enter into military alliances and, even more important, into political subservience.

Finally, one should not underestimate the ideological and cultural component of U.S. hegemony. The immediate post-1945 period may have been the historical high point for the popularity of communist ideology. We easily forget today the large votes for Communist parties in free elections in countries such as Belgium, France, Italy, Czechoslovakia, and Finland, not to mention the support Communist parties gathered in Asia—in Vietnam, India, and Japan—and throughout Latin America. And that still leaves out areas such as China, Greece, and Iran, where free elections remained absent or constrained but where Communist parties enjoyed widespread appeal. In response, the United States sustained a massive anticommunist ideological offensive. In retrospect, this initiative appears largely successful: Washington brandished its role as the leader of the "free world" at least as effectively as the Soviet Union brandished its position as the leader of the "progressive" and "anti-imperialist" camp.

One, Two, Many Vietnams

The United States' success as a hegemonic power in the postwar period created the conditions of the nation's hegemonic demise.

This process is captured in four symbols: the war in Vietnam, the revolutions of 1968, the fall of the Berlin Wall in 1989, and the terrorist attacks of September 2001. Each symbol built upon the prior one, culminating in the situation in which the United States currently finds itself—a lone superpower that lacks true power, a world leader nobody follows and few respect, and a nation drifting dangerously amidst a global chaos it cannot control.

What was the Vietnam War? First and foremost, it was the effort of the Vietnamese people to end colonial rule and establish their own state. The Vietnamese fought the French, the Japanese, and the Americans, and in the end the Vietnamese won—quite an achievement, actually. Geopolitically, however, the war represented a rejection of the Yalta status quo by populations then labeled as Third World. Vietnam became such a powerful symbol because Washington was foolish enough to invest its full military might in the struggle, but the United States still lost. True, the United States didn't deploy nuclear weapons (a decision certain myopic groups on the right have long reproached), but such use would have shattered the Yalta accords and might have produced a nuclear holocaust—an outcome the United States simply could not risk.

But Vietnam was not merely a military defeat or a blight on U.S. prestige. The war dealt a major blow to the United States' ability to remain the world's dominant economic power. The conflict was extremely expensive and more or less used up the U.S. gold reserves that had been so plentiful since 1945. Moreover, the United States incurred these costs just as Western Europe and Japan experienced major economic upswings. These conditions ended U.S. preeminence in the global economy. Since the late 1960s, members of this triad have been nearly economic equals, each doing better than the others for certain periods but none moving far ahead.

When the revolutions of 1968 broke out around the world, support for the Vietnamese became a major rhetorical component. "One, two, many Vietnams" and "Ho, Ho, Ho Chi Minh" were chanted in many a street, not least in the United States. But the 1968ers did not merely condemn U.S. hegemony. They condemned Soviet collusion with the United States, they condemned Yalta, and they used or adapted the language of the Chinese cultural revolutionaries who divided the world into two camps—the two superpowers and the rest of the world.

The denunciation of Soviet collusion led logically to the denunciation of those national forces closely allied with the Soviet Union, which meant in most cases the traditional Communist parties. But the 1968 revolutionaries also lashed out against other components of the Old Left—national liberation movements in the Third World, social-democratic movements in Western Europe, and New Deal Democrats in the United States—accusing them, too, of collusion with what the revolutionaries generically termed "U.S. imperialism."

The attack on Soviet collusion with Washington plus the attack on the Old Left further weakened the legitimacy of the Yalta arrangements on which the United States had fashioned the world order. It also undermined the position of centrist liberalism as the lone, legitimate global ideology. The direct political consequences of the world revolutions of 1968 were minimal, but the geopolitical and intellectual repercussions were enormous and irrevocable. Centrist liberalism tumbled from the throne it had occupied since the European revolutions of 1848 and that had enabled it to co-opt conservatives and radicals alike. These ideologies returned and once again represented a real gamut of choices. Conservatives would again become conservatives, and radicals, radicals. The centrist liberals did not disappear, but they were cut down to size. And in the process, the official U.S. ideological position—antifascist, anticommunist, anticolonialist—seemed thin and unconvincing to a growing portion of the world's populations.

The Powerless Superpower

The onset of international economic stagnation in the 1970s had two important consequences for U.S. power. First, stagnation resulted in the collapse of "developmentalism"—the notion that every nation could catch up economically if the state took appropriate action—which was the principal ideological claim of the Old Left movements then in power. One after another, these regimes faced internal disorder, declining standards of living, increasing debt dependency on international financial institutions, and eroding credibility. What had seemed in the 1960s to be the successful navigation of Third World decolonization by the United States—minimizing disruption and maximizing the smooth transfer of power to regimes that were developmentalist but scarcely revolutionary—gave way to disintegrating order, simmering discontents, and unchanneled radical temperaments. When the United States tried to intervene, it failed. In 1983, U.S. President Ronald Reagan sent troops to Lebanon to restore order. The troops were in effect forced out. He compensated by invading Grenada, a country without troops. President George H.W. Bush invaded Panama, another country without troops. But after he intervened in Somalia to restore order, the United States was in effect forced out, somewhat ignominiously. Since there was little the U.S. government could actually do to reverse the trend of declining hegemony, it chose simply to ignore this trend—a policy that prevailed from the withdrawal from Vietnam until September 11, 2001.

Meanwhile, true conservatives began to assume control of key states and interstate institutions. The neoliberal offensive of the 1980s was marked by the Thatcher and Reagan regimes and the emergence of the International Monetary Fund (IMF) as a key actor on the world scene. Where once (for more than a century) conservative forces had attempted to portray themselves as wiser liberals, now centrist liberals were compelled to argue that they were more effective conservatives. The conservative programs were clear. Domestically, conservatives tried to enact policies that would reduce the cost of labor, minimize environmental Constraints on producers, and cut back on state welfare benefits. Actual successes were modest, so conservatives then moved vigorously into the international arena. The gatherings of the World Economic Forum in Davos provided a meeting ground for elites and the media. The IMF provided a club for finance ministers and central bankers. And the United States pushed for the creation of the World Trade Organization to enforce free commercial flows across the world's frontiers.

While the United States wasn't watching, the Soviet Union was collapsing. Yes, Ronald Reagan had dubbed the Soviet Union an "evil empire" and had used the rhetorical bombast of calling for the destruction of the Berlin Wall, but the United States didn't really mean it and certainly was not responsible for the Soviet Union's downfall. In truth, the Soviet Union and its East European imperial zone collapsed because of popular disillusionment with the Old Left in combination with Soviet leader Mikhail Gorbachev's efforts to save his regime by liquidating Yalta and instituting internal liberalization (perestroika plus glasnost). Gorbachev succeeded in liquidating Yalta but not in saving the Soviet Union (although he almost did, be it said).

The United States was stunned and puzzled by the sudden collapse, uncertain how to handle the consequences. The collapse of communism in effect signified the collapse of liberalism, removing the only ideological justification behind U.S. hegemony, a justification tacitly supported by liberalism's ostensible ideological opponent. This loss of legitimacy led directly to the Iraqi invasion of Kuwait, which Iraqi leader Saddam Hussein would never have dared had the Yalta arrangements remained in place. In retrospect, U.S. efforts in the Gulf War accomplished a truce at basically the same line of departure. But can a hegemonic power be satisfied with a tie in a war with a middling regional power? Saddam demonstrated that one could pick a fight with the United States and get away with it. Even more than the defeat in Vietnam, Saddam's brash challenge has eaten at the innards of the U.S. right, in particular those known as the hawks, which explains the fervor of their current desire to invade Iraq and destroy its regime.

Between the Gulf War and September 11, 2001, the two major arenas of world conflict were the Balkans and the Middle East. The United States has played a major diplomatic role in both regions. Looking back, how different would the results have been had the United States assumed a completely isolationist position? In the Balkans, an economically successful multinational state (Yugoslavia) broke down, essentially into its component parts. Over 10 years, most of the resulting states have engaged in a process of ethnification, experiencing fairly brutal violence, widespread human rights violations, and outright wars. Outside intervention—in which the United States figured most prominently—brought about a truce and ended the most egregious violence, but this intervention in no way reversed the ethnification, which is now consolidated and somewhat legitimated. Would these conflicts have ended differently without U.S. involvement? The violence might have continued longer, but the basic results would probably not have been too different. The picture is even grimmer in the Middle East, where, if anything, U.S. engagement has been deeper and its failures more spectacular. In the Balkans and the Middle East alike, the United States has failed to exert its hegemonic clout effectively, not for want of will or effort but for want of real power.

The Hawks Undone

Then came September 11—the shock and the reaction. Under fire from U.S. legislators, the Central Intelligence Agency (CIA) now claims it had warned the Bush administration of possible threats. But despite the CIA's focus on al Qaeda and the agency's intelligence expertise, it could not foresee (and therefore, prevent) the execution of the terrorist strikes. Or so would argue CIA Director George Tenet. This testimony can hardly comfort the U.S. government or the American people. Whatever else historians may decide, the attacks of September 11, 2001, posed a major challenge to U.S. power. The persons responsible did not represent a major military power. They were members of a nonstate force, with a high degree of determination, some money, a band of dedicated followers, and a strong base in one weak state. In short, militarily, they were nothing. Yet they succeeded in a bold attack on U.S. soil.

George W Bush came to power very critical of the Clinton administration's handling of world affairs. Bush and his advisors did not admit—but were undoubtedly aware—that Clinton's path had been the path of every U.S. president since Gerald Ford, including that of Ronald Reagan and George H.W. Bush. It had even been the path of the current Bush administration before September 11. One only needs to look at how Bush handled the downing of the U.S. plane off China in April 2001 to see that prudence had been the name of the game.

Following the terrorist attacks, Bush changed course, declaring war on terrorism, assuring the American people that "the outcome is certain" and informing the world that "you are either with us or against us." Long frustrated by even the most conservative U.S. administrations, the hawks finally came to dominate American policy. Their position is clear: The United States wields overwhelming military power, and even though countless foreign leaders consider it unwise for Washington to flex its military muscles, these same leaders cannot and will not do anything if the United States simply imposes its will on the rest. The hawks believe the United States should act as an imperial power for two reasons: First, the United States can get away with it. And second, if Washington doesn't exert its force, the United States will become increasingly marginalized.

Today, this hawkish position has three expressions: the military assault in Afghanistan, the de facto support for the Israeli attempt to liquidate the Palestinian Authority, and the invasion of Iraq, which is reportedly in the military preparation stage. Less than one year after the September 2001 terrorist attacks, it is perhaps too early to assess what such strategies will accomplish. Thus far, these schemes have led to the overthrow of the Taliban in Afghanistan (without the complete dismantling of al Qaeda or the capture of its top leadership); enormous destruction in Palestine (without rendering Palestinian leader Yasir Arafat "irrelevant," as Israeli Prime Minister Ariel Sharon said he is); and heavy opposition from U.S. allies in Europe and the Middle East to plans for an invasion of Iraq.

The hawks' reading of recent events emphasizes that opposition to U.S. actions, while serious, has remained largely verbal. Neither Western Europe nor Russia nor China nor Saudi Arabia has seemed ready to break ties in serious ways with the United States. In other words, hawks believe, Washington has indeed gotten away with it. The hawks assume a similar outcome will occur when the U.S. military actually invades Iraq and after that, when the United States exercises its authority elsewhere in the world, be it in Iran, North Korea, Colombia, or perhaps Indonesia. Ironically, the hawk reading has largely become the reading of the international left, which has been screaming about U.S. policies—mainly because they fear that the chances of U.S. success are high.

But hawk interpretations are wrong and will only contribute to the United States' decline, transforming a gradual descent into a much more rapid and turbulent fall. Specifically, hawk approaches will fail for military, economic, and ideological reasons.

Undoubtedly, the military remains the United States' strongest card; in fact, it is the only card. Today, the United States wields the most formidable military apparatus in the world. And if claims of new, unmatched military technologies are to be believed, the U.S. military edge over the rest of the world is considerably greater today than it was just a decade ago. But does that mean, then, that the United States can invade Iraq, conquer it rapidly, and install a friendly and stable regime? Unlikely. Bear in mind that of the three serious wars the U.S. military has fought since 1945 (Korea, Vietnam, and the Gulf War), one ended in defeat and two in draws—not exactly a glorious record.

Saddam Hussein's army is not that of the Taliban, and his internal military control is far more coherent. A U.S. invasion would necessarily involve a serious land force, one that would have to fight its way to Baghdad and would likely suffer significant casualties. Such a force would also need staging grounds, and Saudi Arabia has made clear that it will not serve in this capacity. Would Kuwait or Turkey help out? Perhaps, if Washington calls in all its chips. Meanwhile, Saddam can be expected to deploy all weapons at his disposal, and it is precisely the U.S. government that keeps fretting over how nasty those weapons might be. The United States may twist the arms of regimes in the region, but popular sentiment clearly views the whole affair as reflecting a deep anti-Arab bias in the United States. Can such a conflict be won? The British General Staff has apparently already informed Prime Minister Tony Blair that it does not believe so.

And there is always the matter of "second fronts." Following the Gulf War, U.S. armed forces sought to prepare for the possibility of two simultaneous regional wars. After a while, the Pentagon quietly abandoned the idea as impractical and costly. But who can be sure that no potential U.S. enemies would strike when the United States appears bogged down in Iraq?

Consider, too, the question of U.S. popular tolerance of nonvictories. Americans hover between a patriotic fervor that lends support to all wartime presidents and a deep isolationist urge. Since 1945, patriotism has hit a wall whenever the death toll has risen. Why should today's reaction differ? And even if the hawks (who are almost all civilians) feel impervious to public opinion, U.S. Army generals, burnt by Vietnam, do not.

And what about the economic front? In the 1980s, countless American analysts became hysterical over the Japanese economic miracle. They calmed down in the 1990s, given Japan's well-publicized financial difficulties. Yet after overstating how quickly Japan was moving forward, U.S. authorities now seem to be complacent, confident that Japan lags far behind. These days, Washington seems more inclined to lecture Japanese policymakers about what they are doing wrong.

Such triumphalism hardly appears warranted. Consider the following April 20, 2002, *New York Times* report: "A Japanese laboratory has built the world's fastest computer, a machine so powerful that it matches the raw processing power of the 20 fastest American computers combined and far outstrips the previous leader, an I.B.M.-built machine. The achievement… is evidence that a technology race that most American engineers thought they were winning handily is far from over." The analysis goes on to note that there are "contrasting scientific and technological priorities" in the two countries. The Japanese machine is built to analyze climatic change, but U.S. machines are designed to simulate weapons. This contrast embodies the oldest story in the history of hegemonic powers. The dominant power concentrates (to its detriment) on the military; the candidate for successor concentrates on the economy. The latter has always paid off, handsomely. It did for the United States. Why should it not pay off for Japan as well, perhaps in alliance with China?

Finally, there is the ideological sphere. Right now, the U.S. economy seems relatively weak, even more so considering the exorbitant military expenses associated with hawk strategies. Moreover, Washington remains politically isolated; virtually no one (save Israel) thinks the hawk position makes sense or is worth encouraging. Other nations are afraid or unwilling to stand up to Washington directly, but even their foot-dragging is hurting the United States.

Yet the U.S. response amounts to little more than arrogant arm-twisting. Arrogance has its own negatives. Calling in chips means leaving fewer chips for next time, and surly acquiescence breeds increasing resentment. Over the last 200 years, the United States acquired a considerable amount of ideological credit. But these days, the United States is running through this credit even faster than it ran through its gold surplus in the 1960s.

The United States faces two possibilities during the next 10 years: It can follow the hawks' path, with negative consequences for all but especially for itself. Or it can realize that the negatives are too great. Simon Tisdall of the *Guardian* recently argued that even disregarding international public opinion, "the U.S. is not able to fight a successful Iraqi war by itself without incurring immense damage, not least in terms of its economic interests and its energy supply. Mr. Bush is reduced to talking tough and looking ineffectual." And if the United States still invades Iraq and is then forced to withdraw it will look even more ineffectual.

President Bush's options appear extremely limited, and there is little doubt that the United States will continue to decline as a decisive force in world affairs over the next decade. The real question is not whether U.S. hegemony is waning but whether the United States can devise a way to descend gracefully, with minimum damage to the world, and to itself.

For links to relevant Web sites, access to the *FP* Archive, and a comprehensive index of related Foreign Policy articles, go to www.foreignpolicy.com.

IMMANUEL WALLERSTEIN is a senior research scholar at Yale University and author of, most recently, *The End of the World As We Know It: Social Science for the Twenty-First Century* (Minneapolis: University of Minnesota Press, 1999).

Strategic Fatigue

GRAHAM E. FULLER

In the words of George W. Bush, conducting foreign policy is "hard work." As the immensely ambitious strategic vision of the Bush Administration enters its fifth year, numerous indications of strategic fatigue are in evidence. There is talk of troop withdrawals from Iraq and Afghanistan, even though the insurgencies are not subsiding in either country. The vigor for prosecuting the Global War on Terror is slowing, and, more importantly, the zeal for instigating regime change in other countries—North Korea, Iran, Syria and perhaps Venezuela—has visibly waned. The much scorned, traditional diplomatic processes shepherded by the State Department have returned. Congress is slightly less supine. Changes are evident in both substance and style as Condoleezza Rice demonstrates a new-found preference not to get out too far in front of the creaky wheels of multinational institutions that were the bane of administration activists. The administration's bark is minimized, and much of the bite seems gone.

Has superpower fatigue set in? Clearly so, to judge by the administration's own dwindling energy and its sober acknowledgment that changing the face of the world is a lot tougher than it had hoped. Of course, some degree of wear and tear is normal five years into any administration, regardless of policies. But fatigue emerges in direct proportion to the ambitiousness of the undertaking. From its early days, this administration adopted a strategic vision and peremptory posture whose implementation would prove exhausting under the best of circumstances. Administration documents and statements have regularly indicated that "we are at the beginning" of "a long war" fought globally in well over one hundred countries, probably "lasting for decades", until "victory over terrorism" is achieved. Even more, this all ties in with "the ultimate goal of ending tyranny in our world." The task is Sisyphean, the enemy generalized, the goals unclear, the scope open-ended.

The taxing character of U.S. foreign policy betrays signs of morphing into "imperial overreach." And there should be no doubt that we are talking about empire here, albeit in a new form. Neo-conservatives embrace the term openly, while the ultra-nationalists, headed by Dick Cheney and Donald Rumsfeld, do not disavow the concept. The extent of U.S. global reach—the overseas military installations and complex base-rights agreements that often dominate our relations with small nations, the peripatetic military-command representatives who over-shadow ambassadors, a broad variety of active military presences, a worldwide intelligence and strike capability—is well documented. The U.S. global "footprint"—a revealing word regularly employed by the Pentagon without irony—is massive and backed by the world's most powerful military machine in history. While different in structure and intent than the British, French or even Roman imperial presence, current U.S. ambition for projection of power is sweeping. And pursuit of this goal generates ever newer challenges that quickly contribute to strategic fatigue.

Most empires ultimately founder on economic grounds. But the short-term economic cost of the administration's policies, while high, has not yet become unbearable. Still, there are a number of longer-term indicators that do raise worries about American economic capacities on into this century: massive domestic debt, an ever greater trade imbalance, the extraordinary and broadening gap in domestic wealth between rich and poor that has no parallel in other industrial nations, the growing outsourcing of jobs, and the rise of economic competitors who are hungry for a place in the sun. But it is the immediate political cost of the expansion of empire that is fatiguing, even before the economic cost fully bites in.

"Superpowerdom" imposes the psychological burden of being on the firing line all the time, everywhere—and almost alone. The unprecedented unilateral character of U.S. exercise of global power was of course a conscious choice, reflecting a strong desire to liberate Washington from wearying, nit-picking and encumbering consultations with other world players. It bespeaks a desire to simplify the decision-making process and to clear the decks for action. *Ad hoc* allies were to serve primarily as diplomatic window-dressing and hopefully to pick up some of the bills. But the broader backlash to U.S. unilateralism and its resultant isolation and loneliness it has imposed on Washington were not entirely anticipated.

The administration's foreign policy has been conducted on at least three levels, all of which had an impact on its global reception: strategic, tactical and stylistic. The strategic level could be summed up by the Pentagon's use of the term "full spectrum dominance." Although it specifically refers to desired military capabilities, the choice of words leaves little doubt about its political implications as well. The United States is the globally pre-eminent power, resolved to prevent the emergence of any peer. The task is the indefinite extension and projection of U.S. power to shape the world with little resistance. Entirely predictably, ambitious regional great-power centers—the European Union, China, Russia, India and Brazil to name a few—instinctively objected to this open bid for American hegemony. And their distaste at the strategic level complicates policy acceptance at the *tactical* level, since U.S. tactics, however well conceived in any given situation, nonetheless contribute directly to an unwanted American strategic project. Thus the removal of Saddam Hussein, or even the Taliban, whatever the merits of each case, could not be viewed in isolation but only as key building blocks in a grand U.S. strategic agenda. Similarly, as distasteful and worrying as Tehran's regional and nuclear ambitions might be, neither Russia nor China (nor even Europe) are entirely willing to see Washington crush Iran's independent global posture in a way that leaves the United States entirely free to do its bidding in the Gulf.

Finally, at the level of style, the American dispensation with diplomatic finesse in the lead-up to Iraq and the Global War on Terror alienated many allies in nearly all continents. Washington was willing to make occasional nods to formal multilateralism as long as events closely followed the American script, as with the "coalition" in Iraq. But in the end the gratuitous alienation of many U.S. allies has exacted a measurable and ongoing political cost on U.S. capabilities, now dramatically acknowledged with Condoleezza Rice's new look at the State Department.

But as unpalatable as the uncompromising manner was to so many, it was surpassed by a much more distressing phenomenon: the emergence of a *unipolar world*. The world is quite unaccustomed to the phenomenon of unipolarity and is still trying to cope with its many implications: in politics, economics, energy, war and the fate of international institutions. And, more importantly, the world is now busily engaged in the process of chipping away at that unipolarity wherever it can.

The reality is that no serious player on the international scene can embrace a unipolar world. All states value options. It may well be that if there has to be any sole superpower, most might prefer it to be the United States—at least that appeared to be the case up to five years ago. But what matters is that few accept the status quo. There is genuine global concern with the overwhelming character of American power, against which, it is implied, serious resistance is futile. Major states prefer the more complicated, traditional balances among powers that limit the exercise of excessive power by any state. A multipolar world multiplies the power of smaller states, enabling them to form *ad hoc* coalitions capable of deterring the actions of the dominant power when need be.

There would have been diminished temptation for the Bush Administration to embrace unilateralism as a policy except that the emergence of a unipolar world made unilateralism an option. Our unrivalled power beginning in 1991 was heady brew, liberating the ideological forces of neoconservatism that could, for the first time, credibly speak of imposing an American agenda on the world order.

Yet it is an old political science cliché that a unipolar system over time invariably engenders its own counterweight. Nature abhors a sole superpower; other powers eventually bandwagon against it. So our present strategic fatigue may stem less from the immediate commitments in which we are embroiled and rather more from an unceasing necessity to maintain that sole superpower status against all comers—because that is what the very nature of unipolarity requires.

This exhaustion is perhaps most sapping at the domestic level: Americans are dying in meaningful numbers abroad; there is a lurking fear that the world is not safer, and maybe more dangerous, because of Iraq; Americans prefer to be liked abroad and are uncomfortable with their isolation; U.S. international business is unhappy; and the budget is soaring out of sight, even if its costs haven't yet touched the private pocketbook.

The intensified nationalist and neoconservative agenda within the administration, with its dramatic policy consequences, has greatly divided the nation. While the shock of 9/11 helped create a certain national "can-do" spirit of solidarity against foreign terrorists, that sentiment was rapidly depleted by Bush's broader response to 9/11. The resultant ongoing bitter domestic divisions require the administration's foreign policy architects to drag along a large and hostile domestic minority even before dealing with an unsympathetic world as well.

Abroad, the administration now faces widespread international resistance. The honeymoon of the early post-9/11 days gave way to international reconsideration of the full implications of the Global War on Terror, particularly American doctrines of unilateralism and strategic pre-emption. In the last few years, diverse countries have deployed a multiplicity of strategies and tactics designed to weaken, divert, alter, complicate, limit, delay or block the Bush agenda through a death by a thousand cuts. That opposition acts out of diverse motives, and sometimes narrowly parochial interests, but its unifying theme—usually unspoken—is resistance to nearly anything that serves to buttress a unipolar world.

Regrettably, that kind of resistance now seems nearly indiscriminate. For example, most reasonable people might have agreed that, whatever the merits of the invasion may have been, the overthrow of Saddam is now a *fait accompli* and that further deterioration of the Iraqi scene is in no one's interest. Nonetheless, most of the world has in fact preferred, sometimes almost petulantly, to watch the United States twist in the wind in Iraq, rather than to coordinate an international effort to stabilize a dangerously drifting situation. While the early, gratuitously abrasive American diplomacy contributed to European distancing from Iraq, the unspoken European goal has been to lessen the superpower's freedom of action and to work towards a more multipolar world. This global trend will stamp the character of global politics for a decade or more.

While Europe is more circumspect, other major powers, most notably Russia, China and even India, are more explicitly committed to ending a unipolar world. To be sure, they lack the power—economic, political, military, cultural—to create an alternative power polarity of their own, but they have acted subtly, or even not so subtly, to complicate or block many of Washington's major initiatives. They have worked with European powers to this same end on an *ad hoc* basis. Thus Moscow and Beijing have in one sense or another helped strengthen the ability of Iran, North Korea, Syria, Palestine's Hamas and even Venezuela deflect the broadsides of American power and impose a process-driven, compromising and consultative approach that frustrates American resolve—precisely the nightmare of the Bush unilateralists from the outset.

While no state—not even China—wishes to explicitly declare itself at odds with the United States, the common agenda, almost in principle, remains the ability to stymie Washington's will. As self-defeating, negative and unrealistic as these anti-unipolar tactics may appear to Washington, they happen to drive much of the rest of the world. Furthermore, we witness a growing body of foreign policy observers inside the United States who share that rising doubt: Is a unipolar world truly desirable, even for American interests?

Among the many risks emerging from such unfettered national power has been the growth of an unprecedented American arrogance in its diplomacy—widely discussed by most foreign states. Washington itself is still fiercely driven by the awareness that no alternative forces exist capable of offering an alternative global agenda, much less the capability to implement it. The expectation is that other countries should simply acknowledge the reality of the new world order and get on with it. This creeping arrogance of expectation contributes at a minimum to a kind of "passive aggressive" backlash across the globe.

Finally, the greatest casualty of all is the credibility of American ideology itself. For America as sole superpower, it takes only a short step to conflate our own interests with "universal" interests. Our goals—because of their global reach—seem to take on universal validity. It becomes harder, at least in our eyes, to differentiate between our national interests and the interests of the globe. By one more step of logic, perpetuation of the American imperium becomes openly justifiable in the name of universal values. But what happens when those values then become compromised on the ground?

We may perceive democracy as a universal good—and in principle it may well be. But the ideal now becomes transformed into an *instrument* of U.S. policies. And as a policy tool, the call for democratization in fact has become an instrument to intimidate, pressure or even overthrow regimes that resist the global American project. Yet for Americans, any resistance to democratization becomes an affront to the very principle itself, an irrational, petty act of resistance against the "forces of history." Democratization just might gain some international credence if truly applied across the board as the central principle of U.S. foreign policy. But to date, democratization has largely been a punishment visited upon our enemies, never a gift bestowed upon friends. Selectivity of application heavily undermines Washington's protestations of support for universal principle; in the eyes of others it merely becomes another superpower tool opportunistically employed for its own transient ends. And now even Washington is dismayed and hesitant as democratization fails to produce new governments ready to embrace the American project. This is especially true in the Muslim world, but also in a growing wave across Latin America as well. The administration's extremely spotty and inconsistent record on democratization has heavily damaged our case for democracy. Indeed, is democracy in fact the global ideology most

conducive to a superpower's continuing maintenance of its own hegemony? The democratic process more often than not tends to empower nationalist-minded publics who resent and resist foreign hegemony. Here, the pliable dictators so valued in Washington in the Cold War may soon be on their way back as Washington's most useful instruments for running a U.S.-dominated globe.

Globalization as a "universal" value presents similar problems. History demonstrates that globalization is almost invariably the favored political value of dominant world states—and why not, for which but those states are best poised to benefit from globalization? Economists debate the upsides and downsides of globalization, and each position has its own ideological camp and true believers, but for better or for worse, globalization is now increasingly perceived as a particular American agenda designed to serve American interests. It is therefore held in suspicion by many.

The upshot is that the message, whatever its virtue, becomes fatally tainted by the messenger. George Bush could today proclaim his support for the restoration of the Islamic caliphate and he would be hooted down in Cairo, Riyadh and Islamabad because of deep suspicions now of *any* position adopted by the sole superpower. Such a situation over time saps our best intentions and our wisest steps taken in pursuit of foreign policy, as the audience becomes more obsessed with the messenger than the message.

Many states therefore resist the processes of democratization or globalization simply out of concern that they represent mere instruments in America's tool-kit for promoting the American agenda. Our inevitably selective record of implementation strengthens the perception of American double standards. These international reactions discourage and even embitter an American public and their policymakers who fail to understand how other peoples, except out of sheer perversity, would resist such patently commendable values.

This problem transcends the Bush Administration. The ultimate lesson is perhaps that no sole superpower can promote its "universal values" without tainting them. While not the first U.S. administration to operate in a unipolar world, this administration was the first to drive the logic of such unchecked power to its ultimate unilateral policy conclusions, thereby validating early global fears about a unipolar world.

The setbacks and disappointments for the United States—both in policy failures and their international backlash—are of course intense. Yet our national debate still revolves around only the tactical or the specific—Afghanistan, Iraq, Iran, the Global War on Terror, the Patriot Act, even unilateralism—but there has been no serious discussion at all about the implications of a unipolar world in itself—except to celebrate it.

But by now there is not much celebration left. We are indeed confronted by strategic fatigue. We did not create all of the conditions that led to the emergence of a unipolar world; obviously the collapse of the USSR had much to do with it. But our strategic exhaustion will likely grow as more and more Lilliputians arise to tie new knots in the web of nets that hold down the superpower whose military power is ill suited to changing the existing political situation.

Of course, the United States cannot simply decide to cease being the sole global superpower. But it may have to reconsider the uncertain blessings that emerge from a unipolar world to avoid the costly and growing hostility that hinders American freedom of action as never before, especially at the hands of former friends. Indeed, our revealing national penchant for early and dogged identification of potential "threats" on the horizon that might challenge American hegemony has a strong tendency to create self-fulfilling prophecies. And maybe the emergence of additional great-power centers—dare I say some elements of "balance of power" politics?—might not be quite the disaster it appears, despite Rice's brush-off that we've been there and done that and it doesn't work. It's not as if the world is likely to rally around any of those new contenders, either—except perhaps right now, in an urgent quest for a more multipolar world.

GRAHAM E. FULLER is a former vice-chair of the National Intelligence Council at CIA. His latest book is *The Future of Political Islam* (2004).

From *The National Interest*, Summer 2006, pp. 37-42. Copyright © 2006 by National Interest. Reprinted by permission.

UNIT 2

The United States and the World: Regional and Bilateral Relations

Unit Selections

Key Points to Consider

- Construct a list of the top five regional or bilateral problems facing the United States. Justify your selections. How does this list compare to one that you might have composed 5 or 10 years ago?

- What is the most underappreciated regional or bilateral foreign policy problem facing the United States? How should the United States go about addressing it?

- How much weight should the United States give to the concerns of other states in making foreign policy decisions? Should we listen to some states more than others? If so, who should we listen to?

- What should the United States expect from other states in making foreign policy decisions?

- Looking 5 years into the future, what do you expect to be the most important regional or bilateral issue facing the United States?

- What is the major complaint other states have about U.S. foreign policy today? How should the United States respond to this complaint?

Student Web Site

www.mhcls.com/online

Internet References

Further information regarding these Web sites may be found in this book's preface or online.

Inter-American Dialogue (IAD)
  http://www.iadialog.org

Political Science RESOURCES
  http://www.psr.keele.ac.uk/psr.htm

Russian and East European Network Information Center
  http://reenic.utexas.edu/reenic/index.html

World Wide Web Virtual Library: International Affairs Resources
  http://www.etown.edu/vl/

Possession of a clear strategic vision of world politics is only one requirement for a successful foreign policy. Another is the ability to translate that vision into coherent bilateral and regional foreign policies. What looks clear-cut and simple from the perspective of grand strategy, however, begins to take on various shades of gray as policymakers grapple with the domestic and international realities of formulating specific foreign policy. This will be particularly true in seeking the support of others in pursuing one's foreign policy goals. Cooperation will often come at a price. That price may be as simple as increased access to U.S. officials or it may carry very real military and economic price tags. It may take the form of demands for American acquiescence to the foreign or domestic policies of others.

No single formula exists to guide the Bush administration in constructing a successful foreign policy for dealing with other states and organizations. Still, it is possible to identify three questions that should be asked in formulating a foreign policy. First, what are the primary problems that the United States needs to be aware of in constructing its foreign policy toward a given country or region? Second, what does the United States want from this relationship? That is, what priorities should guide the formulation of that policy? Third, what type of "architecture" should be set up to deal with these problems and realize these goals? Should the United States act unilaterally, with selected allies, or by joining a regional organization?

Each succeeding question is more difficult to answer. Problems are easily catalogued. The challenge is to distinguish between real and imagined ones. Prioritizing goals is more difficult because it forces us to examine critically what we want to achieve with our foreign policy and what price we are willing to pay. Constructing an architecture is even more difficult because of the range of choices available and the inherent uncertainty that the chosen plan will work.

The readings in this section direct our attention to some of the most pressing bilateral and regional problem areas in American foreign policy today. During the Cold War, relations with Europe and the Soviet Union always dominated this list. Today, in spite of disagreements with its European allies over the conduct of the Iraq War and its aftermath, U.S. relations with Europe are relatively calm. Relations with Russia remain more contested. More and more it is relations with Asia that are garnering high level attention in Washington. Relations with the South continue to occupy a low priority except in periods of crisis.

The first readings in this unit examine U.S. relations with Russia. "Exploiting Rivalries, Putin's Foreign Policy," asserts that the core element of Russia's foreign policy toward other countries is that of playing rivals off against one another in order to maximize Russian influence. The next essay, "The United States and Russia in Central Asia," argues that cooperation between Russia and the United States is needed if stability in this region is to be realized. The next section examines U.S. foreign policy toward Asia. "China's Response to the Bush Doctrine" chronicles China's recent foreign policy toward the United States and what it may mean for other Asian states and the United States. "The Fallout of a Nuclear North Korea," presents background information on North Korea's fall 2006 decision to explode a nuclear bomb. It identifies possible North Korean motives for going nuclear and outlines the consequences for the United States and other countries in the region as well as their possible responses. Given the unpredictability of North Korea the authors caution against making overly specific predictions about what will happen next. The emerging relationship between India and the United States is the subject of the final essay in this group. "America's New Strategic Partnership" looks at the pros and cons in the debate over the Bush administration's recent policy shift and finds both sides have overstated their positions.

The final set of readings examines the complex issues of dealing with the South. "The U.S. and Latin America through the Lens of Empire," feels that the window of opportunity for a true hemispheric partnership has passed and that relations have reverted back to a more conflictual pattern. In "Politics on the Edge: Managing the US-Mexico Border," Peter Andreas maintains that a unilateral hardening of the border will do more harm to trade than it will to preventing terrorism, and calls for a new approach to border control between these two states. The final essay in this section looks at US-African relations through the lens of "China's African Policy." It argues that China's increased economic and strategic engagement of Africa should serve as a wake-up call to the United States to become more engaged in the region.

Exploiting Rivalries: Putin's Foreign Policy

"Russian foreign policy-makers seem convinced that playing both sides against the middle with other nations is a clever way to advance Moscow's interests. It may take many more foreign policy setbacks before they are persuaded otherwise."

MARK N. KATZ

Like previous Russian leaders—whether czarist, Soviet, or post-Soviet—President Vladimir Putin is determined to see Russia acknowledged as a great power. Indeed, many Russians across the country's political spectrum share this goal. There is, however, a serious obstacle in the path to achieving it: Russia's diminished military and economic strength. That strength underlay czarist and Soviet Russia's ability to act and be acknowledged as a great power. Today, Russia's ability to credibly threaten the use of force abroad has been undermined by its inability to defeat Chechen rebels within its own borders.

Of course, the fact that Russia no longer is regarded as a threat by most nations (except some of its neighbors) raises the possibility that Moscow can get what it wants through persuasion and cooperation. Moscow's post-Soviet experience, however, has taught it that good relations with Russia are not sufficiently important to most other states that they will alter their policies to accommodate Russian interests. Neither feared as a threat nor valued as a friend, Russia has often found itself simply ignored—much to the chagrin of both the Putin administration and the Russian public generally.

Putin appears to have found a solution to this problem. He has strived to exploit situations in which Moscow, despite its diminished circumstances, can affect the balance between opposing sides on a given issue, thus providing one side or even both an incentive to court Russia. Securing such a position can deliver not just tangible economic benefits for Moscow, but also the gratification that comes with being courted, as well as the self-image of Russia as a great power that this feeds. Of course, Russia is not the only country, nor is Putin the only Russian leader to attempt to exploit rivalries between other states. Putin, however, has made this strategy the centerpiece of Russian foreign policy.

But how successful has the Russian leader been in pursuing this diplomacy? And what has Moscow actually gained by attempting to exploit rivalries between others? A look at the various areas in which Russia has tried this approach shows it has yielded far less than Moscow anticipated.

The Iraqi Oil Game

Well before Putin came to power, Moscow saw Iraqi-American hostility as a golden opportunity for Russia to exploit. With the cooperation of Soviet President Mikhail Gorbachev, stiff international economic sanctions were imposed on Iraq after its 1990 invasion of Kuwait. Although Iraqi President Saddam Hussein was undoubtedly displeased that Moscow, a once-staunch ally, had cooperated with Washington against him in the UN Security Council, his regime soon after the war over Kuwait began negotiating with several Russian firms lucrative oil development contracts that would come into effect once sanctions were lifted. Baghdad thereby provided Moscow with an incentive to seek repeal of the Security Council's sanctions while Saddam was still in power. Moscow, in fact, did repeatedly call for the lifting of the sanctions regime, albeit without success because the United States and Britain used their veto power in the Security Council to block the move. Even under sanctions, Baghdad managed to favor Russian firms when it came to signing oil development agreements under the Security Council imposed "oil for food" program that allowed Iraq to use oil sale revenues only for domestic "humanitarian" purposes.

This practice continued after Putin became president at the end of 1999. Beginning in late summer 2002, however, it became increasingly difficult for Moscow to exploit Iraqi-American hostility after the Bush administration made clear that it sought Saddam's ouster. At this point, the question that concerned Moscow was whether the oil development contracts Russian firms had signed (or initialed, negotiated, or just discussed) with Saddam's regime would be honored after his downfall. Moscow sought assurances both from Washington and American backed Iraqi opposition groups on this score, but they said that only a future Iraqi government could decide this. Further, Saddam became angry about Moscow's making these overtures. So he canceled the one major contract that a Russian oil firm—Lukoil—had actually signed to pump oil from Iraq's West Qurna field, which is believed to contain 15 billion barrels of oil.

Lukoil has insisted that Saddam's regime did not have a legitimate reason to cancel its contract, and that it remains valid. But neither the United States nor the Iraqi government has confirmed this. Lukoil, for its part, has threatened to sue any other company awarded a production contract for West Qurna. On March 9, 2004, the Iraqi oil ministry signed a contract allowing Lukoil to explore West Qurna, but not to extract oil from it. At the end of June 2004—when a new Iraqi interim government came into being—Lukoil's president said that his company would start producing oil in Iraq in 2005, but it is unclear whether the Iraqi government has reached an agreement to allow this to happen.

What Moscow had sought both from Saddam's regime and from Washington was certainty that Lukoil would retain the West Qurna contract even if regime change took place in Iraq. Having received no such certainty, it now faces the very task it had wanted to avoid: obtaining the new regime's permission for Lukoil to exploit West Qurna. Lukoil may yet succeed in operating the field, if only because neither the new Iraqi government nor other oil companies want to deal with the legal hassle Lukoil has threatened to create. But if Lukoil does get its way, Iraqi resentment over Lukoil's and Moscow's behavior in this matter may limit Baghdad's willingness to let Lukoil or other Russian firms develop Iraq's other proven but undeveloped oil fields.

Gaming the Iraq War

Russia was not alone in opposing a US-led intervention in Iraq. France, Germany, and many other countries did as well. French and German opposition offered Putin an opportunity to align Moscow with the impeccably democratic governments of two of the three most important West European states. However, while France opposed an American- led intervention against Iraq unless UN inspectors found incontrovertible evidence of an Iraqi weapons of mass destruction program, and Germany opposed war even if they did, Russia's opposition was far less categorical. Beginning about six months prior to the intervention, Moscow signaled Washington that it would drop its opposition to a Security Council resolution authorizing the use of force against Iraq—for a price.

Accounts of what Moscow demanded included recognition of Russia's economic interests in Iraq (especially oil contracts and debt repayment). Some reports also said Moscow wanted Washington to drop its objections to Russian aid to the Iranian nuclear energy program and to grant Moscow a free hand to intervene in Georgia's Pankisi Gorge (a region where Moscow claimed many Chechen rebels had found refuge). At the same time, Moscow hoped that its alignment with France and Germany would lead those two countries to make certain concessions to Russia, including a halt to their criticism of Russian human rights violations in Chechnya and acceptance of visa-free travel for Russian citizens between Russia and its Kaliningrad exclave after Lithuania joined the European Union (and adopted its immigration policies regarding non-EU citizens). Some Russian commentators also hoped that the schism between Washington and "Old Europe" (as US Defense Secretary Donald Rumsfeld dubbed France and Germany) had become so deep that both sides would need Moscow to mediate between them.

> **Moscow has long recognized Iranian-American hostility as an opportunity for Russia to sell atomic energy technology and weaponry to Tehran.**

In the end Putin did not obtain any of the concessions he had hoped to gain, either from the United States or from France and Germany. Washington intervened in Iraq without conceding to any of Moscow's demands. And France and Germany declined to compensate Russia for siding with them against the United States. The EU and France have continued to criticize Russian policy in Chechnya. And the only concession made on the Kaliningrad issue was to call the papers that Russians must obtain an "expedited travel document" instead of a visa. Neither the Bush administration nor the governments of "Old Europe" called on Moscow to act as a mediator.

Aiding Iran's Nuclear Program

Another conflict that Putin has sought to exploit is between Iran and the United States. Moscow has long recognized Iranian-American hostility as an opportunity for Russia to sell atomic energy technology and weaponry to Tehran. During a more cooperative period of US-Russian relations in 1995, Washington and Moscow reached a secret agreement (signed by Vice President Al Gore and Prime Minister Viktor Chernomyrdin) whereby Russia agreed to limit its military and nuclear cooperation with Iran in exchange for US support for the Russian space program. But in late 2000, at a more acrimonious time in US-Russian relations, Putin renounced the Gore-Chernomyrdin agreement. Partly to assert Russia's independence from the United States and partly to earn money from Iran, the Putin administration indicated it would hasten the completion of the atomic energy reactor it was building for Iran, and expressed a willingness to sell additional reactors as well.

In response to Washington's concern that Tehran might divert spent fuel from its Russian-built nuclear reactors to fabricate nuclear weapons, Moscow publicly parroted Tehran's claims that the Iranian nuclear energy program was for peaceful purposes only and was in full compliance with International Atomic Energy Agency (IAEA) safeguards. Privately, the Putin administration indicated that it was willing to make a deal: Russia would end its assistance to the Iranian nuclear program in return for compensation.

Washington thought it had made just such a deal with the 1995 Gore-Chernomyrdin agreement, whereby the removal of US government obstacles to Russia's launch of communications satellites using American technology was seen as compensation to Russia for limiting its sales of nuclear and military technologies to Iran. Putin's abrogation of the Gore-Chernomyrdin agreement raised doubts that Moscow would honor any other compensation arrangement. Moreover, Putin seemed unwilling or unable to curb the ambitions of Russia's atomic energy agency to sell nuclear reactors to Iran—something the agency saw as vital to its very survival given the dearth of other customers for these products. Finally, as Iran appeared to be inching closer and closer toward being able to build a nuclear weapon, even an end to Russian atomic energy assistance to Iran seemed unlikely to prevent this from happening. Compensating Moscow to halt its nuclear assistance to Tehran appeared increasingly pointless to Washington.

While some Russian commentators have expressed concern about Iran's acquiring nuclear weapons, Putin administration officials insist that Iran cannot do this. Some have even claimed that Washington is not worried about this either, but wants Russia to stop selling nuclear reactors to Iran so that American firms can.

And yet, despite Iran's seeming dependence on Russia for the sale of nuclear reactors and conventional weaponry, Putin's government has been unable to get much of what it wants from Tehran. In an ongoing dispute over the delimitation of the oil-rich Caspian Sea, for example, Tehran has not accepted the "modified median line" proposed by Russia, Azerbaijan, and Kazakhstan that would give Iran 13 percent of the Caspian. Iran has insisted on a 20 percent share—even though it had only 11 percent of the Caspian Sea during the Soviet era.

In addition, as of mid-2004, Tehran had not signed an agreement to return spent fuel to Russia that Moscow says must occur if it is going to provide the uranium to operate the nuclear reactor it is building. Press reports indicate that such an agreement might be signed this fall. Although Russia hopes to build up to five more reactors in Iran, Tehran insists that it will not sign contracts for further construction until the first reactor is completed (there have been numerous delays).

Instead of being able to exploit Tehran's dependence on Moscow to extract concessions from Iran, the Putin administration appears fearful that pressuring Iran on issues of concern to Moscow (not to mention Washington) could result in the Russian atomic energy industry's failure to secure contracts for the additional nuclear reactors it hopes to build for Iran.

Kyoto in the Balance

Putin also has sought international advantage in negotiations over the Kyoto climate treaty. The decision by the Bush administration and the Republican-controlled Senate not to ratify the agreement has provided Russia with extraordinary leverage over the treaty's fate. The Kyoto treaty will take effect only if the industrial nations that were responsible for 55 percent of greenhouse gas emissions in 1990 have ratified it by 2008. So far, the treaty has been ratified by nations—including Japan, Canada, and members of the EU—that produced 44 percent of the 1990 emissions levels. (The United States produced 21 percent.) Because Russia has an emissions share of 17 percent, its ratification alone could bring the treaty into effect. Aware of

this, the Putin administration has sought to exploit Russia's position as the country that determines Kyoto's fate.

The treaty requires that the ratifying industrial nations reduce output of certain emissions to below the levels they were producing in 1990. But it allows states producing over their quota to purchase emissions credits from states producing under theirs. In addition, countries (or companies) producing over their quotas can invest in projects that cut greenhouse gases elsewhere, with the resulting reductions positively affecting the quota of the investing country. Because Russian greenhouse gas emissions have dropped by nearly a third since 1990 (as a result of economic decline—not greater environmental cleanup efforts), Russia would have a massive amount of spare emissions credits to sell and could be an attractive destination for foreign investors seeking credit from projects that cut Russian emissions.

The Putin administration was not satisfied with the potential for making money that ratifying the Kyoto treaty offered. Instead, it wanted guarantees from the EU, Japan, and Canada that they would purchase credits from—or make investments in—Russia in the amount of $3 billion annually. The three refused. Indeed, the EU in particular made clear that it was displeased by this form of bargaining. Putin, after first indicating that Russia would ratify the Kyoto treaty, now raised the possibility in September 2003 that Russia might not do so.

If these tactics were a ploy to pressure the Europeans into meeting Moscow's demands for fear of the treaty's not otherwise coming into effect, they backfired. Instead of giving in to Moscow's demands, the EU made its approval for Russian admission into the World Trade Organization conditional on a pledge that Russia would ratify the Kyoto treaty. Putin himself delivered the pledge at the EU-Russian summit in May 2004. The Russian Duma (the legislative body that must actually ratify the treaty) has not yet acted on it, and Moscow may still attempt to extract "guarantees" from the EU. But in this case it appears the EU has more leverage over Russia than vice versa. For if Moscow does not ratify the treaty by 2008 (when it will lapse if it has not yet gone into effect), the emissions credits and incentives to invest in the Russian energy sector created by Kyoto will not materialize.

Oil Pipeline Politics

Russia's oil riches have created an opportunity to play off China and Japan against each other. Both China and Japan seek to reduce their dependence on oil imports from the volatile Middle East by purchasing oil from Siberia. Because Siberia does not appear to have enough oil to satisfy both China and Japan, a competition between them has emerged over which Siberian oil pipeline route Russia will build. Putin administration machinations and a dispute between two Russian oil companies have complicated the competition. Although there are numerous Russian oil companies, many of which have been privatized, the state-owned (and often slow and inefficient) Transneft exercises monopoly control over the construction and operation of oil pipelines in Russia. Privately owned Yukos, Russia's largest oil company, sought to break this monopoly by building a pipeline that would carry oil from fields it owned in eastern Siberia to Daqing, a city in China's northeastern interior.

> **While the cost of playing games with Beijing over Siberian oil export routes is not yet clear, it is certain that an annoyed China will impose some cost on Russia.**

As this deal was being finalized, the Japanese government proposed that Russia build a pipeline from eastern Siberia to Nakhodka on Russia's Pacific coast. This route would be twice as long (and two to four times more expensive) than Yukos's proposed pipeline to Daqing. But the Japanese argued that the Nakhodka route would benefit Russia more because oil piped there could be exported by sea to many different countries (including both Japan and China), whereas the Daqing route would make purchases of oil through that pipeline dependent on China alone.

Although Tokyo offered to buy all the oil from the Nakhodka route and to provide low-interest loans to cover the cost of its construction, Russian Prime Minister Mikhail Kasyanov indicated in April 2003 that it was the Daqing route that would be built. The following month, Yukos signed an agreement to sell oil to China from the Daqing route, which it expected to complete in 2005. But as the Putin administration turned against Yukos (both in retaliation for the political challenge that its chief, Mikhail Khodorkovsky, posed to the president and possibly as a means for Putin supporters to seize Yukos's assets for themselves), completion of the Daqing route looked less and less likely.

In September 2003, the Russian Ministry of Natural Resources indicated that it would issue a negative assessment of the Daqing pipeline route on environmental grounds (it also had environmental objections to the Nakhodka pipeline route). On a visit to Beijing later that month, Prime Minister Kasyanov informed his Chinese hosts that construction of the Daqing pipeline would be "postponed." Shortly thereafter, Japan offered a beefed up package for the Nakhodka route, including $5 billion in financing to support pipeline construction and $2 billion for Siberian oil field development. Since then, press coverage indicates that Transneft will build the Nakhodka pipeline route, although Moscow will not make a final decision until the end of 2004.

A desire to exploit Sino-Japanese rivalry over export routes has not been the sole factor in the Putin administration's decision making on this issue; Transneft's interest in retaining its pipeline monopoly and Putin's vendetta against Yukos chairman Khodorkovsky also have played a role. Still, the existence of Sino-Japanese competition for Siberian oil certainly pushed Tokyo to provide very generous financial incentives in an attempt to induce Moscow to build the Nakhodka route.

On the other hand, the Putin administration irritated Beijing by derailing the deal for the Daqing pipeline route after it had been agreed to. And Beijing is in a position to impose some

costs on Russia. China's decision in January 2004 to impose anti-dumping tariffs on Russian steel (announced as the Russian foreign minister was arriving in Beijing) was seen as clear retaliation for Moscow's backtracking on the Daqing pipeline deal. Beijing has also revived its efforts to have an oil pipeline built from Kazakhstan to China's western Xinjiang region. Whatever oil China buys from Kazakhstan would represent lost sales for Russia.

The Scorecard

How well has Putin's policy of attempting to exploit rivalries between others worked? There have been some positive results. In Iraq Russia gained the promise of oil deals in the summer of 2002 just as the Iraqi-American crisis was heating up. Its international image may have been burnished as Germany and France and America and Britain courted Russia in the lead-up to the US-led invasion of Iraq. Moscow also appears to have prompted Japan to up the financial ante in the rivalry over where a Siberian oil pipeline should be built.

Often, however, Putin's attempts to exploit rivalries have produced negative results for Russia. Saddam canceled the Lukoil contract for the West Qurna field because Moscow was seeking commitments from Washington and the Iraqi opposition to honor the contract if Saddam was overthrown. The US-led Coalition Provisional Authority did not agree to restore it, nor has the Iraqi interim government done so yet. Despite Iran's dependence on Russia for completion of a nuclear reactor, Tehran has made no concessions to Moscow on the division of the Caspian Sea, and has not yet signed contracts for additional reactors or for the return to Russia of spent fuel from the one reactor Moscow is building. Not only did Moscow fail in its attempts to elicit guarantees that it would receive $3 billion annually from the EU in return for ratifying the Kyoto treaty, but the EU made its approval for Russian admission into the World Trade Organization conditional on a pledge from Putin that Russia would ratify Kyoto. And while the cost of playing games with Beijing over Siberian oil export routes is not yet clear, it is certain that an annoyed China will impose some cost on Russia.

A more general problem associated with attempting to exploit rivalries between other countries is that the other countries resent this approach. They may make some concessions to Moscow to get it to change its behavior. But if the Putin administration continues to play both sides off against each other, other governments may conclude that making concessions to Moscow does not buy them anything—hence concessions are not worth making. When one or both sides to an exploited rivalry decides there is nothing to be gained from acceding to Russia's wishes, then the Putin administration looks weak for setting forth demands that are rejected or ignored. And when this happens, Putin's ultimate goal of having Russia acknowledged by others as a great power becomes increasingly elusive.

Putin's efforts to seek advantage in international rivalries appear to have produced more losses than gains for Russian foreign policy. Yet it is doubtful that his administration will abandon this approach. Even though it has resulted in important setbacks, Russian foreign policy-makers seem convinced that playing both sides against the middle with other nations is a clever way to advance Moscow's interests. It may take many more foreign policy setbacks before they are persuaded otherwise.

MARK N. KATZ is a professor of government and politics at George Mason University.

The United States and Russia in Central Asia: Uzbekistan, Tajikistan, Afghanistan, Pakistan, and Iran

FIONA HILL

I. Overview

Before 1991, the states of Central Asia were marginal backwaters, republics of the Soviet Union that played no major role in the Cold War relationship between the USSR and the United States, or in Soviet Union's relationship with the principal regional powers of Turkey, Iran, and China. But, in the 1990s, the dissolution of the Soviet Union coincided with the re-discovery of the energy resources of the Caspian Sea, attracting a range of international oil companies including American majors to the region. Eventually, the Caspian Basin became a point of tension in U.S.-Russian relations. In addition, Central Asia emerged as a zone of conflict. Violent clashes erupted between ethnic groups in the region's Ferghana Valley. Civil war in Tajikistan, in 1992–1997, became entangled with war in Afghanistan. Faltering political and economic reforms, and mounting social problems provided a fertile ground for the germination of radical groups, the infiltration of foreign Islamic networks, and the spawning of militant organizations like the Islamic Movement of Uzbekistan (IMU). The IMU first sought to overthrow the government of President Islam Karimov in Uzbekistan, later espoused greater ambitions for the creation of an Islamic caliphate (state) across Central Asia, and eventually joined forces with the Taliban in Afghanistan. With the events of September 11, 2001 and their roots in the terrorist groups operating in Afghanistan, Central Asia came to the forefront of U.S. attention.

II. Central Asia: Together but Divided

Central Asia now poses a particular set of challenges for American policy, not least because the U.S. had no history of engagement with the region until the 1990s and thus suffers from a serious lack of expertise in government as well as in academia. In addition, although the Central Asian states occupy a single, shared geographic sphere, they cannot now, in fact, be approached as a single entity. Over the last ten years of independence, the political divisions between and among the Central Asian states have hardened. The borders the states inherited from the USSR in 1991 were created on the principle of divide and rule from Moscow. Without Moscow to play the role of arbiter, these borders have become illogical, contested boundaries—fracturing ethnic groups, rupturing trade and communication routes, and breaking economic and political interdependencies. At the same time, the borders have remained porous to illicit trade, including weapons and drugs smuggling from Afghanistan, and the spread of infectious diseases like HIV/AIDS.

Central Asia's regional context has also become particularly complex since the collapse of the USSR. With the retreat of Russian influence, the states find themselves at the nexus of a number of interlocking regions: Russia and Eurasia, the Middle and Near East, South Asia, and Asia more broadly. Central Asia is simultaneously a buffer zone and a transit area among these regions. Ethno-linguistic and religious groups are spread across the regions, with Russia, Iran, China and Afghanistan sharing groups with Central Asian states, and Turkey representing the western extension of one of Central Asia's broader cultural spheres. Thus, in looking at Central Asia's external security, economic and political environment, *all* the neighboring states have to be factored in as an element in the region's future. In the context of the U.S. war on terrorism, Central Asia's linkages with Afghanistan, Iran, and Pakistan, as well as Russia, have been dramatically underscored.

Finally, the last ten years has also seen the economic, political and military involvement of new states in Central Asia. Northeast Asian countries—China, Japan, Korea—have now become engaged in the region. China has put a particular priority on relations with Central Asia to foster the development and stabilization of its vast western province, Xinjiang. Beijing also sees the region as a potential market, a source of energy and other natural resources, and as a communications bridge to Iran and the Middle East. Japan has become the largest donor country to Central Asia and, like China, sees the region—if it is stabilized and developed—as a potential market, source of raw materials, and bridge to the Middle East. And Korea has a more intimate relationship thanks to the distinct Korean populations deported there under Stalin, who have now become an influential social, political and economic component in Kazakhstan and Uzbekistan. Although China, Japan, and Korea, have only begun to make their presence felt, and their impact on trade and other regional issues has not yet been so substantial, in a sense Central Asia is rapidly becoming the heartland of Asia.

III. What are American Interests in These Countries Since September 11?

In spite of the construction in 2002 of bases in Central Asia to support the military campaign in Afghanistan, the primary U.S. interest in Central Asia is not *strategic*. Central Asia's importance to the United States is not as a bulwark against regional powers such as Russia, China, or even Iran. Nor is it to protect American commercial concerns in the exploitation of Caspian energy resources. The primary American interest is in *security*, in preventing the "Afghanicization" of Central Asia and the spawning of more terrorist groups with transnational reach that can threaten the stability of all the interlocking regions and strike the United States.

As a result, in Central Asia, America's focus is now on creating strong security ties with the states—building on military-military contacts established in the late 1990s—and on securing long-term access agreements to regional bases and military facilities, which can be used to respond to current and future security threats in Afghanistan. However, the primary goal for U.S. policy must also be to enhance Central Asia's *development* not just its military role. Like Afghanistan, if they are to transform themselves from potential breeding grounds for transnational terrorists into viable, stable states, the Central Asian countries must liberalize economically and democratize politically.

IV. What are Russian Interests?

Russia's interests in Central Asia are strikingly similar to those of the United States. Central Asia has lost its former importance to Russia as a military buffer zone—first between the Russian and British Empires, and then between the USSR and U.S. client states in Afghanistan and Pakistan, and between the USSR and China. After the Soviet Union's collapse, Russian troops were withdrawn from all the Central Asian states apart from Tajikistan and some token forces on the Kazakhstan and Kyrgyzstan borders with China.

Today, Russia's paramount concern is also one of security. Russia's own territory has been threatened by the spillover from Afghanistan through Central Asia of Islamic militancy, terrorism, and drug trafficking. Indeed, from the beginning of his presidency in January 2000, Russia's President, Vladimir Putin, pushed the idea of a concerted campaign against terrorism with American as well as European leaders. He was one of the first to raise the alarm about terrorist training camps in Afghanistan, and to warn of linkages between these camps and well-financed terrorist networks operating in Europe and Eurasia. In addition,

Russia actively supported the Northern Alliance in its struggle with the Taliban in Afghanistan. In December 2000, Moscow joined Washington in supporting United Nations sanctions against the Taliban, and later appealed for additional sanctions against Pakistan for aiding the Taliban—all a precursor to cooperation with the United States in the war against terrorism after September 11.

Russia's other major interest in the region is in Central Asian energy development, with a new focus on gas as markets expand in Europe and Asia. Together, Russia, Iran, and the Central Asian states hold more than half of world gas reserves. Gas is not as mobile as oil and is destined for regional rather than world markets. Retaining a major role in Central Asian gas production and export is a key issue for Russia's energy industry. Energy analysts doubt that Russia can both meet its domestic demand and growing ambitions for gas exports in the coming decades without having access to and influence over the flow of Central Asian gas.

In addition, Moscow seeks the restoration of Soviet-era communications and trade infrastructure between Russia and Central Asia, and some capacity for increasing Russian private sector investment in the region beyond the energy sector. In line with this interest, Russia has initiated a major project to revive and revitalize the former North-South transportation corridor from Russian Baltic ports down the Volga River, across the Caspian to Central Asia and Iran, and from there to Pakistan and India. In the Soviet period, this served as a major freight route and an alternative to the transportation of goods from Europe to Asia through the Mediterranean and Suez Canal.

All of this makes for a primary focus on economic rather than military and strategic issues for Russia in the region and, therefore, an increased interest in Central Asia's stability and development.

V. What are the Development Challenges in Central Asia?

American and Russian interests in the stability of Central Asia are challenged by the extreme domestic fragility of the states. Independence has not been kind to Central Asia. The transition from the Soviet command economy and authoritarian political system has been much more complex and difficult than anticipated. The Central Asian states were the poorest and least developed in the USSR and had to begin almost from scratch in their development in the 1990s. In losing Moscow as the center of gravity, the states lost crucial subsidies for budgets, enterprises and households, inputs for regional industries, markets for their products, transportation routes, and communications with the outside world—much of which was filtered through the Soviet capital.

The World Bank estimates that as a result of these losses, between 1990–1996, the Central Asian states saw their economies decline by 20–60% of GDP. Thanks to extensive borrowing from international financial institutions, reforms in the 1990s also saddled regional states with high and unsustainable debt burdens. Landlocked, resource-poor Tajikistan and Kyrgyzstan have fared particularly badly. A staggering 70–80% of their populations have now fallen beneath the poverty line, which puts them among the poorest of the developing countries. Soviet-era attainments in health, education, infrastructure, and industrial development have gradually eroded. As a result of this decline and deprivation, there has been a massive exodus of ethnic Russians and highly-skilled members of indigenous ethnic groups from Central Asia.

In addition, in the last decade, the Central Asian states have largely failed to develop effective post-Soviet state institutions. The legitimacy of their governments remains weak and has not been bolstered by democratic elections. As a result, governments have resorted to authoritarian, Soviet-era methods to retain control of the levers of the state—stifling opposition, clamping down on dissent, harshly cracking down on political manifestations of Islam, and frequently violating political freedoms and abusing human rights. In sum, the prospects for long-term economic and social stability in Central Asia are uncertain.

Before the events of September 11, 2001, there was a growing realization that the accumulation of challenges in Central Asia—especially given the escalating crisis in Afghanistan—demanded attention. But despite these concerns and ten years of development community involvement and engagement in the region, Central Asia was low down the priorities of the United States and other governments. Even for Japan, as the leading bilateral donor in Central Asia, its preeminence was largely the result of the disinterest of others rather than a major priority on the part of the government in Tokyo. In the 1990s, there was no real vision for the regions in world capitals, and no sense of their interaction with issues of global consequence. This changed with the terrorist attacks on the United States and the realization that civil war and acute state failure in Afghanistan had facilitated them.

Within the region, the fate of Uzbekistan is of particular concern. Uzbekistan is the most strategically located of the Central Asian states, with the largest population and the most significant military capabilities and resources, but it has also been a source of regional tension and a logjam for regional development. In the 1990s, a clamp-down on Islamic groups in response to acts of terrorism and militant activities led to the closure of mosques, a ban on political opposition movements, and arrests of practicing Muslims. This forced groups underground and increased support for insurgencies and extremists. In addition, Uzbekistan has had water and territorial disputes with all its neighbors and has used energy exports as a lever to pressure Tajikistan and Kyrgyzstan to make concessions. It has begun to mine its borders against militant incursions, further rupturing communication routes from Tajikistan and Kyrgyzstan. And, domestic economic crisis has become the *status quo*. Through a mixture of currency and exchange rate controls, state orders for its two main export commodities, cotton and wheat, and the good fortune of being self-sufficient in energy, Uzbekistan has muddled along for several years. It has stagnated economically and politically, but defied expectations of collapse and refused to open up and deregulate its economy.

With pressure on Tashkent from the U.S. and other international donors in 2002, it seems that Uzbekistan is now contem-

plating renewed IMF and World Bank programs and a new phase of the macro-economic reforms. Progress in economic reform, an improvement in its economic performance, the removal of currency controls, and increased readiness to deal with regional issues in a cooperative manner would have major benefits for all of Central Asia. However, there is also a serious risk of increased domestic social dislocation, deprivation, and destabilization from new reforms, which could have disastrous implications for Uzbekistan's neighbors.

VI. What are the Prospects for Cooperation Between the United States and Russia in Central Asia?

The U.S. campaign in Afghanistan, its assault on Taliban forces including the IMU, and its military presence in regional bases, has vastly improved the security situation in Central Asia. President Putin and other Russian leaders, as well as the governments of Central Asia, have welcomed American action in Afghanistan, although some in Russian military circles are anxious about the prospects of long-term U.S. engagement on Russia's southern borders. The positive trajectory of overall U.S.-Russian relations fixed at the May 2002 summit meeting between Presidents Bush and Putin in Moscow, and consolidated in subsequent meetings and agreements during the May Russian-NATO summit, and the G8 summit in June 2002, has increased prospects for cooperation between the United States and Russia on a number of issues, including Central Asia.

Indeed, in spite of the decline of its own military influence in Central Asia, Russia remains indispensable to the region's future. Central Asian populations are dependent on Russia for temporary and migrant employment, remittances, and energy subsidies, while Russia is still the primary market for Central Asian goods. To tackle the roots of domestic fragility and prevent Central Asia from becoming a terrorist haven like Afghanistan, the United States will have to work with Russia. Although increased U.S. and international attention to Central Asia has brought additional resources for assistance, international aid will still remain limited and insufficient to cover all pressing development needs. Political interventions will be essential and several critical regional issues will require close cooperation between the United States and Russia, including tackling drug trafficking and HIV/AIDS, promoting energy development, and restoring trade and communications routes.

In the 1990s, Central Asia became the primary conduit for heroin trafficking from Afghanistan to Europe. This has now spawned a huge intravenous drug use problem in Russia, Ukraine, and Iran, and seen the rapid increase of HIV infection and AIDS extending back along the drug routes themselves into Central Asia. Efforts by regional governments to tackle the problem were stymied by the continuation of civil war in Afghanistan and direct linkages between militants and the drug trade. Programs to eradicate heroin production and trafficking, as part of long-term reconstruction efforts in Afghanistan, will require the full cooperation of Russia and all the neighboring states affected. For Russia, drug trafficking, drug use and HIV/ AIDS have become a particular concern and security threat. A recent World Bank study of HIV, for example, notes that Russia has the fastest growing rate of new infection in the world, and estimates that by 2020, Russia will have more than 5 million people infected and face a 10.5 percent loss in GDP.

Energy development is seen as key to Central Asia's economic future and Kazakhstan, Turkmenistan, and Uzbekistan all have considerable oil and gas reserves. Gas is of increasing importance, but Central Asian fields are poorly situated for European and Asian markets and a lack of pipeline infrastructure has constrained the states' efforts to become independent producers and exporters. All existing export pipelines run through Russia, and international energy companies have failed to make the same inroads into regional gas production as they have in Caspian oil. In the 1990s, a series of ambitious international projects to transport Central Asian gas to world markets—from Kazakhstan to China, from Turkmenistan across the Caspian to Azerbaijan and Turkey, and, again, from Turkmenistan across Afghanistan to Pakistan and India—all eventually ran out of steam. In 2002, Russia promoted an Eurasian Gas Alliance to coordinate gas production, guarantee long-term purchases of Central Asian gas for Russia's domestic market, and continue to feed Central Asian gas through Russian export pipelines. Russia's energy industry plays the dominant role in Central Asian gas and Russia's participation is ultimately unavoidable and essential in any projects—U.S. or otherwise—to develop the region's energy potential.

Likewise, Russia is key to restoring trade and communications, and to transforming Central Asia into a route for licit rather than illicit trade between Europe and Afghanistan and South Asia. Projects for transporting gas from Turkmenistan and the broader Caspian Basin across Afghanistan to South Asia, which were precluded by the instability in Afghanistan, could one day be revived in the context of a broader effort to restore and improve road, rail and other transportation and communication links. The future restoration of Central Asia's links with India and Pakistan, which were also ruptured through war in Afghanistan opens up the possibility of access to Pakistani and Indian ports as well as markets for Central Asian goods.

Given Moscow's ongoing interest in reviving the North-South freight transportation corridor, Russia can play a particularly important role in developing infrastructure and bringing the landlocked Central Asian countries into the global marketplace. Here, the United States could also play a role by encouraging and assisting Russia in the development of this route as a complement to the East-West transportation routes from Central Asia across the Caspian, to the Caucasus and the Black Sea, promoted by the U.S in the 1990s. While the East-West route became a focus of early competition between America and Russia, the development of a North-South route that binds Central Asia to Europe and Asia could just as easily become a vehicle for cooperation.

Without cooperation between the U.S. and Russia, the prospects for stability in Central Asia are fairly slim. A renewal of competition will undermine both countries efforts to ensure their security in the region.

China's Response to the Bush Doctrine

PETER VAN NESS

The American political scientist Mike Lampton has captured just the right image in Chinese for understanding America's relationship with China: *tong chuang yi meng* ("same bed, different dreams"). America and China are like two lovers in bed, with very different understandings about why they are there and what the future may hold.[1]

For more than 30 years, beginning with Richard Nixon's accommodation with Mao Zedong in 1971-72, capitalist America and communist China have cooperated with each other off and on, but always with very different agendas in mind. This is no less true today. After 9/11, the People's Republic of China (PRC) sided with the United States in Bush's "war on terror," but virtually every aspect of the Bush Doctrine (e.g., unilateralism, preemption, and missile defense) raises serious security problems for China. Faced with this series of strategic initiatives from Washington, Beijing is responding in an unexpected way, and has now begun to lay down an alternative strategic design to the Bush Doctrine. How relations between the United States and China evolve will probably be decisive in determining whether there is peace or war in the region.

In this essay, I first examine the strategic implications of the Bush Doctrine to date, then analyze the PRC's response, and, finally, highlight key issues for the next four years.

Understanding the Bush Doctrine

From the presidential election campaign of 2000 through George W. Bush's first months in office before the attacks of 9/11, there were strong indications of what was to come. Bush had staffed his administration with conservative Republicans, who, especially on defense and security issues, had articulated a hard-line, unilateralist position. Their strategic priorities included missile defense, withdrawal from the Anti-Ballistic Missile Treaty, the creation of a high-tech, rapid-reaction military of overwhelming scope and power, and the revitalization of the U.S. nuclear weapons industry. Their Manichean worldview led them to view U.S. security in terms of the development of such overwhelming capabilities (military, economic, and technological) that no other state or coalition of states would dare confront the United States.

To some people, it looked as though the Bush leadership did not understand what international relations theorists call the "security dilemma," the idea that when one country builds up its military capability to enhance its defense, an adversary may see that buildup as an offensive threat and increase its own military capabilities, thereby igniting an arms race in which both countries become less secure.

Other commentators thought that President Bush and his advisors understood the security dilemma only too well. The Chinese strategic analyst Yan Xuetong, in an interview in Beijing in April 2001, agreed that when the power capabilities of two states are roughly equal, the security dilemma is likely to have the expected outcome: namely, neither side benefits. But, he said, when one state is much stronger than other states it might deliberately create a security dilemma between itself and its perceived adversaries in order to intimidate and dominate them. That, Yan argued, is what the Bush administration was trying to do.

Writing in these pages after 9/11 but before the invasion of Iraq, the political scientist David Hendrickson explained the logic of the Bush Doctrine as a "quest for absolute security." Unilateralism and a strategic doctrine of preventive war were the key elements of this futile search. Hendrickson argued that these were "momentous steps," standing in "direct antagonism to fundamental values in our political tradition," which threaten "to wreck an international order that has been patiently built up for 50 years, inviting a fundamental delegitimation of American power."[2] Hendrickson concluded his essay with a quote from Henry Kissinger that sums up the basic flaw in a search for absolute security: "The desire of one power for absolute security means absolute insecurity for all the others."[3]

The invasion of Iraq, for the Bush leadership, became the prototype of this search for absolute security: "regime change" by military force to punish any adversary who dared to stand up to American power. The overthrow of Saddam Hussein in Iraq was intended to show the world that opposition to the Bush grand design was futile. Washington would have its way, through the use of overwhelming military force if necessary, even in the face of opposition by major allies. However, the deteriorating security situation in Iraq and Afghanistan and the continued bloodletting in the Israel-Palestine conflict have demonstrated that there are limits to what even the most powerful state in the world can do in imposing its will on other nations.[4]

President Bush, at his first press conference after his reelection, told the world: "I earned capital in the campaign, political capital, and now I intend to spend it. It is my style. That's what happened in the—after the 2000 election, I earned some capital.

I've earned capital in this election—and I'm going to spend it for what I told the people I'd spend it on, which is—you've heard the agenda: Social Security and tax reform, moving this economy forward, education, fighting and winning the war on terror."[5] So, presumably, the Bush Doctrine will remain firmly in place.

The contrast between the preferences of the U.S. electorate and world opinion is sharp and potentially calamitous. While George Bush won reelection in 2004 with markedly improved margins of support over 2000, including clear control of both houses of Congress, world opinion has shifted sharply against his policies. The terrorist attacks of September 2001 on the World Trade Center and the Pentagon prompted almost universal sympathy for the victims and support for the United States, but President Bush has squandered that "capital" over the past three years by his contempt for international law and institutions, and his disdain for any who might dare to disagree with him. His administration has shown little concern for either legitimacy or the moral dimensions of the exercise of power.[6]

During the past two years, I have worked on a collaborative project with colleagues from around the Asia-Pacific on responses to the Bush Doctrine.[7] From our discussions, and informed by the insights of other colleagues like Yan Xuetong and David Hendrickson, we can infer four general propositions that are amply illustrated by the efforts of the Bush administration to date.

First, there is no such thing as absolute security, which is simply unattainable for any country, including the United States, the most powerful state the world has ever seen.

Second, the world is confounded by a unique and complex range of military, political, economic, environmental, and public health insecurities that we are only beginning to comprehend. For example, some scientists cogently argue that climate change, by itself, is the greatest threat to our existence. At the same time, specialists on Islam are convinced that if we do not treat the global problems of human security seriously, terrorism will be with us forever.

Third, no individual state, no matter how powerful, can adequately manage this range of insecurities alone. An effective response to the broad range of threats to national security presented by these problems requires a multilateral response. Obviously, the leaders of every independent state will attempt to advance their own interests as best they can, but the realist assumption that strategies based on narrow self-interest might be adequate to protect the security of a country are utopian in today's world.[8]

Fourth, the more the most powerful states seek to achieve absolute security by building up their economic and military power and operating with impunity to advance their perceived national interests, the more insecure the world—and they themselves—become.[9]

The Bush Doctrine is simply not sustainable in its current form.

It is often remarked that, since the collapse of the Soviet Union, there is no longer any state or group of states with the political will and material capabilities to balance U.S. power,

and that following the delegitimation of socialism as a developmental alternative to capitalism, there is no longer any ideological alternative to market economics and representative democracy. Where does one stand intellectually in response to the Bush Doctrine, one is asked, other than to argue that the neoconservatives are not practicing what they preach when they say that what they are trying to do is to bring freedom and democracy to the world? On what basis can a systematic alternative to the Bush Doctrine be built?

The most substantive and promising international reaction to date has been Beijing's response. Rather than initiate an arms race to challenge U.S. hegemonic power directly, as one might expect, China reacted cautiously at first and then began to promote a fully elaborated response to the Bush Doctrine.

The Chinese Response

The Chinese leadership was aware of the hard-line political views of many of the people chosen for top positions in the new administration when George W. Bush was inaugurated in January 2001. Right-wing opinion in the United States had it that China was the most likely challenger to U.S. hegemony and that the "China threat" should be a priority for the new administration. When President Bush chose to identify certain "rogue states" as the main danger in his early speeches on national security, many analysts inferred that the main, unnamed rogue that the administration had in mind was China. When the classified Nuclear Posture Review of 2002 was leaked to the press, it identified China as one of seven possible targets for nuclear attack by the United States, and a PRC-Taiwan confrontation as one of three likely scenarios in which nuclear weapons might be used.[10] The administration's commitment to both missile defense and preemptive or preventive war further raised Chinese concerns.[11]

Official Chinese reaction to the Bush Doctrine has gone through three distinct stages: *avoidance, collaboration, and strategic response.* At first, Chinese policy seemed designed to avoid confrontation with the new president. As the administration set about putting its foreign and security policies in place, Beijing could see that many of the Bush initiatives clashed with China's interests. But rather than confront the new president directly, the Chinese leadership appeared determined to stand aside from the hard-line bulldozer, apparently hoping that Washington's enthusiasm for missile defense and preventive action against "rogue states" would wane over time.

However, September 11 changed all that. The terrorist attacks on the United States provided China with an opportunity to find common ground with the new administration—to collaborate with Washington in the new "war on terror." This second stage began almost immediately after the attacks, when Chinese president Jiang Zemin telephoned Bush to offer his sympathy and support. In effect, Beijing's message was: We have terrorists too (among China's 10 million Muslims), and we want to work with you in the struggle against terrorism.[12] When it came to invading Iraq, however, China joined France and Russia in opposition. If the United Nations Security Council had put a second resolution on Iraq to a vote, one that proposed to endorse a U.S.-led invasion, it was unclear whether China would have joined France and Russia in vetoing that resolution. But China clearly opposed the invasion. Nor did China join in other U.S. undertakings, such as the Proliferation Security Initiative, a multilateral effort to interdict shipments of weapons of mass destruction and missile delivery systems.

Meanwhile, Beijing began to implement a strategic response to the Bush Doctrine. In this third stage, the focus has been on Asia. The core of the Chinese alternative has been a cooperative security response to Bush's unilateralist, preventive war strategy. In response to America's determination to reshape the world by force, China now proposed to build cooperation among different groupings of states in creating new international institutions for achieving solutions to common problems.

For Beijing, these initiatives were unprecedented. From dynastic times to the present, China had adopted a largely realist view of the world, and, like the United States, it had preferred a bilateral approach to foreign relations. Moreover, neither in its dynastic past nor in its communist present had China been any more benevolent toward its neighbors, or more hesitant to use military force than most major powers.[13] For China now to adopt a multilateral, cooperative-security design was something new and important.

By the mid-1990s, some analysts had begun to identify China as a "responsible" power, pointing to Beijing's increasing participation in international institutions like APEC (Asia-Pacific Economic Cooperation), the Association of Southeast Asian Nations (ASEAN) Regional Forum, and the World Trade Organization. By seeking and winning the opportunity to host the Olympics in 2008, and in other ways, Beijing began to signal that it was aware of its growing stake in the status quo and was prepared to help in maintaining the strategic stability that is a prerequisite for the continued economic prosperity of East Asia.

From this beginning emerged the strategic response to the Bush Doctrine. Some called this "China's new diplomacy,"[14] but it was much more than that. Beijing followed the establishment of "ASEAN+3" (yearly meetings between the ten member countries of ASEAN with China, Japan, and South Korea) with the establishment of "ASEAN+1" (the ASEAN countries and China alone). China took the lead in creating the first multilateral institution in Central Asia, the six-member Shanghai Cooperation Organization (China, Russia, Kazakhstan, Tajikistan, Uzbekistan, and Kyrgyzstan),[15] and worked to demonstrate to its neighbors that both economic and strategic security could be based on a new design: cooperation for mutual benefit among potential adversaries rather than the building of military alliances against a perceived common threat.

In the name of "nontraditional" security cooperation to deal with terrorism and other transnational crime, Beijing even normalized its relations with its former adversary India,[16] and conducted unprecedented, joint naval exercises with both India and Pakistan in the East China Sea near Shanghai in late 2003. Chinese commentators emphasized the cooperative-security theoretical basis for these initiatives: "China has been a proponent of mutual understanding and trust through international security cooperation and opposed any military alliance directed at any

other countries," and "China won't accept any military cooperation that is directed at other countries."[17]

In October 2003, China signed the ASEAN Treaty of Amity and Cooperation (the first non-ASEAN country to do so), and negotiated a "strategic partnership for peace and prosperity" with the ten ASEAN member countries. The objective is to build an East Asian Community founded on economic, social, and security cooperation.[18] Beijing also demonstrated its new approach by offering to host the six-party negotiations to find a peaceful solution to the North Korean nuclear crisis.

The key distinguishing features of the Bush administration's and Beijing's very different approaches to dealing with the post–Cold War world, stated schematically, are the following:

Bush	PRC
Absolute security for the United States	Cooperative security (seeking to work *with* potential adversaries, rather than to make war against them)
Unilateral	Multilateral
Preventive war and regime change	Rules-based collective action, and conflict resolution diplomacy
Zero-sum strategic games	Positive-sum strategic games, designed to achieve win-win outcomes
Disdain for international law, treaties, and institutions	International institution building

Beijing's approach is by no means a pacifist design. China is clearly seeking to modernize its military capability and giving very serious thought to exactly what kind of military would be most effective in dealing with the dangers of today's world, including a potential U.S. threat.[19] The military specialist Paul Godwin notes that "a primary objective of the PLA [People's Liberation Army] is to exploit perceived U.S. vulnerabilities."[20] For example, the PRC has made a careful study of so-called asymmetrical warfare and how weaker powers might successfully confront stronger powers. But it would be a mistake to understand the Chinese modernization project as predicated on launching an arms race with the United States—at least not yet.

To date, Chinese nuclear doctrine has focused on maintaining a "minimum nuclear deterrent" capable of launching a retaliatory strike after surviving an initial nuclear attack, rather than on building huge arsenals of more and more powerful nuclear weapons.[21] Beijing is well aware of the great disparity in military capabilities between China and the United States, as well as the disparity in financial and technological capacity. It is also aware of the argument that one of the key factors that finally broke the back of the former Soviet Union was its inability to sustain the arms race with the United States. It does not want to fall into that trap.

Chinese analysts have described their strategy as a design for *heping jueqi*, or "peaceful rise." Zheng Bijian, former vice president of the Central Chinese Communist Party School, says that this approach is prompted by the conviction that "China must seek a peaceful global environment to develop its economy even as it tries to safeguard world peace through development."[22] Building relations based on mutual benefit with all of its neighbors is a central objective of this strategy. Beijing wants to demonstrate that closer trade, investment, and even security relations with China can be beneficial to its neighbors.

Singapore commentator Eric Teo Chu Cheow has suggested that this new strategy resembles an old one: "China's Ming/Qing tributary system was based on three cardinal points: First, China considered itself the 'central heart' of the region; this tributary system assured China of its overall security environment. Second, to ensure its internal stability and prosperity, China needed a stable environment immediately surrounding the Middle Kingdom. Third, the Chinese emperor would in principle give more favors to tributary states or kingdoms than he received from them; for this generosity, the emperor obtained their respect and goodwill."[23]

Obviously, the international relations of the twenty-first century are very different from China's imperial relations during the Ming and Qing dynasties, but the idea of establishing mutually beneficial economic and security ties with neighboring states makes sense for everyone in Asia. Meanwhile, if successful, such a concert of power (in this case, among states that are formally equals rather than dependents of China) would help to maintain the strategic stability that China needs for its economic modernization. Critics, like activist Cao Siyuan, argue that to be successful, the "peaceful rise" strategy must be accompanied by substantial domestic political liberalization and greater transparency with respect to China's military posture: "Diplomacy is often the extension of domestic policy. A leadership's commitment to global fraternity and solidarity will be called into doubt if it is so reluctant to give its own people adequate human rights."[24] Can China practice at home what it has begun to preach abroad?

Beijing's new strategy has yet to be tested. How will Beijing's commitment to cooperative security hold up when disputes with neighbors over territory or political differences reemerge? Will it also apply to cross-strait relations with Taiwan? Yet when compared with Bush's record of making war to achieve peace in Afghanistan and Iraq, the Chinese response has substantial appeal, especially among the ASEAN countries, where cooperative security ideas have long been popular.

Clearly, China wants to avoid a conflict with the United States. The Japanese journalist Funabashi Yoichi quotes one Chinese think tank researcher as saying: "We are studying the origin of the U.S.-Soviet Cold War. Why did it happen? Was there no way to prevent it? Some see that a U.S.-China cold war is inevitable, but what can we do to prevent it?"[25] China's strategic response to the Bush Doctrine is not confrontational toward the United States and does not require China's Asian neighbors to choose between Beijing and Washington, something none of them wants to have to do.[26] Though it is not a design for what realists would call "balancing" against the United States, it challenges Washington to think and act in ways quite different from the policies pre-scribed by the Bush Doctrine when trying to resolve problems in international relations.

What Is to Come?

Leaders in both the United States and the PRC have recently consolidated their power: George W. Bush has been reelected, and Hu Jintao has finally moved former president Jiang Zemin into retirement from his Central Military Commission chairmanship and assumed the preeminent leadership of China's party, army, and state institutions. But there the similarities end.

While Beijing has been preoccupied with trying to cool down its burgeoning economy, which has been growing at the astonishing rate of some 9 percent a year, the United States appears stretched to the breaking point to meet its global commitments as the world's sole superpower. And despite the customary statements made by Secretary of State Colin Powell and his PRC counterpart about Sino-America cooperation and harmony, Qian Qichen, China's former vice premier and foreign minister, published an attack on the Bush Doctrine just before the U.S. presidential election that perhaps presented a more accurate picture of Chinese leadership thinking than the official Foreign Ministry statements.

Although it was immediately disowned by Beijing as in any sense reflecting official PRC views, Qian's article charged that the Bush Doctrine had opened a Pandora's box in advancing the notion that the United States "should rule over the whole world with overwhelming force, military force in particular." The Iraq war, Qian wrote, "has made the United States even more unpopular in the international community than its war in Vietnam." Washington, he said, was practicing "the same catastrophic strategy applied by former empires in history." But, he concluded, "it is incapable of realizing [its] goal." In his view, "the troubles and disasters the United States has met do not stem from threats by others, but from its own cocksureness and arrogance."[27]

China is not without its own problems, of course. A society of 1.3 billion people ruled by a Communist Party that insists on a monopoly of political power while trying to manage an increasingly open market economy is never going to be short of problems. Corruption, growing income inequality, and devastating environmental problems lead the list. Meanwhile, in terms of purchasing power parity, China is already the second-largest economy in the world. It is also second to the United States in energy consumption, having shifted over the past decade from being an oil exporter to an oil importer: China is now dependent on foreign sources for some 40 percent of its crude oil requirements, a number that is expected to rise to as much as 75 percent by 2025.[28]

But while China may be suffering from too much exuberance, the United States appears to be increasingly overextended. Nearly two decades ago, the historian Paul Kennedy sounded a warning about what he called "imperial overstretch," when a state's geopolitical ambitions exceed its material capabilities to sustain such ambitions.[29] In early 2001, when George W. Bush first took office, the Congressional Budget Office projected a federal budget surplus of $5 trillion over the next ten years; but following what the *Economist* has characterized as Bush's "binge of tax-cutting and spending," economists are now projecting instead a $5 trillion budget deficit.[30] Since Bush took office, the federal debt has increased by 40 percent, or $2.1 trillion, and Congress has been required to raise the federal debt ceiling several times already.[31] Meanwhile, the burden of U.S. military commitments in Afghanistan and Iraq, where tours of duty have been extended to keep sufficient troops on the ground, appears to preclude any new "preemptive" assaults on additional countries.

China, for its part, is concerned about Japanese participation in the U.S. missile defense system, new legislation to permit Japanese forces to play a larger supporting role in Bush initiatives, and the possible revision of Japan's constitution to facilitate a more substantial military modernization;[32] but except for possible miscalculation over the issue of Taiwan, there appears to be little likelihood of direct confrontation between the United States and China. Beijing and Washington understand each other much better today than they did in 1995-96 when China launched its "missile exercises" in a failed effort to influence the presidential elections in Taiwan, and since then, they have established a variety of communication links in order to avoid misperception and miscommunication if tensions in the Taiwan Strait should reemerge.

Taiwan will continue to be an issue in Sino-American relations, but it is Iraq, Iran, and North Korea that should provide the best indicators of their strategic competition. China and the United States take very different positions with respect to each of the three states demonized by President Bush as an "axis of evil" in his 2002 State of the Union Address, and each one raises a separate kind of problem for the Bush Doctrine.

The most serious and immediate case is, of course, Iraq. China opposed the U.S. invasion and totally rejects the doctrine of preventive war. The PRC, like the other major powers, fears a disruption in petroleum imports from the Middle East if the U.S. intervention fails and Iraq descends into chaos, but Beijing clearly does not want the U.S. policy of unilateral military intervention to become the norm.

Iran's nuclear program raises a different issue, since it is unlikely that the United States will have the military capability in the near future to threaten an invasion of the country. It is possible that Bush might endorse at some point an Israeli air assault on the Iranian nuclear facilities, like the Israeli "surgical strike" on Iraq's plutonium-producing Osirak research reactor in 1981, but rather than a site for a new preventive war, Iran is currently a test case for Under Secretary of State John Bolton's policy of "counterproliferation," a coercive-diplomacy strategy designed to use international pressure to force Iran to give up its potential nuclear weapons capability.[33] China, like many of the European allies, rejects this approach in favor of a more conventional "arms control" or "nonproliferation" approach.[34]

Finally, by hosting the six-party talks on North Korea, China directly confronts the Bush Doctrine with its own cooperative security approach to conflict resolution.[35] China is no less concerned to stop nuclear weapons proliferation in Northeast Asia

than the United States, fearing that a nuclear North Korea could prompt Japan, South Korea, and possibly even Taiwan to follow suit. But having rejected the coercive U.S. Proliferation Security Initiative, China is proposing instead a multilateral security mechanism for the region to engage and to incorporate the existing North Korean regime.

When Beijing and Washington come face to face, there are always a great many issues to discuss: Taiwan, the U.S. trade deficit with the PRC, and Beijing's concern about the falling U.S. dollar (China is heavily invested in U.S. Treasury bonds), as well as North Korea, Iraq, Iran, and other security problems. Beijing will wait to see who will hold the key foreign policy and security posts in the second Bush administration, and it will have to learn to work more closely with Condoleezza Rice as secretary of state after Colin Powell is gone.

China and the United States are still "in the same bed but dreaming different dreams," as Beijing and Washington each appeal to the world to support their distinctive approaches to resolving the problems of the twenty-first century. President Chen Sui-bian's failure to win a majority for his pro-independence position in Taiwan's legislature in the December 11 elections should help ease tensions over the Taiwan issue, but policies toward the "axis of evil" countries remain in dispute. For the next chapter in the Sino-American saga, it would be a good idea to keep a close watch on North Korea, Iran, and Iraq.

Notes

1. David M. Lampton, *Same Bed, Different Dreams: Managing U.S.-China Relations, 1989-2000* (Berkeley: University of California Press, 2001).

2. David C. Hendrickson, "Toward Universal Empire: The Dangerous Quest for Absolute Security," *World Policy Journal,* vol. 19 (fall 2002), pp. 1-2.

3. Ibid., p. 7.

4. See, for example, Ahmed Rashid, "The Mess in Afghanistan," *New York Review of Books,* February 12, 2004, pp. 24-27; Jamie Wilson, "Attacks Halt Rebuilding Work in Iraq," *Guardian Weekly,* April 29-May 5, 2004, p. 1; Scott Wilson, "US Abuse Worse Than Saddam's, Say Inmates," *Sydney Morning Herald,* May 4, 2004; and Sarah Boseley, "100,000 Iraq Civilians Have Died Since Invasion, Survey Finds," *Guardian Weekly,* November 5-11, 2004, p. 4.

5. "President Holds Press Conference," November 4, 2004, www.whitehouse.gov.

6. See Robert W. Tucker and David C. Hendrickson, "The Sources of American Legitimacy," *Foreign Affairs,* vol. 83 (November/December 2004), pp. 18-32. Regarding the issue of torture, which has so undermined the legitimacy of the U.S. role, see also Seymour M. Hersh, *Chain of Command: The Road from 9/11 to Abu Ghraib* (New York: HarperCollins, 2004); and Mark Danner, *Torture and Truth: America, Abu Ghraib, and the War on Terror* (New York: New York Review Books, 2004).

7. Melvin Gurtov and Peter Van Ness, eds., *Confronting the Bush Doctrine: Critical Views from the Asia-Pacific* (New York: RoutledgeCurzon, 2004).

8. See Peter Van Ness, "Hegemony, Not Anarchy: Why China and Japan Are Not Balancing US Unipolar Power," *International Relations of the Asia-Pacific,* vol. 2, no. 1 (2002), pp. 131-50.

9. For example, Richard Clarke, former head of counterterrorism in the White House during both the Clinton and George W. Bush administrations, found that for Bush and his neoconservative advisers "Iraq was portrayed as the most dangerous thing in national security. It was an idée fixe, a rigid belief, received wisdom, a decision already made and one that no fact or event could derail." Invading Iraq constituted "a rejection of analysis in favor of received wisdom. It has left us less secure. We will pay the price for a long time" (Richard A. Clarke, *Against All Enemies: Inside America's War on Terror* [New York: Free Press, 2004], pp. 265, 287).

10. See Timothy Savage, "Letting the Genie Out of the Bottle: The Bush Nuclear Doctrine in Asia," in Gurtov and Van Ness, eds., *Confronting the Bush Doctrine;* and David S. McDonough, *The 2002 Nuclear Posture Review: The "New Triad," Counterproliferation, and U.S. Grand Strategy* (Vancouver, B.C.: Centre of International Relations, University of British Columbia, Working Paper No. 38, August 2003).

11. Li Bin, "China: Weighing the Costs," *Bulletin of the Atomic Scientists,* March/April, 2004, pp. 21-23. Paul Godwin argues that "assuring a reliable second-strike capability in the shadow of US ballistic missile defense programs is unquestionably China's highest priority" (Paul H. B. Godwin, "The PLA's Leap into the 21st Century: Implications for the US," Jamestown Foundation, *China Brief,* vol. 4, no. 9, April 29, 2004).

12. You Ji, "China's Post 9/11 Terrorism Strategy," Jamestown Foundation, *China Brief,* vol. 4, no. 8, April 15, 2004.

13. See, for example, Alastair Iain Johnston, *Cultural Realism: Strategic Culture and Grand Strategy in Chinese History* (Princeton, NJ: Princeton University Press, 1995); Allen S. Whiting, "The Use of Force in Foreign Policy by the People's Republic of China," *Annals of the American Academy of Political and Social Science,* no. 402 (July 1972), pp. 55-65; and Allen S. Whiting, *The Chinese Calculus of Deterrence: India and Indochina* (Ann Arbor: University of Michigan Press, 1975).

14. Evan S. Medeiros and M. Taylor Fravel, "China's New Diplomacy," *Foreign Affairs,* vol. 82 (November-December, 2003), pp. 22-35.

15. For the Shanghai Cooperation Organization statement on terrorism, see *Beijing Review,* January 17, 2002, p. 5.

16. For agreements signed and a chronology of Sino-Indian contacts, April-June 2003, see *China Report* (New Delhi), vol. 39 (October-December 2003).

17. Xiao Zhou, "China's Untraditional Thoughts on Security," *Beijing Review,* November 27, 2003, pp. 40-41.

18. "East Asian Community Now Possible," *Beijing Review,* October 30, 2003, pp. 40-41. *China: An International Journal,* published by the East Asia Institute, National University of Singapore, has taken a special interest in China's relations with ASEAN. This new journal publishes a chronology of events and documents on the relationship in each issue.

19. See David Shambaugh, *Modernizing China's Military: Progress, Problems, and Prospects* (Berkeley: University of California Press, 2002).

20. Godwin, "PLA's Leap into the 21st Century"; see also William S. Murray III and Robert Antonellis, "China's Space Program: The Dragon Eyes the Moon (and Us)," *Orbis,* vol. 47 (fall 2003), pp. 645-52.

21. Joseph Cirincione, with Jon B. Wolfsthal and Miriam Rajkumar, *Deadly Arsenals: Tracking Weapons of Mass Destruction* (Washington, D.C.: Carnegie Endowment for International Peace, 2002), pp. 141-64.

22. Willy Wo-Lap Lam, "China Aiming for 'Peaceful Rise,'" **www.cnn.com,** February 2, 2004.

23. Eric Teo Chu Cheow, "An Ancient Model for China's New Power: Paying Tribute to Beijing," *International Herald Tribune,* January 21, 2004.

24. Quoted in Lam, "China Aiming for 'Peaceful Rise.'"

25. Funabashi Yoichi, "China's 'Peaceful Ascendancy,'" December 2003, YaleGlobal Online, at www.yaleglobal.yale.edu.

26. Amitav Acharya, "Will Asia's Past Be Its Future?" *International Security,* vol. 28, (winter 2003/04), pp. 149-64.

27. Qian Qichen, "US Strategy Seriously Flawed," *China Daily Online,* November 1, 2004.

28. Pam Woodall, "The Dragon and the Eagle," *Economist,* October 2, 2004; and "Asia's Great Oil Hunt," *Business Week,* November 15, 2004.

29. Paul Kennedy, *The Rise and Fall of the Great Powers* (New York: Vintage, 1987), pp. 514-15.

30. *Economist,* October 9-15, 2004.

31. *International Herald Tribune,* October 16-17, 2004, p. 2.

32. Richard Tanter, "With Eyes Wide Shut: Japan, Heisei Militarization, and the Bush Doctrine," in Gurtov and Van Ness, eds., *Confronting the Bush Doctrine.*

33. John R. Bolton, "An All-Out War on Proliferation," *Financial Times,* September 7, 2004.

34. Li Bin, "China: Weighing the Costs."

35. Peter Van Ness, "The North Korean Nuclear Crisis: Four-Plus-Two—An Idea Whose Time Has Come," in Gurtov and Van Ness, eds., *Confronting the Bush Doctrine.*

PETER VAN NESS is a visiting fellow in the Contemporary China Centre and lectures on security in the Department of International Relations at Australian National University. His new book, *Confronting the Bush Doctrine: Critical Views from the Asia-Pacific,* edited with Melvin Gurtov and published by RoutledgeCurzon, is the basis for this essay.

From *World Policy Journal,* Winter 2004/2005, pp. 38-47. Copyright © 2005 by MIT Press. Reprinted by permission.

The Fallout of a Nuclear North Korea

"The nuclearization of North Korea will have a profound impact on Northeast Asia. If Pyongyang opts for crash nuclearization through a weapon test, that could bring the countries of the region together in opposition. This reaction is far from assured, however . . . ."

ANDREW SCOBELL AND MICHAEL R. CHAMBERS

North Korea kept the rest of the world on the edge of their seats during the first half of 2005. Six-party talks on the future of North Korea's nuclear program had stalled for eight months before Pyongyang announced in February that it was indefinitely withdrawing from the negotiations and that it already possessed nuclear weapons. By May, the crisis seemed about to boil over, as US intelligence agencies indicated that North Korea might be preparing to test a nuclear device, thereby proving its nuclear weapon status.

No test occurred, and South Korea's unification minister traveled to Pyongyang in mid-June to present a new proposal for massive economic and energy aid to the north. He returned with new assurances that North Korean leader Kim Jong-il was prepared to give up his country's nuclear weapons program and rejoin the multilateral talks if US officials would treat North Korea with "respect." After weeks of clarifications and wrangling, the United States and North Korea agreed to participate in a fourth round of the talks. These began in Beijing on July 26 and included bilateral discussions between Washington and Pyongyang. The talks ended inconclusively 13 days later with a promise to resume discussions in three weeks.

Yet, even if the six parties to the negotiations (the United States, North Korea, South Korea, China, Japan, and Russia) make some measure of progress, it is doubtful that the talks will result in Pyongyang's forsaking its nuclear weapons program. North Korea has a long-standing interest in nuclear weapons, and Kim Jong-il believes in the security such weapons will provide his regime. The real question then is: How will the United States and North Korea's neighbors respond to Pyongyang's nuclearization? To a large extent, this will depend on which path North Korea takes—whether it continues on its current course of gradually revealing its nuclear capabilities, or opts for the sudden clarity of a nuclear test. Whichever path Pyongyang takes, its nuclear weapons status will remain of great concern to the United States and others. Not only does North Korea's nuclearization challenge the international nonproliferation regime, but the risk of Pyongyang's transferring nuclear material or technology to other countries or terrorist groups is too high to ignore.

From the outset it is important to acknowledge the challenges of analyzing, understanding, and forecasting the actions and intentions of the Pyongyang regime. North Korea has an extremely opaque political system and its inner workings and policy-making process are impossible to discern with any high degree of certainty. Indeed, former US Ambassador to South Korea Donald Gregg, who has spent virtually his entire professional career studying the country, has called North Korea "the longest running intelligence failure in US history." Predicting the reactions of the United States and the major regional actors to North Korea's nuclearization is somewhat easier, but still not fool-proof.

A Continuing Obsession

The current nuclear crisis erupted in October 2002 when North Korean diplomats admitted to US Assistant Secretary of State James Kelly that Pyongyang possessed an active nuclear weapons program. This startling admission meant that North Korea had violated the 1994 Agreed Framework, under which Pyongyang had agreed to halt nuclear weapons development in return for aid from a consortium of countries that included the United States. While it is now commonly assumed that North Korea does indeed possess a small number of nuclear weapons, no conclusive evidence exists to corroborate the assumption.

Some analysts argue that Pyongyang only began seeking nuclear weapons in the early 1990s as a deterrent when its two major sponsors, Moscow and Beijing, severed or substantially cut back military aid to North Korea and the government witnessed a significant erosion of its conventional military capabilities. Other analysts, including many in China, contend that the primary goal of North Korea's nuclear program is to use it as a bargaining chip to obtain much-needed economic assistance from abroad and that Pyongyang is prepared to relinquish its program in return for ironclad security guarantees from the United States. The problem with both of these explanations is that neither fits the messy reality of the North Korean experience with weapons of mass destruction (WMD).

North Korea's obsession with WMD predates its 15-year-old heightened security concerns and chronic economic woes. Indeed, North Korea has possessed chemical and biological weapons for at least several decades. The available evidence suggests that North Korea has actively pursued a nuclear program for almost 50 years. Pyongyang began a "peaceful" nuclear program in the 1950s with Soviet and Chinese assistance and apparently made the decision to pursue weaponization in the late 1970s.

Pyongyang, thus, is not faking an interest in nuclearization. North Korea does appear to be drawing out its rhetoric and actions to extract maximum concessions in what amounts to an extended game of nuclear brinkmanship or blackmail. But, while the regime might bargain on aspects of its nuclear activities, it is highly unlikely to negotiate away the entire program. Even though North Korea agreed to halt work on its plutonium-based nuclear weapons program under the 1994 Agreed Framework, it commenced a second weapons program based on highly enriched uranium by 1997. The message seems clear: North Korea wants to become a nuclear weapons state.

Indeed, North Korea's historical experience suggests that it views WMD and nuclear weapons in particular as central to its identity and critical to its survival. Three factors point to this conclusion. First, the regime traces its lineage to a band of communist guerrillas led by Kim Il Sung that battled Japanese occupation forces in China's Manchuria in the 1930s. While they accepted Soviet assistance, the fighters espoused an ideology of extreme self-reliance on the assumption that no one outside the band could be fully trusted. Second, the only reliable form of security was the acquisition of sufficient military capabilities to make their own destiny. For Kim, who would go on to lead North Korea, and his band of rugged partisans, the most fundamental form of power was military might. This became the top priority after the formal establishment of North Korea in 1947, and was reinforced following the 1953 Korean War armistice. The emphasis on military power has continued, and is manifested in the current "military first" policy espoused by Pyongyang.

Third, WMD represents for Pyongyang the ultimate form of national power, security, and status. The government sincerely believes that Korea and Koreans have been victims of the threatened or actual use of WMD from early on. Thousands of Korean laborers working in Japan were killed and maimed by the atomic blasts at Hiroshima and Nagasaki. Pyongyang apparently honestly believes (as does Beijing) that Washington used biological agents in the Korean War. (Although the United States reportedly considered using biological weapons, the available evidence indicates that they were never actually employed.) North Korea also believes that the United States has repeatedly issued nuclear threats, beginning with the Korean War and continuing since. Given this experience and these perceptions, it is not surprising that North Korea has doggedly sought to acquire an arsenal of chemical, biological, and nuclear weapons and the delivery systems for them. Pyongyang has learned that a country in possession of WMD can use that power to influence others. And the most effective way to counter and deter such threats is to possess these weapons.

"Striptease" or "Big Bang"?

States can take two main routes to nuclear power status: through creeping nuclearization or crash nuclearization. The first route would simply involve a continuation of existing policy in a kind of nuclear "striptease," in which Pyongyang would persist in gradually revealing tantalizing tidbits about the extent of its nuclear program and its nuclear status would become less and less ambiguous. The second route would involve a sudden detonation that would dramatically make clear North Korea's nuclear status. The striptease approach offers Pyongyang the advantage of continuing to make countries pay to get the regime to remove items of nuclear clothing, drawing this process out as long as possible while skillfully maneuvering so as not to give up its program completely. Creeping nuclearization would inhibit the strong negative reactions from the United States and neighboring Northeast Asian countries that would follow a North Korean nuclear test. It would also allow Pyongyang to benefit from tensions among the other members of the six-party talks—especially between the United States and South Korea—as they continue with their different approaches to dealing with the North Korean nuclear challenge.

If the benefits of creeping nuclearization are so significant, under what conditions would Pyongyang abandon this lucrative course of action? North Korea is likely to carry out a nuclear test only in extreme conditions: in a climate of heightened fear or heightened confidence. In the former situation, Pyongyang would fear that an external attack was imminent or that domestic instability had reached a critical point and the only hope of regime survival was to test. In the second case, Pyongyang might become convinced that it could escape severe international repercussions and that it could continue to use the nuclear program as a bargaining chip even after testing. The regime might calculate that the United States and other governments would be willing to provide aid and security assurances in exchange for North Korea's agreement to limit its nuclear arsenal and not proliferate. Pyongyang might also conclude that a test could create tensions in the US–South Korea alliance.

North Korean overconfidence may be avoided by a continued hard-line stance on the part of the United States and Japan, and by China's pursuit of its stated interest in a non-nuclear Korean Peninsula. Avoiding heightened North Korean fears may require further American security reassurances to Pyongyang that it will not attack, as well as additional economic assistance from China and South Korea (conditional on progress by North Korea on freezing and then dismantling its nuclear program). Coordinating such an approach would be difficult, and of course there is no guarantee that it would prevent Pyongyang's nuclearization even if a multilateral deal were struck.

The Regional Fallout

Whether North Korea continues its course of creeping nuclearization or adopts crash nuclearization, the decision will have enormous consequences for the balance of power in Northeast Asia. Testing a nuclear weapon would be clearly in defiance of the interests of North Korea's neighbors and the international community, and would increase the prospects for a strong reaction. Revealing its nuclear capability bit by bit would maintain for some time—perhaps several years—a degree of ambiguity that would allow some countries, such as China and South Korea, to continue to downplay North Korea's actions and thereby inhibit a strong, unified international response. How might the United States, China, Japan, and South Korea respond to either course?

United States

The United States has consistently expressed the greatest alarm about—and been the most focused on—North Korea's nuclear program. Whether Pyongyang's program proceeds by increments or with a "bang," Washington will approach the situation with great seriousness and will be inclined to take a hardline response.

If North Korea tests a nuclear weapon, the US response would likely be relatively swift and tough. The Bush administration would almost certainly take the matter to the United Nations Security Council, seeking a resolution condemning North Korea and supporting sanctions of some kind, probably economic. Washington would also work with friends and allies to impose sanctions against Pyongyang and to strengthen the Proliferation Security Initiative (PSI), a multilateral effort launched by President Bush in 2003, to block exports of nuclear technology or materials. It is unlikely that America would undertake military action except as a last resort, since there do not appear to be any good military options.

> **While the regime might bargain on aspects of its nuclear activities, it is highly unlikely to negotiate away the entire program.**

If, however, Pyongyang were to continue its policy of gradually enhancing its nuclear capabilities while revealing them to the outside world in a slow-motion striptease, that would complicate and possibly frustrate Washington's efforts at a strong response. Whether or not the six-party talks continue, the United States would almost certainly ratchet up pressure on North Korea if Pyongyang appeared to be enhancing its nuclear capability. The United States would likely pursue a UN Security Council resolution condemning North Korea for its behavior and seek sanctions in coordination with other countries. Washington would also continue to pursue the PSI. Yet the lack of strong international support, especially from Beijing and Seoul, under this scenario would impede the American efforts and reduce their chances of success.

China

Beijing is increasingly concerned about the protracted crisis over North Korea, but there is no consensus among Chinese leaders as to what should be done. Three schools of thought appear to have formed: the "no matter what" school; the "just say no" school; and the "wait and see" school.

The "no matter what" school advocates Chinese support for North Korea irrespective of what Pyongyang does because of the abiding friendship and alliance between the two countries that date back to the Korean War. Adherents of this school appear to be in a distinct minority, but they can count on additional support from a widespread unease among Chinese elites about the possible collapse of a buffer between China and US military forces in South Korea.

Adherents of the "just say no" school are more numerous. They are adamant that China must oppose North Korea's nuclearization and insist that Beijing would make a "strong response" to a Pyongyang test. This appears to be the stance of many current and retired senior Chinese officials, who routinely assure their American counterparts that China considers a nuclear test by North Korea to be a clear "red line" and that Beijing has firmly communicated this to Pyongyang. Their tough rhetoric, however, does not seem to be backed by any real commitment to tough action, and in reality many of these purported adherents probably belong to the third school of thought.

The "wait and see" adherents evidently have convinced themselves that even if North Korea tests, the outcome would be something that China could live with. Several Chinese analysts have opined that they are not certain whether a test by Pyongyang would actually constitute a red line for Beijing. These analysts are not convinced that China would crack down hard on North Korea in this eventuality despite US expectations of a strong Chinese reaction. What seems to concern Chinese analysts of all three schools most about Pyongyang's nuclear program is not the prospect of a nuclear North Korea, but that this development would put China in a difficult spot diplomatically.

According to Chinese analysts in Beijing and Shanghai interviewed earlier this summer, the Chinese government, lacking internal consensus on the matter, would confront a dilemma if North Korea tested. Along with the United States, Japan, South Korea, and Russia, China has stated that it desires a non-nuclear Korean Peninsula. Because of this public stance and its cooperation with Washington on the issue, the Bush administration would expect China to firmly back a stern response: support a UN Security Council resolution, join in sanctions, and cooperate more closely on counterproliferation efforts. Beijing has reportedly warned Pyongyang that a nuclear test would prompt a serious reaction by China. These measures could include a reduction in food aid to North Korea and refusal to block a UN Security Council resolution critical of North Korea.

Yet, despite the stern talk in line with its "just say no" school, China does not appear to be seriously considering tough measures because of concerns that sanctions and punishment might lead to political and economic instability in North Korea. The result, Beijing fears, could include massive refugee flows into northeast China—one of China's worst nightmares when it comes to its eastern neighbor. This development could disrupt northeastern China's social and economic stability. It could also bring a US military ally directly onto China's border if the North Korean regime collapsed (with the possibility of armed conflict during the collapse). Consequently, China has continued publicly to oppose the use of sanctions to resolve the nuclear crisis. How the Chinese leadership would resolve this dilemma, and which of the three schools of thought on North Korea would prove triumphant, remains an open question. Meanwhile, the reactive and passive mood evident in Beijing in the summer of 2005 suggests that the "wait and see" school will determine policy.

Surprisingly, South Korea is not terribly concerned about the prospect of the nuclearization of its northern neighbor.

Because of the enormous stakes involved with a North Korean nuclear test, China would much prefer a creeping nuclearization program. That would allow Beijing to argue that Pyongyang's nuclear weapons development is not as advanced as Washington claims it is. But China would also like to see a de-escalation in tensions, including an end to North Korean nuclear brinkmanship and progress in the six-party negotiations. Absent an actual test, Beijing's response to creeping nuclearization is likely to be a continued emphasis on a diplomatic track (which would include economic or other incentives to keep Pyongyang talking) in tandem with continued opposition to the use of sanctions.

South Korea

Like Beijing, Seoul is extremely concerned about the stability of the Korean Peninsula and its northern neighbor. This concern underlies South Korea's "sunshine policy." Launched in 1998 by President Kim Dae Jung and continued by President Roh Moo Hyun, the sunshine policy is an attempt to expand cooperation and contacts with Pyongyang through public diplomacy and economic interaction. The Roh administration has, like Beijing, also opposed the use of UN sanctions to curb Pyongyang's nuclear ambitions.

Surprisingly, South Korea is not terribly concerned about the prospect of the nuclearization of its northern neighbor. In fact, the primary military threat to Seoul from Pyongyang remains conventional. South Korea's capital is well within the range of North Korea's forward-deployed long-range artillery. In any event, many South Koreans believe there is little likelihood that North Korea would attack, and the possibility of its communist neighbor employing nuclear weapons against fellow Koreans south of the demilitarized zone is unthinkable.

Still, it is difficult to forecast Seoul's reaction to a nuclear test by Pyongyang because it will be influenced by a host of factors, including the climate between Seoul and Pyongyang, domestic politics in South Korea, and the state of the economy. All these will come into play over the next two years as prospective candidates jockey for position in the lead-up to the presidential election scheduled for December 2007. While it is conceivable that South Korea's response to a nuclear test would be relatively subdued and accepting, it is also possible that South Korea might react angrily, agreeing with the United States and Japan to impose sanctions or take other assertive steps, such as using the PSI to quarantine arms shipments.

A North Korean nuclear test would challenge the underpinnings of the sunshine policy, but might not suffice to overturn it. Significant numbers of South Koreans seem to have persuaded themselves that they could live with a nuclear North Korea. If Pyongyang publicly justified a nuclear detonation as a purely defensive step forced on it by the increasing hostility of the United States and openly declared that nuclear weapons would never be used against the people of South Korea, many South Koreans might be receptive to such rhetoric.

South Korea's reluctance to take strong actions against Pyongyang is likely to continue if the north maintains its policy of creeping nuclearization. This softer policy approach would frustrate US and Japanese efforts to tighten the screws on North Korea as it gradually nuclearizes, such as the imposition of economic sanctions or tightening of the PSI. (South Korea is not a member of the PSI states, fearing that its membership would irritate the north.) Such differences could exacerbate existing strains in the US–South Korean relationship.

Japan

Other than the United States, the country most alarmed about the prospect of a nuclear North Korea is undoubtedly Japan. Tokyo's security apprehensions were greatly magnified following the 1998 flight of a North Korean Taepodong I missile over northern Japan, and were raised further with the onset of the current nuclear crisis in fall 2002. As a result, Tokyo's thinking is much closer to that of Washington's than either Beijing's or Seoul's. Not surprisingly, Japan closely monitors developments in North Korea and, in particular, the status of Pyongyang's nuclear and ballistic missile programs. Japanese nationalists have used North Korea's nuclear and missile programs as a catalyst for conversations about whether Japan should become a "normal country"—that is, one with a military worthy of its international status. These conversations have included discussions about alterations to Article 9 of the constitution (which renounces war) as well as the possibility that in the future Japan might develop and deploy nuclear weapons.

In December 2003 the government decided to purchase and deploy a ballistic missile defense (BMD) system with the United States as a response to the increasing North Korean threat. Earlier that year, Shigeru Ishiba, the director general of the Japanese Defense Agency, had warned that Japan might launch a "preemptive" strike against North Korea if Tokyo determined that Pyongyang was about to launch a missile attack on Japan. In addition to strengthening Japan's military capabilities, Tokyo has issued tough rhetoric on economic means to pressure North Korea. In the spring of 2005, senior politicians—such as Shinzo Abe, the secretary general of the ruling Liberal Democratic Party—called for UN sanctions should North Korea test a nuclear weapon.

Many observers continue to speculate that, if North Korea tests, Japan may follow suit. But this is unlikely to happen, at least anytime soon. Tokyo almost certainly has the technical capability to test and weaponize, and a North Korean nuclear test possibly would increase popular support for Japanese nuclearization. But the political impediments to such moves are significant. These barriers include long-standing domestic Japanese opposition to the acquisition of nuclear weapons, concern among Japan's regional neighbors, and pressures from the United States to halt further proliferation in East Asia. Although these impediments are not insurmountable, they would mean that any steps toward nuclearization would take years rather than months.

Almost certainly, however, a test by Pyongyang would spark a major reassessment of Tokyo's defense policy. At a minimum Japan would accelerate plans to deploy a BMD system and further strengthen its security relationship with the United States. A test could also catalyze Japanese efforts to develop a more active defense policy and to acquire weapons congruent with this policy (such as cruise missiles). In addition to these military measures, Japan would be certain to call for the UN Security Council to take up the issue and pass a sanctions resolution. Tokyo would also join the United States in any efforts to use the PSI to disrupt North Korea's arms trade.

If North Korea continues its nuclear striptease, Japan would adhere to its circumspect policy toward North Korea. It is also virtually inconceivable that bilateral relations would improve. This is so in part because Pyongyang's nuclear and missile programs are only one of a number of thorny issues complicating relations with Japan. (Others that remain unresolved include a full accounting of Japanese citizens believed to have been abducted by North Korea and reparations for Japanese atrocities committed during the extended occupation of the Korean Peninsula in the first half of the twentieth century.) If Pyongyang gradually reveals its nuclear capabilities, Tokyo would join with Washington to ratchet up the pressure, using economic measures as well as military cooperation to achieve this. Many of the reactions under this scenario would resemble those under crash nuclearization, but would be drawn out over a longer period without the drama of a nuclear test.

Perils of Prediction

The responses by the United States, China, South Korea, and Japan to North Korea's nuclearization may themselves trigger reactions among the regional powers. In particular, efforts by Washington and Tokyo to invoke UN-approved sanctions or to use the PSI to inhibit Pyongyang's arms trade might increase tensions with Beijing and Seoul, fraying cooperative relations. Similarly, efforts by Japan to enhance its military capabilities—especially if it procures weapons (for example, cruise missiles)

with an offensive strike capability to neutralize the increased North Korean threat—would probably be met with strong negative reactions from China and perhaps South Korea, and could provoke public protests in both countries. These developments could aggravate the deteriorated state of Japan's relations with both of these neighbors and raise regional concerns over rising Japanese assertiveness.

The nuclearization of North Korea will have a profound impact on Northeast Asia. If Pyongyang opts for crash nuclearization through a weapon test, that could bring the countries of the region together in opposition. This reaction is far from assured, however, because of the uncertainties surrounding Chinese and South Korean responses to a test. Creeping North Korean nuclearization holds the real prospect of frayed relations between the United States and Japan on the one side and China and South Korea on the other, with the US–South Korean alliance suffering. It seems unlikely, however, that Seoul would break the US alliance to form one with Beijing. South Korea would be reluctant to reject a battle-tested ally in favor of an unproven strategic partner with questionable designs on the Korean Peninsula.

It is also difficult to predict how a nuclear North Korea may act within the region. Conceivably, the possession of nuclear weapons will make the paranoid regime in Pyongyang feel more secure, and thus willing to engage more openly with its neighbors—and perhaps even agree to negotiate on other issues. However, it is also possible that the stability-instability paradox may come into play: believing that the United States and others will not dare to retaliate militarily for fear of a conflict escalating to the nuclear level, North Korea might engage in reckless and aggressive behavior, creating further instability in the region.

While Pyongyang tends to engage in identifiable patterns of behavior, it is also prone to surprise. In comparison, the reactions of Washington, Beijing, Seoul, and Tokyo seem more predictable. One prospect does seem certain: barring the imminent collapse of North Korea (which cannot be ruled out but appears highly unlikely), analysts will be forced to speculate about Pyongyang's nuclear intentions until the ruling North Korean regime decides to provide clarity.

ANDREW SCOBELL is an associate research professor at the Strategic Studies Institute of the US Army War College. **MICHAEL R. CHAMBERS** is an associate professor of political science at Indiana State University. The views expressed here are solely those of the authors.

Reprinted from *Current History*, September 2005, pp. 289-294. Copyright © 2005 by Current History, Inc. Reprinted with permission.

America's New Strategic Partner?

Ashton B. Carter

Seeing the Big Picture

Last summer, Indian Prime Minister Manmohan Singh announced that India and the United States had struck a deal for a far-reaching "strategic partnership." As part of the agreement, President George W. Bush broke with long-standing U.S. policy and openly acknowledged India as a legitimate nuclear power, ending New Delhi's 30-year quest for such recognition. Much of the debate surrounding "the India deal," as the agreement has come to be known since it was finalized last March, has focused on nuclear issues. Opponents charge that Bush's historic concession to India could deal a serious blow to the international nonproliferation regime and could set a dangerous precedent for Iran, North Korea, and other aspiring nuclear powers. They also note that the Bush administration obtained no meaningful commitments from New Delhi—no promises that India would limit its growing nuclear arsenal or take new steps to help combat nuclear proliferation and international terrorism. Why, the critics ask, did Washington give India so much for so little?

These detractors are both right and wrong. They are right to say that the deal is unbalanced and seems to have been struck with little regard for some of its implications. But they overstate the damage it will do to nonproliferation—an important cause, without doubt—and their understanding of the deal's objectives is too narrow. When the nuclear arrangements of the agreement are understood—as they should be—as just one part of a sweeping strategic realignment that could prove critical to U.S. security interests down the road, the India deal looks much more favorable. Washington gave something away on the nuclear front in order to gain much more on other fronts; it hoped to win the support and cooperation of India—a strategically located democratic country of growing economic importance—to help the United States confront the challenges that a threatening Iran, a turbulent Pakistan, and an unpredictable China may pose in the future. Washington's decision to trade a nuclear-recognition quid for a strategic-partnership quo was a reasonable move.

Critics rightly note, however, a serious asymmetry in the arrangement: whereas the deal is clear about what the United States conceded, it is vague about what India will give in return. India obtained nuclear recognition up front; the gains for the United States are contingent and lie far ahead in the uncertain future. This imbalance leaves Washington at the mercy of India's future behavior: there is still a chance that India will not deliver on the strategic partnership, especially if cooperating with the United States means abandoning positions it once endorsed as a leader of the Nonaligned Movement (NAM) and siding decisively with Washington on a range of security issues. It remains to be seen, for example, if India, once a staunch detractor of the nonproliferation regime, will now become one of its supporters.

The truth is that it is too soon to tell whether the promise of the India deal will be realized. It is too soon to tell even whether the deal will be consummated at all. To take effect, the White House's nuclear concessions to India must be written into U.S. law. Only Congress can do that, and many of its members are seeking to rebalance the deal in the United States' favor. Some legislators are eager to do so by taking back some of Washington's nuclear concessions, including on nuclear recognition—a recanting that would cast a lasting cloud over U.S.–Indian relations. Recognizing the danger of this approach, other legislators, backed by reputable nonproliferation experts, are advocating imposing new technical conditions on India. They hope to limit what they perceive to be the danger posed by the India deal to the nonproliferation regime. But the damage will likely be manageable, and haggling over technical details is unlikely to restore whatever loss to its reputation as a proponent of nonproliferation Washington has already suffered. New Delhi might view such conditions as punitive or as only a begrudging acceptance of the deal, a result that would undermine the goodwill Washington sought to build by launching a broad strategic partnership.

The deal, no matter how problematic its nuclear provisions, should not be recast or curtailed. Rather, Congress must support it in its entirety and approve it with implementation language that clearly states the concrete geopolitical advantages the United States expects to gain from a strategic partnership with India.

Recognition at Last

Previous U.S. administrations adopted the stance that India's nuclear arsenal, which was first tested in 1974, was illegitimate and should be eliminated or at least seriously constrained. They did so for two reasons. First, they feared that legitimating the Indian arsenal might spur an arms race in Asia because Pakistan, India's archrival, and China might be tempted to keep pace with India's activities. Second, Washington wanted to stick strictly to the principles underlying the Nuclear Nonproliferation

Treaty (NPT): parties to the treaty could engage in peaceful nuclear commerce; states that stood outside the NPT regime, such as India, could not. U.S. policymakers feared that compromising these principles might both give states with nuclear aspirations reason to think they could get around the NPT if they waited long enough and dishearten those other states that loyally supported the treaty against proliferators.

A stance, however, is not a policy. And eliminating India's arsenal became an increasingly unrealistic stance when Pakistan went nuclear in the 1980s—and then became a fantasy in 1998, when India tested five bombs underground and openly declared itself a nuclear power. After India's tests, the Clinton administration sought to nudge New Delhi in directions that would limit counteractions by China and Pakistan and above all prevent an Indo-Pakistani nuclear war. All the while Washington firmly maintained that U.S. recognition of India's nuclear status was a long way off. After the attacks of September 11, 2001, which prompted Washington to take a fresh look at U.S. policies in South Asia, the Bush administration first reached out to Pakistan to secure its help against Islamist terrorists.

But then it also turned toward New Delhi, and in the summer of 2005 finally granted India de facto nuclear recognition. In a stroke, Washington thereby invited India to join the ranks of China, France, Russia, the United States, and the United Kingdom—the victors of World War II—as a legitimate wielder of the influence that nuclear weapons confer. When, earlier this year, the Bush administration negotiated the specific terms of its nuclear arrangement with New Delhi, Washington abandoned, against the advice of nonproliferation specialists, any efforts to condition the deal on constraints that would keep India from further increasing its nuclear arsenal.

Under the terms of the deal, the United States commits to behave, and urges other states to behave, as if India were a nuclear weapons state under the NPT, even though India has not signed the treaty and will not be required to do so. (Even if the Bush administration had wished to make India a de jure nuclear weapons state under the NPT, such a change probably would not have been possible, as it would have required unanimous approval by all 188 parties to the treaty.) Washington has also undertaken to stop denying civil nuclear technology to India and has determined to require India to apply the safeguards of the International Atomic Energy Agency (IAEA) only to nuclear facilities it designates as being for purely civil purposes. India is now also authorized to import uranium, the lack of which had long stalled the progress of its nuclear program.

Nuclear recognition will bring enormous political benefits to the Indian government. Naturally, the deal is popular with domestic constituencies, which were already well disposed toward the United States. (In 2005, a poll by the Pew Research Center found that 71 percent of Indian respondents had a favorable view of the United States—the highest percentage among the 15 leading nations polled.) Singh supporters in the National Congress Party have downplayed the importance of the few obligations that India has undertaken, such as the commitment to voluntarily subject some of its nuclear facilities to inspections, a routine practice in all the other recognized nuclear states, including the United States. Criticism from the opposition BJP (Bharatiya Janata Party) has been narrow and technical—and it probably reflects the BJP's chagrin that the agreement was secured while the National Congress Party was in power. Although some members of the marginal Left Front parties have criticized the terms of the deal, their complaints have smacked of antiquated NAM politics, and the detractors are unlikely to be able to block the deal's approval by the Indian Parliament. Barring the imposition of new conditions by the U.S. Congress, the deal is thus likely to sail through the legislature in India.

American critics of the deal contend that India's past behavior does not warrant this free pass. They argue that Washington should at least ask India to stop making fissile material for bombs, as the NPT's acknowledged nuclear powers have already done, rather than wait for the proposed fissile Material Cutoff Treaty to come into existence. Others contend that India should be required to place more nuclear facilities under IAEA safeguards, to prevent any diversion of fissile materials from its nuclear power program to its nuclear weapons program. Still others want India to sign the Comprehensive Test Ban Treaty rather than be allowed merely to abide by a unilateral moratorium on further underground testing, as it has done since 1998.

The Indian government, backed by Indian public opinion, has resisted all attempts to impose such technical constraints on its nuclear arsenal. So far, the U.S. government has effectively supported New Delhi's position by insisting that the India deal is not an arms control treaty but a broader strategic agreement. The Bush administration has described the nuclear issue as the "basic irritant" in U.S.–Indian relations and has argued that once the issue is out of the way, India will become a responsible stakeholder in the nonproliferation regime, jettison its vestigial NAM posturing, take a more normal place in the diplomatic world—and become a strategic partner of the United States.

Collateral Damage

The most serious charge against the deal is that Washington, by recognizing India's de facto nuclear status and effectively rewarding noncompliance, hurt the integrity of the nonproliferation regime. There is no question that such an abrupt reversal of U.S. policy was a blow to nonproliferation efforts, but the damage is manageable and will not affect the most worrisome near-term cases.

To begin with, the impact of the Bush-Singh deal on so-called rogue states is likely to be minimal. It is safe to assume that as North Korea's Kim Jong Il calculates how far he can go with his nuclear breakout, he hardly worries about the internal consistency of the NPT regime (much like Saddam Hussein, who eventually stopped paying it any heed). Pyongyang's governing ideology is not communism so much as a fanatical embrace of autarky and self-reliance, which seems to include open defiance of international norms such as nonproliferation. North Korea's tolerance for ostracism by the international community is legendary. Stopping its nuclear program—by measures short of war—would require tough and focused diplomacy, with incentives and sanctions, in which the NPT would play little part.

The India deal's impact on Iran, another country driving for nuclear power status, will also be modest. Tehran's ongoing cat-and-mouse game with the IAEA, the United States, the United Kingdom, France, and Germany suggests that Iranian leaders have at least a smidgen of sensitivity to international opinion. India's nuclear recognition may give Tehran a new talking point—if India gets a free pass, why not Iran?—but that is about it. Iran's nuclear program, like that of North Korea, has deep roots in the country's sense of insecurity and its national pride, and these factors matter far more than the NPT. Besides, because Tehran continues to claim that it seeks only nuclear power, not nuclear weapons, it would be hard-pressed to point to India as a relevant precedent.

The deal's impact will mostly be felt among two other groups of countries: states that are not rogues but have flirted or continue to flirt with nuclear status ("the in-betweens") and states that faithfully uphold the rules, whether or not they have nuclear weapons ("the stalwarts"). South Africa, Argentina, Brazil, Ukraine, Kazakhstan, Belarus, South Korea, Taiwan, and, more recently, Libya have all been in-betweens at some point. Although they eventually forwent nuclear weapons for reasons specific to their own circumstances, all of them were in some way swayed by the fear that they would suffer lasting international ostracism if they flouted the NPT regime. With India's sweet deal now suggesting that forgiveness comes to proliferators who wait long enough, some states might be tempted to stray. (Brazil, which is now trying to enrich uranium, comes to mind.)

Curiously, the India deal might have the greatest effect on the stalwarts of nonproliferation, including the five states that are formally entitled to hold nuclear weapons under the NPT. Not only do these countries play an important role in confronting rogue states and keeping in-betweens in bounds; they also provide direct technical support to the nonproliferation regime by denying critical exports to governments that infringe the NPT's rules. The Nuclear Suppliers Group, in particular, coordinates controls on exports by nations with advanced nuclear power technology. The NSG was the result of a U.S. initiative, and the United States has long helped prevent the group's members from giving in to pressure from their nuclear industries to sell technology more liberally abroad. Now that Washington has suddenly changed its policy, the NSG states might consider themselves free to pick and choose when they will and will not apply nonproliferation rules. The Chinese could be tempted to make deals with Pakistan, the Russians with Iran, and the Europeans with everyone else.

Limiting the damage caused by the Bush-Singh deal must therefore center on managing the in-between and stalwart states. (Developing a plan for doing so would have been a logical part of the U.S. diplomatic initiative toward India in 2005–6, yet the Bush administration failed to devise one.) Such an effort should be possible, and the U.S. government's belated consultations with the leaders of such states have had promising results. In fact, most of the countries whose adherence to the NPT regime remains critical will wind up supporting the deal or at least acquiescing in it, for three reasons. First, they tend to accept Washington's arguments that New Delhi's possession of nuclear weapons is an irreversible fact and that India has controlled the transfer of sensitive technology responsibly—there

has apparently been no Indian Abdul Qadeer Khan (known as A. Q. Khan, he ran a black-market nuclear supply ring from Pakistan). Second, India is not a rogue state but a stable democracy that is likely to play a large and constructive role in the global order in the years to come. Third, India's 30 years in the penalty box, which long exacted a heavy price from New Delhi in terms of both prestige and technology, should be sufficient to establish that adherents to the nonproliferation regime are serious about punishing those who infringe its norms. Such arguments have won over many members of the nonproliferation community, notably Mohamed ElBaradei, the IAEA director general and a Nobel Peace Prize laureate. Although the Bush–Singh deal has caused some grumbling within the NPT regime, a revolt of its members or the regime's collapse is not likely. The damage to nonproliferation will ultimately be limited.

The Real Deal

Just as the deal's critics have exaggerated its costs to the nonproliferation regime, its proponents have exaggerated—or misstated—its benefits. The Bush administration claims, for example, that the India deal will require New Delhi to improve its laws and procedures for controlling exports or diversions of sensitive nuclear technology. But India already is bound to exert such controls under the U.S.-sponsored UN Security Council Resolution 1540. Moreover, Washington is touting better compliance as a plus of the deal, even as it lauds India's apparently solid record of controlling nuclear exports—effectively trying to argue the point both ways.

Bush administration spokespeople have also defended the deal as critical to preventing India's economic rise from posing a threat to the world's oil security and to the environment. Both New Delhi and Washington want India to be able to satisfy its huge population's spiking energy needs—which are projected to grow fourfold within 25 years (faster than the country's GDP is expected to increase)—without aggravating its dependence on oil from the Middle East or excessively contributing to pollution and global warming. Nuclear power can play a part in helping India address these problems, but it will not make a critical difference. It can do little to slake the thirst of the principal oil-consuming sector in India—transportation—because cars and trucks do not run off the electrical grid and will not for a long time. Electricity in India will be mostly produced by coal-burning power plants for the foreseeable future; even under the most extravagant projections, nuclear plants will provide less than ten percent of India's electricity. (Today, they produce only three percent.) Burning coal more cheaply and more cleanly would do more for India's economy and the environment than would expanding the country's nuclear power capacity.

The real benefits of the India deal for Washington lie in the significant gains, especially in terms of security, that the broader strategic relationship could deliver down the road. For one thing, with New Delhi as an informal ally, Washington should expect to have India's help in curbing Iran's nuclear ambitions, even if India's assistance would risk compromising its friendly relations with Iran. There have been some promising signs. At meetings of the IAEA Board of Governors over the past year, India joined the United States and its European partners in finding that Iran had violated its NPT obligations and then in referring the matter to the UN Security Council—two welcome signs that India supports the international campaign to curb Iran's nuclear ambitions. Whether India actively cooperates with the United States against Iran or persists in offering rhetorical support for the spread of nuclear-fuel-cycle activities (uranium enrichment and plutonium reprocessing) will be the clearest test of whether nuclear recognition "brings India into the mainstream" of nonproliferation policy, as the Bush administration predicts will happen.

The United States will also want India's assistance in dealing with a range of dangerous contingencies involving Pakistan. Pakistan's stock of nuclear weapons, along with Russia's, is the focus of urgent concern about nuclear terrorism. Whatever version of the A. Q. Khan story one believes—that the Pakistani government and military were unaware of Khan's activities or that they permitted them—its moral is worrisome. It suggests that terrorists could buy or steal the materials (namely, plutonium or enriched uranium) necessary to building nuclear bombs from Pakistan thanks to diversion by radical elements in the Pakistani elite or if the Musharraf regime crumbles. And if an incident were to originate in Pakistan, the United States would want to respond in concert with as many regional players as possible, including India.

Such risks are still difficult for Washington and New Delhi to acknowledge publicly, however, as both governments try to maintain a delicately balanced relationship with Islamabad. The United States needs Pervez Musharraf's support to search for Osama bin Laden and other terrorists on Pakistani territory, prevent the radicalization of Pakistan's population, and stabilize Afghanistan; it can ill afford to be perceived as tilting too far toward India. The Indian government, for its part, also seems intent on improving its relations with Islamabad. But it is still reeling from the fallout of the bombings on the Indian Parliament last year, which have been attributed to Pakistani terrorists. And India, too, could be a victim of loose nukes in the event of disorder in Pakistan.

Down the road, the United States might also want India to serve as a counterweight to China. No one wishes to see China and the United States fall into a strategic contest, but no one can rule out the possibility of such a competition. The evolution of U.S.–Chinese relations will depend on the attitudes of China's younger generation and new leaders, on Chinese and U.S. policies, and on unpredictable events such as a possible crisis over Taiwan. For now, the United States and India are largely eager to improve trade with China and are careful not to antagonize it. But it is reasonable for them to want to hedge against any downturn in relations with China by improving their relations with each other. Neither government wishes to talk publicly, let alone take actions now, to advance this shared interest, but they very well might in the future.

The India deal could also bring the United States more direct benefits, militarily and economically. Washington expects the intensification of military-to-military contacts and hopes eventually to gain the cooperation of India in disaster-relief efforts,

humanitarian interventions, peacekeeping missions, and post-conflict reconstruction efforts, including even operations not mandated by or commanded by the United Nations, operations in which India has historically refused to participate. Judging from the evolution of the United States' security partnerships with states in Europe and Asia, the anticipation of such joint action could lead over time to joint military planning and exercises, the sharing of intelligence, and even joint military capabilities. U.S. military forces may also seek access to strategic locations through Indian territory and perhaps basing rights there. Ultimately, India could even provide U.S. forces with "over-the- horizon" bases for contingencies in the Middle East.

On the economic front, as India expands its civilian nuclear capacity and modernizes its military, the United States stands to gain preferential treatment for U.S. industries. The India deal theoretically creates economic opportunities in the construction of nuclear reactors and other power infrastructures in India. These should not be exaggerated, however. The United States would have to secure preferences at the expense of Russian and European competitors and would need to persuade India's scientific community to focus its nuclear power expansion on conventional reactors rather than on the type of exotic and expensive technologies (for example, fast-breeder reactors) it currently favors. India is also expected to increase the scale and sophistication of its military, in part by purchasing weapons systems from abroad. The United States can reasonably anticipate some preferential treatment for U.S. vendors. Early discussions have concerned the sale of F-16 and F-18 tactical aircraft and P-3C maritime surveillance aircraft.

The Only Way to Go

Of course, there can be no guarantees that the United States will benefit from India's partnership in these matters. As befits a great nation on its way to global prominence, India will have its own opinions about how best to live up to the deal—or not, as the case may be—while pursuing its own interests.

Proponents of the India deal have compared it to President Richard Nixon's opening to China in 1971. It is true that both overtures were bold moves based on a firm foundation of mutual interest and that both were leaps of trust rather than shrewd bargains. But there are sobering differences between the two fledgling partnerships. Nixon and Mao Zedong shared a clear and present enemy—the Soviet Union—not an uncertain set of possible future dangers, as do Bush and Singh now. More important, India today, unlike Mao's China, is a democracy. No government in New Delhi can turn on a dime in regard to a policy followed for decades or suddenly commit India to a broad set of actions that support U.S. interests; only a profound and probably slow evolution in the views of India's elites could produce such changes. India's diplomats and civil servants are notorious for adhering to independent positions regarding the world order, economic development, and nuclear security. The architects of the India deal have suggested that such habits will quickly yield in the face of the United States' recent accommodations on the nuclear issue. But their expectation is naive. Americans may see Washington's turnabout on long-standing

U.S. nonproliferation policy as a serious concession, but Indians view it as a belated and much deserved acknowledgment. The United States could come to regret having played its trump card so early.

Although the deal's critics are understandably worried, they risk expressing their concern in counterproductive ways, most notably by seeking to rebalance the U.S.–India deal by imposing additional constraints on India's nuclear program. Preventing an arms race between India, China, and Pakistan is an important goal, but it is best pursued in nontechnical ways. New Delhi has stated its intention to pursue a "minimum deterrent"—not an all-out arms race—and the Bush administration should hold it to this pledge.

Rather than pull back, the Bush administration and Congress should move forward. A better approach than subtracting benefits from India's side of the ledger would be to add benefits to the United States' side so as to ensure that Washington will obtain what it rightly expects of New Delhi: not just nuclear restraint and a new level of support in handling potential proliferators such as Iran, but a broad strategic realignment. It is too soon to tell whether the United States' goals are shared by India and whether they will be reached. But the United States can do no better to serve its interests than to state its high expectations of this strategic partnership and then give it a real chance of being fully realized.

Reprinted by permission of *Foreign Affairs*, July/August 2006, pp. 33-44. Copyright © 2006 by the Council on Foreign Relations, Inc.

The US and Latin America Through the Lens of Empire

"An unvarnished sense of superiority, displayed proudly on the regional and global stage, has revived the resentment and distrust of Latin Americans toward the United States that had recently shown signs of receding."

MICHAEL SHIFTER

For many Latin Americans, President George W. Bush's November 6, 2003, speech before the National Endowment for Democracy touched on an all-too-familiar theme. Bush boldly called for a democratic revolution, led by the United States, in Iraq and the Middle East. Two decades earlier, President Ronald Reagan had delivered a similarly audacious address to the British Parliament, one that laid the groundwork for the creation of the endowment itself. Just as Bush has now targeted the "axis of evil," Reagan had assailed the Soviet Union's "evil empire." Then, however, the principal theater the US president had in mind for his democracy mission was not thousands of miles away, in the Middle East, but much closer to home, in Central America.

Not surprisingly, Latin Americans are perhaps peculiarly sensitive to the stunning projection of US power in Iraq in 2003. The terms that are increasingly fashionable in describing international affairs—"unilateralism," "hegemony," "empire"—have long been used in analyses of inter-American relations. The vast asymmetry of power between the United States and the countries to its south has been a fundamental feature of the region's historical landscape. The Manichaean "you're either with us or against us" formulation has been implicit, and long assimilated.

With the collapse of the Berlin Wall, the use of terms such as empire and hegemony, tailored over decades to cold war realities, was substantially attenuated. Starting with the administration of George H. W. Bush (1988-1992), a window of opportunity opened for referring, without irony, to the prospect of constructing political partnerships and striving to become "enterprises of the Americas." Fresh and original ideas for defending democracy and extending commerce in the Americas offered considerable promise for more productive hemispheric cooperation.

Today that promise has largely faded. Relations between the United States and Latin America have acquired a rawness and a level of indecorum that recall previous eras of inter-American strain and discord. In the past, the rough edges had occasionally been blunted and softened, not only during the post-cold war interlude of the 1990s, but also at various other moments, such as the 1930s and early 1960s. Although Latin Americans have always resisted and opposed US power, from time to time their demands have been at least partially addressed.

Yet, at the beginning of the twenty-first century, the quality of American "exceptionalism" that sociologist Seymour Martin Lipset called a "doubleedged sword"—characterized, on the one hand, by generosity and democratic openness and, on the other, by unbridled moralism, bordering on intolerance—has tilted decidedly toward the latter. An unvarnished sense of superiority, displayed proudly on the regional and global stage, has revived the resentment and distrust of Latin Americans toward the United States that had recently shown signs of receding. It is an attitude captured in a November 2003 survey by Zogby International among key opinion makers in six Latin American countries, which showed that a startling 87 percent of respondents had a negative opinion of President Bush.

Historical Baggage, and Lessons Learned

The United States has rarely exhibited the characteristics of an empire or imperial power in a classical sense. Unlike Britain, France, or Spain in previous eras, the United States has shown little propensity to completely take over another territory and control its institutions. Instead, since the elaboration of the Monroe Doctrine in 1823, there has been a tendency to keep other great powers out of the Western Hemisphere and permit national, independent development—provided that it posed little threat to the region's stability and assured the primacy of US interests.

In the early part of the twentieth century especially, the US role in Central America and the Caribbean was marked by various occupations carried out by the US armed forces when it was deemed necessary to protect American economic and strategic interests and to spread American values. Nicaragua, Haiti, the Dominican Republic—all at one time were occupied, often for considerable stretches. The occupations, which generally came to an end by the 1930s, proved difficult, and had mixed results at best. These experiences account, in part, for the enormous skepticism in much of Latin America about the current US occupation of Afghanistan and Iraq.

The cold war saw the United States return to Latin America in an attempt to assert its ideological hegemony and maintain the hemisphere as its sphere of influence, if not control. Whatever Washington perceived as an extension of Soviet influence in the hemisphere was typically met with a swift and severe response. This was the case even before the 1959 Cuban revolution (for example, in Guatemala in 1954), but became especially pronounced after the installation of a Communist government just off the US mainland. It would be hard to overstate the effect of Fidel Castro's regime in shaping US Latin America policy through the cold war—and even since the cold war's end. The US intervention in the Dominican Republic in 1965, and the US pressure that helped result in the 1973 military coup against Chile's elected president, Salvador Allende, can best be understood against this cold war backdrop.

In the 1980s, the cold war's intense ideological battle became concentrated in Central America, where the Reagan administration backed an authoritarian government in El Salvador to prevent a powerful leftist insurgency from taking over. The United States also waged a proxy war through the "contras" in Nicaragua, then controlled by a Sandinista government with close ties to Cuba and the Soviet Union.

The US obsession with security questions in the 1980s rendered a productive relationship with Latin America virtually impossible. Sharp differences in priorities had always existed, but occasional US initiatives in response to Latin American concerns attempted to bridge them. Franklin Roosevelt's Good Neighbor Policy of the 1930s, a serious effort to engage constructively with the region, was one example. Another was John Kennedy's lofty Alliance for Progress. No doubt calculated to counter the appeal of Castro's regime, it nonetheless projected a commitment to Latin America's social reform agenda. Although these initiatives did not transform the hemisphere's power relations, they did display a concern for Latin America's acute social conditions and reflect an effort to identify common interests, thereby cushioning the negative effects of US hegemony.

The Bush I and Clinton Era

In fundamental respects, the first Bush administration reflected continuity with the US policies toward Latin America whose antecedents were Roosevelt's Good Neighbor Policy and Kennedy's Alliance for Progress. Transformations on the world stage—most notably the fall of the Berlin Wall— coupled with important changes in Latin America's political landscape toward more democratic rule, created fertile and favorable conditions for a more serious engagement with the region.

This period saw new precedents set in the critical areas of democracy and trade. Roughly coinciding with the end of Chilean dictator Augusto Pinochet's extended military rule, member governments of the Organization of American States, meeting in Santiago, Chile, in June 1991, approved a resolution that marked a sharp departure in inter-American norms. For the first time, any interruption in democratic, constitutional rule would become a matter of regional concern and would trigger a hemispheric response. That resolution, which has been invoked four times since its adoption, formed the cornerstone of the widely touted Inter-American Democratic Charter that was approved a decade later at an OAS General Assembly in Lima, Peru. The charter codified or systematized all the democracy-related declarations and resolutions that had been adopted over the previous decade, essentially giving these declarations and resolutions greater force.

The notion of creating a hemisphere-wide free trade area can also be traced to the first Bush administration. The Enterprise of the Americas initiative, launched in 1990, recognized the concerns of Latin American leaders who had expressed keen interest in securing greater access to US markets for their countries' products. Such responsiveness and engagement were welcomed south of the Rio Grande, and especially in Mexico. It was during the first Bush administration that the final terms of the North American Free Trade Agreement (NAFTA), involving the United States, Canada, and Mexico, were negotiated and signed. The US Congress approved the treaty in 1993, under the Clinton administration. The first Bush administration was responsive to Latin American concerns about foreign debt as well, devising the Brady Plan—after Treasury Secretary Nicholas Brady—to reduce the region's $450 billion in foreign debt.

Other nods to Latin America did not go unnoticed in the region. With the end of the cold war, Washington became more committed to achieving a peaceful resolution to longstanding conflicts in Central America—in Nicaragua in 1990 and El Salvador in early 1992 under the first Bush administration, and then in Guatemala under Clinton in 1996. The US role helped overcome doubts about whether the United States was prepared to apply its power constructively in former cold war battlegrounds. The first Bush administration also participated in two anti-drug summits—in Cartagena, Colombia, and San Antonio, Texas—during which the US president met with his Andean counterparts in a multilateral framework.

The momentum toward greater cooperation continued into the two terms that Bill Clinton served between 1992 and 2000. This era saw not only the passage of NAFTA, but also the convening of the Summit of the Americas, featuring all the hemisphere's elected leaders, in December 1994 in Miami. The summit was the first meeting of its kind in a quarter of a century. It set the goal of negotiating a Free Trade Area of the Americas (FTAA) by January 2005.

Two months before the summit, the Clinton administration used the threat of force to return to office the democratically elected leader of Haiti, Jean-Bertrand Aristide. This was in striking contrast to historical images of the United States propping up authoritarian regimes. It offered further evidence that the US government could use its power to advance legitimate democratic rule in the hemisphere.

The momentum stalled, however, in the latter part of the 1990s. Economic and political conditions in many Latin

American countries deteriorated. In Venezuela, which endured two successive lost decades, strongman Hugo Chávez was elected president in December 1998, while in Peru, President Alberto Fujimori further entrenched his authoritarian rule. In short, a malaise gripped much of the region, making it less attractive to Washington. In addition, the US Congress continually denied Clinton the "fast track" authority he sought to negotiate trade agreements without congressional amendment, reflecting a more inward-looking society and the growing salience of domestic politics—in this case, pressure from labor unions identified with the Democratic party—in shaping US hemispheric policy.

Relations between the United States and Latin America have acquired a rawness and a level of indecorum that recall previous eras of inter-American strain and discord.

Latin Americans were deeply suspicious of what they regarded as unilateral moves in Colombia that culminated in the July 2000 approval of some $1.3 billion in US security aid to fight the drug war in that country. To be sure, Washington was responding to a deeply troubling situation: a democracy under siege. But the elements of the final assistance package nonetheless centered chiefly on combating drugs, a narrow piece of the wider problem, and mostly through law enforcement efforts. A more comprehensive strategy, embracing key dimensions of social development and institutional reform, was lacking.

Bush II and 9-11

The election in November 2000 of George W. Bush generated varied expectations about how the United States would approach hemispheric relations. Two separate tendencies within the executive branch could be discerned. That Bush appeared comfortable with Latin America—he had served as governor of Texas—and had initially evinced great enthusiasm for a tightly knit inter-American community, seemed to bode well for hemispheric relations. At the same time, senior officials such as national security adviser Condoleezza Rice showed little sympathy for the kind of "nation-building" mission the Clinton administration had carried out in Haiti and instead signaled that the new administration would pursue hardheaded policies, emphasizing the defense of vital national interests.

The first nine months of the Bush administration provided evidence of both of these tendencies. Bush met with many of the region's leaders, attended the third Summit of the Americas in Quebec, and cultivated a particularly close relationship with Mexican President Vicente Fox. At the White House on September 5, 2001, Bush famously referred to Mexico as "our most important relationship." Unlike its predecessor, however, Bush's team at the Treasury Department eschewed anything resembling a bailout in dire financial situations like the rescue the Clinton administration had provided to Mexico during the 1995

peso crisis. Thus, the deepening Argentine predicament in 2001—marked by unsustainable deficits, which resulted in widespread social unrest and the forced resignation of the country's president—was treated as merely a fiscal problem and initially elicited indifference from Washington. Eventually, however, the United States voted in favor of an IMF loan of nearly $3 billion to Argentina in January 2003, and also participated in an IMF aid package to Brazil.

The United States has instruments and resources at its disposal to mollify the virulent anti-Americanism that has returned to Latin America.

The attacks on the World Trade Center and Pentagon on September 11, 2001, dramatically eclipsed the incipient Bush administration approach to Latin America. The traumatic events engendered a sense of vulnerability and fear in American society, and transformed Bush into a wartime president. The moralist side of American exceptionalism described by Lipset was activated with unprecedented force. Crystallizing the emerging foreign policy concept was a new doctrine of "preemption," developed in the Bush administration's September 2002 *National Security Strategy*. The strategy made it clear that America would not hesitate to use power preemptively to protect itself. For the United States, this marked a departure. As historian Arthur Schlesinger noted in the October 23, 2003, *New York Review of Books*, "Mr. Bush has replaced a policy aimed at peace through the prevention of war by a policy aimed at peace through preventive war."

Much of the rest of the world overwhelmingly rejected this formulation. The response in Latin America was similar, but it had a distinctive twist. For Latin Americans, the practice of preventive military action by the United States had a long history, especially in Central America and Caribbean countries. It can be plausibly argued that the use of US force in 1983 in Grenada, or in 1989 in Panama, were early examples of preventive military action. But making the practice a matter of doctrine touched a raw nerve in Latin America, since it showed a blatant disregard for the precepts of international law. It also raised the specter of future US military adventures in the region, employing the war on terror as a justification.

The region has been sensitive as well to the treatment of prisoners of America's "war on terror" that are being held at the detention center in Guantánamo, Cuba. In this US-controlled territory, secured as a result of what many Latin Americans see as an imperialist war, basic standards of due process have not been respected and followed. Although, at the end of 2003, US courts had begun to raise serious objections to such treatment, the reports from Guantánamo have not helped enhance US credibility as a guardian of human rights and constitutional protections. Some comments in the Latin American press have been unsparing (one Colombian columnist referred to Guantánamo as the US "gulag"). Guantánamo, and the specter of military tribunals for suspected terrorists, raised the perennial question of double standards, and supplied ammunition for Latin Americans subjected to US sermons on the importance of adhering to the rule of law.

As the war on terror became the overriding priority of US foreign policy, claims of interest in and concern for Latin America within the Bush administration rang increasingly hollow. Senior officials became more and more distracted from a region that was supposed to be high on Washington's agenda. It is true that in September 2003 the US Congress, for the first time in five years, confirmed an assistant secretary of state for Western Hemisphere affairs, Roger Noriega. But, given that US prestige and credibility were on the line in Iraq and the war on terror, it would take a superman to successfully engage interest in Latin America among the most senior-level decision makers in Congress and the administration. Latin Americans hoped not so much for increased attention—the demand, after all, has a paternalistic ring to it—but rather a strategy that sought to take better advantage of the many mutual interests shared by the United States and Latin America.

Washington's distraction, indifference, and failure to seriously consider Latin America's own concerns have exacted considerable costs. The Bush administration's initially mishandled response to the April 2002 military coup against Venezuelan President Hugo Chávez—failing to show any concern and instead expressing undisguised glee—eroded the administration's credibility on the democracy question. That blunder effectively sidelined any potential US leadership role in trying to assure a peaceful, constitutional resolution to Venezuela's political crisis.

From Latin America's perspective, Washington also bore some responsibility for the democratic setback that Bolivia suffered in October 2003. The government of President Gonzalo Sánchez de Lozada, which had faithfully implemented the various economic and drug policy recipes advocated by Washington, could not withstand the enormous social pressure brought by a variety of angry and frustrated sectors, particularly the well-organized indigenous groups and coca growers. As was widely reported after the collapse of his government, President Sánchez de Lozada had in 2002 requested some $150 million in development assistance from Washington to deal with growing strain and unrest. He was rebuffed by the Bush administration, which offered merely $10 million. The Bolivian president was prescient in anticipating that, without the requested aid, he would have trouble surviving in office.

The Bolivia case underscores the myopia of a longstanding US drug policy excessively focused on law enforcement objectives—a policy that gives scant attention to social development issues and fails to take into adequate account its effects on democratic governance. More important, what happened in Bolivia illustrates a deeper malaise throughout the troubled Andean region that also extends to other pockets of concern in Latin America. Bolivia conveys a sense of an already fragile region breaking further apart, devoid of a coherent framework for political and economic development.

In this regard, the Latinobarómetro's comparative surveys offer little to cheer about. As the October 30, 2003, *Economist*

summed it up, "A bare majority of Latin Americans are convinced democrats, but they are deeply frustrated by the way their democratic institutions work in practice." In 10 of the 17 Latin American countries polled, support for democracy has dropped significantly, and steadily, since 1996. Notably, 52 percent of the sample agreed with the statement: "I wouldn't mind if a non-democratic government came to power if it could solve economic problems." Levels of confidence and trust in the region's political leaders and institutions—political parties are particularly discredited— remain alarmingly low.

Such worrying results are impossible to separate from Latin America's stubbornly stagnant economies. Many of the region's citizens are profoundly disenchanted with market-oriented prescriptions that they see as having yielded only greater corruption, few tangible benefits, and deepening social inequalities. Whether one refers to the precepts of "neoliberalism" or, as shorthand, the "Washington consensus," there is clearly a major backlash in much of Latin America. Bolivia highlights the spreading angst about lack of national control in the context of globalization as indictments of privatization gain growing support.

Increasing social dislocations and rising tensions are understandably of primary concern for most Latin Americans. Yet, in Washington, the war on terror, perhaps also understandably, is of overriding concern. The result is a disturbing disconnect that, as Latin America's social disintegration and the US-led war continue, could become even wider. The common language of open democracies and free markets used in the past decade by reform-minded opinion leaders throughout the hemisphere has less and less resonance. And, as the Latinobarómetro poll reports, at least among Mexicans and South Americans, regard for the United States in the past two years has fallen sharply. True, the unilateral US military adventure in Iraq in large measure accounts for the drop. But the sense that the United States has mainly been unresponsive to and disengaged from Latin America's deepening concerns—while expecting unquestioning support and loyalty for its own specific agenda—also helps to explain the growing anti-American sentiment in the region.

The Test Of Hegemony: Trade And Brazil

Although the Bush administration has not strayed from Washington's traditional indifference to Latin America's social distress and political turmoil, it has been far more engaged and energetic in seeking to advance the trade agenda. President Bush managed to secure the "fast track" trade authority that President Clinton failed to obtain, and achieved a long-awaited bilateral trade agreement with Chile. In late 2003, the United States announced a free trade agreement with four Central American countries, and prospects for reaching deals with Colombia and Peru looked promising. US trade representative Robert Zoellick has, more than any other senior Bush administration official, engaged Latin America—responding to the region's interest in obtaining access for its products to US markets.

Although there has been undeniable progress in this area, trade issues also pose significant challenges to inter-American relations and represent a fundamental test of the relationship between the United States and Brazil. Agreement between these two large countries is essential if there is to be any possibility of moving toward the goal of a Free Trade Area of the Americas, which has been generally supported by the hemisphere's elected governments since 1994. And on a wide array of other critical issues affecting the hemisphere, it is difficult to imagine important advances without close cooperation between the United States and Brazil.

The election of Luiz Inácio Lula da Silva as Brazil's president in October 2002 left Washington palpably nervous; it did not know what to expect from the leftist leader of the Workers Party. Yet 2003 proved to be the year of Lula (as he is commonly known) in Latin America. Impressively, he has so far sustained what might ultimately prove an impossible balancing act: straddling the worlds of the financial establishment and its critics. No other leader, for example, participated in both the World Economic Forum in Davos, Switzerland, and its counterpoint, the Social Forum in Porto Alegre, Brazil. Lula appears to be the quintessential pragmatist, displaying a penchant for fiscal discipline and other economic policies associated with the Washington consensus. At the same time, unless he can make progress in tackling Brazil's immense social agenda and particularly its glaring inequalities, Lula risks disappointing many of his supporters, in Brazil and throughout Latin America, who have high hopes and expectations for another "way" in a frustrated region searching for alternatives.

Lula has surprised many observers not only with his pragmatism in national policies, but also because of his assertive role in regional affairs. Building on Brazil's self-image as a regional power, with disproportionate significance in South America, Lula has taken initiative in dealing with difficult situations in Venezuela, where he launched a Group of Friends mechanism to deal with the clash between President Chávez and his opponents, and in Colombia, where he offered support to President Álvaro Uribe in his pursuit of democratic security. Lula has also sought to strengthen his relationship with Argentina, particularly the government of Néstor Kirchner, to further consolidate MERCOSUR, the Southern Cone trade group. Indeed, Lula has staked out a position on reaching an FTAA pact, consistent with his predecessors, that emphasizes the importance of US concessions in lifting agricultural subsidies as a precondition for corresponding concessions on the Brazilian side.

Questions related to a trade agreement aside, what is crucial in the coming period will be the capacity of both the United States and Brazil to reach an accommodation and tolerate what are bound to be inevitable differences on policy issues. From all indications, the US government is split on how to deal with Brazil's attempt to establish itself as a regional power. (The Brazilian government appears similarly divided regarding the United States.) Growing strains between the two countries were apparent during the World Trade Organization meeting in Cancún, Mexico, in September 2003, and the gathering of trade ministers in Miami in November 2003. But the question is: will the United States exercise its hegemonic presumption in this context and show little tolerance for Brazil's heightened activism, or will it pursue an understanding with another regional power in this hemisphere? Will accommodation or an adversarial posture prevail? Can the United States accept real policy differences for the sake of building a broader relationship? There is no better opportunity for Washington to forge a strategic partnership and restore the declining goodwill among many Latin Americans toward the United States.

Back To The Backyard?

How the United States deals with Brazil's evolving role in the hemisphere in the coming years will largely determine America's ability to adjust its thinking to the region's new realities. Analysts have long used the image of the "backyard" to depict US conceptions of Latin America, especially Central America. But in the context of globalization—where national problems have worldwide ramifications— such conceptions are woefully inadequate.

The regional test for the United States also includes its relationship with Mexico, which is fundamental to constructing a vital hemispheric community. After the September 11 attacks, no country has experienced more friction with the United States at the highest political levels than Mexico. Perhaps expectations were unrealistically high, but President Bush, based on his previous foreign policy experience and friendship, initially looked south, toward President Fox. The strain that developed after the attacks—Washington felt that Mexico did not show sufficient solidarity—was exacerbated once the Iraq enterprise started, and Mexico, as a member of the United Nations Security Council, had to take a public stand on the US decision to go to war. Mexico's opposition to the US position did not sit well with Congress and, especially, the Bush administration.

Not surprisingly, toward the end of 2003 signs appeared that the bilateral relationship was on the road to repair. Summits held in Mexico in October 2003 and January 2004 should help re-engage Washington with the bilateral agenda. Electoral politics in advance of the US presidential election of 2004—Mexicans make up a growing share of the voting population in key states—have also prompted another glance south.

President Fox, for his part, dismissed Mexico's ambassador to the United Nations, Adolfo Aguilar Zinser, in November 2003 for suggesting in a speech that the United States treats Mexico like its "backyard." While one can question Aguilar Zinser's discretion and diplomacy for such a remark, a shrinking number of Mexicans—and Latin Americans generally—would probably take issue with his characterization. It is a measure of how sour feelings have become since NAFTA was signed a decade ago.

Relations between the United States and Latin America—like those between the United States and Mexico—have often suffered from unrealistic expectations. Unless vital national security interests have been perceived to be at stake, as was the case in Central America in the 1980s, Latin America has not been a top priority for Washington, and that is unlikely to change in the foreseeable future. Still, the unmitigated projection of US power in the world, combined with the assumption that Latin America will automatically go along with any policy put forward by Washington, creates an unnecessary rift and strain in the Western Hemisphere.

The United States has instruments and resources at its disposal—and there are ample historical precedents—to mollify the virulent anti-Americanism that has returned to Latin America. Higher levels of engagement and greater responsiveness from Washington to the region's agenda—to create jobs, stimulate growth, and reduce crime—could once again put the first Bush administration's vision of a productive partnership in the Americas within reach.

MICHAEL SHIFTER, a *Current History* contributing editor, is vice president for policy at the Inter-American Dialogue and an adjunct professor at Georgetown University.

Politics on Edge: Managing the US–Mexico Border

"The politically tricky challenge is to tap heightened attention and concern over border security in a manner that promotes rather than poisons cross-border cooperation."

PETER ANDREAS

It is perhaps only a slight exaggeration to say that relations between the United States and Mexico begin and end at their shared 1,933-mile-long border. Indeed, the degree of harmony or conflict in the relationship increasingly depends on how the border and border-control matters are politically managed. The territorial line between Mexico and the United States is both one of the busiest and one of the most heavily policed borders in the world, where many of the most critical and sensitive issues in the bilateral relationship—such as trade, migration, and drug trafficking—come together.

Much of US policy toward Mexico has been driven by the twin objectives of facilitating authorized border crossings and deterring unauthorized crossings. Balancing these tasks has always been politically and bureaucratically frustrating and cumbersome, but both the challenge and the stakes have grown substantially as counterterrorism has been added to and redefined the border-control agenda since September 11, 2001.

While the post–9-11 security context has created new frictions about border control, it has also presented a new opportunity to reconceptualize the border and border controls. The political challenge for policy makers on both sides of the border is to creatively harness and channel the heightened border-security attention and anxiety in a manner that promotes greater cross-border cooperation and a more rational approach to border control. The alternative—a unilateral hardening of the borderline—would probably do more to deter legitimate trade and travel than to prevent terrorism.

The most promising approach to border management is to "de-border" traditional border-control tasks—that is, to move more inspection and control functions beyond the physical border itself. A number of policy measures can help to cushion if not entirely avert a collision between economic and security imperatives at the border. Successful implementation of these measures, however, ultimately will require not only more resources and cooperation but also a fundamental shift in the way policy makers and the Mexican and American publics think about border control.

The NAFTA Effect

During the 1990s, border control was transformed from a low-priority and politically marginalized activity into a high-intensity campaign commanding significant resources and media attention. Driven primarily by concerns over the large influx of unauthorized migrants across the border, the size of the US Border Patrol more than doubled between 1993 and 2000. New personnel were matched by new border fencing, equipment, and surveillance technologies. Highly concentrated and high-profile border enforcement operations were launched at major border crossings, such as "Operation Gatekeeper" south of San Diego and "Operation Hold the Line" in El Paso. Both sides of the border also became partly militarized in an effort to reduce Mexico's role as the transit point for roughly 60 percent of the cocaine destined for the US market and as a major supplier of heroin, marijuana, and methamphetamines.

Remarkably, this unprecedented border-enforcement buildup took place at the same time as—and did not significantly interfere with—the rapidly accelerating process of US–Mexico economic integration. Even as new police barriers were going up, old economic barriers were coming down, formalized through the North American Free Trade Agreement (NAFTA). Cross-border trade more than tripled between 1993 and 2000, from $81 billion to $247 billion, making Mexico the second-largest trading partner of the United States. By the end of the decade, nearly 300 million people, 90 million cars, and 4 million trucks and railcars were entering the United States from Mexico every year.

Equally remarkable, policy discussions of economic integration and border control largely remained compartmentalized and divorced from each other—even while the boom in cross-border economic exchange made the border-control task of "weeding out" illegal border flows from legal flows increasingly difficult. (As the haystack grew, finding the needle became harder.) Also, even though migrant labor was a leading Mexican export, it was treated as a border-control matter rather than an economic issue of labor market regulation.

Meanwhile, more intensive border control did not significantly deter illegal crossings but rather prompted shifts in the location and methods of entry. In the case of cocaine trafficking, for example, smugglers increasingly turned to camouflaging their illicit shipments within the growing volume of commercial cargo conveyances crossing the border. In the case of unauthorized migration, tighter border control fueled more sophisticated and well-organized migrant smuggling operations. While hiring the services of a smuggler had traditionally been optional for unauthorized crossers, this was now more of a necessity, and often required attempting entry in more remote and dangerous terrain away from urban areas.

Thus, while entry was less visible and involved more physical risks (with hundreds of migrants dying annually), hundreds of thousands of migrants entered the United States illegally every year during the 1990s. The unauthorized resident Mexican population had reached nearly 5 million by 2000—double the number of a decade earlier. Although not officially recognized or discussed as such, this essentially represented an informal, clandestine form of economic integration.

After 9-11

On September 11, 2001, the US–Mexico border was virtually shut down, squeezing the arteries that provided the lifeblood to the border economies and to the larger US–Mexico economic integration process. US border inspectors were put on a Level 1 alert, defined as a "sustained, intensive, antiterrorism operation." The resulting traffic jams and other border delays sent shockwaves through the local economies on both sides of the border. Mexican trade to the United States contracted by 15 percent in the weeks that followed. Most severely affected were electronics, textiles, chemicals, and Mexican factories supplying just-in-time parts to American automobile plants. Even though border delays today are not as long as they were in the immediate wake of the attacks, the new security context has introduced added border anxieties and uncertainties that have had a chilling effect on cross-border exchange.

The virtual shutdown of the border signaled that security can trump trade. Before 9-11, it was the other way around: despite more intensive and more high-profile border control in the decade preceding the attacks, trade clearly trumped security. The worry is that border controls may become a new kind of trade barrier—a security tariff that replaces the economic tariffs of old. The heightened post–9-11 importance of border security has been reflected not only in the allocation of more border control resources but also in the reorganization of multiple agencies (including the US Immigration and Naturalization Service and the Customs Service) under a newly formed Department of Homeland Security—the largest restructuring of the federal government in half a century. In terms of border control, this reorganization has essentially consisted of taking the old drug and immigration control infrastructure and adapting it to previously low-priority counterterrorism efforts.

The same groups, methods, and routes employed to smuggle migrants and drugs across the border can now be used to smuggle terrorists and weapons of mass destruction.

The border-control crackdown sparked by the terrorist events on 9-11 also starkly illustrated the high price of asymmetric interdependence for Mexico. Mexico is far more dependent on an open economic border and is therefore far more vulnerable to security-related border closings than the United States is. Almost 90 percent of Mexican trade goes to the United States, but only 15 percent of US trade goes to Mexico. Some Mexicans may understandably consider this asymmetric vulnerability to be a security concern. The border policy agenda is, more than ever, driven by US worries and anxieties irrespective of Mexican priorities and concerns. This has had a number of troubling implications for Mexico, including a hardening of the US immigration policy debate as immigration matters are now inescapably viewed through the prism of national security. The upside of the new security context has been far greater US and Mexican recognition of the need to more closely coordinate and creatively integrate enforcement and facilitation strategies in managing cross-border flows. Because of the high stakes involved, there has been growing policy awareness that the economic integration process cannot be maintained simply by the spontaneous logic of the market. Integration requires active government intervention and management to avoid being slowed down or even derailed in the new security environment.

The "Smart Border"

As the task of border controls has become more difficult, looking for answers beyond physical borderlines has been an increasingly attractive way to enhance security while encouraging economic integration. This is most clearly articulated in the US–Mexico Border Partnership Agreement (better known as the Smart Border Accord), signed on March 22, 2002. The 22-point agreement calls for the creation of a "smart border" for the twenty-first century, focusing on the safe and secure flow of people and goods and major improvements in border infrastructure.

This pact should be viewed not only as a bilateral agreement but also as a distinct approach to border control that, if fully pursued, would constitute a major departure from the inefficiencies and impracticality of traditional borderline inspections. The Smart Border Accord promotes various forms of pre-inspection and pre-sorting to reduce congestion and separate out low-risk from higher-risk border flows. This risk management strategy, heavily based on the use of new tracking and surveillance technologies, is designed to allow inspectors to focus more of their attention on higher-risk cases. Some of these innovations were in place before 9-11, but have received renewed attention and are being expanded.

Border-control strategists have developed a number of innovative cargo-tracking systems, inspection technologies, and traffic-management strategies to extend policing beyond ports of entry. These measures are designed to ease border congestion and enhance security at the same time. For example, regular business travelers can be prescreened and provided with an identification card with biometric information (such as handprint or retina data), and their vehicles can be equipped with electronic transponders. To facilitate border inspections and ease congestion, passenger information can be transmitted to border agents in advance. Manufacturers and transport companies can beef up internal security measures to seal their cargo and use new information and tracking systems to assure the accountability of drivers and shipments. The entire inspection process could potentially even be pushed away from the physical border into a joint NAFTA inspection facility.

Granted, the Smart Border Accord is very much a general "wish list" that is still at an early stage of implementation. Nevertheless, it represents an important departure from the past because it explicitly recognizes that more effective border controls require pushing such controls beyond the border (essentially a "de-bordering" of border controls) through a multilayered monitoring and inspection strategy that by its very nature requires much greater US–Mexico cooperation. In the case of travel, for instance, it calls for consultation on visa policies and greater screening of third-country nationals, the development of pre-clearance procedures and provision of advanced passenger information, and the creation of compatible databases that foster information sharing between US and Mexican authorities.

A growing fear that has preoccupied both US and Mexican authorities is that the same groups, methods, and routes employed to smuggle migrants and drugs across the border can now be used to smuggle terrorists and weapons of mass destruction. Similarly, the same fraudulent document industry that has long provided identification cards for unauthorized migrants can also potentially provide these services to terrorists. Thus, even while continuing to disagree sharply on aspects of border control related to unauthorized Mexican migration, the United States and Mexico share a strong pragmatic interest in close counterterrorism cooperation.

Moreover, US–Mexico counterterrorism cooperation does not face the same level of domestic resistance and political sensitivity within Mexico that has traditionally plagued cooperation on counter narcotics efforts and migration control. Cooperation in this area has been promising, reflected, for example, in the heightened level of coordination between the US Department of Homeland Security and the Mexican Secretariat of Government in overseeing the implementation of the Smart Border Plan.

The Political Challenge

The new security context presents an obstacle and an opportunity. Nothing illustrated the former more starkly and bitterly for Mexicans than the quick demotion of Mexico on the Bush administration's policy agenda following 9-11 and the de-

railing of momentum that had developed for a new dialogue on migration. However, the heightened prioritization of border security also presents a window of opportunity to reevaluate the border and border control. Whether the new security context can be more of an enabling rather than a constraining factor in US–Mexico relations will depend on political leadership and commitment on both sides of the border. The politically tricky challenge is to tap heightened attention and concern over border security in a manner that promotes rather than poisons cross-border cooperation.

The trajectory of border-control efforts no doubt will be significantly shaped by the location, method, timing, intensity, and frequency of any future terrorist incidents. As noted earlier, the dramatic events of 9-11 were not directly border-related but had profound border ripple effects. A more directly border-related incident, such as the smuggling of a weapon of mass destruction, would likely provoke a powerful political backlash and fuel calls for a dramatic hardening of the border. US and Mexican counterterrorism-related border initiatives to date should therefore be viewed as confidence-building measures designed to avoid precisely this kind of impulsive finger-pointing response.

In this regard, there is an urgent need to establish clear rapid-response protocols and procedures in the event of a terrorist attack in order to avoid another virtual shutdown of the border similar to what happened on 9-11. Strategic planning in the area of border control should include measures to minimize and contain border collateral damage from any future terrorist-related incidents.

As outlined in the policy recommendations of a recent report on border security by the US–Mexico Binational Council, new policy measures should build on the US–Mexico Smart Border Accord. Reducing cross-border friction and enhancing communication and cooperation will help to produce an increasingly dense web of cross-border linkages and can help facilitate the "de-bordering" of border control functions where there is the greatest convergence of interest.

The full potential of these steps, however, is unlikely to be realized without a more fundamental rethinking of the border and the paradigm of border control. Although politically awkward, this should start with a new domestic and bilateral conversation about the border that overcomes the politics of denial that has long afflicted US–Mexico border-control issues. This starts by acknowledging rather than continuing to conveniently deny the inherent limitations of borderline policing as a meaningful deterrent.

The Border Reality

Regardless of the popular rhetoric in the United States about having "lost control" of the border, the border in fact has never been "under control" and is unlikely to ever be fully controlled in the future. The fact that the US–Mexico border is the single busiest land border in the world makes the limitations of relying on the border as the centerpiece of policing even more apparent.

In the case of drug control, for example, the amount of cocaine necessary to satisfy US consumers for one year can be transported in just nine of the thousands of large tractor-trailers that cross the border every day. Given this sobering reality, relying on random inspections at the border is more likely to impede legal rather than illegal trade. In the case of immigration control, adding thousands of new Border Patrol agents has had the perverse effect of enriching smugglers more than deterring migrants, creating a more serious organized crime problem on the border. Operational success against particular smuggling organizations has not translated into a successful reduction of smuggling.

Even if the border is often the focus of political attention, it is rarely the underlying source of the problem or the site of the most effective policy solutions. All nations have the right and obligation to protect their borders, but a narrow and intense focus on policing the physical borderline creates unrealistic expectations and can distract attention from pursuing more effective solutions.

Unless these uncomfortable facts and their equally uncomfortable implications are fully incorporated into the policy debate, there will always be a powerful urge to harden the border as a visible and symbolic show of force in moments of crisis when the pressure to "do something" is greatest. While perhaps politically irresistible, such a response is highly inefficient, and it can be enormously damaging.

The fallout from building a barrier along the entire US–Mexico borderline would be a diplomatic and humanitarian disaster.

The most difficult part of this new conversation about the border is to redefine Mexican migration as an issue of labor market regulation rather than border control. Identifying Mexican nationals in search of employment as "low risk" (the vast majority of unauthorized border crossers) would allow border inspectors to concentrate on the much smaller number of "high risk" crossers.

This would essentially push the risk-management approach to creating a "smart border" to its logical conclusion. Emphasizing labor market regulation with a focus on the workplace and more tamperproof documents rather than on border control with a narrow focus on the borderline would put most migrant smuggling organizations out of business. That in turn would contribute to the goal of enhancing border security. The post–9-11 security environment has made this an even harder sell politically than before, but it is precisely because of this new security context that it is even more urgently needed.

Walls, Minutemen, and Taboos

Ultimately, the greatest obstacle to a meaningful policy shift in this direction is an old and familiar one: US domestic politics, driven by opportunistic politicians and easily manipulated societal anxieties and nativist fears. Nowhere is this more apparent than in recent calls by some conservative congressional leaders in Washington to build a vast border fence from the Pacific

Ocean to the Gulf of Mexico and to hire thousands of additional Border Patrol agents to patrol it. The border fence proposal is actually a revival of an old idea: more than a decade ago the conservative commentator Pat Buchanan gained momentary fame and notoriety by proposing a 2,000-mile-long border wall. Such a project is certainly technologically feasible.

But the fallout from building a barrier along the entire US–Mexico borderline would be a diplomatic and humanitarian disaster. It would cost many billions of dollars to build and maintain (even if one assumes that labor costs would be kept down, ironically, by hiring migrant workers). Currently, more than 400 migrants already die each year attempting to cross the border, and the number of deaths would likely escalate. Although the border crossing would become more lethal, determined migrants would more likely be redirected rather than deterred—tunneling under or going around or over the new border barrier. And the boom in professional smuggling services would further skyrocket. Predictably, Mexico and other southern neighbors would consider the new fence a symbolic slap in the face, further stoking the already intense fires of anti-Americanism throughout the region. Much needed cooperation on issues ranging from trade to counterterrorism would surely suffer.

The continued domestic popularity of a narrowly border-focused immigration control strategy is also powerfully illustrated by the high-profile "Minuteman Project," a militia-style border-monitoring effort launched in early 2005 involving armed civilians taking up patrol positions along the Arizona-Mexico border. This initiative—essentially a border publicity stunt designed to embarrass the federal government—is actually a variation on an old strategy. It is not so different from the "light up the border" campaign of the early 1990s, when local anti-immigration activists drove south of San Diego and collectively shined their headlights on the borderline to draw attention to illegal crossings and prompt a reaction from the federal government. The subsequent infusion of border-control resources in the area prompted migrants and smugglers to simply shift their entry efforts eastward—to the Arizona-Mexico border, which in turn would become the focus of the Minuteman Project. This time, however, the initiative would draw recruits from across the country, aided by the use of the Internet and national media coverage.

Ultimately, unless there is the political will to try to "seal" the US workplace with tighter regulations and tougher employer penalties (an unlikely outcome that employers find difficult even to contemplate), popular calls to "seal the border" are little more than distracting political theatre. They also distract attention from the reality that there are some 11 million unauthorized migrants already residing in the country. The closest the US government has come to dealing with this awkward fact have been much-debated proposals to create a new guest worker program.

President George W. Bush has stressed that this is not an amnesty program—indeed, any talk of "amnesty" is taboo in Washington policy circles. Nevertheless, without the prospect of eventual legalization and assurance against deportation, it is difficult to imagine that millions of unauthorized migrants in the country will come out of the shadows and sign up. Guest worker programs have never functioned as an effective immigration-control tool; the lesson of past guest worker programs in the United States and elsewhere is that there is nothing more permanent than a temporary worker. Perhaps not surprisingly, the current immigration policy debate remains conveniently afflicted by historical amnesia. At least for the time being, it seems that policy escalation is politically more palatable than any fundamental reevaluation.

PETER ANDREAS is an assistant professor of political science and international studies at Brown University. He is the author of *Border Games: Policing the US–Mexico Divide* (Cornell University Press, 2000). An earlier version of this article appeared as a background paper for the Woodrow Wilson Center's Mexico Institute project on "The Parameters of Partnership in US–Mexico Relations."

China's Africa Strategy

"Beijing has enjoyed considerable success in Africa, building close ties with countries from Sudan to South Africa, becoming a vital aid donor ..., and developing military relationships with many of the continent's powers."

JOSHUA EISENMAN AND JOSHUA KURLANTZICK

The streets of Maputo, the capital of the former Portuguese colony of Mozambique, look little different from those of other sub-Saharan African cities. Open sewers overflow with rotting fruit, beggars harass pedestrians for 1,000 meticals (the equivalent of less than 10 cents), and young mothers walk past in dirty rags, carrying emaciated children. Yet Maputo is also hopeful. After decades of brutal civil war, Mozambique has enjoyed peace since the early 1990s and has built a nascent, if fragile, democracy. Mozambican entrepreneurs have reconstructed the shattered economy of their capital, whose business district has even sprouted a small skyline.

Amid the pink and green Mediterranean-style buildings on Maputo's oceanfront, signs of its Portuguese colonial heritage, one structure stands out—an enormous, blocky building with an Asian pagoda roof that hardly resembles the surrounding architecture. It is the Ministry of Foreign Affairs, and it has been built, as part of a larger initiative, with Chinese aid. Indeed, in recent years China has become a major provider of aid to Mozambique, launching an investment- and trade-promotion center in Maputo, offering debt reduction, and promising significant other economic assistance.

Perhaps unsurprisingly, Mozambique now regards China as one of its most important allies outside of Africa. On one visit to Beijing, Mozambique's prime minister announced that his country supports China's "independent foreign policy"—a term Beijing uses to denote independence from American power—and called for China to play a larger role on the African continent.

Mozambique is hardly unique. Over the past decade, while the United States has too often ignored sub-Saharan Africa policy other than counterterrorism cooperation and aid initiatives, Beijing has quietly established relationships with the continent's political and business elites. And Beijing has enjoyed considerable success in Africa, building close ties with countries from Sudan to South Africa, becoming a vital aid donor in many African nations, signing trade initiatives with more than 40 African states, and developing military relationships with many of the continent's powers.

Into Africa

A decade ago, China's influence in Africa was limited. Its aid programs were hardly significant, its diplomats relatively unskilled. And many Chinese were unsure about their country's role as an international actor. In most international forums, China did little other than defend core interests, like the "one China" principle. Recently, however, continued strong economic growth, a more sophisticated generation of Chinese leaders, better scholarship in China on Africa, and a domestic population more confident in China as a global actor have encouraged Beijing to take a more proactive approach to foreign affairs.

Beijing's motives are clear. China's growing industries demand new energy and raw material suppliers; its exporters want markets; its diplomats require support in international organizations; and its propaganda still seeks support from allies to advance Chinese interests and, when necessary, to counter the United States.

Africa has become central to these strategies. In part, China's courtship of Africa is a resource grab. Rapid Chinese economic growth coupled with dwindling domestic Chinese petroleum and mineral deposits have encouraged Beijing to look abroad for resources. Last year, China became the world's second-largest consumer of petroleum products, and its imports of natural gas, copper, cobalt, and other key resources are rising by as much as 20 percent annually.

Within the next decade, China's domestic oil production is likely to continue diminishing, and the country will surpass the United States as the largest global consumer of oil. And China possesses no significant strategic petroleum reserve. According to energy analysts such as Erica Downs of the Brookings Institution, who follows the debate on oil within the Chinese leadership, Beijing is convinced that it must become less dependent on market-dictated pricing in case of a global crisis or a deliberate US attempt to cut China's energy supply lines.

This search for resources takes Chinese officials to commodity-rich Africa, home to major oil producers, including Nigeria, Sudan, Angola, and Gabon, as well as some of the richest deposits of minerals in the world. China already imports about 28 percent of its oil and gas from sub-Saharan Africa, compared with about 15 percent for the United States, and it has made sizable copper purchases in Zambia, the Democratic Republic of Congo, and other African states. Although Zimbabwe lacks oil, it has the second-largest deposits of platinum in the world; those riches remain largely untapped, as do Zimbabwe's deposits of more than 40 other minerals, including ferrochrome, uranium, gold, silver, and copper.

But China's Africa strategy is about more than resources. As in other parts of the developing world, Chinese businessmen are looking to open new markets for their products. They have been surprisingly successful: according to Chinese government reports, trade between China and Africa jumped over 35 percent between November 2004 and 2005.

In fact, Chinese merchants may have been too successful. In 2004, Chinese exports to Ethiopia made up over 93 percent of the two nations' bilateral trade, and in the first half of 2005, Chinese purchases from Djibouti, Eritrea, and Somalia/Somaliland were negligible, an imbalance that could alienate these countries in the long run, as Beijing's trade imbalance has already begun to alienate Latin American states. In an attempt to ease the lopsided trade relationship, this year Beijing scrapped tariffs on 190 commodities from 25 African nations.

African leaders are increasingly treating China like a great power on the continent.

Yet, despite claims by Beijing that this initiative marks an "important commitment to help African countries develop their economies," the decision is unlikely to dramatically change China's trade relationships in the region. Meanwhile, aided by its undervalued currency, China's unparalleled competitiveness in developed international markets like those of the United States and Europe have hurt African exports, such as textiles.

China's efforts to win friends across Africa also are aimed at safeguarding its interests in international forums and institutions, such as the UN Commission on Human Rights. The commission is to be replaced by the Human Rights Council in part because China helped fill it with Africa's worst human rights abusers, including Zimbabwe, Sudan, and Eritrea. At every turn these African nations then have supported Beijing's efforts to sideline attempts to redress abuses throughout China and Africa. In the case of Sudan, China has used its status as a member of the UN Security Council to block real measures intended to address genocide in Darfur. By leveraging its seat, China has driven a further wedge between Sudan and the West, a move that only bolsters Beijing's importance to the oil-rich Khartoum regime.

Africa is one of two parts of the world, along with Latin America, with sizable numbers of states that still recognize Taiwan. Taiwan's remaining allies are vital to preventing the island from becoming isolated diplomatically, and Beijing clearly wants to reduce Taiwan's influence on the continent. In late 2005, China lured Senegal, one of the most important West African states, back to its camp. African rulers affirm their support for the "one China" principle at nearly every official meeting with their Chinese counterparts. Earlier this year, Ethiopia's parliament even approved a resolution in support of Beijing's anti-secession law.

How to Win Friends

Since at least the 1980s, US scholars on Africa have focused primarily on developments within the continent, or on Africa's relations with Western nations and international aid and financial institutions. American China scholars, by contrast, tend to focus on Chinese domestic developments, US–China relations, and China's relations with the Asian region. As a result, there has been limited research on how China has pursued influence in Africa over the past two decades. Understanding these tools of influence offers a window into China's strategies on the continent, and whether they could be replicated in other parts of the developing world.

How does China obtain resources, build trade, and win African nations to its side? In January, Beijing released an official China–Africa policy white paper, a document remarkable for the broad range of issues it covers. The white paper offers some clues into Beijing's strategy in Africa. First, China is dramatically boosting its aid and economic support to Africa—aid it can provide with few strings, at the same time as international financial institutions, like the World Bank, increasingly link aid disbursements in the developing world to good governance and anticorruption initiatives.

Chinese aid to the continent has become more sophisticated. While China once focused on large buildings—sports stadiums in Gambia and Sierra Leone, for example—it has increasingly used aid to support infrastructure creation that then also helps Chinese companies, and to directly woo African elites. In 2002, China gave $1.8 billion in development aid to its African allies. (Beijing has since then stopped officially reporting its aid, making a complete and accurate tally impossible.)

China has also used debt relief to assist African nations, effectively turning loans into grants. Since 2000, Beijing has taken significant steps to cancel the debt of 31 African countries. In 2000, China wrote off $1.2 billion in African debt; in 2003 it forgave another $750 million. Ethiopian Prime Minister Meles Zenawi has proclaimed that "China's exemplary endeavor to ease African countries' debt problem is indeed a true expression of solidarity and commitment." Debt relief has been an excellent public relations tool for Beijing because it not only garners popular support but also allows for two positive press events: the first to provide the loan, the second to relieve the debt.

In addition to increased aid, China's outreach includes efforts to boost its soft power in Africa. This is evident in a growing focus on promoting Chinese cultural and language studies on the continent. In 2003, 1,793 African students studied in China, representing one-third of total foreign students that year. Indeed, China plans to train some 10,000 Africans per year, including many future African opinion leaders who once might have trained in the West.

Beijing also seeks to establish "Confucius Institutes" in Africa—programs at leading local universities, funded by Beijing and devoted to China studies and Chinese language training. Already, in Asia, Confucius Institutes have proved effective in encouraging graduate students to focus on China studies and, ultimately, to study in China. Meanwhile, Chinese medical schools and physicians train African doctors and provide medicine and equipment free of charge to African countries.

Through these programs and exchanges, China develops trust by investing in long-term relationships with African elites that formerly might have been educated in London or Washington. Beijing is also working to encourage tourism in Africa, partly in an effort to develop cultural ties. The government has approved 16 African countries as outbound destinations for Chinese tourists, including Ethiopia, Kenya, and Zimbabwe. This pushed the number of Africa's Chinese tourists to 110,000 in 2005, a 100 percent increase over 2004, according to Chinese government figures.

Trade Summits and Arms Deals

On the trade front, Beijing has enacted policies to encourage greater Chinese investment in Africa. It has launched centers for "investment and trade promotion," providing business and consultation to Chinese enterprises in Africa. Beijing has also created special funds and simplified procedures to promote Chinese investment.

As Chinese investment in the continent has grown, some 80,000 migrant workers from China have moved to Africa, creating a new Chinese diaspora that is unlikely to return home. (In some cases, this diaspora, along with imports of cheap Chinese goods, has sparked anger in Africa. Many African businesspeople believe that Chinese goods are unfairly undercutting them, and fear the diaspora is remitting nearly all of its money back to China rather than reinvesting it into local economies. These are the kinds of concerns that once led to anger against Indian populations on the continent.)

In a strategy Washington would be wise to emulate, China uses summits and informal meetings to reach out to African business leaders. The first Sino–African business conference was held in Ethiopia in December 2003. It resulted in agreements on 20 projects with a total value of $680 million. In August 2004, China held a China–Africa Youth Festival in Beijing, and in 2006 Beijing will host the third ministerial meeting of the China–Africa Cooperation Forum. Events like these provide a venue for rolling out Beijing's technical assistance, and where the idea of China as a benign actor in Africa can be tacitly emphasized.

Finally, Beijing increasingly views Africa as a center for military-military cooperation and a market for China's growing arms industry. Today, Chinese firms rank among the top suppliers of conventional arms in Africa. Between 1996 and 2003, Chinese arms sales to Africa were second only to Russia's. In particular, China has developed close military ties with Zimbabwe, Sudan, and Ethiopia, three of Africa's most strategically important states.

In April 2005, Zimbabwe's air force received six jet aircraft for "low-intensity" military operations. The year before, a Chinese radar system was installed at President Robert Mugabe's mansion in the Harare suburbs. Most important, in June 2004, Zimbabwe reportedly purchased 12 jet fighters and 100 military vehicles, worth an estimated $240 million. This order, which had been kept secret, was also reported to have circumvented the state procurement board tasked with appropriating Zimbabwe's $136 million defense budget.

China has become the largest supplier of arms to Sudan, according to a former Sudanese government minister. Chinese-made tanks, fighter planes, bombers, helicopters, machine guns, and rocket-propelled grenades supplied Khartoum's forces in the north-south civil war.

And even as world leaders remain fearful of new conflict between Ethiopia and Eritrea, China has extended arms sales to both nations. (During the war between Ethiopia and Eritrea from 1998 to 2000, China bypassed a UN arms embargo and sold over $1 billion in weapons to both states.) Ethiopian Prime Minister Meles Zenawi and Chinese Lieutenant General Zhu Wenquan met in Addis Ababa in August 2005. They agreed that "Ethiopia and China shall forge mutual cooperation in military training, exchange of military technologies, and peacekeeping missions, among others." The previous week, Zhu had met with the commander of the Eritrean Air Force. At that gathering, Zhu had said it was China's desire "for the armies of the two sisterly countries to cooperate in various training."

"Number One Friend"

These tools and strategies have proved effective. China has gained access to sizable resources across the continent. It has been offered exploration rights to important Nigerian oil fields. Beijing already dominates Sudan's oil industry and has the inside track to Angola's and Algeria's oil industries. More Chinese companies, too, are proving successful in mining African markets. The Chinese telecommunications giant Huawei, for instance, now holds contracts worth $400 million to provide mobile phone service in Kenya, Zimbabwe, and Nigeria. In Zambia, Chinese investors are working on a $600 million hydroelectric plant at Kafue Gorge. They are also active in South Africa and Botswana's hotel and construction industries. Chinese firms dominate the recovering economies of Sierra Leone and Angola, and China has become an increasingly close trade partner with South Africa, the region's largest economy.

African leaders are increasingly treating China like a great power on the continent, affording Chinese officials and businesspeople the type of welcome and access once reserved for Western leaders. Beijing's outreach has been well received by many African leaders, who welcome China's rhetoric of noninterference and constant inveighing against American "hegemonism."

Just as Gabon, Sudan, Angola, and other nations now look to China first, so too Mugabe now calls China his "number one friend," while the leaders of Rwanda, where the government is accused of rigging polls and locking up opposition leaders, have lavished praise on Beijing. "It's a different way of doing business," Rwanda's finance minister told reporters, pleased that China has offered aid without any preconditions, such as improving Rwanda's human rights record. Sudanese officials, too, give thanks to Beijing: "We have our supporters," the deputy head of Sudan's parliament said wryly after Washington attempted, with little luck, to sanction Sudan at the United Nations. As Mugabe put it, China is becoming "an alternative global power point."

This growing influence comes at some US expense. Africa has not been a priority for US foreign policy, other than counterterrorism cooperation with states in North and East Africa. Meanwhile, in some democratic African nations, the war in Iraq, the use of the term "empire" in relation to elements of US foreign policy, and the American focus on transparency, sometimes seen as meddling, genuinely anger average citizens. The White House has held few bilateral meetings with the continent's most important players, and, according to a report on West Africa by the Center for Strategic and International Studies, it has cut back on American energy attachés to the continent, even as African oil becomes more important to the United States. At the same time, restrictive US policies on student visas have led many Africans studying abroad, historically a vanguard of pro-American sentiment, to look outside the United States for their education.

In Africa, where the rule of law often does not exist, China's state-led business model could prove a disaster.

Yet the fact that some African leaders welcome Beijing does not mean that average Africans will always benefit from China's influence. Although much of Africa has rid itself of dictators, the continent is still left with fragile, poor pseudodemocracies that lack strong civil societies, independent media, and other important pillars of democracy. These nations could go either way. Like Benin and Botswana, they could blossom into consolidated, mature democracies. Or, like Zimbabwe and Rwanda, they could deteriorate into one-party states that hold elections but lack other essential elements of a democracy.

Setting a Poor Example

In this fragile environment, Chinese influence could complicate democratic consolidation and good governance. It might also undermine China's own efforts to be seen as a responsible global power. In Zimbabwe last year, the country held a dismal election; before the vote, candidates and poll workers from the Movement for Democratic Change, the leading opposition party, were threatened, beaten, and even killed. Mugabe had gerrymandered parliament so he would be guaranteed to start with more seats than the MDC before votes were even counted. On Election Day, when Mugabe unsurprisingly won a smashing victory, and the MDC unsurprisingly cried foul, no major international power would endorse the outcome—except China.

In the run-up to the election, China had delivered to Zimbabwe agricultural equipment, electricity transformers, and planeloads of T-shirts bearing the insignia of Mugabe's party. Chinese businesses also reportedly offered the government jamming devices to be used against Zimbabwean opposition radio

stations, and Beijing is said to have sent Harare riot control gear, in case of demonstrations. Mugabe was ecstatic at his good fortune. "The Chinese are our good friends, you see," he told a British interviewer.

Beyond Zimbabwe, Beijing has been criticized for blocking Western efforts to isolate and punish the Sudanese government. In the fall of 2004, when the United States submitted draft resolutions to the United Nations that would have called for tough action against ethnic cleansing in Darfur, China's UN ambassador quietly defanged the drafts, rendering them useless.

Chinese support also has helped African leaders maintain controls on information. Beijing aids African regimes with training on press and Internet monitoring. Tracing China's efforts in this area is difficult, but China's official press even alluded to these media initiatives. On November 11, 2005, the *People's Daily* proclaimed, "In the information sector, China has trained dozens of media from 35 African countries for the past two years." The day before, the group Reporters without Borders released an analysis of Mugabe's media activities, finding that "the use of Chinese technology in a totally hypocritical and non-transparent fashion reveals the government's iron resolve to abolish freedom of opinion in Zimbabwe."

China's unwillingness to put any conditions on its assistance to Africa could undermine years of international efforts to link aid to better governance. Already, international corruption watchdogs like Global Witness have warned that China's $2 billion aid to Angola, given in advance and without pressure for poverty reduction, will allow the Angolan government to revert to its old habits, skimming the petroleum cream for itself. Today, the majority of Angola's roughly 13 million people still live in poverty, while elites have siphoned off much of the nation's oil wealth. Yet in November 2005, José Pedro de Morais, Angola's finance minister, said he expected future Chinese loans would exceed $2 billion. "When we ask our Chinese counterparts if they are willing to provide more loans, they say yes," he remarked.

More generally, the state-led business model that China suggests to visiting African leaders could prove problematic in Africa. Chinese firms with state links often have poor standards of corporate governance, including a lack of transparency. In Africa, Chinese firms, many of them owned by the Chinese state, have been known to submit bids below cost in an effort to break into a market. Examples include Asmara's Oratta Hospital in Eritrea and a $300 million hydroelectric dam and power plant on Ethiopia's Tekeze River.

Notably, the Tekeze project is behind schedule and the Ethiopian government is insisting the Chinese construction firm pay for the delays. Because of below-cost bids and a desire to save money, some of the buildings Chinese firms have built in Africa are already crumbling, leading to fears about whether much of the new Chinese-built infrastructure will stand the test of time.

In China, this poor corporate governance has led to fiscal meltdowns. Yet the Chinese government, constrained by its need to demonstrate some rule of law to foreign investors, has managed to prosecute the most egregious white-collar criminals, including some corrupt officials. In Africa, where the rule of law often does not exist, China's state-led business model could prove a disaster, an invitation for rapacious governments and companies.

Competing Values

Ultimately, Africa will provide a test of whether Beijing can be a successful great power, exerting influence far from its borders. In some respects, China's influence may prove benign, as China shares burdens in Africa with other nations like the United States, becomes a greater source of investment in the continent, and funds much-needed aid programs.

Even as the United States has largely ignored African nations in UN forums, China has supported a range of proposals favored by African countries on UN Security Council reform, peacekeeping, and debt relief. In so doing, Chinese officials often portray Beijing as a champion of the developing world that listens to other countries, drawing an implicit contrast with the United States, which China portrays as uninterested in developing nations' needs. As Chinese Prime Minister Wen Jiabao put it, "As a permanent member of the UN Security Council, China will always stand side by side with developing countries in Africa and other parts of the world."

Yet Beijing's influence must be weighed in light of the fact that China, at least for now, does not share American values of democratization and good governance—in Africa or anywhere else. Because China's influence might constrain the existing powers in Africa, including the United States and France, the temptation may be to match some of China's efforts on the continent in order to win resources. But it is more important that the United States leverage its values, which are still more appealing to average Africans.

For the United States, China's growing role in Africa should be a wakeup call. Washington needs to convince both average Africans and their leaders that their future is better served, over the long term, by working more closely with the United States, the European Union, and international financial institutions. After all, a Chinese victory on the continent could come back to haunt the struggling residents of Maputo and other African capitals.

JOSHUA EISENMAN, a fellow in Asia studies at the American Foreign Policy Council, is coeditor of *China and the Developing World: Beijing's Strategy for the 21st Century* (M.E. Sharpe, 2006). **JOSHUA KURLANTZICK**, a *Current History* contributing editor, is a visiting scholar at the Carnegie Endowment, where he is writing a book on the emergence of China's foreign policy.

UNIT 3

The Domestic Side of American Foreign Policy

Unit Selections

Key Points to Consider

- Should policymakers listen to the U.S. public in making foreign policy decisions? Defend your answer.

- What types of foreign policy issues is the American public most informed about?

- Construct a public opinion poll to measure the relative support for internationalism and isolationism among students. What do you expect to find? Were your expectations correct?

- In what ways is U.S. foreign policy true to traditional American values?

- What is the most effective way for Americans to express their views to policymakers on foreign policy?

- What should be the major foreign policy issue debated in the next presidential campaign?

- Does global involvement threaten to destroy American national values? If so, what steps might be taken to prevent this from happening?

- Where do you draw the line between the public's right to know about foreign policy matters and the governments desire to keep information secret?

Student Web Site
www.mhcls.com/online

Internet References
Further information regarding these Web sites may be found in this book's preface or online.

American Diplomacy
   http://www.unc.edu/depts/diplomat/
Carnegie Endowment for International Peace (CEIP)
   http://www.ceip.org
RAND
   http://www.rand.org

Conventional political wisdom holds that foreign policy and domestic policy are two very different policy arenas. Not only are the origins and gravity of the problems different, but the political rules for seeking solutions are dissimilar. Where partisan politics, lobbying, and the weight of public opinion are held to play legitimate roles in the formulation of health, education, or welfare policy, they are seen as corrupting influences in the making of foreign policy. An effective foreign policy demands a quiescent public, one that gives knowledgeable professionals the needed leeway to bring their expertise to bear on the problem. It demands a Congress that unites behind presidential foreign policy doctrines rather than one that investigates failures or pursues its own agenda. In brief, if American foreign policy is to succeed, politics must stop "at the water's edge."

This conventional wisdom has never been shared by all who write on American foreign policy. Two very different groups of scholars have dissented from this inclination to neglect the importance of domestic influences on American foreign policy. One group holds that the essence of democracy lies in the ability of the public to hold policymakers accountable for their decisions and therefore that elections, interest group lobbying, and other forms of political expression are just as central to the study of foreign policy as they are to the study of domestic policy. A second group of scholars sees domestic forces as important because they feel that the fundamental nature of a society determines a country's foreign policy. These scholars direct their attention to

studying the influence of such forces as capitalism, American national style, and the structure of elite values.

The terrorist attack of September 11, 2001, altered the domestic politics of American foreign policy—at least for the short run. Unity replaced division in the aftermath of the attacks as the public rallied behind President Bush. This unity began to fray somewhat as the George W. Bush administration made its case for war with Iraq but overall it remained in place. Domestic political forces began to reassert themselves after President Bush declared that major fighting had ended. Now issues such as the cost of the war, the length of time American forces would remain in Iraq, the constant attacks on American occupying forces, and the handling of pre-war intelligence came under close scrutiny. By June 2004, for the first time, public opinion polls showed a majority of Americans (54.6 percent) saying sending troops to Iraq was a mistake and that the war had made the United States less safe from terrorism.

As George W. Bush's second term got underway the influence of domestic politics on the conduct of American foreign policy had become more visible and has remained so. His nomination of John Bolton to be ambassador to the United Nations produced a lengthy and highly charged debate in the Senate that focused as much on Bush's foreign policy as it did on Bolton's qualifications. The rising tide of imports from China brought forward complaints from domestic producers and workers and led the administration to file complaints against it with the World Trade Organization for illegal trade practices. Allegations of the mistreatment of prisoners and the Koran at Guantanamo Bay brought forward vigorous defenses and condemnations of American foreign policy and the role of the media. Most recently, revelations of spying on Americans in the name of the war on terrorism brought forward protests, and the question of how to deal with illegal immigration became a thorny political issue that divided the Republican Party.

The readings in this section provide us with an overview of the ways in which U.S. domestic politics and foreign policy interact. The first reading in this unit focuses on the influence that American values have on U.S. foreign policy as well as the impact American foreign policy has on those values. In "The Author of Liberty: Religion and U.S. Foreign Policy," John Judis argues that religion plays an important role in how Americans understand the US role in the world and defines its responsibilities. In the second reading, "The Tipping Points" pollster Daniel Yankelovich provides us with recent evidence of how Americans think about specific foreign policy issues. He is most concerned with identifying those at or near the tipping point: issues which most Americans hold important and which they feel the government is not responding to in an appropriate fashion. The final essay, "Trade Talk" contends that presidents can no longer make trade policy in a political vacuum. The author presents three iron laws of trade politics that help to explain the current political debate over American trade policy.

The Author of Liberty

Religion and U.S. Foreign Policy

JOHN B. JUDIS

As the U.S. occupation of Iraq dragged on, George W. Bush declared in April 2004 that the United States is "the greatest power on the face of the earth," and that "we have an obligation to help the spread of freedom. ... That is what we have been called to do, as far as I'm concerned." In his inaugural address in January this year, Bush declared that the United States had been given a "mission" by the "Maker of Heaven" and "Author of Liberty" to spread freedom and democracy. And in May, Bush again asserted that encouraging "freedom's advance" is the "calling of our time. And America will do its duty."

In these and many other statements, Bush invoked religious ideas to justify U.S. foreign policy: the idea of "calling," for example, has its origins in Calvinist theology. Bush has often been criticized for invoking religious belief in this manner. After his April 2004 speech, *U.S. News and World Report* commented, "Listening to President Bush's religious rhetoric, some Americans may wonder if they elected a president or a pastor."

In fact, there was nothing exceptional about Bush's resort to religion. Since the country's founding, Americans have invoked the Bible and Christian, often specifically Protestant, beliefs to explain their role in the world. Presidents from John Adams and Andrew Jackson to Franklin Roosevelt and Ronald Reagan attributed America's role to "Providence" or "Destiny." In his inaugural address, Adams thanked an "overruling Providence which has so signally protected this country from the first." During the Second World War, Roosevelt told Congress, "We on our side are striving to be true to [our] divine heritage."

Many high officials have invoked an American "mission" or "calling" to "further freedom's triumph." Woodrow Wilson saw America's leadership in the new League of Nations as leading to the "liberation and salvation of the world." During the 1960 presidential campaign, Richard Nixon said that America had come "into the world 180 years ago not just to have freedom for ourselves, but to carry it to the whole world ..." And in his second inaugural, Reagan described Americans as "one people under God, dedicated to the dream of freedom that He has placed in the human heart, called upon now to pass that dream on to a waiting and hopeful world."

In short, many presidents before Bush have invoked religious concepts or quoted the Bible to justify or explain a foreign policy dedicated, they claimed, to the spread of freedom and democracy. What has differentiated their foreign policies is how each of them attempted to make good on this commitment. What strategy did they pursue in order to spread freedom? And more important, did they allow religious beliefs not only to define America's ultimate objectives, but also to color their understanding of the challenge that America faces in achieving them. America's more difficult moments—and those of George W. Bush's presidency—have come when its leaders have allowed religion not only to shape their vision of the future but also their understanding of the present.

Religion has entered into Americans' thinking about foreign policy primarily by framing how Americans understand their role and responsibilities in the world. There are three key components of this framework.

The first is the idea of America as God's "chosen nation"—from Abraham Lincoln's "the last, best hope of earth" to Madeleine Albright's "indispensable nation," to George W. Bush's claim that the United States has "a unique role in human events." The second is the idea that America has a "mission" or a "calling" to transform the world. God, Senator Albert Beveridge declared during the debate over the annexation of the Philippines, had "marked the American people as His chosen nation to ... lead in the redemption of the world."

The third component of the framework is the idea that the United States, in carrying out its mission, represents the forces of good against those of evil. William McKinley's secretary of state, John Hay, described the Indian wars as "the righteous victory of light over darkness ... the fight of civilization against barbarism." In 1942, Roosevelt warned that in the war with Germany and Japan, "There never has been—there never can be—successful compromise between good and evil." Reagan referred to the Soviet Union as "the evil empire." And George W. Bush declared at West Point in May 2003, "We are in a conflict between good and evil, and America will call evil by its name."

The specific terms of this framework—exactly what kind of world Americans want to create and exactly who stands in the way—have changed over the last two and a quarter centuries. The first generation of Americans, for instance, saw themselves creating what Thomas Jefferson called an "empire of liberty" against the opposition of Old World tyranny; Jacksonian Democrats wanted to build a continental Christian civilization against the opposition of "red demons"; Theodore Roosevelt's generation envisioned the spread of Anglo-Saxon civilization against the opposition of barbarians and savages; and Wilson, Franklin Roosevelt, and their successors wanted to create a global democratic order against the opposition, first, of imperial Germany, then of fascism, and then of communism.

Obviously, this framework doesn't fully explain why the United States has adopted one foreign policy rather than another. There have been significant variations in the use of the framework—by isolationists, for example—and even explicit repudiation of it by what I will call the "strict realists." Americans have been driven to make foreign policy decisions by a range of considerations that don't necessarily fit within the framework—acting sometimes in immediate self-defense (for instance, after the September 11, 2001, attacks) as well as for broader economic or geopolitical reasons. As one State Department official quipped prior to the invasion of Iraq, the Bush White House would probably not have decided to go to war if the Gulf 's main product were kumquats instead of oil. Yet on major questions involving war and peace, the idea of a chosen nation, attempting to transform the world in the face of evil, has recurred and played a significant role in justifying and explaining American actions.

In addition to its formulation in explicitly religious terms, the framework is religious in two other important ways. First, it is specifically rooted in the Protestant millennialism that was brought to America from England in the seventeenth century. The English Puritans originally believed that England was to be the "new Israel"— the site of the millennium and of the climactic battle of Armageddon predicted in the Book of Revelation. After the collapse of Oliver Cromwell's revolution in 1658, they transferred their hopes to the New World. New England, Cotton Mather wrote in 1702, is "the spot of Earth, which the God of Heaven spied out as the center of the future kingdom." Jonathan Edwards, the leading figure of the Great Awakening of the 1740s, predicted that "the dawning, or at least the prelude, of that glorious work of God ... shall begin in America."

In the late eighteenth century, America's founders transformed this biblical millennialism into what historian Nathan Hatch has called America's "civil millennialism." They translated Protestant millennialist doctrine into the language of American nationalism and exceptionalism. The chosen people—whom Edwards and Mather had identified with the Visible Saints of New England's Congregational churches—became the citizens of the United States; and the hopes for New England were transferred to the new United States, which, Thomas Barnard declared, "are now His vineyard." The millennium became a thousand-year-reign of religious *and* civil liberty where, in Timothy Dwight's words, "Peace and right and freedom greet the skies." And the adversary became English tyranny and an Old World Catholicism that was trying to destroy "the church in the wilderness."

Second, Americans approached these grand objectives, and the obstacles that seemed to stand in their way, with a religious *mentality*, characterized by an apocalyptic outlook characteristic of seventeenth-century Protestant millennialism. In 1777, for instance, Abraham Keteltas, a chaplain in the Revolutionary Army, declared that what was at stake in the war was "the cause of trust against error and falsehood; the cause of righteousness against iniquity; the cause of the oppressed against the oppressor; the cause of pure and undefiled religion against bigotry, superstition, and human inventions. ... In short, it is the cause of heaven against hell—of the kind Parent of the universe, against the prince of darkness and the destroyer of the human race."

According to this apocalyptic outlook, major international conflicts involving the United States will be resolved through a cataclysmic transformation, not gradual or subtle change. By defeating England, or seizing Texas from Mexico, or driving the Indians out of the Black Hills, or defeating Kaiser Wilhelm and then Adolf Hitler, or even driving Saddam Hussein out of Kuwait, the United States would secure not merely a temporary reprieve from further conflict but a triumph of civilization, a new world order, and an end to war. The First World War was "the war to end all wars." The cold war was "Armageddon." In addition, Americans would expect the conflict to be sudden, quickly concluded, and transformative, with the opposition capitulating to the superior force and virtue of the Americans. On the eve of war with Mexico in 1846, a New York poet wrote that Mexicans would greet American conquerors with the shout, "The Saxons are coming, our freedom is nigh."

This religious mentality can inspire dedication to a difficult goal, and it certainly did so during the Second World War and the cold war. It can also shape the way people see reality, inclining them toward revolutionary rather than evolutionary change. It discourages complex distinctions and shadings in favor of generalities and absolute dichotomies. It looks toward immediate resolution of conflict through an Armageddon-like event and discourages the postponement or modification of ultimate objectives. In some instances, of course, reality matches these ideas, but even when it does not, as it usually does not, the apocalyptic mentality can impose itself.

The United States is not the only country to have imagined itself bringing on the millennium. The British had similar illusions from the seventeenth through the early twentieth century; as did the Nazis and the Soviet communists. Historian Ernest Tuveson once argued that Marxism—with its stages of history culminating in revolution and communist utopia—was itself a product of Protestant millennialism. Where these peoples have been defeated or have abandoned their millennial hopes, the United States has retained its own. That's not because the religious framework has been genetically transmitted to Americans, but because America, unlike Britain, Nazi Germany, or the Soviet Union, has yet to suffer a crushing setback to its hopes. Over the last three centuries, America has steadily risen in prosperity and power. As a result, successive generations have passed on the belief that the United States has a special role in the world.

There have, of course, been times when this outlook did not prevail or when it was seriously challenged. During the early years of the nineteenth century, the Civil War, the 1930s, the 1970s, and even the early 1990s, many Americans believed that they were better off seeking salvation at home while avoiding what Jefferson called the "exterminating havoc" beyond America's shores. In the 1930s, many Americans saw Europe as beyond redemption. In the early 1990s, some Americans worried that their country had fallen behind Europe and Japan and was no longer capable of world leadership. In September 1991, Republican Pat Buchanan evoked religion in opposition to George H. W. Bush's focus on foreign policy, "What doth it profit a nation if it gain the whole world, and lose its own soul?" This view was not so much a repudiation of Protestant millennialism as a variation of it, rejecting a transformative role for America, but retaining the view of America as the place where the hopes of humanity stand the best chance of being realized.

This view of America and of world history has a correlate in a dissenting version of Protestant millennialism—introduced to the United States in 1859 by English theologian John Nelson Darby and made popular among fundamentalists and Pentecostals—which holds that the world will end before the millennium and that the primary responsibility of Christians is to lead sinless lives so that Jesus will "rapture" them out of the world before the final, climactic wars take place. At best, they see foreign policy as a means of carrying out "God's commission" to evangelize the world before the seven violent years of tribulation take place.

But this dissenting faith has run up against the success of the American dream. The American economy has always seemed to recover its buoyancy; victories in war blotted out the memory of past failures. As a result, any pessimism about the future, any restrictive view of America's role in the world has periodically given way to the more expansive millennialism of Wilson, Franklin Roosevelt, Reagan, and Clinton. George W. Bush began with a more pessimistic view of America's role, only to embrace a full-blown version of Protestant millennialism after America's military success in Afghanistan. Even many religious conservatives—once they have entered politics—have turned from a pessimistic, pre-millennial to a more optimistic, post-millennial outlook on America's role in the world.

Most of the great debates in American foreign policy have not been about the framework itself, but about how America should act to transform the world according to its ideal image of itself. From the nation's founding until the 1890s, most American policymakers believed that the best means to transform the world was by example—by creating what John Winthrop called a "city on the hill" that all nations could emulate. During most of the nineteenth century, American foreign policy was principally concerned with continental expansion and with acquiring lands formerly occupied by Indians and Mexicans. Jefferson and George Washington both conceived of continental expansion as the basis for what Washington called a "rising American empire." Neither envisaged a colonial empire along the lines of the British. Instead, they conceived of a large federation of equal states and citizens that by its size and population would command the attention of, and serve as an example to, other nations.

In the last two decades of the nineteenth century, however, as Britain, France, Germany, Russia, and Japan began to carve the world into colonies, Theodore Roosevelt, Henry Cabot Lodge, and other prominent statesmen and intellectuals advocated that the United States seek to transform the world by becoming an imperial power—not simply by establishing a model republic on the continent, but by seeking what Roosevelt called the "domination of the world." After the United States drove Spain out of the Caribbean and the Pacific in 1898, William McKinley's administration, goaded by the would-be imperialists, decided to annex the Philippines and other Spanish possessions in order, McKinley said, "to educate the Filipinos, and uplift and civilize and Christianize them."

This experiment with imperialism proved ill-fated. The annexation of the Philippines led to a four-year war that claimed the lives of more than four thousand Americans and more than two hundred thousand Filipinos. By his second term in office, Theodore Roosevelt had abandoned the imperial strategy and sought instead to position the United States as a mediator between the other warring imperial powers.

Woodrow Wilson was initially a proponent of American imperialism, but, chastened by his own unsuccessful intervention in Mexico in 1914 and by the outbreak of the European war, he developed a new strategy for transforming the world. Its aim was to "make the world safe for democracy" by dismantling the imperial system, which Wilson blamed for the war. That would entail removing the sources of conflict among the advanced nations and aiding the transition of former colonies to self-government. Wilson didn't think that the United States—or, for that matter, Britain or France—could achieve this alone without perpetuating imperialism and provoking a nationalist backlash. He wanted the advanced nations to work cooperatively in international organizations to guide the former colonies toward self-government and to prevent the outbreak of wars among themselves. Wilson was foiled by opposition at home and abroad, but his overall approach was at least partly adopted by American presidents from Franklin Roosevelt to Bill Clinton. While reserving America's right to defend itself, and (after the Second World War) circling America's adversaries with military bases, these presidents vested the effort to transform the world in an array of American-led international and regional organizations, including the UN, the International Monetary Fund, the World Bank, the North Atlantic Treaty Organization, and the World Trade Organization.

During the last century, most of the heated foreign policy debates have been between proponents of these competing strategies for changing the world. During World War I, Wilson's secretary of state, William Jennings Bryan, championed the strategy of transformation-through-example in opposition to direct intervention. "Our mission is to implant hope in the breast of humanity," he said, "and substitute higher ideals for the ideals which have led nations into armed conflicts." During the 1930s, isolationists mixed a lingering commitment to changing the world by example with a distaste for the world and all its works. And during the debate over whether to invade Iraq in 2003, Bush administration supporters counterposed the young Theodore Roosevelt's imperial strategy to a Wilsonian strategy of seeking "liberation and salvation" through international cooperation.

What has distinguished the most successful from the least successful American policymakers has been their ability to focus on America's objectives, as given by the millennialist framework, while still retaining a complex and non-apocalyptic view of means and ends, capabilities and challenges. In the early 1790s, some Americans dreamed of making a world revolution by supporting the French. In his "Farewell Address" in 1796, Washington warned against involving the United States, which was a minor power, with either side in the European struggle. He cautioned against "permanent inveterate antipathies against particular nations and passionate attachments for others." Washington was not arguing for what would later be called isolationism; he wanted to ground the country's ultimate objectives in a sober appraisal of America's power and of foreign threats.

During and after the First World War, Wilson resisted the widespread perception that German ambition was the sole cause of the war. During the Second World War, Roosevelt rejected plans, based on a view of Germany as inherently evil, for dismembering and deindustrializing the country. In 1963, Kennedy looked beyond the "long twilight struggle" of the cold war and backed a test ban treaty with the Soviet Union. In 1971, Nixon put aside his own demonizing of "Red China" and sought to normalize relations. And in 1987, to the consternation of many conservatives, Reagan signed an arms control agreement with the country he had once called the evil empire.

At other times, and particularly after the shock of a new overseas threat or the euphoria bred by a success at war, American officials have become captive of the religious mentality handed down from Protestant millennialism. In the late 1890s, the young Theodore Roosevelt and other imperialists, writing in the wake of the American victory in the Spanish-American war and ignoring ample evidence of discord in the world, maintained that the race to carve up colonies was leading to a more peaceful, prosperous world. "Fundamentally, the cause of expansion is the cause of peace," Roosevelt wrote in 1899, justifying the annexation of the Philippines.

Although Wilson had a realistic view of World War I, he had an entirely unrealistic view, nourished by Protestant millennialism and by America's decisive role in the war (and by the adulation visited upon him), of the kind of international organization that could be created in the wake of the war and of its possible accomplishments. Wilson's vision of a new millennium blinded him to enduring conflicts in Europe and Asia. In Great Britain, on the eve of the Versailles peace conference, Wilson insisted that "as this war had drawn the nations temporarily together in a combination of physical force, we shall now be drawn together in a combination of moral force that will be irresistible."

During the early cold war, many American officials, stunned by the Soviet Union's acquisition of the bomb and its domina-

tion of Eastern Europe, succumbed to a view of the Soviet Union as the demonic center of a seamless world conspiracy. A few arrests at home fed fears that this conspiracy threatened not only Western Europe, but also Phoenix, Boise, and San Diego. These exaggerated fears led policymakers to ignore Sino–Soviet tensions for at least a decade and to discount the strong nationalist element in communist movements in Vietnam and Latin America. During the height of this hysteria, Reinhold Niebuhr, a supporter of Harry Truman's cold war policies, took aim at the mentality that America's millennialist view was nurturing. "Success in world politics," Niebuhr wrote in *The Irony of American History*, "necessitates a disavowal of the pretentious elements in our original dream, and … requires a modest awareness of the contingent elements in the values and ideas of our devotion, even when they appear to us to be universally valid; and a generous appreciation of the valid elements in the practices and institutions of other nations though they deviate from our own."

In the wake of the September 11, 2001, attacks, George W. Bush fully embraced the same overall view of America's role as his predecessors. Clinton's "indispensable nation" became Bush's "unique role." Clinton's commitment to "democratic engagement and enlargement" became Bush's pledge to "the spread of freedom." Bush simply made the Protestant roots of this outlook more explicit by his references to the "Author of Liberty" and the "Maker of Heaven." Where Bush differs from Clinton (and from his own father), however, is in the way he applied this framework to the development of foreign policy.

Some of Bush's supporters have described his foreign policy as "Wilsonian," but what he shares with Wilson—a commitment to global democracy—he shares with most of Wilson's successors. More to the point, Bush repudiated Wilson's liberal internationalist strategy for bringing about global democracy. He spurned working through international organizations—whether to protect the environment, prosecute war crimes, or wage war—except on a purely ad hoc basis and under American control. His was a strategy based on what his supporters called a "unipolar" vision of the world.

To a greater extent than his immediate predecessors, Bush has also allowed the millennialist framework and its accompanying mentality to color his view of reality. That was not so much a product of his peculiar psychology but of the circumstances in which he found himself in early 2002—facing an unexpected threat from al-Qaeda, on the one hand, and buoyed by an initial success in Afghanistan, on the other. Bush, his top advisers, and some part of the foreign policy elite began to see the world through the prism of Protestant millennialism. A case in point was the administration's decision to go to war in Iraq.

There are a host of reasons why the administration went to war. Vice President Richard Cheney and Secretary of Defense Donald Rumsfeld appear to have been determined even before September 11 to oust Saddam Hussein in order to assert American power in the oil-rich Middle East. But an apocalyptic mentality certainly played a role in giving strategic urgency to what had formerly been a secondary concern. Administration members continually referred to Saddam Hussein as "evil." This was not simply a way of condemning his inhumanity toward his own citizens, but of endowing him with attributes that threatened global havoc. Bush saw Saddam as a "madman." That meant that Saddam might unleash destruction on the United States even if he and his regime were destroyed in the process. "I acted," Bush would later say, "because I was not about to leave the security of the American people in the hands of a madman. I was not about to stand by and wait and trust in the sanity and restraint of Saddam Hussein."

Many members of the policy elite, including former Clinton administration officials, shared some version of this outlook. In *The Threatening Storm*, Kenneth Pollack rejected the idea of deterring Saddam without an invasion. He conjured up an image of a deranged Saddam at the end of his life using nuclear weapons to revenge himself on the United States or Israel. "What bizarre notions would run through his mind as he confronted his own mortality without having achieved any of his grandiose visions?" Pollack's book had the imprimatur of the Council on Foreign Relations and was written in the style of the dispassionate expert, but its conclusions were informed by an apocalyptic view.

A millennialist mentality was also evident in the administration's belief that invading Iraq would set off a chain reaction that would transform the entire Middle East. It would lead, administration officials maintained, to democratic regimes in Syria, Iran, and Saudi Arabia; the marginalization of Palestinian militants; and the end of the Organization of Petroleum Exporting Countries. At a speech in Nashville, Tennessee, in August 2002, Cheney claimed that as a result of Saddam's ouster "extremists in the region would have to rethink their strategy of jihad. Moderates throughout the region would take heart." That could eventually happen, but it was certainly not an immediate result of the invasion.

Similarly, in an interview with the *New York Times Magazine* in September 2002, Deputy defense secretary Paul Wolfowitz, a key administration ideologue, predicted that after Iraq became "the first Arab democracy," it would "cast a very large shadow, starting with Syria and Iran, but across the whole Arab world." Clearly, the invasion cast a shadow, but not one that encouraged democracy in those two countries. These statements by Bush administration officials were, of course, for public consumption, but administration officials made similar statements privately to academics and journalists.

Certainly, one can attribute these errors of judgment to factors other than America's millennial heritage. Government officials make mistakes all the time for perfectly mundane reasons. Still, the Bush administration's mistakes echo a pattern that runs through American history. From the Indian wars to the Mexican War of 1846 to the Philippine War of 1899 to Vietnam in the 1960s, Americans erroneously believed, just as they did before the Iraq War, that they would be welcomed as agents of political transformation. These beliefs reflected error and ignorance as well as the blindness that a millennial mentality encourages. In 1899, McKinley ignored reports from military men in the field in deciding to spurn the Filipino independence movement. In 2003, the Bush administration ignored its own military experts, intelligence services, and allied experts in planning for the invasion and occupation of Iraq.

As Bush's foreign policy in Iraq failed to meet its initial expectations, foreign policy experts in Washington put forth an alternative version of international politics called "realism." The Coalition for a Realistic Foreign Policy drew together political scientists with policy analysts from the Cato Institute, the New America Foundation, and the Carnegie Endowment for International Peace. In its founding statement, it argued for a "restrained and focused foreign policy [that] will best protect the liberty and safety of the American people in the twenty-first century."

Over the last fifty years, at least two different foreign policies have been called "realist." One, inspired by European practices and theories, has enjoyed considerable support in international relations departments and at the mid-levels of the State Department and Central Intelligence Agency. Its practitioners believe that policy decisions should be based strictly upon calculations of national interest and aimed only at maintaining a favorable balance of power. The United States shouldn't worry about spreading freedom, but about making its citizens safe and prosperous. Political scientist Hans Morgenthau wrote in *Politics Among Nations* that "the state has no right to let moral disapprobation of the infringement of liberty get in the way of successful political action, in itself inspired by the moral principle of national survival."

The other kind of realism is a prudential version of Protestant millennialism. It argues that the United States should be "realistic" about how quickly and easily it can transform the world in its image. Although George Kennan would later embrace a strict realism, his theory of cold war containment was prudential realism. Similarly, neoconservative Jeane Kirkpatrick's essay "Dictatorships and Double Standards," while rejecting the Carter administration's human rights diplomacy, did not reject the spread of freedom as an overall objective.

Although strict realism is popular among political scientists, it has never gained a foothold in the national debate over foreign policy. The millennialist framework is too deeply embedded in Americans' understanding of their role in the world. Writing in 1985, Robert Bellah, who pioneered the study of America's "civil religion," criticized the Reagan administration for depicting its intervention in Central America as an attempt to help "democratic angels" who were battling "hellish fiends and brutish men." But Bellah cautioned against alternative foreign policy doctrines that abandon "the notion of any divine mission" in favor of "the practical pursuit of national interest":

> That advice … presumes a nation other than the one in which we live. The best that we have achieved as a people, a people that really has brought hope to millions all over the world, is tied up with our sense that

we are a special people, that ours is a noble experiment upon which much depends ...

Reinhold Niebuhr, who described himself as a "Christian realist," makes a similar point in analyzing America's entry into World War I. Rejecting critics who charged that "making the world safe for democracy" was "moral cant," Niebuhr wrote: "For the fact is that every nation is caught in the moral paradox of refusing to go to war unless it can be proved that the national interest is imperiled, and of continuing in the war only by proving that something much more than national interest is at stake."

One can argue that the framework itself, prudentially adapted to reality, could achieve results that accord with what strict realists would call the national interest. Wilson was the first president to argue that the spread of democracy would make America safer and more prosperous. This argument can be abused, as it has been by the Bush administration. But the United States has certainly been far better off with a democratic Europe than it was with a Europe divided between autocracies and democracies, and it would be better off still if other parts of the world followed Europe's example. How the United States can best encourage that to happen is another question entirely.

Americans who want to influence our foreign policy have to recognize the existence of a guiding framework inherited from Protestant millennialism. And that certainly includes critics of George W. Bush. Bush's belief that America has a "mission" or a "calling" from the "Maker of Heaven" to spread freedom around the world puts him in a mainstream of American foreign policy. Yet the critics who point to the influence of the role of religion in Bush's foreign policy still have a point. What sets this president off from some of his more illustrious predecessors is that in making foreign policy—a task that requires an empirical assessment of means and ends—he has been guided both by the objectives of Protestant millennialism and by the mentality it has spawned. That has made for some stirring oratory, but it has detracted from a clear understanding of the challenges facing the United States. Indeed, it has laid the basis for the greatest American foreign policy disaster since the war in Vietnam.

JOHN B. JUDIS is a senior editor of the *New Republic,* a visiting scholar at the Carnegie Endowment for International Peace, and author most recently of *The Folly of Empire* (Scribner, 2004). A shorter version of this essay has appeared as a policy brief for the Carnegie Endowment for International Peace.

Originally published in *Dissent* Magazine, Fall 2005, pp. 54-61. Copyright © 2005 by Foundation for Study of Independent Ideas, Inc. Reprinted by permission. www.dissentmagazine.org

The Tipping Points

Daniel Yankelovich

From Bad to Worse

Terrorism and the war in Iraq are not the only sources of the American public's anxiety about U.S. foreign policy. Americans are also concerned about their country's dependence on foreign energy supplies, U.S. jobs moving overseas, Washington's seeming inability to stop illegal immigration, and a wide range of other issues. The public's support for promoting democracy abroad has also seriously eroded.

These are a few of the highlights from the second in a continuing series of surveys monitoring Americans' confidence in U.S. foreign policy conducted by the nonprofit research organization Public Agenda (with support from the Ford Foundation), of which I am chair. The first survey, conducted in June of last year, found that only the war in Iraq had reached the "tipping point"—the moment at which a large portion of the public begins to demand that the government address its concerns. According to this follow-on survey, conducted among a representative sample of 1,000 American adults in mid-January 2006, a second issue has reached that status. The U.S. public has grown impatient with U.S. dependence on foreign countries for oil, and its impatience could soon translate into a powerful demand that Washington change its policies.

Overall, the public's confidence in U.S. foreign policy has drifted downward since the first survey. On no issue did the government's policy receive an improved rating from the public in January's survey, and on a few the ratings changed for the worse. The public has become less confident in Washington's ability to achieve its goals in Iraq and Afghanistan, hunt down terrorists, protect U.S. borders, and safeguard U.S. jobs. Fifty-nine percent of those surveyed said they think that U.S. relations with the rest of the world are on the wrong track (compared to 37 percent who think the opposite), and 51 percent said they are disappointed by the country's relations with other countries (compared to 42 percent who are proud of them).

As for the goal of spreading democracy to other countries, only 20 percent of respondents identified it as "very important"—the lowest support noted for any goal asked about in the survey. Even among Republicans, only three out of ten favored pursuing it strongly. In fact, most of the erosion in confidence in the policy of spreading democracy abroad has occurred among Republicans, especially the more religious wing of the party. People who frequently attend religious services have been among the most ardent supporters of the government's

policies, but one of the recent survey's most striking findings is that although these people continue to maintain a high level of trust in the president and his administration, their support for the government's Iraq policy and for the policy of exporting democracy has cooled.

What Matters, and Why

A question always hovers in the background whenever public attitudes on foreign policy are reported: What influence do shifts in such attitudes have on the actual day-to-day conduct of foreign policy? Unlike for domestic policy, where it is clear that public opinion is always relevant, for foreign policy it is often difficult to understand whether changes in public opinion lead to changes on the ground.

The reason for this murkiness is that the public grants the president and Congress far more authority for decision-making on foreign policy than on domestic affairs. Americans assume that the president and his advisers have special information about international relations to which they are not privy. Some Americans may also lack confidence in their ability to judge the wisdom of particular foreign policies. All of this translates into a good deal of leeway for policymakers. Still, the public puts limits on this freedom and sometimes takes it away abruptly. Under certain conditions, public opinion can have a decisive influence. The trick is understanding what those conditions are.

In mid-2005, we found that in addition to the war in Iraq, three other issues were moving toward the tipping point, where public opinion would become strong enough to influence policy. These issues were the outsourcing of jobs to other countries, illegal immigration, and the United States' deteriorating relations with the Muslim world. Based on the January survey, concern over outsourcing and illegal immigration has grown a bit more intense, and the worry about the growing hatred of the United States in Muslim countries has modestly receded. On the other hand, U.S. dependence on foreign energy sources, which was not an urgent issue in mid-2005, has leapt to the forefront of the public's consciousness.

In studies that track attitudes, there are always more views that do not change than views that do. This survey is no exception. It is a striking—and encouraging—illustration of the public's thoughtfulness and consistency. Respondents still awarded the government high marks (an A or a B) on its performance in achieving foreign policy goals such as helping other nations when natural disasters strike and making sure the United States has a strong and well-supplied military. Respondents continued to believe that the government deserves intermediate ratings on its efforts to make peace between the Israelis and the Palestinians and help improve the lives of people in the developing world. And respondents still gave the government failing grades on issues such as stopping the importation of illegal drugs. This context of overall stability makes any changes in opinion that the survey did find all the more striking and significant.

The war in Iraq, already at the tipping point in mid-2005, remains the primary foreign policy issue on which public pressure continues to mount. Although illegal immigration and outsourcing moved closer to the tipping point in the January 2006 poll, neither has actually reached it. In contrast, the public's concern over U.S. relations with the Muslim world moved slightly away from the tipping point. And the issue of energy dependence, which had ranked far down the list, leapfrogged ahead to move into tipping-point territory.

No change is more striking than that relating to the public's opinion of U.S. dependence on foreign oil. Americans have grown much more worried that problems abroad may affect the price of oil. The proportion of those who said they "worry a lot" about this occurring has increased from 42 percent to 55 percent. Nearly nine out of ten Americans asked were worried about the problem—putting oil dependence at the top of our 18-issue "worry scale." Virtually all Americans surveyed (90 percent) said they see the United States' lack of energy independence as jeopardizing the country's security, 88 percent said they believe that problems abroad could endanger the United States' supply of oil and so raise prices for U.S. consumers, and 85 percent said they believe that the U.S. government would be capable of doing something about the problem if it tried. This last belief may be the reason that only 20 percent of those surveyed gave the government an A or a B on this issue; three-quarters assigned the government's performance a C, a D, or an F.

The oil-dependency issue now meets all the criteria for having reached the tipping point: an overwhelming majority expresses concern about the issue, the intensity of the public's unease has reached significant levels, and the public believes the government is capable of addressing the issue far more effectively than it has until now. Should the price of gasoline drop over the coming months, this issue may temporarily lose some of its political weight. But with supplies of oil tight and geopolitical tensions high, public pressure is likely to grow.

The only other issue that has reached the tipping point is the war in Iraq. It continues to be the foreign policy issue foremost in the public's mind, and respondents consistently deem the war (along with the threat of terrorism) to be the most important problem facing the United States in its dealings with the rest of the world. Concern about mounting U.S. casualties in Iraq is particularly widespread—82 percent of respondents to the June 2005 survey said they cared deeply about the issue; in January 2006, 83 percent said they did. Although the level and intensity of concern about Iraq has remained fairly stable, the public's appraisal of how well the United States is meeting its objectives there has eroded slightly. Last summer, 39 percent of respondents gave the government high marks on this issue; 33 percent

did in January. The erosion, moreover, comes almost entirely from Republicans: 61 percent gave the government an A or a B on Iraq in the first survey, but only 53 percent did in the second. Confidence in U.S. policy on Iraq is also down significantly among those who regularly attend religious services, who also show rising levels of concern about casualties.

One reason for the downward trend is skepticism about how truthful Washington has been about the reasons for invading Iraq. Fifty percent of respondents said they feel that they were misled—the highest level of mistrust measured in the survey. Another source of skepticism may be more troublesome for the government: only 22 percent of Americans surveyed said they feel that their government has the ability to create a democracy in Iraq.

What's on Deck

Three other issues are approaching the tipping point but have not yet reached it: the outsourcing of jobs, illegal immigration, and U.S. relations with the rest of the world, and especially Muslim countries.

An impressive 87 percent of respondents expressed some degree of concern about outsourcing, 52 percent said they "worry a lot" about it, and 81 percent of respondents gave the government poor grades (a C, a D, or an F) on its handling of the issue. Thus, outsourcing now meets two of the three criteria for reaching the tipping point. But it falls short on the third criterion, the ability of the government to take effective action on the issue. Most Americans surveyed (74 percent) felt that it was unlikely that U.S. companies would keep jobs in the country when labor is cheaper elsewhere. And 52 percent of respondents believed it was unrealistic to think that the government could do anything to stop corporations from sending jobs abroad. On the other hand, a large plurality (44 percent) said they believe the U.S. government could do a lot to prevent jobs from moving overseas if it really tried. Should this plurality become a majority—which we suspect will happen during 2006—outsourcing will have reached the tipping point.

Concern about illegal immigration has also grown. Two out of five Americans surveyed (41 percent) said they "worry a lot" about this issue, and half (50 percent) said they believe that tighter controls on immigration would greatly enhance U.S. security. Almost half (48 percent) also said they believe the government could do a lot to slow illegal immigration, and respondents gave Washington even lower grades on protecting U.S. borders in the most recent survey than they did in mid-2005.

Interestingly, the public's feelings on a third issue have moved in the opposite direction. This issue is the intangible but important question of U.S. relations with the rest of the world, and specifically with Muslim countries. During the period between the two surveys, the U.S. public grew marginally less worried about anti-Americanism in the Muslim world and elsewhere. The number of respondents who said they "worry a lot" about growing hatred of the United States in the Muslim world decreased from 40 percent to 34 percent, and the share of those who were deeply concerned about losing the trust of people in other countries declined from 40 percent to 29 percent, one of the larger changes in the survey. The reasons for these changes are not self-evident. The sense of shame about the treatment of prisoners at Abu Ghraib, so strong in 2005, seems to have receded with the passage of time.

Only about a third of Americans surveyed (35 percent) said they think the U.S. government could do a lot to establish good relations with moderate Muslims—but almost two-thirds (64 percent) nevertheless gave the government poor marks because of its failure to do so. We expect opinions on this issue to be volatile in the future. Nearly a third of respondents said they "worry a lot" about the rise of Islamic extremism around the world (31 percent) and the possibility that U.S. actions in the Middle East have aided the recruitment of terrorists (33 percent). Almost half (45 percent) said they believe that Islam encourages violence, and survey respondents estimated that about half or more of all Muslims in the world are anti-American. But a clear majority (56 percent) continued to have confidence that improved communications with the Muslim world would reduce hatred of the United States.

Americans may also be getting used to the once-shocking notion that they are not well loved abroad. A majority of respondents (65 percent) have realized that the rest of the world sees the United States in a negative light. When Americans are asked to describe the image of the United States in other countries, the results show a great deal of ambivalence and confusion. Even though a majority said they believe the United States is seen negatively, large majorities ascribed positive elements to the country's image abroad. Four out of five respondents said they think the United States is seen as "a free and democratic country" (81 percent) and "a country of opportunity for everyone" (80 percent). Nearly as many said they believe the United States is seen as generous to other countries (72 percent) and as a strong leader (69 percent). But equal numbers said the United States is seen as "arrogant" (74 percent), "pampered and spoiled" (73 percent), "a bully" (63 percent), and a "country to be feared" (63 percent).

Unity and Division

The U.S. public holds a strikingly clear view of what Washington's foreign policy priorities should be. The goals the public highlights range widely. Those that receive the most public support are helping other nations when they are struck by natural disasters (71 percent), cooperating with other countries on problems such as the environment and disease control (70 percent), and supporting UN peacekeeping (69 percent). A surprisingly high level of support shows up for goals that represent the United States' humanitarian (as distinct from its political) ideals, such as improving the treatment of women in other countries (57 percent), helping people in poor countries get an education (51 percent), and helping countries move out of poverty (40 percent). Receiving less support are goals such as encouraging U.S. businesses to invest in poor countries (22 percent). And receiving the least support is "actively creating democracies in other countries" (20 percent).

Not surprisingly, there are partisan differences over what the United States' goals should be. The largest gap between Repub-

licans and Democrats relates to "initiating military force only when we have the support of our allies." Almost two-thirds of Democrats surveyed (64 percent) endorsed this multilateralist principle, in contrast to slightly more than a third of Republicans (36 percent). There are no significant differences between Republicans and Democrats on humanitarian ideals. The parties do differ, however, on the desirability of promoting democracy in other countries (30 percent of Republicans surveyed supported this goal, compared to only 16 percent of Democrats). But even a majority of Republicans have little stomach for this priority of the Bush administration.

This last point merits some elaboration. A majority of the U.S. public supports the ideal of spreading democracy (53 percent of respondents said they believe that "when more countries become democratic there will be less conflict"), but Americans are skeptical that an activist U.S. policy can contribute much to this outcome. A majority of those surveyed (58 percent) said they feel that "democracy is something that countries only come to on their own." As such skepticism grows, support for trying to create democracies abroad declines. In the 2005 survey, 50 percent of respondents thought that the United States was doing well at that task; in the more recent survey, the number fell to 46 percent, and only 22 percent said they believe that Washington can do a lot to build a democratic Iraq.

The 2005 survey described the huge gap that divided Republicans and Democrats on most aspects of foreign policy. The most recent survey found that partisan differences remain pronounced. The gap between the parties is at its widest with regard to how the United States is doing in its foreign policy and how much the Bush administration can be trusted. The most striking difference is in the expression of pride in the nation's foreign policy, with a whopping 58-point spread between the percentage of Republicans and the percentage of Democrats who believe that there is "plenty to be proud of" in U.S. dealings with the world. Essentially, Republicans think the country is doing well in foreign policy, whereas Democrats think it is failing miserably.

But digging into the numbers reveals that although Republicans generally endorse the country's current foreign policy, they share with Democrats a critical appraisal on a number of specific issues. Both groups are reluctant to give an A or a B to the government for its efforts to stop illegal immigration, achieve energy independence, block drugs from entering the country, limit the extent of foreign debt, or negotiate beneficial trade agreements.

Back to the Fold?

The first survey showed a remarkable parallel between the views of Republican respondents and the views of those respondents who said they frequently attend religious services. (By "religious services," we mean services of any kind—in churches, synagogues, mosques, or elsewhere.) The second survey showed reduced enthusiasm for some of the administration's policies among devoted service attendees, especially regarding the war in Iraq. In fact, most of the erosion in confidence in the government's foreign policy in the seven

Reduced Polarization of Opinion Between Americans Who Frequently Attend Religious Services and the U.S. Population at Large

STATEMENT:	Respondents who agreed		Respondents who frequently attend religious services who agreed		Opinion gap	
	2005	2006	2005	2006	2005	2006
"Worry a lot" that the war in Iraq is leading to too many casualties	56%	56%	45%	52%	11	4
"Worry a lot" that the war in Iraq is requiring too much money and attention	44%	43%	32%	40%	12	3
The U.S. is "generally doing the right thing, with plenty to be proud of," in its relations with the rest of the world	40%	39%	52%	46%	12	7
The U.S. can help other countries become democracies	38%	36%	48%	37%	10	1

months between the two surveys came from this source. Although there are still striking differences between the views of Americans who do not attend religious services frequently and the views of those who do, the gap has started to narrow, suggesting reduced polarization on the basis of religion.

In the first survey, a minority of frequent attendees at religious services (45 percent) expressed serious worry about casualties in Iraq, compared to 56 percent of the total sample. Now that number has increased to 52 percent, closer to the proportion of the population as a whole, which has remained at 56 percent. Although people who frequently attend religious services are still the respondents most supportive of U.S. policy in Iraq, fewer of them (41 percent of those surveyed) gave a high grade to the government on meeting U.S. objectives there than did seven months earlier (46 percent). In the first survey, 32 percent of those who frequently attend religious services said they worried a lot that the war in Iraq was taking up too much money and attention; in January, 40 percent did. Almost half of those surveyed in June 2005 (48 percent) said they believed that the United States could help other countries become democracies; in January, that number had dropped to 37 percent, in line with the 36 percent of the general population. And in the more recent surveys only 46 percent agreed that the United States was "generally doing the right thing" in its relations with the rest of the world, down from 52 percent in the earlier survey.

These are not big changes, but they follow a consistent pattern, suggesting that the most actively religious Americans are starting to react more like the rest of the public. This conclusion is supported by the results of the broad overview question asking whether U.S. foreign policy is going in the right or the wrong direction: 57 percent of those who frequently attend religious services said the latter in January, matching the 58 percent of the rest of the population who said this. Still, despite the

mounting reservations of actively religious Americans about some policies, a majority (54 percent) continue to trust the government to tell them the truth about the country's relations with others, in contrast to the 37 percent of respondents who do not frequently attend religious services.

A recent survey of public opinion in Arab countries, conducted in late 2005 by Zogby International and University of Maryland Professor Shibley Telhami, showed results that are dismaying from the United States' point of view, with large majorities believing that the war with Iraq will make Iraqis worse off and the region less peaceful, breed more terrorism, and worsen the prospects for settling the Arab-Israeli dispute. Comparably large majorities said they consider U.S. foreign policies to be driven not by a desire to spread democracy, but by oil, a quest to dominate the Middle East, the goal of protecting Israel, or a desire to weaken the Muslim world.

Nevertheless, one ray of light shines through. Asked what the primary motivation for Bush's Middle East policy is, only 13 percent of those Arabs surveyed in the Zogby/Telhami poll cited "the need to spread . . . Christian religious convictions"; most (61 percent) chose instead "the pursuit of [the United States'] national interest." Why does this offer grounds for hope? Because our most recent survey showed that the religious divide over U.S. foreign policy seems to be narrowing, and the Zogby/Telhami survey revealed a similar finding: that the Arab world sees secular, rather than religious, motivations as crucial to U.S. foreign policy. However difficult differences rooted in interests might be to solve, and however long it might take to solve them, clashes rooted in identity and religion are even more problematic and take far longer to surmount.

DANIEL YANKELOVICH is Chair and Co-founder of the organizations Public Agenda, DYG, and Viewpoint Learning.

Trade Talk

Daniel Drezner

American perceptions about international trade have changed dramatically in the past two decades. Presidents can no longer craft positions on foreign economic policy in a vacuum. Trade now intersects with other highly politicized issues, ranging from the war on terror to environmental protection to bilateral relations with China. Old issues such as the trade deficit and new issues such as offshore outsourcing have made a liberal trade policy one of the most difficult political sells inside the Beltway.

Indeed, shifts in domestic attitudes have created the least hospitable environment for trade liberalization in recent memory. Unfortunately, this inhospitable environment has arisen at a time when trade is more vital to the U.S. economy than ever. The challenge for this President and for those who succeed him will be to reinvigorate U.S. trade policies despite the current public mood. In short, it is the challenge to lead.

The first thing any president must do to lead effectively on economic issues is to persuade the country that trade matters. This should not be that hard, for trade manifestly does matter. In 1970 the sum of imports and exports accounted for less than 12 percent of U.S. GDP; by 2004 that figure had doubled to 24 percent. Approximately one out of every five factory jobs in the United States depends directly on trade. U.S. exports accounted for approximately 25 percent of economic growth during the 1990s, supporting an estimated 12 million jobs. U.S. farmers export the yield of one out of every three acres of their crops. In 2003 the United States exported $180 billion in high-tech goods and more than $280 billion in commercial services. From agriculture to manufacturing to technology to services, the U.S. economy needs international trade to thrive.

Researchers at the Institute for International Economics recently attempted to measure the cumulative payoff from trade liberalization since the end of World War II. Scott Bradford, Paul Grieco and Gary Hufbauer conservatively estimated that free trade generates economic benefits ranging from $800 billion to $1.45 trillion dollars per year in added output. This translates into an added per capita benefit of between $2,800 and $5,000—or, more concretely, an addition of between $7,100 and $12,900 per American household. The gains from future trade expansion have been estimated to range between $450 billion and $1.3 trillion per year in additional national income, which would increase per capita annual income between $1,500 and $2,000. There are few tools in the U.S. government's policy arsenal that consistently yield rewards of this magnitude.

Trade expansion brings several benefits to the U.S. economy. It allows the United States to specialize in making the goods and services in which it is most productive. The bigger the market created by trade liberalization, the greater the benefits from specialization. Trade also increases competition within economic sectors. Over the past decades economists have repeatedly shown that industries exposed to trade are more productive than sectors in which cross-border exchange is limited or impossible. As available markets expand, the rate of return for technological and organizational innovations increases. With freer trade, firms and entrepreneurs have a greater incentive to take risks and to invest in new inventions and innovations.

These benefits also make it easier for the Federal Reserve to run a bullish monetary policy. An open market is a significant reason why the United States has been able in recent years to sustain robust economic growth, dramatic increases in labor productivity, low unemployment, modest inflation and historically low interest rates. The combination of these effects boosts the trajectory of feasible economic growth without triggering inflation, which in turn has allowed the Fed to pursue more expansionary monetary policies than would otherwise have been possible.

Trade is equally vital to American foreign policy. The regions of the world that have embraced trade liberalization—North America, Europe and East Asia—contain politically stable regimes and, despite some problems with radical Islamist minorities, make our best partners in the war on terror. The regions of the world with the most tenuous connection to global markets—the Middle East and Africa—are plagued by unstable regimes and remain hotbeds of terrorist and criminal activity. Trade is not a silver bullet for U.S. foreign policy; many other factors affect the rise of terrorism and political instability. Nevertheless, trade is a handmaiden to hope. It provides significant opportunity to individuals in poor countries, offering a chance for a better life for them and their children. Creating hope among people is a powerful long-term weapon in the war on terror.

Multiple economic analyses demonstrate that trade promotes economic freedom and economic development. Trade will be essential to advancing the Millennium Development Goals of halving global poverty by 2015. Exposure to the global economy correlates strongly with the spread of democracy, the rule of law and the reduction of violence.

Over the long term, trade liberalization is a win-win proposition among countries and therefore serves a useful purpose in promoting American interests and values. Most of the time, trade helps to reduce frictions between countries and serves as one of the most powerful tools of soft power at America's disposal. Bilateral relations have improved with every country that has signed a free-trade agreement (FTA) with the United States. If countries perceive that the rules of the global economic game benefit all participants—and not merely the United States— these countries will be more favorably disposed toward the United States on other foreign policy dimensions.

Over the very long term, U.S.-led trade expansion can cement favorable perceptions of the United States among rising powers. Both the CIA and private sector analysts project that China and India will have larger economies than most G-7 members by 2050. Decades from now, it would serve American interests if these countries looked upon the United States as a country that aided rather than impeded their economic ascent. Trade liberalization undertaken now serves as a down payment for good relations with rising great powers in the future.

Our Ambivalent Public

Despite these significant economic and diplomatic benefits, the American public is increasingly hostile to freer trade. Between 1999 and 2004, public support for free trade dropped off a precipice. The most dramatic shift in opinion came from Americans making more than $100,000 a year: Support for promoting trade dropped from 57 percent to 28 percent in this group. According to a July 2004 poll jointly conducted by the Pew Research Center and the Council on Foreign Relations, 84 percent of Americans thought that protecting the jobs of American workers should be a top priority of American foreign policy. The same month, a poll conducted by the German Marshall Fund of the United States concluded that only 4 percent of Americans still supported NAFTA. Americans are also less enthusiastic about further international trade deals than are Europeans: 82 percent of the French and 83 percent of the British want more international trade agreements, compared to just 54 percent of Americans.

Hostile attitudes toward trade liberalization are even more concentrated when the focus turns to newer forms of trade, such as outsourcing. In 2004 at least ten different surveys asked Americans how they felt about the growing number of jobs being outsourced overseas. The results were consistently and strongly negative. Depending on the poll, between 61 and 85 percent of respondents agreed with the statement that outsourcing is bad for the American economy. Between 51 and 72 percent of Americans were even in favor of the government penalizing U.S. firms that engage in outsourcing. In a Harris poll taken in May and June of 2004, 53 percent of Americans said U.S. companies engaging in outsourcing were "unpatriotic." This hostility remains consistent regardless of how respondents are categorized. A 2004 *CFO Magazine* survey of chief financial officers revealed that 61 percent of them believed outsourcing was bad for the economy, while an April 2004 Gallup poll showed 66 percent of investors believed outsourcing was hurting the investment climate in the United States.

Free traders assert that greater liberalization will always benefit the economy. The polling data reveal that most Americans do not buy the "always", and instead believe in "fair trade." They believe that the expansion of trade leads to an increase in economic insecurity that outweighs any increase in national income. A fair-trade doctrine recommends the use of safeguards, escape clauses and other legal protections to slow down the economic and social effects of import competition. Such views have become dominant in the United States over the past two decades. But why?

The Iron Laws of Trade Politics

Three political facts of life have caused many Americans to shift their support from free trade to fair trade. First, during economic downturns or periods of slack job growth, public suspicion of free-trade policies explodes into hostility. Inevitably, foreign countries become the scapegoat for business cycle fluctuations that have little to do with trade. When presented with economic theories and statistical data on the one hand showing that trade is good for the economy, and anecdotes of job losses due to import competition on the other, most Americans are swayed by the anecdotes. There may be no discernible economic correlation between trade and overall employment, but many Americans believe there is one—a belief that policymakers ignore at their peril.

Combine this with a massive trade deficit and the perception problem becomes even more acute. Most Americans think a large trade deficit is bad for the economy, even though such deficits correlate *positively* with strong economic growth. Indeed, the growth in the trade deficit since 1998 has been accompanied by strong GDP growth and excellent productivity gains. Nevertheless, the U.S. trade deficit is projected to top $670 billion this year—in absolute dollar terms, the largest trade deficit in world economic history. In an uncertain economy, that number will lead to greater public skepticism about the merits of freer trade. To be sure, there are valid reasons to be concerned about the size of the current account deficit, but even those economists who voice such concerns do not recommend higher tariffs as the answer.

The second reason American support for free trade has dropped is that it is particularly difficult to make the case for trade expansion during election cycles. Trade generates large, diffuse benefits but concentrated—if smaller—costs. Those who bear the costs are more likely to vote on the issue—and make campaign contributions based on it—than those who reap the benefits. In this situation, politicians will always be tempted to engage in protectionist rhetoric. The latest example of this came when politicians on both sides of the aisle demanded government action to halt outsourcing. As election cycles continue to lengthen, this political temptation will only get stronger.

The third iron law of trade politics is that both advocates and opponents talk about trade in ways that simultaneously inflate its importance and frame the issue as a zero-sum proposition. Trade is both blamed and praised for America's various economic strengths and ills, even though domestic factors such as macroeconomic policy, stock market fluctuations and the pace of innovation are far more significant determinants of America's overall economic performance. Politicians routinely address trade issues by discussing how changes in policy will affect the trade deficit. The implicit understanding in their arguments is that it is better to run a trade surplus than a deficit, even though there is no economic data to support that view. Debates about trade inevitably revolve around the question of jobs, even though trade has a minimal effect on aggregate employment levels.

We should be used to this by now. A decade ago, the political debate over NAFTA was framed in terms of job creation and job destruction, despite the fact that every sober policy analysis concluded that NAFTA would not significantly affect the employment picture in the United States one way or the other. As a result, even politicians who advocate trade liberalization do so by focusing on increasing American exports and downplaying imports. If politicians talk about trade in a mercantilist, zero-sum way, Americans will be led to think about the issue this way as well.

New Constraints on Trade Politics

The next presidential election is three years away. The economy has created a net gain of nearly 2 million new jobs in the past year, so the public should be more receptive to a discussion of free trade now than it was a year ago. Public opinion polls, however, say otherwise. Part of the reason is that, in a world of high oil prices and frequent natural disasters, many Americans remain nervous about the state of the American economy. A bigger part of the problem, however, is that new trade-related issues have made talking about trade policy more difficult than before. Even as the economy continues to add jobs, there are sound reasons to believe that public antipathy toward trade liberalization will not abate. If anything, it will increase.

One new problem is that the percentage of the American economy exposed to international competition is on the rise. Over the next decade, technological innovation will convert what have been thought to be nontradable sectors into tradable ones. Trade will start to affect professions that have not changed their practices all that much for decades—fields such as accounting, medicine, education and law. This will increase the number of Americans who perceive themselves to be vulnerable to international competition and economic insecurity. This insecurity is the driving force behind the growing hostility to free trade among the upper income brackets.

Another relatively new issue is the rise of China. Twenty years ago, there was a great deal of American hand-wringing at the prospect of Japan "overtaking" the U.S. economy. For *realpolitik* reasons, the current fear of China's economic rise will be worse. At least Japan was a stable democratic ally of the United States. China is neither democratic nor an ally, and the jury is still out with respect to its long-term stability.

Beijing has brought some of this enmity on itself. China's central bank has increasingly intervened in foreign exchange markets to maintain the dollar's strength against the yuan, even though China's currency has risen in value compared to other major currencies. In July 2005, China's central bank announced a slight devaluation against the dollar, with an intention to move to a managed float. However, Beijing has continued to purchase dollars at an extraordinary rate, ensuring that the yuan will not appreciate significantly anytime soon. China's interventions have exacerbated the U.S.-China trade deficit: In 2004 the bilateral deficit was a record $162 billion.

These practices—combined with China's high growth rate, the media firestorm over outsourcing and a recent flurry of Chinese corporate takeover efforts directed at U.S. firms—have created intense domestic pressures for some kind of retaliatory policy. In April 2005, a bill was introduced in the U.S. Senate that threatens a 27.5 percent tariff on Chinese goods unless Beijing revalues its currency; the bill garnered a veto-proof majority. In May, the House of Representatives proposed a different piece of legislation to widen the definition of exchange-rate manipulation to include China as an offender. Many congressmen reacted negatively to the proposed takeover of Unocal by the China National Offshore Oil Corporation, with the House passing a measure urging the President to block the purchase on national security grounds. This congressional hostility helped to scotch the proposed takeover.

China's energy diplomacy has led to ambitious deals with authoritarian regimes.

China's economic growth and aggressive trade diplomacy also pose significant challenges to the United States from a security perspective. In 2004 China accounted for 31 percent of global growth in the demand for oil. China's energy diplomacy has led to ambitious deals with authoritarian regimes in Myanmar, Iran and Sudan, and has placed China's diplomacy in all three cases at loggerheads with that of the United States. China's growing interest in commercial relations with other Pacific Rim countries contrasts with U.S. regional policy, which prioritizes the war on terror. At a fundamental level, even if the United States benefits from the bilateral trading relationship, China appears to benefit more—and that could clash with the stated *National Security Strategy* objective of "dissuad[ing] potential adversaries from pursuing a military buildup in hopes of surpassing, or equaling, the power of the United States."

The content of current trade negotiations has also made trade a tougher sell. World Trade Organization negotiations have shifted much of their focus away from tariff reduction to ensuring that disparities in national regulations do not interfere with international trade. In large part this is due to the WTO's success at reducing border-level trade restrictions. For most areas of merchandise trade (agricultural, textile and clothing products excepted), tariffs and quotas have been at nominal levels since completion of the Uruguay Round in 1994. As for agriculture and textiles, liberalization of either sector will not be an easy sell. The end of the Multi-Fibre Agreement in January 2005 has led to "bra wars" between the developed world and China, with the Bush Administration using every tool at its disposal to staunch the flow of textile imports. As for agriculture, the lack of progress in those negotiations now threatens to derail the upcoming WTO's Ministerial Conference in Hong Kong.

Increasingly, trade negotiations inside and outside the WTO have revolved around the residual non-tariff barriers to trade—social and business regulations. The most obvious examples include labor standards, environmental protection, consumer health and safety, antitrust, intellectual property rights and immigration controls. Because most regulatory policies were originally devised as domestic policies, they are more politically difficult to change than tariffs or quotas.

Some of these new trade negotiations will touch third rails of American politics. For example, developing countries are pushing in the WTO for greater liberalization in the trade of "Mode 4" services, in which the person performing the service crosses a border to do his or her job. The benefits of such liberalization for the United States economy would be significant; Microsoft chairman Bill Gates warned early this year that visa restrictions were limiting U.S. access to highly trained computer engineers from other countries, undercutting America's ability to innovate. Despite the economic advantages, however, such a move raises politically sensitive questions. One obvious concern would be the effect this kind of liberalization would have on homeland security. Another prominent concern would be the effect on U.S. immigration policies: Opponents would claim that the liberalization of trade in services was back-door immigration.

The American public's growing hostility to freer trade has made congressional passage of trade agreements more difficult, and this in turn has worsened the public image of trade. The victory margins in congressional votes for trade legislation have narrowed over the years. In December 2001, the Bush Administration secured Trade Promotion Authority by a single vote in the House of Representatives. (Trade Promotion Authority—which used to be called "fast track"—allows the president to submit trade deals for congressional approval via a simple up-or-down vote, preventing any poison-pill amendments.) In July 2005, the Central American Free Trade Agreement passed by only two votes, and that was after significant White House lobbying of wavering representatives. The smaller the margin of victory, the more leverage wavering representatives have to extract district-specific spending or trade-distorting measures that undercut the original purpose of the trade deal. As a result, congressional negotiations over trade agreements have begun to give off the same whiff of pork that comes with transportation and agricultural bills.

What Can Be Done?

Can the public's turn against free trade perhaps be ignored? Political analysts and trade experts alike argue that the political significance of this attitudinal shift remains an open question. Americans are skeptical about the benefits of trade, but they are not particularly passionate about it. Polling data, purchasing behavior and experimental evidence all suggest that American consumers talk like mercantilists but purchase goods like free traders. It is difficult to point to specific members of Congress

who have lost their seats because they adopted an unpopular position on trade policy.

That said, international trade is viewed as increasingly salient by many Americans. Now is not the time for a policy of trade expansion to lose political legitimacy. This is particularly true given the Bush Administration's full plate of trade issues for the next several years. At the top of the list is the Doha Round of WTO talks. Thorny negotiations remain on the liberalization of trade in services and the reduction of internal price supports and market restrictions for agricultural producers. The nominal deadline for these negotiations is the Hong Kong Ministerial Conference scheduled for December 2005. That deadline will not be met, but it cannot be extended indefinitely, since other countries will want to see the Doha Round completed well before the expiration of U.S. Trade Promotion Authority in 2007.

At the regional level, efforts to advance the Free Trade Area of the Americas and the Middle Eastern Free Trade Area Initiative are continuing, albeit at less than breakneck speed. At the bilateral level, the Administration has stepped up its use of free-trade agreements with favored allies. In the first term, FTAs were ratified with Singapore, Australia, Morocco and Chile. FTAs have been negotiated and signed with Bahrain and Oman. Negotiations with Panama, Peru, Ecuador, Colombia, Thailand and the United Arab Emirates are ongoing.

Can public attitudes be changed? The primary impediment to boosting public support for trade liberalization is not one of economics but of psychology. People *feel* that their jobs and wages are threatened. Even if the probability of losing one's job from import competition or outsourcing is small, the percentage of workers who know someone who has lost his or her job because of trade is much larger. In this sense, public perceptions about trade are akin to perceptions about crime: Knowing a victim of crime often makes the problem appear to be greater than it actually is. While these fears may be exaggerated, they are nonetheless real.

Psychology, not economics, holds down public support for freer trade.

If the Bush Administration decides to follow through on its ambitious trade agenda, it will need new strategies to counteract shifts in public opinion. The good news is that while the current political environment is challenging, it is not hopeless. Polling strongly suggests that a healthy majority of Americans—including skeptics of freer trade—supports policies that pair liberalization with policies that reduce the disruptions to groups that are negatively affected. These policies can take the form of expanded insurance opportunities, greater public investment in research and development, and retraining programs. The 2002 expansion of the Trade Adjustment Assistance program is a good first step, but more steps are needed: a wider use of wage insurance schemes, increased portability of health care coverage and including service-sector workers in assistance programs.

Another useful tactic would be to link trade to larger foreign policy priorities. One reason the United States was able to advance trade liberalization during the Cold War was the bipartisan consensus that a liberal trading system aided the cause of containment. Trade expansion can and should be presented as a critical element of the long-term grand strategy of the United States to spread democracy and defeat terrorism. Security arguments resonate with a broad majority of the American public. According to new polls, a large majority of Americans support promoting international trade with poor, democratic governments—a message consistent with President Bush's second Inaugural Address. As with the Cold War, a communications strategy that markets economic diplomacy as "America's first line of offense" would blunt the arguments of protectionists while promoting the virtues of trade liberalization. Greater presidential involvement in shifting public attitudes—including aggressive use of the bully pulpit—will be needed.

The alternative to blunting the shift in public opinion is to go with the flow. While politically expedient, adopting a more protectionist foreign economic policy will hurt the U.S. economy and ultimately undermine global stability. If barriers are placed on trade, the effect would be to preserve jobs in less competitive sectors of the economy and destroy current and future jobs in more competitive sectors. Trade protectionism would therefore lead to higher consumer prices, lower rates of return for investors and reduced incentives for innovation in the United States. The International Monetary Fund recently warned that trade protectionism in the United States would also magnify the negative effects of any global economic shock.

Ignoring public attitudes about trade is dangerous in the long run, and following the public mood on trade would be an unfortunate abdication of leadership by the Bush Administration in the short run. If the first step to recovery is recognizing that there is a problem, then responsible policymakers in Washington need to appreciate the extent to which the political terrain has shifted. The next step will be changing the American public's mind—a difficult but achievable task, if there is true leadership in the White House.

DANIEL DREZNER is assistant professor of political science at the University of Chicago and author of *U.S. Trade Strategy: Choices and Consequences*, published by the Council on Foreign Relations in December 2005. This article is adapted from a chapter of the book.

UNIT 4

The Institutional Context of American Foreign Policy

Unit Selections

Key Points to Consider

- How relevant is the Constitution to the conduct of American foreign policy? Do courts have a legitimate role to play in determining the content of U.S. foreign policy?

- To what extent should the United States adjust its foreign policy and laws because of decisions made by international bodies such as the World Trade Organization or the International Criminal Court?

- What is the proper role of Congress in making foreign policy?

- How much power should the president be given in making foreign policy?

- Make a case for or against the creation of a Department of Globalization Affairs.

- Which of the foreign affairs bureaucracies, discussed in this unit, is most important? Which is the most in need of reform? Which is most incapable of being reformed?

Student Web Site

www.mhcls.com/online

Internet References

Further information regarding these Web sites may be found in this book's preface or online.

Central Intelligence Agency (CIA)
http://www.cia.gov

The NATO Integrated Data Service (NIDS)
http://www.nato.int/structur/nids/nids.htm

U.S. Department of State
http://www.state.gov/index.html

United States Institute of Peace (USIP)
http://www.usip.org

U.S. White House
http://www.whitehouse.gov

Central to any study of American foreign policy are the institutions responsible for its content and conduct. The relationship between these institutions often is filled with conflict, competition, and controversy. The reasons for this are fundamental. Edwin Corwin put it best: The Constitution is an "invitation to the president and Congress to struggle over the privilege of directing U.S. foreign policy." Today, this struggle is not limited to these two institutions. At the national level the courts have emerged as a potentially important force in the making of American foreign policy. State and local governments have also become highly visible actors in world politics.

The power relationships that exist between the institutions that make American foreign policy are important for at least two reasons. First, different institutions represent different constituencies and thus advance different sets of values regarding the proper direction of American foreign policy. Second, decision makers in these institutions have different time frames when making judgments about what to do. The correct policy on conducting a war against terrorism looks different to someone coming up for election in a year or two than it does to a professional diplomat.

This close linkage between institutions and policies suggests that if American foreign policy is to successfully conduct a war against terrorism, policy-making institutions must also change their ways. Many commentators are not confident of their ability to respond to the challenges of the post–September 11 foreign policy agenda. Budgetary power bases and political predispositions that are rooted in the cold war are seen as unlikely to provide any more of a hospitable environment for a war against terrorism than they were for promoting human rights or engaging in peacekeeping operations. The creation of the Department of Homeland Security was a first institutional response to the terrorist attacks of September 11. The appointment of a Director of National Intelligence, a post advocated by investigative reports of why 9-11 happened and how intelligence was handled in the lead up to the Iraq War, was a second.

We can organize the institutions that make American foreign policy into three broad categories. The first are those composed of elected officials and their staffs: the Presidency and Congress. One topic of enduring interest is the relationship between these bodies. Considerable variation has existed over time with such phrases as the "imperial presidency," "bipartisanship," and "divided government" being used to describe it. A more contemporary issue that has raised considerable concern is the ability of elected officials to manage and organize their appointed staffs effectively so as to retain control over, and responsibility for, making decisions.

Bureaucratic organizations constitute a second set of institutions that need to be studied when examining American foreign policy. The major foreign policy bureaucracies are the State Department, Defense Department, and the Central Intelligence Agency. Often agencies with more of a domestic focus such as the Commerce Department and Treasury Departments also play important foreign policy roles in highly specialized areas. The Department of Homeland Security might be described as the first foreign policy bureaucracy to have a domestic mandate. Bureaucracies play influential roles in making foreign policy by supplying policymakers with information, defining problems, and implementing the selected policies. The current international environment presents these bureaucracies with a special challenge. Old threats and enemies have declined in importance or disappeared entirely and new ones have arisen. To remain effective these institutions must adjust their organizational structures and ways of thinking—or risk being seen by policymakers as irrelevant anachronisms.

The final institutional actor of importance in making American foreign policy is the courts. Their involvement tends to be sporadic and highly focused. Courts serve as arbitrators in the previously noted struggle for dominance between the president and Congress. A key issue today involves determining the jurisdictional boundary of the American legal system and international bodies such as an International Criminal Court and the World Trade Organization. Another involves determining the boundary of legitimate national security concerns and Constitutional rights and protections of those accused or suspected of engaging in terrorist activities.

The essays in this section survey recent developments in and controversies surrounding the key institutions that make American foreign policy. The first essay, "The Return of the Imperial Presidency?" looks at the relationship between Congress and the president. The author cautions against becoming overly enamored with the concept of an imperial presidency and urges that presidential power be examined in the context of congressional power and the influence of the public. In the next essay, "The Truman Standard," the authors examine the oft made comparison between George W. Bush and Harry Truman. This is an analogy favored by the Bush administration but the authors caution it may highlight its weaknesses more than its strengths.

The next series of essays look at the bureaucracy. "In Defense of Striped Pants" reviews the pattern of presidential relations with career foreign policy professionals focusing on the common strategies presidents use to "fix" the bureaucracy problem. The next essay in this group, "The Need for a Military Draft," argues that the all-volunteer army is not up to the task of protecting America's superpower status. The authors call for a reintroduction of the draft and explain what it might look like. The final essay in this section "Checks, Balances, and Wartime Detainees," reviews the Supreme Court's ruling on the enemy combatant cases and the implications of Congress' lack of involvement in this policy dispute. The case they review is the precursor to the Supreme Court's June 2006 decision that the Bush administration had overstepped its powers in detaining suspected terrorists at Guantanamo Bay.

The Return of the Imperial Presidency?

One lesson of American politics since September 11 is that some tensions between presidents and Congress spring from a deeper source than the partisan passions of the moment.

DONALD R. WOLFENSBERGER

Moments after President George W. Bush finished his stirring antiterrorism speech before Congress last September, presidential historian Michael Beschloss enthusiastically declared on national television that "the imperial presidency is back. We just saw it."

As someone who began his career as a Republican congressional staff aide during the turbulence of Vietnam and Watergate in the late 1960s and early 1970s, I was startled by the buoyant tone of Beschloss's pronouncement. To me, "imperial presidency" carries a pejorative connotation closely tied to those twin nightmares. Indeed, *Webster's Unabridged Dictionary* bluntly defines *imperial presidency* as "a U.S. presidency that is characterized by greater power than the Constitution allows."

Was Beschloss suggesting that President Bush was already operating outside the Constitution in prosecuting the war against terrorism, or did he have a more benign definition in mind? Apparently it was the latter. As Beschloss went on to explain, during World War II and the Cold War, Congress deferred to presidents, not just on questions of foreign policy and defense, but on domestic issues as well. Whether it was President Dwight D. Eisenhower asking for an interstate highway system or President John F. Kennedy pledging to land a man on the moon, Congress said, "If you ask us, we will." Without such a galvanizing crisis, the president would not be able to define the national interest so completely. "Now," continued Beschloss, "George Bush is at the center of the American solar system; that was not true 10 days ago." In fact, just nine months earlier Beschloss had described Bush as "the first post-imperial president" because, for the first time since the Great Depression, "we were not electing a president under the shadow of an international emergency like the Cold War or World War II or an economic crisis." Then came September 11.

Still, it's hard to join in such a warm welcome for the return of an idea that was heavily burdened just a generation ago with negative associations and cautionary experiences. Presidential scholars understandably become admirers of strong presidents and their presidencies. But a focus on executive power can become so narrow as to cause one to lose sight of the larger governmental system, with its checks and balances. To invest the idea of the imperial presidency with an aura of legitimacy and approbation would be a serious blow to America's constitutional design and the intent of the Framers.

It was historian Arthur M. Schlesinger, Jr., who popularized the term *imperial presidency* in his 1973 book by that title. Schlesinger, who had earlier chronicled the strong presidencies of Andrew Jackson and Franklin D. Roosevelt in admiring terms, admits in *The Imperial Presidency* his own culpability in perpetuating over the years "an exalted conception of presidential power":

> American historians and political scientists, this writer among them, labored to give the expansive theory of the Presidency historical sanction. Overgeneralizing from the [pre-World War II] contrast between a President who was right and a Congress which was wrong, scholars developed an uncritical cult of the activist Presidency.

The view of the presidency as "the great engine of democracy" and the "American people's one authentic trumpet," writes Schlesinger, passed into the textbooks and helped shape the national outlook after 1945. This faith of the American people in the presidency, coupled with their doubts about the ability of democracy to respond adequately to the totalitarian challenge abroad, are what gave the postwar presidency its pretensions and powers.

Uniforms redolent of imperial pomp briefly appeared on White House guards in the Nixon administration, only to vanish after a public outcry.

"By the early 1970s," Schlesinger writes, "the American President had become on issues of war and peace the most absolute monarch (with the possible exception of Mao Tse Tung of China) among the great powers of the world." Moreover, "the claims of unilateral authority in foreign policy soon began to pervade and embolden the domestic presidency."

The growth of the imperial presidency was gradual, and occurred "usually under the demand or pretext of an emergency," Schlesinger observes. Further, "it was as much a matter of congressional abdication as of presidential usurpation." The seeds of the imperial presidency were sown early. Schlesinger cites as examples Abraham Lincoln's 1861 imposition of martial law and his suspension of habeas corpus, and William McKinley's decision to send 5,000 American troops to China to help suppress the Boxer Rebellion of 1900. It is a measure of how much things have changed that Theodore Roosevelt's 1907 decision to dispatch America's Great White Fleet on a tour around the world was controversial because he failed to seek congressional approval. Then came Woodrow Wilson's forays into revolutionary Mexico, FDR's unilateral declaration of an "unlimited national emergency" six months before Pearl Harbor, and Harry Truman's commitment of U.S. troops to the Korean War in 1950, without congressional authorization, and his 1952 seizure of strike-threatened steel mills.

I n 1973, the year *The Imperial Presidency* was published, Congress moved to reassert its war-making prerogatives during non-declared wars by enacting the War Powers Resolution over President Nixon's veto. The following year, prior to Nixon's resignation under the imminent threat of impeachment, Congress enacted two more laws aimed at clipping the wings of the imperial presidency and restoring the balance of power between the two branches. The Congressional Budget and Impoundment Control Act of 1974 was designed to enable Congress to set its own spending priorities and prohibit the president from impounding funds it had appropriated. The Federal Election Campaign Act of 1974 was supposed to eliminate the taint of big money from presidential politics. Subsequent years witnessed a spate of other statutes designed to right the balance between the branches. The National Emergencies Act (1976) abolished scores of existing presidential emergency powers. The Ethics in Government Act (1978) authorized, among other things, the appointment of special prosecutors to investigate high-ranking executive branch officials. The Senate, in 1976, and the House, in 1977, established intelligence committees in the wake of hearings in 1975 revealing widespread abuses; and in 1980 the Intelligence Oversight Act increased Congress's monitoring demands on intelligence agencies and their covert operations.

Since those Watergate-era enactments, presidential scholars have decried the way Congress has emasculated the presidency. As recently as January of last year, political scientist Richard E. Neustadt, author of the classic *Presidential Power* (1964), lamented that "the U.S. presidency has been progressively weakened over the past three decades to the point where it is probably weaker today than at almost any time in the preceding century." Neustadt cited congressional actions as one of several causes of the decline.

As one who worked in the House of Representatives from 1969 to 1997, I have long been puzzled by such complaints. They have never rung true. What I witnessed during those years was the continuing decline of the legislative branch, not its ascendancy. Even Congress's post-Watergate efforts to reassert its authority look rather feeble in the harsh light of reality. The War Powers Resolution has been all but ignored by every president since Nixon as unconstitutional. They have abided by its reporting requirements, but presidential military forays abroad without explicit congressional authority continue unabated. Bosnia, Kosovo, Haiti, Somalia, and Serbia come readily to mind.

The congressional budget act has been used by every president since Ronald Reagan to leverage the administration's priorities by using budget summits with Congress to negotiate the terms of massive reconciliation bills on taxes and entitlements. The independent counsel act has been allowed to expire twice—though, in light of the unbridled power it gives counsels and the potential for abuse, this may have been wise. Federal funding of presidential campaigns has not stopped campaign finance abuses. And congressional oversight of perceived executive abuses has met with mixed results at best.

In the meantime, presidents have been relying more heavily than before on executive agreements to avoid the treaty ratification process, and on executive orders (or memorandums) of dubious statutory grounding in other areas. Administrations have defied Congress's requests for information with increasing frequency, dismissing the requests as politically motivated. And they have often invoked executive privilege in areas not previously sanctioned by judicial judgments.

T he most recent example is Vice President Richard Cheney's refusal, on grounds of executive privilege, to turn over to the General Accounting Office (GAO), an arm of Congress, information about meetings between the president's energy task force and energy executives. The controversy took on added interest with the collapse of Enron, one of the energy companies that provided advice to the task force. Vice President Cheney, who served as President Gerald R. Ford's White House chief of staff, said his action was aimed at reversing "an erosion of the powers" of the presidency over the last 30 to 35 years resulting from "unwise compromises" made by past Administrations. President Bush backed Cheney's claim of executive privilege, citing the need to maintain confidentiality in the advice given to a president.

It is revealing in this case that the congressional requests for information came not through formal committee action or subpoenas but more indirectly from the GAO, at the prompting of two ranking minority committee Democrats in the House, even though their Senate party counterparts are committee chairmen with authority to force a vote on subpoenas. The committee system, which should be the bulwark of congressional policymaking and oversight of the executive branch, has been in steady decline since the mid-1970s. Not the least of the causes is the weakening of committee prerogatives and powers by Congress itself, as a response to members' demands for a more participatory policy process than the traditional committee system allowed. Party leaders eventually replaced committee leaders as the locus of power in the House, a shift that was not altered by the change in party control of Congress in 1995.

Another contributing factor has been the shift in the Republican Party's base of power to the South and West, which has given a more populist and propresidential cast to the GOP membership on Capitol Hill.

Even with recent promises by Speaker of the House Dennis Hastert (R-Ill.) and Senate Majority Leader Tom Daschle (D-S.D.) to "return to the regular order" by giving committees greater flexibility and discretion in agenda setting and bill drafting, Congress is hamstrung by self-inflicted staff cuts and three-day legislative workweeks that make deliberative lawmaking and careful oversight nearly impossible. The "permanent campaign" has spilled over into governing, diminishing the value members see in committee work and encouraging partisan position taking and posturing. (It also makes members eager to get back to their districts for the serious work of campaigning, which explains the three-day work week in Washington.) It is easier to take a popular campaign stand on an unresolved issue than make a painful policy choice and explain it to the voters.

Bill Clinton had the common touch—and an imperial taste for sending U.S. troops abroad without congressional approval.

Is it any wonder that even before the current emergency the executive was in a stronger position than Congress? Such power alone is not necessarily a sign of an imperial presidency. But testing the limits of power seems to be an inborn trait of political man, and presidents are no exception. Even presidential power proponent Richard Neustadt, who sees the presidency at the beginning of this 21st century as the weakest it's been in three decades, concedes that none of the formal limits on presidential powers by Congress or the courts have managed to eliminate those powers of greatest consequence, including the "plentitude of prerogative power" (a Lockean concept of acting outside the constitutional box to save the nation) that Lincoln assumed during the Civil War.

Both presidents George H. W. Bush and George W. Bush, to their credit, sought authorization from Congress for the use of force against Iraq and international terrorists, respectively, before committing troops to combat. Yet both also claimed they had inherent powers as president to do so to protect the national interest. (The younger Bush was on firmer ground since even the Framers explicitly agreed that the president has authority to repel foreign invasions and respond to direct attacks on the United States.)

The presidency is at its strongest at the outset of a national crisis or war. Just as President Franklin D. Roosevelt was encountering public and congressional wariness over his depression-era policies in the late 1930s, along came World War II and a whole new lease on the throne. Presidential power tends to increase at the expense of Congress. Alexander Hamilton put it succinctly in *The Federalist* 8: "It is of the nature of war to increase the executive at the expense of the legislative authority."

One way to gauge this balance of power is to look at the extent to which Congress deliberates over policy matters and the extent to which it gives the president most of what he requests with minimal resistance. Two weeks after Congress passed a $40 billion emergency spending bill and a resolution authorizing the president to use force against those behind the World Trade Center attacks, Senator Robert S. Byrd (D-W.Va.) rose in a nearly empty Senate chamber to remind his colleagues of their deliberative responsibilities. "In the heat of the moment, in the crush of recent events," Byrd observed, "I fear we may be losing sight of the larger obligations of the Senate."

> Our responsibility as Senators is to carefully consider and fully debate major policy matters, to air all sides of a given issue, and to act after full deliberation. Yes, we want to respond quickly to urgent needs, but a speedy response should not be used as an excuse to trample full and free debate.

Byrd was concerned in part about the way in which language relating to the controversy over adhering to the 1972 antiballistic missile treaty had been jettisoned from a pending defense authorization bill in the interest of "unity" after the terrorist attacks. But he was also disturbed by the haste with which the Senate had approved the use-of-force resolution "to avoid the specter of acrimonious debate at a time of national crisis." Byrd added that he was not advocating unlimited debate, but why, he asked, "do we have to put a zipper on our lips and have no debate at all?" Because of the "paucity of debate" in both houses, Byrd added, there was no discussion laying a foundation for the resolution, and in the future "it would be difficult to glean from the record the specific intent of Congress."

A review of the *Congressional Record* supports Byrd's complaint. Only Majority Leader Daschle and Minority Leader Trent Lott (R-Miss.) spoke briefly before the Senate passed the emergency spending bill and the use-of-force resolution. The discussion was truncated chiefly because buses were waiting to take senators and House members to a memorial service at the National Cathedral.

The House, to its credit, did return after the service for five hours of debate on the resolution, which it passed 420 to 1. Some 200 members spoke for about a minute each—hardly the stuff of a great debate. At no time did any member raise a question about the breadth, scope, or duration of the authority granted by the resolution. The closest some came were passing references to the way in which President Lyndon B. Johnson had used the language of the 1964 Gulf of Tonkin Resolution as authority to broaden U.S. involvement in Vietnam.

To the credit of Congress, a small, bipartisan leadership group had earlier negotiated a compromise with the White House to confine the resolution's scope to "those nations, organizations or persons" implicated in the September 11 attacks.

The original White House proposal was much broader, extending the president's authority "to deter and pre-empt any future acts of terrorism or aggression against the United States." The language change is significant. If President Bush cannot demonstrate that Iraq was somehow involved in the September 11 attacks but decides to take military action against it, he will have to decide whether to seek additional authority from Congress or act without it, as President Bill Clinton did before him.

In times of war or national emergency, presidents have always acted in what they thought to be the national interest. That is not to say that Congress simply becomes a presidential lap dog. While it tends to defer to the commander in chief on military matters once troops have been committed to combat, it continues to exercise oversight and independence on matters not directly affecting the war's outcome. For example, President Bush was forced to make drastic alterations in his economic stimulus package by Senate Democrats who disagreed with his tax relief and spending priorities. And even in the midst of the war on terrorism, the House and Senate intelligence committees launched a joint inquiry into why our intelligence services were not able to detect or thwart the September 11 terrorist plot. In the coming months, moreover, Congress is sure to have its own ideas on how the federal budget can best be allocated to meet the competing demands for defense, homeland security, and domestic social-welfare programs.

I s the imperial presidency back? While at this writing the White House has not overtly exercised any extraconstitutional powers, the imperial presidency has been with us since World War II, and it is most likely to be re-energized during times of national crisis. Every president tends to test the limits of his power during such periods in order to do what he deems necessary to protect national security. To the extent that Congress does not push back and the public does not protest, the armor of the imperial presidency is further fortified by precedent and popular support against future attacks.

What is the danger in a set of powers that have, after all, evolved over several decades into a widely recognized reality without calamitous consequences for the Republic? As James Madison put in *The Federalist* 51, "The separate and distinct exercise of the different powers of government… is admitted on all hands to be essential to the preservation of liberty." The "great security against a gradual concentration of power in the same department," he went on, is to provide each department with the "necessary constitutional means and personal motives to resist…. Ambition must be made to counteract ambition."

The Constitution's system of separated powers and checks and balances is not a self-regulating machine. Arthur M. Schlesinger, Jr., observed in *The Imperial Presidency*, that what kept a strong presidency constitutional, in addition to the president's own appreciation of the Framers' wisdom, was the vigilance of the nation. "If the people had come to an unconscious acceptance of the imperial presidency," he wrote, "the Constitution could not hold the nation to ideals it was determined to betray." The only deterrent to the imperial presidency is for the great institutions of our society—Congress, the courts, the press, public opinion, the universities, "to reclaim their own dignity and meet their own responsibilities."

DONALD R. WOLFENSBERGER is director of the Congress Project at the Wilson Center and the author of *Congress and the People: Deliberative Democracy on Trial (2000).* He retired as chief of staff of the House Rules Committee in 1997 after a 28-year career on the staff of the U.S. House of Representatives.

The Truman Standard

DEREK CHOLLET AND JAMES M. GOLDGEIER

"Soon after arriving at the State Department", Secretary of State Condoleezza Rice wrote in December 2005, "I hung a portrait of Dean Acheson in my office." The reason for choosing the visage of Harry Truman's second Secretary of State to gaze down upon her? "Like Acheson and his contemporaries, we live in an extraordinary time—one in which the terrain of international politics is shifting beneath our feet and the pace of historical change outstrips even the most vivid imagination."[1]

In and of itself, this is nothing new. Since the end of the Cold War, it has become customary for American secretaries of state to compare the challenges before them to those confronted by Truman and his two distinguished top diplomats, Acheson and his predecessor, General George C. Marshall. But the second term Bush team has taken this comparison to a new level. Particularly at the State Department, the Truman-Acheson reference has become a mantra, part of the standard, bedrock rhetoric of the Secretary both in her prepared and extemporaneous remarks. Secretary Rice and President Bush clearly want this comparison to be accepted and made by others. But in some important ways the analogy, if thought through, highlights more of the Administration's shortcomings than its strengths. What, then, is the Truman Standard, and how does the Bush Administration really measure up to it?

Analogies, Intended and Not

It's easy to see why Secretary Rice, President Bush and others in the Administration invoke Truman and Acheson when explaining their own circumstances and choices. Like Truman, Bush takes pride in being plainspoken and enjoys needling Washington's political and policy elite. The Truman Administration, facing novel and unexpected challenges, rose to the occasion with sharp analysis, bold policy change and courageous leadership in the face of much hidebound skepticism and fear. The principals of the Bush Administration fancy themselves as having done the same thing.

In a way, this has been inevitable. After all, the Cold War story of danger, struggle, determination and victory is the happy-ending story they know best. Rice often mentions that when she was watching the USSR break apart as the White House Soviet specialist during 1989-1991, she "was only harvesting the good decisions that had been taken in 1947, in 1948, and in 1949." A half century from now serious historians may conclude that the British success at defeating the Indian Rebellion of 1857—which sparked broad unrest against British rule on the subcontinent—is a better analogy to the American "war on terror", but no one should expect American leaders to draw from that or any other similarly distant historical event.

Besides, there are arguable parallels between the late 1940s and the early years of this century. Then, some sixty years ago, the Soviet Union had occupied half of Europe and exploded an atomic bomb, and with communism sprouting up in Asia, Africa and elsewhere, Truman and his team feared a new existential threat to the United States just a few short years after the defeat of fascism. Now, the challenges posed by the nexus of al-Qaeda and the perils of WMD proliferation seem similarly to pose an existential threat, and again a threat rising unexpectedly just after a great victory. So as the Truman Administration recognized the scope of the threat and responded to scale, the Bush Administration strives to do the same. Just as freedom and democracy were the guiding inner lights of Truman's vision, so they are for George W. Bush. And just as building democratic allies in Germany and Japan were the key arenas for the success of containment, so the Bush team views the creation of a democratic Iraq and Afghanistan as similar in importance to the success of its long-term strategy. None of this is far-fetched.

No less important a Truman parallel is the belief that George W. Bush will be vindicated by history, despite his increasing unpopularity among the American people today—not to speak of how unpopular he may be when he leaves office in January 2009. In this way, the Truman comparisons offer a kind of psychological comfort for the beleaguered Bush team. As Secretary of Defense Rumsfeld said at a press briefing late last year, Truman, who is

> now remembered as a fine president, [left] office in 1953 with an approval rating of about 25 percent, one of the lowest recorded ratings since folks started measuring those things. ... Back then, a great many people questioned whether young Americans should face death and injury in Korea, thousands of miles from home, for a result that seemed uncertain at best. And today the answer is the Korean peninsula.[2]

Former *New York Times* columnist William Safire predicted for 2006 that, "As Bush's approval rises, historians will begin to equate his era with that of " Truman.[3]

It is true that Harry Truman is held in far higher esteem today than when he left office. He is now considered one of America's greatest presidents, much admired for his humble style and his decisive, gutsy leadership. Yet what such comparisons overlook is that the Truman Administration not only helped build up two major new democracies and established the strategy of containment, but developed the tools to implement its policy over the long haul. That Administration created the United Nations, the Marshall Plan, NATO, the General Agreement on Tariffs and Trade, the IMF and the World Bank, institutions that have underpinned American leadership in world politics for more than half a century.

There is yet another Truman parallel that, unsurprisingly, the Bush team does not go out of its way to emphasize. In the 1952 election, with an unpopular president mired in war in Korea, both Democratic candidate Adlai Stevenson and Republican candidate Dwight Eisenhower ran against the Truman legacy. The year 2008 will witness the first presidential election since 1952 in which, presumably, neither the sitting president nor the vice president is running. If George W. Bush cannot turn things around in Iraq—which appears depressingly likely—candidates from both parties may well run against his record, and not just in foreign policy. The skyrocketing budget deficit, lagging health care reform, the prescription drugs-for-seniors mess, and the continuing ethics scandals that often plague second-term administrations are available as campaign grist, as well. The Republicans are already heading into a difficult mid-term election in November (in the 1950 midterm elections, Truman's Democrats were trounced, losing 5 Senate seats and 28 in the House). So at least in the short run, Bush might prove to be a lot like Truman, leaving office with little popularity and a legacy that politicians from both parties treat as a liability.

But will Bush win big in his long-term gamble—that, as with Truman, future historians will esteem him as a visionary leader? That is not clear on account of the biggest difference between the Truman of 1950 and the Bush of 2006. Truman not only created international institutions, but he also built his foreign policy with bipartisan support, so that his successors—Republican and Democratic alike—were destined to operate within the framework he created. So far, President Bush has done nothing of that scale and scope. Not only has he largely disdained formal institutions, he has also spurned bipartisanship. There is thus no lasting institutional or political legacy to ensure that his successors will adopt his general approach to world affairs.

Work to Do

What would President Bush have to accomplish in the final three years of his presidency to make his Truman show—and Rice's supporting act to compare herself to Acheson—less a theatrical slogan than an achievement historians and the public will truly come to appreciate?

The Truman Administration faced five unprecedented challenges: turning vanquished adversaries into democratic allies; defending the free states of Europe from possible Soviet aggression; developing a new architecture for managing the global economy; creating international legitimacy for American ac-

tions abroad; and deterring the Soviet nuclear threat. As President Bush and Secretary Rice have asserted, today's challenges are somewhat comparable. It is in America's interest to spread freedom in the broader Middle East, not just in Afghanistan and Iraq, but in the Palestinian Authority, Iran and Syria. Strong alliances continue to be important for that and other purposes. The global economy is under significant strain. America needs to ensure that its foreign policy actions are perceived as legitimate. And the United States faces a range of foreign policy threats, including nuclear programs in North Korea and Iran, the continued threat posed by al-Qaeda, the uncertain future of a growing China, and the reassertion of Russian power, this time not least in tightening global energy markets.

The Administration has a long way to go to meet the Truman Standard, and its most serious impediment is the Iraq problem. In the 1950s, America ensured that Germany and Japan became pro-American allies because they had been occupied after the war with sufficient numbers of American troops and protracted American oversight. In Iraq, the United States bungled badly the postwar occupation. And if Iraqi democracy—or chaos and collapse—leads to greater Iranian dominance of the region, the effort will hardly be compared to postwar American leadership in Europe and Asia.

There are some areas where the Bush team is showing promising course corrections. For example, the Administration did not necessarily need to create new alliances because it inherited those created during the Cold War. But having initially decided not to work through NATO in Afghanistan and then splitting the alliance over Iraq, the Administration recognized early in its second term a need to repair the damage it had done. Deciding that the first overseas trip of his second term would be to Europe, the President stirred hopes for better relations by visiting not only NATO but the European Union in Brussels. And with an increasing NATO role in Afghanistan, Iraq and Darfur, it appeared in 2005 and early this year that Bush might yet infuse the alliance with new shared purpose. Unfortunately, the disputes over treatment of terrorist suspects on European territory and U.S. policies of preventive detention have complicated efforts to forge that renewed sense of purpose.

On trade, the Administration decided early in its tenure to pursue bilateral deals and the relatively small Central American Free Trade Agreement rather than to reach for more ambitious multilateral accords. This left tough issues of the Doha Round on the back burner until it was too late to forge a comprehensive agreement at the WTO's December meeting in Hong Kong. There is no question that concluding the Doha Round would be a real challenge for any administration given the range of demands from Europe and some of the leading developing countries, but rising to that challenge would go a long way toward defining Bush as Trumanesque.

Having soured relations with the United Nations, and alienated much of the world by the way it has handled its policies toward terrorist detainees and interrogations, the Administration seems unable to decide where to turn to rebuild American legitimacy in global affairs. The September deal with North Korea appears insubstantial; negotiations with Iran have faltered; bin Laden and Zarqawi remain at large, China has begun to dominate Asian affairs, and a more authoritarian Russia has been working to counter American democratization efforts along its borders. The Administration has made clear that it does not trust formal institutions and does not want to create new bureaucracies to develop global governance. It has preferred to work through less formal structures like the G-8, the loose framework Bush used to promote his Broader Middle East and North Africa Initiative, and the Six Party Talks for solving the North Korean nuclear problem. Some of these informal structures have been useful, but they are hardly firstorder institutions. And they often exclude countries whose cooperation is essential to solving global problems. It seems unlikely, for example, that the G-8 can really handle major transnational issues like proliferation, terrorism and global health when countries like China, India and Brazil stand on the sidelines.

There is also the question of how lasting Bush's grand strategy, defined by preemption and democracy promotion, will really be. Will preemption get enshrined in the first half of the 21st century as containment did in the second half of the 20th? Perhaps. After all, any president faced with imminent threats of the kind that struck the United States on September 11, 2001 will want to preempt them. Yet the first test of the new strategy, Iraq, was sold as preemption in the face of an imminent weapons of mass destruction threat. Since we now know that there was no such imminent threat, the American public and the Congress might be much less compliant in future crises. A debacle in Iraq could well be the undoing of the Bush team's efforts to develop an enduring grand strategy for the post-9/11 era.

The future of the other strategic pillar of the Bush policy, democracy promotion, is also uncertain. Secretary Rice speaks often of "transformational diplomacy", which is underpinned by the idea (if not the practice) of promoting freedom everywhere. She has made some sensible reforms in the way professional diplomats are trained and where they are stationed. What's missing from this notion, however, is a coherent strategy for pursuing not only democratization but other American interests as well. Few would argue against the idea that a freer and more democratic world is in America's interests. This idea is not new; "transformational diplomacy" is little different from the doctrine of "democratic enlargement" enunciated by Bill Clinton's first National Security Advisor, Anthony Lake, in 1993. Yet what the idea lacked in 1993, and still lacks today, is a way to apply it globally in a meaningful way. In the Cold War we knew what we wanted to contain, and where we wanted to contain it. Clinton and Bush have stated a desire to enlarge the community of democracies, but there is no consensus domestically on where, how or when to do so.

■

So, what can President Bush do? Like Truman, he has already shuffled some key personnel. But as even sympathetic observers have suggested, he could do a lot more in this regard and make an honest stab at bipartisanship. It might go against his every instinct and anger his base, which, with the exception of the immigration issue, he has been unwilling to do so far. But he has to do it if he is to meet the Truman Standard. To gain support for the Marshall Plan, Truman reached out to Republican

senator Arthur Vandenberg and chose Republican businessman Paul Hoffman to head the agency that would oversee disbursement of the funds. Would George Bush work in partnership with the Vandenbergs of today, like Delaware Senator Joseph Biden? Would he choose a Democrat with experience in foreign aid to head his Millennium Challenge Corporation? If he did, it would be a sign that he was not simply talking about Truman but actually taking a page from the Truman playbook.

The President could also do some second-term institution building. New domestic and international institutions were critical to the Cold War strategic framework. Truman engineered the National Security Act of 1947 and the institutional architecture of America's modern foreign policy and military establishment. Bush has taken major steps to reform intelligence and homeland security, but he still has a long way to go to reform how we go about promoting democratization and development. Without fundamental changes to the ways we use our so-called soft power—or what Pentagon planners call the tools to win the "long war"—the U.S. approach will continue to be piecemeal, lack focus, and ultimately fall short.

International institutions embedded American ideals and habits of cooperation into the structure of global politics, and they helped lend legitimacy to American actions. This has hardly worked perfectly, as the deep flaws of institutions like the United Nations make clear. Yet despite the boldness of his rhetoric, President Bush's efforts to create new avenues for American legitimacy—through institutions or otherwise—have been underwhelming. The Administration's most successful new international programs—the Proliferation Security Initiative and the Millennium Challenge Account—hardly compare with the creation of NATO or the World Bank. To meet the Truman Standard, Bush will have to develop new ways to build American legitimacy to act internationally. Perhaps transforming the Community of Democracies from an ineffectual and occasional talk-fest into a real, working alliance, with a permanent secretariat and a real budget, would be one way to do this. But the Administration has consistently opposed any such idea—at least up to now.

Finally, there is the political reality of the Bush legacy. Unless the President can find a way to turn the Iraq situation around and get American troops out gracefully, and without leaving behind a civil war, by 2008, the next presidential election will be defined by which candidates can better distinguish (and distance) themselves from the current Administration. And to leave something lasting behind, the Administration will need to reinvigorate NATO and elevate U.S. cooperation with the EU; find the key to success in the Doha Round; gain consensus with Europe, China and Russia on containing the threats posed by North Korea and Iran; capture or kill bin Laden and Zarqawi; and counter Russian and Chinese diplomacy in places like Ukraine, the Caucasus, Central Asia and Southeast Asia while finding ways to engage those two countries on matters of common strategic interest.

If Bush fails to do any of this, he will likely leave office politically hobbled, with his opponents emboldened and a country deeply disillusioned about his policies around the world. He will be remembered as a leader who tried to do big things and articulate a new vision for America, but because of his stubbornness and insularity failed to garner the support to sustain his policies beyond his term in office. The result might be an America more withdrawn from the world and reluctant to take on significant challenges. And instead of evoking comparisons to Harry Truman, President Bush will leave a more mixed legacy closer to another of his predecessors—Woodrow Wilson.

Notes

1. Condoleezza Rice, "The Promise of Democratic Peace", *Washington Post*, December 11, 2005.

2. Rumsfeld quoted in Al Kamen, "Bush and Turman Don't Match Up", *Washington Post*, November 7, 2005.

3. Safire, "The Office Pool, 2006", *New York Times*, December 30, 2005.

DEREK CHOLLET is a fellow at the Center for Strategic and International Studies and a non-resident fellow at the Brookings Institution. **JAMES GOLDGEIER** is a professor of political science at George Washington University and an adjunct senior fellow at the Council on Foreign Relations.

From *The American Interest*, Summer 2006, pp. 107-112. Copyright © 2006 by American Interest. Reprinted by permission.

In Defense of Striped Pants

MORTON ABRAMOWITZ AND LESLIE H. GELB

From the day after the United States toppled the regime of Saddam Hussein, it has run into one problem after another in Iraq. We failed to establish security. We steadily lost support from Arab Sunnis and Shi'a. We entered the war with limited international support and have even less today. However encouraging the January elections, Iraq is a work in progress, and it is straining our resources, roiling our military and complicating our diplomacy. How long public support will last is uncertain. So who is responsible for our current predicament, and what can we learn from a serious answer to that highly charged question?

Politics requires scapegoats, whether they bear guilt or not. And the media seem less interested in discovering who is responsible than in providing a megaphone for the accusations. But the questions need to be asked. We cannot begin to fix the policymaking process until we see who broke it—and even then, the damage may be beyond repair.

Cheered on by conservative think tanks and journals, the administration has focused on the sins of that easiest of targets, the career professionals. That requires bloodletting, and it has gushed at the top levels of the CIA. The State Department was expected to be next, but Secretary of State Condoleezza Rice thus far has selected very able foreign service officers for a number of top positions. It is, of course, unclear how she will want to use their advice—or whether she will be able to do so. The Pentagon had already experienced significant bloodletting in the ranks of the career military through Secretary of Defense Donald Rumsfeld's highly personal and unorthodox choices for top jobs.

The administration, and even more its vocal outside supporters, assert that Iraq, as well as democracy promotion and other important policies, have not gotten traction because career professionals are incompetent, unable to see the merit of these policies, unwilling to carry them out, or insufficiently aggressive in explaining their wisdom to a skeptical world. They blame the CIA for faulty information, and military leaders for not insisting on more troops. Some conservative critics even blame the State Department and the CIA for the occupation of Iraq, when it could have been avoided, they say, by just installing Ahmed Chalabi and withdrawing U.S. troops quickly thereafter. (Are George Bush, Dick Cheney and Donald Rumsfeld such pussy cats for State and the CIA?) Many career professionals were indeed skeptical of the Iraq enterprise as conceived, publicly ex-

plained and carried out. These views were hardened by the persistent internal warfare between the Pentagon and other agencies, where battles were frequently denied publicly while Mr. Rumsfeld was mostly winning them.

Conservative critics also generally believe that the top bureaucratic ranks are essentially inhabited by cautious officials overly wed to international institutions and fearful of wholesale change or the pursuit of a foreign policy mission with big, politically difficult objectives. They also see many career officials as Democrats, disloyal or at least unsympathetic to the Bush Administration, who will often try to undermine policy by leaking secret information that casts doubt on the effectiveness of administration policies. They point to the CIA's allowing the publication before the November election of a book by a relatively senior official that was highly critical of the administration's Iraq and counter-terrorism policies. Indeed, some of the usually quasi-public statements of several CIA officials were surprising in their direct criticism of the Bush Administration, particularly in comments denying Iraq's ties to international terrorism. Unidentified officials in all agencies were also frequently quoted in the press, questioning what the U.S. government was publicly saying about Iraq.

A more detached view that partially supports this perspective comes from the 9/11 Commission (and more recently the CIA's inspector general). The commission found the federal bureaucracy under at least two administrations to have been mostly out of touch with the threat posed to the United States by Islamic jihadism. But the commission did not focus on the road to Iraq, the administration's role, or the interplay between political leaders and career professionals.

The opposite perspective—one shared by many Democrats, editorialists, academics and senior officials—regards these charges as little more than scapegoating of the bureaucracy by the administration and its supporters—a way to hide its own massive mistakes in Iraq. Vice President Cheney's visits to the CIA notwithstanding, the bureaucrats' defenders charge the administration with failure to seriously consult the bureaucracy, and with pushing aside uniformed officers in the Pentagon who were upset with the planning for war. As a matter of historical fact, this group does have a big truth on its side: The administration did little to encourage any serious internal debate or real consideration of alternate policy approaches.

Some holding this view consider the Iraq War a historic policy mistake based on profound ignorance and the arrogance of administration "ideologues." They also believe that the administration has been mendacious in shaping the limited public debate, and that the mainline agencies are being punished while the principal authors of Iraq policy and their cheerleaders are allowed to remain in office—another expression of the administration's inability to admit the slightest error. And they assert that the Bush foreign policy has been run without diplomacy, almost purposefully, in order to avoid the kind of compromises that presumably might have avoided armed conflict in Iraq.

When the debris of charges and counter-charges is set aside, two broad conclusions remain. First, even had the bureaucratic professionals had their full say on Iraq policy, it is far from clear that President Bush would have changed his basic decision and policy to remove Saddam Hussein from power by force of arms. It seems the odds are that he would have resorted to arms in any event. Second, even with war as a given, a strong case can be made that the president's Iraq policy would have been strengthened had he listened to the career professionals on three critical issues: better mobilizing international support by giving the UN inspections some additional time; better managing the postwar occupation; and the need for far more troops to establish and maintain security.

It is too soon to measure the ultimate impact of our Iraq effort. But with the war still underway and with other major problems between political masters and career professionals, it is none too soon to re-examine, and hopefully fix, the policymaking process.

Tension between presidential administrations and their foreign affairs, intelligence and career military bureaucracies is hardly a new phenomenon. Since the centralization of national security decision-making in the White House in the 1960s, most presidents and their national security advisors—Democratic and Republican— have been distrustful of the bureaucracies. They have often viewed them as disloyal competitors and as resistant to change. And often, the political masters have excluded them from high-level considerations of critical issues, relegating them to producing unneeded papers or busying them with planning trips and motorcades.

This now built-in tension becomes acute when there is a major foreign policy discontinuity or a radical change in course or style. We saw it in the Reagan Administration and in the first George W. Bush Administration in spades. From the very start of the current administration, internal tensions grew over what was immediately seen as an unnecessarily unilateralist and arrogant White House style. That seemed immediately "proven" when Mr. Bush publicly told South Korean President Kim Dae Jung that his policy toward North Korea was totally wrong (a view and an act held to be destructive by many career officials). Simmering feelings then exploded from many quarters over Iraq. Most professionals adjusted, but some found ways of going to war with the administration and its policy. Very few left, particularly those in the senior ranks.

But the administration does have legitimate gripes about the capabilities of two key agencies, the State Department and the CIA. (The serious limitations in the Defense Department are of a different character.) The State Department is not now, to put it charitably, at its zenith. Its policymaking capabilities and functions have declined, it has reduced its interest in field reporting, and its implementation of policy sometimes has been taken over by Defense or the CIA. State also has not exhibited much imagination. Nor has it honed its political skills. For example, State put its highly regarded study of postwar Iraq under the aegis of a very capable midlevel foreign service officer whose name was not known far beyond his own office. This valuable study was shunted aside, possibly by the senior officials surrounding Colin Powell in the officer's own building.

Nevertheless, the State Department remains a great source of talent, information and analytical skills. Its international experience is unrivaled and can be applied on numerous issues. It has a wealth of important and often unique associations, and it is filled with people dedicated to pursuing our national interests. And for all its complaining about political masters, it does try hard to satisfy them. State is almost Zelig-like in its capacity to adjust to political leadership, whatever the personal views of its professionals. Many administrations fail to take advantage of this trait and prefer to talk about the disloyalty of the State Department. But most political appointees to Foggy Bottom will tell you, correctly, that the department responds to anyone who takes the institution seriously. Taking the place seriously will not stop all the leaks—that's life. But it will reduce them.

The CIA's reputation, never very high, has significantly declined despite a huge infusion of resources. But its recent roguish behavior is not typical. Indeed, quite the opposite. When the U.S. government embarks on a major effort, its employees, including the CIA, usually salute. Top officials want very much to please their big bosses, and they usually find ways to match the intelligence to the policy proclivities. And when things go wrong, their political masters inevitably turn against the agency. None of this should obscure the general capability of CIA analysts and their dedication to preserving the integrity of the intelligence process.

The CIA's analytical product faces some serious hurdles. First, its importance is inflated in the public eye, even as its reports go mostly unread by top policymakers. And second, if there are intelligence errors on big issues, it casts a pall over the whole intelligence analysis effort. The agency's failure on Iraq's WMD, and its lack of understanding of the potemkin and dysfunctional nature of the Saddam regime, have had a serious impact on American credibility as well as attitudes toward the agency.

It is not the CIA's analytical directorate but the operations directorate— the field-agent effort and the one so important to dealing with terrorism— that has been getting most of the flak, and the one whose career senior leaders have been summarily fired by Mr. Goss. They have been variously accused of delinquencies ranging from gross incompetence to extreme caution—no "risktakers there." That may be one reason the Defense Department is taking over many of the CIA's activities. This part of the CIA has had trying times, from the Church Committee in the

1970s to their involvement in the Iran-Contra affair to their difficulties in the early Clinton years. They have gone up and down in manpower. In the last few years they have been the beneficiaries of a significant infusion of resources, but if the recent firings are any indication, the enhancements have not yet paid off.

It is difficult for the outsider to draw any conclusion about the effectiveness of the CIA's clandestine efforts. Congressional oversight cannot be given much credence. The agency claims that only its failures become public, that there are many unheralded and unknown achievements, particularly in preventing terrorist incidents. One thing is clear: Greater risk-taking and reorganization of the whole intelligence community does not necessarily produce more intelligence on extremely difficult targets like North Korea. The challenges in acquiring such information are enormous. The Clandestine Service is not likely to be "transformed" by simply changing the organization's wiring diagram and the top people.

The fixes to these "problems" within the professional bureaucracy and between it and the political masters have mainly taken three forms. First, there are times when the political masters have grown so exasperated or so eager to place blame elsewhere that they have fired senior career people. On many occasions, these firings are justified, as with some of the recent moves in the upper reaches of the CIA. But it is hard for senior professionals to swallow righteous firings when those whose mistakes are seen as even more egregious, like several high-level Pentagon officials, retain their positions and are praised for performance. While bloodletting is needed at times to get rid of particular problems, it does not solve systemic ones.

A second tried-and-true formula has been to reorganize the bureaucracy, redirect supporting lines, and move boxes for whole agencies from one place to another. Most times these reorganizations are a waste of time and money. Moving bureaucrats does not necessarily change the culture or the performance. And wherever they are moved. Congress is almost always unmoved. Organizational changes that occur within administrations are often negated by unchanged and parochial congressional relationships—as demonstrated by the utter disregard with which Congress has treated the reforms to its own operations that were recommended by the 9/11 Commission. It is argued that the recent attempts to improve counter-terrorism efforts have proven successful. But a serious evaluation will take several more years.

Third, the final fix resorted to by political masters has been to rail against or ignore the bureaucracy. That is the approach discussed in this article. It has proven very costly to the nation. As we have noted, it is clear in retrospect that U.S. policy in Iraq could have benefited at almost every turn from the advice and information of the professional bureaucracy. From the president on down, political appointees must realize that, yes, bureaucracy is sluggish and out of touch, resistant to change, lacking in imagination, and often wrong, but career professionals can save them from disastrous mistakes. By virtue of having worked seriously on these problems, countries and cultures for years, no one is better than they are at spotting obstacles and landmines. No policy can be successful that fails to anticipate these hurdles. Political masters ignore this expertise at their peril.

Every administration must be zealous in the pursuit of important national security goals. Political appointees, however, must not confuse an absence of candor with loyalty in their career subordinates. Career professionals are being most loyal when they are being candid with their bosses about situations and when they press for a serious examination of policy. They have a sense of American national interests that tries to transcend an individual administration and should be fully and fairly examined before administrations change course.

This will not stop all leaking to the press. But the kind of draconian measures that would be needed to prevent all significant leaks would be bad for the policymaking process and, it could well be argued, worse for the democratic process. Sometimes the people know what's going on or what the choices are only because of these leaks. Ditto for Congress.

Thus, probably the most effective way to address the bureaucracy's weaknesses and take advantage of its strengths is not bloodletting, or reorganization, or ignoring and condemning the bureaucrats. It is having a sensible attitude at the top, starting with presidents and secretaries. Beneath them, the key to making the system work is to have appointees at the assistant secretary level who are responsive to the policy imperatives of the political leadership and willing to engage and draw on the skills of their career experts. The assistant secretary jobs are where the proverbial rubber meets the road.

At this time, the country has a particular need for preserving candor in the departments and a variety of viewpoints from different agencies, particularly in the intelligence world. The War on Terror has given the U.S. government enormous power to do what it thinks is necessary to protect this country. Today, everything done in the name of that effort seems to be acceptable to, even demanded by, the public. The mechanisms for self-examination or self-correction either do not work or are diminishing. Congress provides little serious oversight. The media, particularly on television, are disadvantaged by the secrecy of subject matter and often by their lack of interest. In this post-9/11 environment, the permanent bureaucracy is the last line of defense in possibly subjecting critical policy considerations to the most informed scrutiny. If the administration does not want to consult them seriously, they must themselves persist in trying to make their views known to their leaders in constructive ways that go beyond anonymous leaks to the *Washington Post*.

MORTON ABRAMOWITZ is senior fellow at the Century Foundation and former Assistant Secretary of State for Intelligence and Research. **LESLIE H. GELB** is president emeritus of the Council on Foreign Relations.

From *The National Interest*, Spring 2005, pp. 73-77. Copyright © 2005 by National Interest. Reprinted by permission.

The Need for a Military Draft

Protecting Superpower Status

PHILLIP CARTER AND PAUL GLASTRIS

The United States has occupied many foreign lands over the last half century—Germany and Japan in World War II, and, on a much smaller scale, Haiti, Bosnia, and Kosovo in the 1990s. In all these cases, we sponsored elections and handed-off to democratic governments control of countries that were relatively stable, secure, and reasonably peaceful.

In Iraq, we failed to do this, despite heroic efforts by U.S. and coalition troops. The newly-elected Iraqi government inherits a country in which assassinations, kidnappings, suicide bombings, pipeline sabotages, and beheadings of foreigners are daily occurrences. For the last eight months, the ranks of the insurgency have been growing faster than those of the security forces of the provisional Iraqi government—and an alarming number of those government forces are secretly working for the insurgency. American-led combat operations in Ramadi and Fallujah killed large numbers of the enemy, but at the price of fanning the flames of anti-American hatred and dispersing the insurrection throughout Iraq. Despite nearly two years of effort, American troops and civilian administrators have failed to restore basic services to much of the central part of the country where a majority of Iraqis live. The U.S. military has not even been able to secure the 7-mile stretch of highway leading from the Baghdad airport to the Green Zone where America's own embassy and the seat of the Iraqi government are headquartered.

How we got to this point is by now quite obvious. Even many of the war's strongest supporters admit that the Bush administration grievously miscalculated by invading Iraq with too few troops and then by stubbornly refusing to augment troop numbers as the country descended into violent mayhem after the fall of Saddam.

This analysis, of course, presumes that it was ever possible to invade and quickly pacify Iraq, given the country's religious-ethnic divisions and history of tyranny. But it also presumes that the fault is primarily one of judgment: that the president and key senior military officials made a mistake by accepting Defense Secretary Donald Rumsfeld's theory that a "transformed" American military can prevail in war without great masses of ground troops. That judgment was indeed foolish; events have shown that, while a relatively modest American force can win a stunning battlefield victory, such a force is not enough to secure the peace.

But there's a deeper problem, one that any president who chose to invade a country the size of Iraq would have faced. In short, America's all-volunteer military simply cannot deploy and sustain enough troops to succeed in places like Iraq while still deterring threats elsewhere in the world. Simply adding more soldiers to the active duty force, as some in Washington are now suggesting, may sound like a good solution. But it's not, for sound operational and pragmatic reasons. America doesn't need a bigger standing army; it needs a deep bench of trained soldiers held in reserve who can be mobilized to handle the unpredictable but inevitable wars and humanitarian interventions of the future. And while there are several ways the all-volunteer force can create some extra surge capacity, all of them are limited.

Updating the Draft

The only effective solution to the manpower crunch is the one America has turned to again and again in its history: the draft. Not the mass combat mobilizations of World War II, nor the inequitable conscription of Vietnam—for just as threats change and war-fighting advances, so too must the draft. A modernized draft would demand that the privileged participate. It would give all who serve a choice over how they serve. And it would provide the military, on a "just in time" basis, large numbers of deployable ground troops, particularly the peacekeepers we'll need to meet the security challenges of the 21st century.

America has a choice. It can be the world's superpower, or it can maintain the current all-volunteer military, but it probably can't do both.

Plowing a Field with a Ferrari

Before the invasion of Iraq, Army Chief of Staff Eric Shinseki and Army Secretary Thomas White advised Rumsfeld that many more troops would be needed to secure Iraq (something on the order of 250,000 to 300,000). Secretary of State Colin Powell, whose State Department was shut out of the post-war planning process, also privately argued for a bigger force. A RAND Corporation analysis, published in summer 2003, offered a range of estimates for what size force would be necessary in Iraq. Using troops-to-population ratios from previous occupations, RAND projected that, two years after the invasion, it would take anywhere from 258,000 troops (the Bosnia model), to 321,000 (post-World War II Germany), to 526,000 (Kosovo) to secure the peace.

None of these figures seems, at first glance, unachievable for a U.S. military comprised of 1.4 million active-duty troops, 870,900 reservists, and 110,000 individual ready reservists (soldiers who have served their tour of duty and are not training with the reserves but who can by statute still be called up for service). And yet an Iraq deployment that has never exceeded 153,000 ground personnel has put so much stress on the military that a senior Army Reserve official has candidly stated that current rotation policies will lead to a "broken force." How can that be?

To answer that question, begin by deducting virtually the entire Navy and Air Force from the head count; the Iraq occupation has been almost exclusively a ground game, hence an Army and Marine operation. Next, consider that the United States sends into combat not individual soldiers but units, complete with unit equipment sets, unit leaders, and an organizational structure that facilitates command, control, and logistical support. So instead of counting individual soldiers—a meaningless exercise—one must look at how many *units* the United States could theoretically put on the ground if it wanted to mobilize every active and reserve soldier available. And if you do that, you come to a figure of roughly 600,000 troops. That's the total number of deployable soldiers that the United States could theoretically have called upon to man the initial invasion.

In practice, however, the Pentagon would never have sent that many troops to Iraq, for good reasons: It would have left the defense cupboard bare and served as an open invitation to America's enemies to make trouble elsewhere in the world. Massing a 600,000 force would have meant not only pulling nearly all front-line troops out of Korea, but also mobilizing the poorly-resourced divisions of the National Guard, the third-string crew that the president can call on when the first string (active troops) and the second string (the Guard's elite "enhanced" reserve brigades) are depleted.

Given the need to hold troops in reserve for deterrence purposes, the Pentagon had perhaps 400,000 troops available for the invasion. Yet that number includes many troops in specialized fields that are of little or no use in desert warfare or peacekeeping—off-loading equipment in sea ports, for instance. Such troops could have been reshaped into provisional infantry units, as the Army has done with artillery and air-defense formations, but that would've taken time. The number of troops with units that would actually have been of use in Iraq was probably closer to the figures that Gen. Shinseki and Secretary White have suggested: 250,000 to 300,000—in other words, the lower end of what RAND estimated would be required for success.

Deceptive Numbers

But even that number is deceptive. It is the size of the force that could have been initially sent into Iraq, not the number that could have realistically been *sustained* there. Because so many soldiers in the all-volunteer military are married with families (compared to conscript armies), and because soldiers must periodically be induced or persuaded to voluntarily reenlist, the Pentagon must rotate its forces in and out of theater every 12 months or so in order to maintain morale and reenlistment. Thus, just as a civilian police department must hire three to four police officers for every one cop on the beat, so too must the U.S. military have three to four soldiers for every one serving in Iraq.

The Pentagon, then, could have realistically kept those initial 250,000 to 300,000 troops in place only for a limited time—perhaps a year, certainly not more than two. That might have been enough time to pacify the country, especially if higher troop numbers at the outset would have quelled the early looting and disorder. Then again, a year or two might not have been sufficient time to beat back an insurgency which, we now know, was to some extent planned in advance of the invasion. In that case, keeping 250,000 to 300,000 troops in Iraq for two years or longer would have risked so lowering morale and reenlistment rates as to destroy the all-volunteer force. It would have been like plowing a field with a Ferrari; it could have been done, but only once.

Taking the need for rotations into account, then, the U.S. military can comfortably handle something like 80,000 troops in Iraq at any one time. The actual number on the ground has averaged 133,286 for the last two years, and more than 150,000 soldiers are in Iraq now.

That's a woefully insufficient number for the task. Yet it is pushing the outside limits of what the current force structure can handle. It has meant imposing "stop-loss" emergency measures to prevent soldiers from exiting the service. It has required deploying nearly every active-duty brigade, including one previously committed elsewhere in Korea. It has meant raiding the seed corn of military readiness by deploying the Army's elite "opposing force" training units—seasoned soldiers who play the enemy in mock exercises to build the skills of greener troops before they are sent into battle. It has necessitated calling up all 15 of the National Guard's enhanced readiness brigades, as well as poorly-resourced National Guard divisions that have not been mobilized *en masse* since the Korean War. It has led the Army Reserve Chief Lt. Gen. James Helmly to write in a recent memo that the Reserve will be unable to meet its commitments without substantial use of the Army's *involuntary* mobilization authorities under federal law. As of Dec. 15, 2004, the Army Reserve retained just 37,515 deployable soldiers out of a total of 200,366—almost no cushion at all. And in the final two months of last year, the Reserves missed their enlistment targets last year by 30 percent—a sign of even greater problems to come.

All this for a war that most planners consider to be a medium-sized conflict—nothing like what the United States faced in World War I, World War II, or the Cold War. And while threats of that magnitude aren't anywhere on the horizon, there are plenty of quite possible scenarios that could quickly overwhelm us—an implosion of the North Korean regime, a Chinese attack on Taiwan, worsening of the ethnic cleansing in the Sudan, or some unforeseen humanitarian nightmare. Already we have signaled to bad actors everywhere the limits of our power. Military threats might never have convinced the Iranians to give up their nuclear program. But it's more than a little troubling that ruling Iranian mullahs can publicly and credibly dismiss recent administration saber-rattling by pointing to the fact that our forces are pinned down in Iraq.

Stress Test

Every 20 years or so for the past century, America has found it necessary, for national security reasons, to send at least half a million troops overseas into harm's way, and to keep them there for years at a time. It did so in World War I, sending 4.1 million doughboys and Marines to Europe. In World War II, it mobilized 16 million for the war effort. America sent more than 3 million grunts to fight in Korea against the North Koreans and Chinese, in the first hot war of the Cold War. It rotated 5.1 million soldiers and Marines through Vietnam over a decade, with 543,400 stationed there at the height of that war in April 1969. And more recently, America sent 550,000 ground troops to eject Saddam's forces from Kuwait, as part of a ground force which totaled 831,500 with allied contributions from dozens of nations. Along the way, the United States military simultaneously fought small wars in Greece, Lebanon, El Salvador, Somalia, Haiti, Bosnia, and Kosovo, requiring the commitment of thousands more. This ability to deploy large numbers of troops overseas for long periods of time has been the price of America's superpower status—what President John Kennedy alluded to in his inaugural address when he said America would bear any burden to assure the survival and the success of liberty.

There's no reason to think that America will be exempt from paying that price in the future. Even those who don't support the Bush policy of using unilateral force to democratize the Middle East (and we don't), and who prefer to work through military alliances whenever possible (and we do), should understand the need to increase American troop strength. The international community failed to act in Rwanda largely because the United States chose not to send troops; our NATO allies sent soldiers into Bosnia and Kosovo only because we put substantial numbers of ours in, too. The same will hold true for just about any other major war or humanitarian intervention in the future.

Built to Purpose Army

What we're increasingly learning from Iraq is that the all-volunteer force, as presently built, cannot do that—indeed, it was consciously designed to be incapable of such deployments. Today's force was built for precisely the kinds of wars that Caspar Weinberger and Colin Powell envisioned in their doctrines: wars with explicit purposes, narrow parameters, and clear exit strategies. In other words, it was built for the kinds of wars the military prefers to fight, not necessarily the kinds of wars we have, as a nation, historically fought.

The evolution of this force owes much to Vietnam. After that war ended, the nation's senior generals devised a military structure called the "total force" concept to circumvent two of the great moral hazards they identified with Vietnam: the failure to mobilize the nation, with all of its strata and segments, for the war; and the reliance on young American conscripts, who were coerced by the state to kill or be killed.

Vietnam had been fought almost entirely by active-duty volunteers and conscripts. A great number of young men, including many from the nation's privileged classes, sought refuge in the reserves as a way out of duty in Vietnam. The total force concept entailed, first of all, the splitting of key war-fighting and support functions. Henceforth, active-duty troops would perform nearly all the traditional combat roles; reservists would provide most of the support functions, such as logistics and military policing. This ensured that future wars could not be fought without the heavy involvement of the reserves. Army Gen. Creighton Abrams and other leaders felt that this would be a check on the power of presidents to go to war because mass reserve call-ups typically require a great deal of political capital.

Second, Pentagon leaders replaced the conscripted military with an all-volunteer force that would recruit enlistees with pay and benefits like the civilian world. This all-volunteer model, they believed, would improve morale for the simple reason that all soldiers would be in the service by choice. It would also improve military effectiveness because if soldiers could be lured to stay longer by reenlisting, they could acquire higher levels of skill. The mantra of the new military became "send a bullet, not a man"; the modern American military came to embrace precision firepower over manpower in what historian Russell Weigley called the "American way of war."

The Last Four Decades

This all-volunteer military made good on nearly all these promises. After a rough period in the late 1970s, the U.S. military emerged a leaner, better force in the 1980s, proving itself in the small wars of that decade—Grenada, Libya, and Panama. Then came the first Gulf War—the apothesis of the all-volunteer, total force model. Coming off the Cold War, the Army had 18 divisions on active duty, in comparison to 10 today, and had little in the way of a pressing commission with the imminent collapse of the Soviet Union. By mobilizing seven of these Army divisions and two Marine divisions, in addition to the reserves and ready reserves, military leaders were able to send half a million troops to the Saudi desert. But because that war lasted just months, largely due to U.S. reluctance to invade and occupy Iraq, the system worked. Active-duty soldiers deployed for less than a year, without fear of immediately being sent back to fight; reservists were similarly tapped just once. Desert Storm did not break the all-volunteer force because that war was precisely the kind that the force had been designed to fight: a limited campaign for limited ends, of limited duration, and with a defined exit strategy.

Unfortunately, national security threats don't always conform to the military's precise specifications. The 1990s brought two wars, in Bosnia and Kosovo, requiring the long-term commitment of U.S. troops for peacekeeping. These were relatively modest-sized deployments. Yet the military leadership complained that they put undo stress on the system, and, indeed, then-Gov. George Bush lambasted the Clinton administration in 2000 for the way it managed military readiness, charging that the Kosovo war put two of the Army's 10 divisions out of action, hurting the nation's ability to respond to threats abroad. In the wake of

September 11, the U.S. military mobilized tens of thousands of reservists for homeland security and sent thousands of elite infantrymen and special forces into the mountains of Afghanistan; neither mission conformed to the model of past wars.

Then came Operation Iraqi Freedom, and the real stress test began.

Five Bad Options

In theory, there are several ways to get out of the military manpower bind we find ourselves in. In reality, there are inherent limits to almost all of them. The first option—at least the one Democrats and moderate Republicans have talked most about—is to convince other countries to share the burden in Iraq. But that's not likely. Even if the security situation in Iraq improves and the Bush administration begins to share decision-making—something it's so far refused to do—European leaders would be extremely wary of trying to sell their citizens on sending troops to keep the peace in a war they expressly opposed. It may be possible to convince the Europeans and other developed nations to be more willing to contribute troops the next time there's an international need. But that, as we've seen, will require more U.S. troops, not fewer. Nor should it be the policy of the United States to have to rely on other countries' troops. We must be prepared to intervene unilaterally if necessary.

A second solution to the manpower crisis would be to rely more on private military contractors, whose use has exploded in recent years. Currently, more than 40,000 government contractors are on duty in Iraq, working in myriad jobs from security to reconstruction. The advantage of using contractors is that they provide surge capacity; they are hired only for the duration of an engagement. But according to Peter W. Singer, a research fellow at the Brookings Institution, these private armies also create problems. First, all costs considered, they're not necessarily less expensive for the military. Second, private military contractors often compete with the military for personnel, so any growth in these contractors usually results in tension between military retention and contractor recruiting efforts. Third, contractors operate in a legal gray area where their financial and accounting activities are heavily regulated, but their operations are barely looked at. It's one thing to contract for truck drivers; it's another to hire contractors to guard Afghan President Hamid Karzai or work as interrogation linguists in the Abu Ghraib prison because the military has too few commandos or linguists in its own ranks. The military has probably already pushed the contractor concept about as far as it will go; expecting much more surge capacity from private industry is probably unrealistic.

A third possibility might be to follow the advice of several cutting-edge military reformers to radically transform today's military. According to these reformers, today's force was drawn up for a bygone age of massed superpower armies; it does not reflect today's threats. These visionaries would downsize the Navy, scrap some of the Army's mechanized divisions, and in these and other ways free up tens of thousands of troops to be redeployed into "soldier centric" units capable of doing everything along the spectrum from humanitarian relief in Banda Aceh to combat patrols in Baghdad. Under pressure from the Iraq mission, the military has taken some steps in this direction—for instance, by retraining and reequipping some army artillery and air defense units into military police units. But such moves have been incremental in nature thus far; the true scope of the problem is orders of magnitude larger than the Pentagon's current solution. And some day, a war may come which requires all kinds of combat power—from large land-based formations to ships capable of sailing through the Taiwan strait to legions of peacekeepers. The military cannot build additional capability simply by playing a shell game with its personnel; at some point, it must genuinely add more soldiers too, and in large numbers.

Simple Increase

A fourth option, and the most obvious one, would be to simply increase the size of the active-duty force. This too has been discussed. During the 2004 campaign, Sen. John Kerry called for increasing the active-duty force by 40,000 troops. More recently, a bipartisan group of hawkish defense intellectuals published an open letter on *The Weekly Standard* Web site calling on Congress to add 25,000 ground troops each year for the next several years. And the Pentagon has announced some money for extra troops in the administration's latest budget. The problem with such proposals is that they underestimate both current manpower needs and the cost of forcing the all-volunteer military to grow.

In theory, one can always lure the next recruit, or retain the next soldier, by offering a marginally higher monetary incentive—but in reality, there are practical limits to such measures. The pool of people who might be convinced to join the Army is mainly comprised of healthy young people with high school degrees but no college plans. That pool is inherently limited, especially when the economy is heating up and there's a shooting war on. Last year, despite signing bonuses in the tens of thousands and other perks, military recruiters had to lower entry standards to meet their enlistment goals. The active force met its recruiting targets for 2004, but the reserves have found themselves increasingly struggling to bring enough soldiers in the door.

But it's the long-term cost issues that most militate against making the all-volunteer force bigger. Generals today are fond of saying that you recruit a soldier, but you retain their families. One reason the Army has resisted Congress' attempts to raise its end strength is that it does not want to embrace all of the costs associated with permanently increasing the size of the military, because it sees each soldier as a 30-year commitment—both to the soldier and his (or her) family. According to the Congressional Budget Office, each soldier costs $99,000 per year—a figure which includes medical care, housing, and family benefits.

The United States does not necessarily need a massive standing military all the time. What it needs is a highly trained professional force of a certain size—what we have right now is fine—backed by a massive surge capacity of troops in reserve to quickly augment the active-duty force in times of emergency. Sure, right now, the Army is light several hundred thousand deployable ground troops. But over the long term, the demands of Iraq will subside, the need for troops will decline, and it could be another decade or two before another mission that big comes along.

Short-Term and Long-Term Problems

The problem is that under the all-volunteer system it's hard to fix the short-term problem (too few troops now) without creating long-term problems (too many troops later). And so, paying for the salaries and benefits and families of 50,000 or 500,000 extra soldiers on active duty over the course of their careers doesn't, from a military standpoint, make sense. Politically, it would put the senior military leadership in the position of convincing the American people to keep military budgets extremely high to pay for a huge standing army that isn't being used and might not be for years. It might be possible now to convince the public to add another 100,000 soldiers (annual cost: about $10 billion in personnel costs alone, not including equipment and training). But the generals rightly worry that this support will evaporate after Iraq stabilizes. Indeed, Americans have a long tradition dating back to the writing of Constitution, of refusing to support a large standing military unless the need is apparent. (The public paid for a much bigger all-volunteer military in the 1970s and 1980s, but only because of the obvious need to deter a massive Soviet army from threatening Europe; after the Berlin Wall fell, both political parties supported big cuts in troop strength). What we really need is the capability to rapidly mobilize and deploy a half million troops to project U.S. power abroad, and to be able to sustain them indefinitely while maintaining a reserve with which to simultaneously engage other enemies.

A fifth option would be to build this surge capacity into the reserves, instead of the active force. Under this plan, which some military personnel planners are already discussing, the army would radically bump up enlistment bonuses and other incentives to lure vastly more young people directly into the reserves than are being recruited now. Such a plan would have the advantage of creating the surge capacity the nation needs without saddling the nation with a large, standing professional army. But the disadvantages are substantial, too. For such a plan to work, the military would have to make a commitment, which thus far it never has, to fix the legendary resources problems and anemic readiness of the reserves. A great many reservists have gone through the crucible of combat in Afghanistan and Iraq, and yet still cope with vehicles that lack armor, weapons older than they are, and a paucity of training dollars. Also, the army would always (and rightly) insist that signing bonuses for reservists be substantially below those offered by to active-duty recruits. And even if bonuses and other reenumeration for both the active-duty and the reserves were to rise substantially, it is hard to see how the reserves could lure in a sufficient number of recruits without significantly lowering admissions standards. The real advantage of the all-volunteer force is its quality. If the military tries to recruit so many soldiers that it must substantially lower its entry requirements, then the all-volunteer force will lose its qualitative edge. This decrease in quality will have a cascade effect on discipline within the ranks, degrading combat effectiveness for these units.

A 21st-Century Draft

That leaves one option left for providing the military with sufficient numbers of high-quality deployable ground forces: conscription. America has nearly always chosen this option to staff its military in times of war. Today, no leading politician in either party will come anywhere near the idea—the draft having replaced Social Security as the third rail of American politics. This will have to change if the United States is to remain the world's preeminent power.

Traditional conscription has its obvious downsides. On a practical level, draftees tend to be less motivated than volunteers. Because they serve for relatively short periods of time (typically two years), any investment made in their training is lost to the military once the draftees return to civilian life. And despite the current manpower shortage, there's no foreseeable scenario in which all 28 million young Americans currently of draft age would be needed.

Above all else, there's the serious ethical problem that conscription means government compelling young adults to risk death, and to kill—an act of the state that seems contrary to the basic notions of liberty which animate our society.

In practice, however, our republic has decided many times throughout its history that a draft was necessary to protect those basic liberties. Even if you disagreed with the decision to invasion of Iraq, or think the president's rhetoric is demagogic and his policies disastrous, it is hard to argue that Islamic terrorism isn't a threat to freedom and security, at home and abroad. Moreover, any American, liberal or conservative, ought to have moral qualms about basing our nation's security on an all-volunteer force drawn disproportionately, as ours is, from America's lower socioeconomic classes. And the cost of today's war is being borne by an extremely narrow slice of America. Camp Pendleton, Calif., home to the 1st Marine Expeditionary Force, is also home to approximately one-seventh of the U.S. fatalities from Iraq. In theory, our democracy will not fight unpopular wars because the people who must bear the casualties can impose their will on our elected leaders to end a war they do not support. But when such a small fraction of America shoulders the burden—and pays the cost—of America's wars, this democratic system breaks down.

Nor are the practical considerations of a draft impossible to overcome. A draft lottery, of the kind that existed in the peacetime draft of the 1950s, with no exemptions for college students, would provide the military an appropriate and manageable amount of manpower without the class inequities that poisoned the national culture during Vietnam. Such a system, however, would not avoid the problem of flooding the military with less-than-fully-motivated conscripts.

Adding Choice

A better solution would fix the weaknesses of the all-volunteer force without undermining its strengths. Here's how such a plan might work. Instead of a lottery, the federal government would impose a requirement that no four-year college or university be allowed to accept a student, male or female, unless and until that student had completed a 12-month to two-year term of service.

Unlike an old-fashioned draft, this 21st-century service requirement would provide a vital element of personal choice. Students could choose to fulfill their obligations in any of three ways: in national service programs like AmeriCorps (tutoring disadvantaged children), in homeland security assignments (guarding ports), or in the military. Those who chose the latter could serve as military police officers, truck drivers, or other non-combat specialists requiring only modest levels of training. (It should be noted that the Army currently offers two-year enlistments for all of these jobs, as well as for the infantry.) They would be deployed as needed for peacekeeping or nation-building missions. They would serve for 12-months to two years, with modest follow-on reserve obligations.

Whichever option they choose, all who serve would receive modest stipends and GI Bill-type college grants. Those who sign up for lengthier and riskier duty, however, would receive higher pay and larger college grants. Most would no doubt pick the less dangerous options. But some would certainly select the military—out of patriotism, a sense of adventure, or to test their mettle. Even if only 10 percent of the one-million young people who annually start at four-year colleges and universities were to choose the military option, the armed forces would receive 100,000 fresh recruits every year. These would be motivated recruits, having chosen the military over other, less demanding forms of service. And because they would all be college-grade and college-bound, they would have—to a greater extent than your average volunteer recruit—the savvy and inclination to pick up foreign languages and other skills that are often the key to effective peacekeeping work.

A 21st-century draft like this would create a cascading series of benefits for society. It would instill a new ethic of service in that sector of society, the college-bound, most likely to reap the fruits of American prosperity. It would mobilize an army of young people for vital domestic missions, such as helping a growing population of seniors who want to avoid nursing homes but need help with simple daily tasks like grocery shopping. It would give more of America's elite an experience of the military. Above all, it would provide the all-important surge capacity now missing from our force structure, insuring that the military would never again lack for manpower. And it would do all this without requiring any American to carry a gun who did not choose to do so.

The war in Iraq has shown us, and the world, many things: the bloody costs of inept leadership; the courage of the average American soldier; the hunger for democracy among some of the earth's most oppressed people. But perhaps more than anything, Iraq has shown that our military power has limits. As currently constituted, the U.S. military can win the wars, but it cannot win the peace, nor can it commit for the long term to the stability and security of a nation such as Iraq. Our enemies have learned this, and they will use that knowledge to their advantage in the next war to tie us down and bleed us until we lose the political will to fight.

If America wishes to retain its mantle of global leadership, it must develop a military force structure capable of persevering under these circumstances. Fortunately, we know how to build such a force. We have done it many times in the past. The question is: Do we have the will to do so again?

PHILLIP CARTER is an attorney and former Army captain who writes on national security issues for *The Washington Monthly*. **PAUL GLASTRIS** is the editor-in-chief of *The Washington Monthly*.

Checks, Balances, and Wartime Detainees

BENJAMIN WITTES

The day the Supreme Court handed down what have collectively become known as the enemy combatant cases—June 28, 2004—was both widely anticipated and widely received as a legal moment of truth for the Bush administration's war on terrorism. The stakes could not have been higher. The three cases came down in the midst of election-year politics. They each involved challenges by detainees being held by the military without charge or trial or access to counsel. They each divided the Court. And they appeared to validate or reject core arguments that the administration had advanced—and had been slammed for advancing—since the fight against al Qaeda began in earnest after September 11, 2001.

The dominant view saw the cases as a major defeat for President George W. Bush—and with good reason. After all, his administration had urged the Court to refrain from asserting jurisdiction over the Guantanamo Bay naval base in Cuba, and it did just that in unambiguous terms: "Aliens held at the base, no less than American citizens, are entitled to invoke the federal courts' authority."[1] The administration fought tooth and nail for the proposition that an American citizen held domestically as an enemy combatant has no right to counsel and no right to respond to the factual assertions that justify his detention. The Court, however, held squarely that "a citizen-detainee seeking to challenge his classification as an enemy combatant must receive notice of the factual basis for his classification, and a fair opportunity to rebut the Government's factual assertions before a neutral decision-maker."[2] It held as well that "[h]e unquestionably has the right to access to counsel" in doing so. These holdings led the *New York Times* (June 29, 2003) to call the cases "a stinging rebuke" to the administration's policies, one that "made it clear that even during the war on terror, the government must adhere to the rule of law."

A dissident analysis of the cases, however, quickly emerged as well and saw them as a kind of victory for the administration dressed up in defeat's borrowed robes. As David B. Rivkin Jr. and Lee A. Casey put it in the *Washington Post* (August 4, 2004):

> In the context of these cases, the court accepted the following critical propositions: that the United States is engaged in a legally cognizable armed conflict with al

Qaeda and the Taliban, to which the laws of war apply; that "enemy combatants" captured in the context of that conflict can be held "indefinitely" without criminal trial while that conflict continues; that American citizens (at least those captured overseas) can be classified and detained as enemy combatants, confirming the authority of the court's 1942 decision in *Ex Parte Quirin* (the "Nazi saboteur" case [317 U.S. I (1942)]); and that the role of the courts in reviewing such designations is limited. All these points had been disputed by one or more of the detainees' lawyers, and all are now settled in the government's favor.

Even among those who celebrated the administration's defeat, this analysis had some resonance. Ronald Dworkin, for example, began his essay on the cases in the *New York Review of Books* ("What the Court Really Said," August 12, 2004) by triumphantly declaring, "The Supreme Court has finally and decisively rejected the Bush administration's outrageous claim that the President has the power to jail people he accuses of terrorist connections without access to lawyers or the outside world and without any possibility of significant review by courts or other judicial bodies." But he then went on to acknowledge that the Court had "suggested rules of procedure for any such review that omit important traditional protections for people accused of crimes" and that the government "may well be able to satisfy the Court's lenient procedural standards without actually altering its morally dubious detention policies." How big a rebuke could the cases really represent if they collectively entitle the president to stay the course he has chosen?

The court managed to leave all of the central questions unanswered.

In my view, both strains of initial thought have considerable merit. The administration clearly suffered a "stinging rebuke" in rhetorical terms. But Dworkin, Rivkin, and Casey (an unlikely meeting of the minds if ever there were one) were quite correct that, in the long run, the president's actual power to detain enemy combatants may not have been materially damaged either with respect to citizens domestically or with respect to enemy fighters captured and held abroad. In a profound sense, the Supreme Court, despite delivering itself of 178 pages of text on the subject of enemy combatant detentions, managed to leave all of the central questions unanswered. In fact, if a new front in the war on terrorism opened tomorrow and the military captured a new crop of captives, under the Court's rulings, the administration would face very nearly the same questions as it did in 2002. Can the military warehouse foreign citizens captured overseas at a military base abroad without intrusive interference by American courts keen to protect their rights under either American or international law? What process must the military grant to an American citizen it wishes to hold as an enemy combatant, and is that process different if the citizen is detained domestically by law enforcement, rather than overseas by the military? Must such a person be granted immediate access to a lawyer or can he be held incommunicado for intelligence-gathering purposes? And if he can be so detained, for how long? The answers to these questions are only a little clearer today than they were a few months ago. The Court has only begun to forge the regime that, in the absence of congressional intervention, will govern the detention of enemy combatants. Until that regime comes into clearer focus, it will be too early to determine the real winners and losers in this landmark struggle.

It is not, however, too early to begin assessing the performance of the responsible institutions of American government and civil society with respect to the forging of this regime—that is, to look seriously at the engagement so far among the courts, the administration, Congress, and the civil liberties and human rights groups that have opposed the administration's policies. The exercise, in my judgment, flatters none of the aforementioned institutions. Congress has simply abandoned the field, leaving a series of questions which obviously require legislative solutions to a dialogue between the executive and judicial branches. The administration has encouraged this abdication by, instead of seeking legislative input, consistently asserting the most needlessly extreme vision of executive power to resolve novel problems unilaterally. By doing so, it has all but guaranteed a skeptical reception for even its stronger arguments. The courts, meanwhile, have proven uneven in the extreme both at the lower court level and at the Supreme Court. For their part, the human rights and civil liberties communities have responded to the cases with an almost total lack of pragmatism, advancing a reading of federal and international law no less selective and convenient than the administration's own and consistently failing, over the three years since these cases arose, to offer a plausible alternative to the administration's proposed regime.

In the end, the enemy combatant cases—at least so far— stand as a kind of case study of the consequence of abandoning to the adversarial litigation system a sensitive policy debate in which powerful and legitimate constitutional concerns animate both sides. By nearly universal agreement, these cases were submitted to common-law decision making in the face of almost-as-universal agreement that the extant body of law did not fully address the novel conditions of the war on terrorism. As a result,

as I shall attempt to show, nuance was lost, flexibility and imagination in envisioning an appropriate regime were jettisoned, and the courts were left to split the difference between polar arguments to which few Americans would actually sign on and which should not have defined the terms of the discussion. It needn't have been this way. But until Congress assumes responsibility for crafting a system to handle enemy combatants, the regime necessarily will remain a crude, judge-made hybrid of the criminal and military law traditions that will, I suspect, satisfy nobody save the judges who—piece by piece, bit by bit, question by question—will decree it into existence.

What the Court Ruled

It overstates the matter to say that the enemy combatant cases were full of sound and fury and signifying nothing, but they certainly signified a great deal less than their sound and fury portended. It is worth, therefore, beginning by examining exactly what the Court did, what it didn't do, and what questions it left unaddressed.

To begin with the least consequential case, in *Padilla v. Rumsfeld,* the Court did virtually nothing at all—clarifying only that a habeas petitioner in military custody must bring suit in a court with jurisdiction over his immediate physical custodian.[3] While this holding was in considerable tension with the Court's ruling concerning Guantanamo—where it divined jurisdiction for seemingly any federal court in the country—it was neither especially surprising nor substantively important. It affects, after all, not one jot the procedural rights an accused enemy combatant will enjoy, nor does it alter at all the substantive standard the government must satisfy in order to justify the combatant's detention. It affects only the question of what court he must appear in to challenge that detention.

So far Padilla stands for nothing but a perfectly pedestrian jurisdictional point.

The only feature of *Padilla* that seems important at all is a footnote in the dissent, in which four members of the Court appear to address the case's merits head on and dismiss the government's substantive position that President Bush could, under current authorities, designate Jose Padilla—a citizen suspected of planning terrorist attacks on al Qaeda's behalf—as an enemy combatant and hold him as such. "Consistent with the judgment of the Court of Appeals," wrote Justice John Paul Stevens, "I believe that the Non-Detention Act, I 8 U.S.C. § 4 0 0 I (a), prohibits—and the Authorization for Use of Military Force Joint Resolution, 115 Stat. 224, adopted on September 18, 2001, does not authorize—the protracted, incommunicado detention of American citizens arrested in the United States." This language, though certainly dicta, suggests that a majority on the Court may exist for the proposition that someone in Padilla's position, a suspected al Qaeda operative arrested domestically, must either be charged criminally and prosecuted or else released—at least in the absence of a more explicit congressional authorization for enemy combatant detentions. Justice Antonin Scalia wrote in dissent in *Hamdi* that he did not believe a citizen could be detained as an enemy combatant at all, an opinion Justice Stevens joined. Combine the two opinions, and you may have a glimmering of the Court's future direction on this question. So far, however, *Padilla* stands for nothing but a perfectly pedestrian jurisdictional point: that an enemy combatant detained domestically has to go to his local federal court for relief. Which court should hear the claims of detainees was hardly the question that animated the spirited public discussion of enemy combatants over the past three years. So clearly, *Padilla* answers nothing.

The Court said a lot more in *Hamdi*, and in important respects, it did repudiate the military's position. The government, after all, had argued that the courts should show nearly total deference to the executive branch's determinations concerning citizens alleged to be enemy combatants: They should rely entirely on the government's factual allegations, as laid out in a hearsay affidavit by a midlevel Defense Department official. The detainee need not have any ability to contest these allegations or any assistance of counsel in challenging his detention. And the standard of review itself should be trivial, merely whether the material in the cursory, page-and-a-half affidavit would, if presumed true, support the designation. Eight members of the Court rejected each of these suggestions. The controlling plurality opinion insisted that Yaser Esam Hamdi had a right to contest his designation and to submit evidence to the court in doing so, that he had a right to the assistance of counsel, and, it insisted, that the government's designation be supported with "credible evidence." Rivkin's and Casey's contention that the decision was really a victory is belied by the fact that the plurality opinion in Hamdi tracks closely with—indeed, in critical respects, is less favorable to the government than—the district court's opinion in *Padilla*, an opinion the government aggressively appealed.

The plurality reaffirmed the power of the president to detain a citizen as an enemy combatant.

But if *Hamdi* establishes that the executive's hand is not entirely free, it by no means clarifies that judicial review—even in cases involving citizens—will function as a meaningful, as opposed to a symbolic, restraint on executive behavior. For starters, the government won on a truly fundamental point in the case: The plurality reaffirmed the power in principle of the president to detain a citizen as an enemy combatant—a power it articulated in *Ex parte Quirin*—writing that "[there is no bar to this Nation's holding one of its own citizens as an enemy combatant." In other words, the plurality allowed the military to exempt an individual from the full protections of criminal process on the basis of a finding that he has enlisted in a foreign military struggle against the United States in the context of a use of force authorized by Congress. The Court's acceptance of this basic premise of the government's argument is no small matter.

Moreover, Justice Sandra Day O'Connor was a bit cagey on the subject of Hamdi's access to counsel, and what she doesn't hold is as important as what she does. "Hamdi asks us to hold that the Fourth Circuit also erred by denying him immediate access to counsel upon his detention and by disposing of the case without permitting him to meet with an attorney," she noted at the end of the plurality opinion. "Since our grant of certiorari in this case, Hamdi has been appointed counsel, with whom he has met for consultation purposes on several occasions, and with whom he is now being granted unmonitored meetings. He unquestionably has the right to access to counsel *in connection with the proceedings on remand.* No further consideration of this issue is necessary at this stage of the case" (emphasis added). The language granting Hamdi access to counsel is ringing. It is framed in the language of constitutional rights, not—as the district courts in both *Hamdi* and *Padilla* envisioned it—as a discretionary grant of access for the purpose of airing all the issues in the case fully. But as the italicized language indicates, the "right" is only clear prospectively. Justice O'Connor did not address the question of whether Hamdi had this right from the outset of the litigation, when the right attached, or whether it was appropriate for the government—in the interests of interrogating him for intelligence—to have withheld it for two years.

What's more, Justice O'Connor left open the possibility that her due process concerns could be satisfied by tribunals within the military and that had such military process been available to Hamdi, judicial review would have been far more deferential as a consequence. "Plainly, the 'process' Hamdi has received is not that to which he is entitled under the Due Process Clause," she wrote. But "[t]here remains the possibility that the standards we have articulated could be met by an appropriately authorized and properly constituted military tribunal. Indeed, it is notable that military regulations already provide for such process in related instances, dictating that tribunals be made available to determine the status of enemy detainees who assert prisoner-of-war status under the Geneva Convention. … In the absence of such process, however, a court that receives a petition for a writ of habeas corpus from an alleged enemy combatant must itself ensure that the minimum requirements of due process are achieved." The tribunals to which she refers are, historically speaking, cursory affairs that do not involve a right to counsel or contemplate a great deal of factual development. If the import of *Hamdi* is that the military can, in the future, buy the total judicial deference it sought in this case by affording citizens alleged to be enemy combatants the limited process contemplated by Article 5 of the Third Geneva Convention, then the military has lost little and gained much in its apparent defeat this time around.

In short, although the government was rebuked by the Court, it is by no means clear that the next time an American citizen is captured abroad while apparently fighting for the other side, the military will not be able to behave very nearly as it behaved toward Hamdi—that is, hold him incommunicado for an extended period of time while interrogating him for intelligence. Nor are we likely to find out the answer to this question any time soon. The *Hamdi* case, after all, has been settled, and Hamdi himself released. While clarity could come as a consequence of future developments in *Padilla,* there is a substantial possibility that it too will become moot, not because of Padilla's release but because of his criminal indictment.[4] The question of whether enemy combatant detention is a legally tenable approach for the government toward citizens remains, despite the cases, very much an open one.

The high court's pronouncements with respect to the detainees at Guantanamo Bay, Cuba, were just as Delphic. The justices, by a 6–3 vote, declared that the federal courts had jurisdiction to consider habeas petitions filed on behalf of inmates at the facility. Indeed, the justices formulated the question posed by the case in language emphasizing the stakes for liberty and the rule of law: "What is presently at stake is only whether the federal courts have jurisdiction to determine the legality of the Executive's potentially indefinite detention of individuals who claim to be wholly innocent of wrongdoing," Justice Stevens wrote. The assertion of jurisdiction necessarily cast the Bush administration's conduct in a negative light, implying that there were substantial questions to litigate concerning the legality of the detentions—questions that rendered the Court's jurisdiction significant. And, to be sure, Justice Stevens's language did nothing to dispel this impression. He noted at one point in a footnote, for example, that "Petitioners' allegations—that, although they have engaged neither in combat nor in acts of terrorism against the United States, they have been held in Executive detention for more than two years in territory subject to the long-term, exclusive jurisdiction and control of the United States, without access to counsel and without being charged with any wrongdoing—unquestionably describe 'custody in violation of the Constitution or laws or treaties of the United States.'"

Heartless as it may sound, however, this apparently unobjectionable statement may not actually be true. That is to say, even if all of the Guantanamo inmates were completely innocent of any wrongdoing—which they most assuredly are not—and, more important, even were they all demonstrably not combatants, it would remain something of a puzzle what, if any, judicially enforceable law would be implicated by such reckless executive behavior. Indeed, the court has not generally held that the protections of the Bill of Rights apply to aliens overseas.[5] The Geneva Conventions have not traditionally been regarded as self-executing, and Congress has never explicitly given the courts power to enforce the terms of the conventions, which have been generally guaranteed by diplomatic pressures and reciprocity, not by litigation.[6] Exactly what does American law promise a suspected Taliban soldier—much less an al Qaeda operative—that a court in this country can ensure he gets?

Since only the jurisdictional question was before it, the Court avowedly declined to answer this question. "Whether and what further proceedings may become necessary after respondents make their response to the merits of petitioners' claims are matters that we need not address now," Justice Stevens wrote. And this coyness can, I suppose, be reasonably defended as judicial restraint—an unwillingness to address questions before they are fully presented and briefed. But the result is that nobody knows today what the great rebuke to the executive branch that the Court delivered in *Rasul* means in practice. Detainees have filed numerous claims since the decisions, alleging treaty, statutory, and constitutional deprivations. The great rebuke could be a giant nothing, If the Court has, in fact, asserted jurisdiction in order to determine later that no judicially cognizable rights have been violated, the executive will have lost nothing save a certain embarrassment and the inconvenience of having to brief and argue the subsequent legal questions.[7] Civil libertarians and human rights groups—not to mention the detainees—will have won nothing more than the satisfaction of having lost on the merits, rather than on a jurisdictional point. The litigation will have rendered the executive branch barely more accountable than had it won on the jurisdictional point—indeed, the administration will have had its legal position actively *affirmed*, not just deemed unreviewable. The detainees will certainly be no freer as a consequence of their victory. On the other hand, if the Court is truly prepared to act as the enforcer of legal rights toward alien detainees who have never set foot in this country, *Rasul* heralds a sea change in judicial power in wartime, an earthquake of untold magnitude and importance. The Court could also attempt some kind of intermediate step.

What does American law promise a Taliban soldier that a court can ensure he gets?

But the fog does not even end there. For the Court was less than clear about precisely what it was holding, even with respect to mere jurisdiction. At times, the majority opinion seemed to depend on the unique legal status of Guantanamo Bay, which is leased on an indefinite basis to the United States and subject during that time to the "exclusive jurisdiction and control" of the United States. At other times, however, the decision appears to rest on no such gimmick, relying instead only on the allegation of an illegal detention and the Court's proper jurisdiction over the Pentagon: "Petitioners contend that they are being held in federal custody in violation of the laws of the United States. No party questions the District Court's jurisdiction over petitioners' custodians. ... [The habeas statute], by its terms, requires nothing more." So while it is clear, after the court's decision, that the federal courts have the power to decide legal questions concerning the Guantanamo detainees, it is no clearer than before that decision whether the detentions at Guantanamo are in fact legally defective, nor is it clear whether the executive could still evade federal court oversight altogether by simply avoiding detention facilities abroad that happen to be formally leased to exclusive, indefinite American jurisdiction. Once again, the Court left all of the fundamental questions unanswered.

In short, while it is indisputable that the administration suffered a major atmospheric defeat at the hands of solid, though shifting, majorities of the Court, it remains premature to describe the true winners and losers in the cases. One cannot, at this stage, say—with Rivkin and Casey—that the administration has won the fight. But one has to acknowledge the possibility that the doctrinal seeds of its ultimate victory are germinating in the Court's decisions, and one cannot dismiss the possibility that in the long run, the true import of the decisions will lie more in what they permit than in what they forbid.

Article 2 Fundamentalism

Even in this moment of uncertainty as to the ultimate significance of the cases, however, one can attempt to assess the performance of the institutions, governmental and other, that have brought us to this point. The one that has attracted the most attention—criticism, controversy, and defense—is the executive branch. This is natural enough given the president's necessary leadership role in moments of national crisis, his control over the military, and, in this instance, his personal responsibility for many of the policies in question. Padilla was, after all, plucked out of the criminal justice system on the personal order of President Bush. It is right and proper that President Bush should be held accountable for the detention policies practiced by his administration. Still, in my judgment, the centrality of executive branch decisions in the public discussion of detention policies seems slightly too forgiving of the failures of other institutions. What's more, the criticism seems, in a fundamental sense, misdirected. For the president's original sin lay not simply—or even chiefly—in the substance of the positions he took with respect to captured enemy fighters. It lay, rather, in his utter unwillingness to seek legal sanction from Congress for those positions.

When you step back and examine the detention policies of the war on terrorism from the highest altitude, the administration's posture is not quite as outrageous as it seems from the ground. After all, countries at war detain the enemy. They interrogate those captured enemy fighters not entitled to privileged treatment. They don't usually provide foreign fighters with lawyers, except when those fighters are tried for war crimes. And they claim the right to hold those fighters until hostilities end. In the broadest sense, therefore, there is nothing exceptional about the Bush administration's position toward those it has detained. What's more, the civil liberties intrusion of these policies is quite constrained compared with past wars. The affected universe of detainees is limited to those the military believes to be fighters for the other side—neither large civilian populations (like the Japanese Americans interned during World War II) nor opponents of the war (like socialists during World War I). And in contrast to the Civil War, the writ of habeas corpus has not been suspended, so the courts remain at least formally open for business in judging any challenges to detentions. There is, quite simply, nothing intrinsically unreasonable about the administration's desire to use the traditional presidential wartime power to detain enemy combatants in this particular conflict.

What is unreasonable, however, is the pretense, almost since the beginning of the conflict, that the proper altitude for considering this problem is that of a jetliner. For zoom in only a little, and the differences between this conflict and those that have preceded it make the clean application of prior law and precedent nearly impossible. What does it mean to detain combatants for the duration of hostilities in a conflict that may never end? In a conflict with a shadowy, international, nonhierarchical, nonstate actor as enemy, what would victory look like if we

achieved it? If we then released detainees, as international law requires, wouldn't that act merely restart the conflict? More immediately, given that al Qaeda does not fight along a front but seeks to infiltrate American society and destroy it from within, how can one reliably distinguish between combatants and mere sympathizers or even uninvolved parties caught in the wrong place at the wrong time? These differences are not mere oddities of the current conflict. They are fundamental challenges to the legal regime that governs traditional warfare, which presupposes clearly defined armies and a moment of negotiated peace, after which those captured will be repatriated as a consequence of diplomatic negotiation. The premise of detention in traditional warfare is that the warring parties have no issue with the individual soldier detained, who is presumed to be honorable. That premise is simply false in the current war, in which America's battle is very much with the individual jihadist. After all, unlike, say, Germany or Japan, al Qaeda is nothing more than the sum of its members.

Given the profound differences between the war on terror and past conflicts, there was no good reason for the administration to treat the resolution of questions as simple matters of executive discretion. They are essentially legislative in character—for notwithstanding the administration's pretenses, they go far beyond questions of how to apply old law to new circumstances. Rather, they represent the questions that will define the legal regime we, as a society, create in order to govern a situation never fully imagined, let alone encountered, in the past. As such, it was sheer folly for the Bush administration to attempt to answer them on its own—and that folly was as profoundly self-destructive as it was injurious to liberty and fairness.

The simple truth is that the administration could have gotten almost anything it wanted from Congress in the way of detention authority for enemy aliens abroad in the wake of September 11. If the debate over the USA Patriot Act proved anything, it was that Congress had little appetite for standing in the way of the most robust response the executive could muster. The administration would likely have had to stomach a certain amount of process for the detainees, particularly for citizens held domestically. One can imagine that Congress might have required some eventual provision of counsel for some detainees, perhaps even mandated a forum in which the evidence against them in some form could be tested. The administration may even have been forced to provide the process contemplated by Article 5 of the Third Geneva Convention for distinguishing between lawful and unlawful combatants—a process it certainly should have been granting in any event. In my estimation, however, it is simply inconceivable that Congress would have crafted a regime that did not amply accommodate the president's wartime needs, particularly if President Bush had been clear about what he needed, why he needed it, and what the stakes were if he didn't get it. Going to Congress would have required two things of President Bush: a willingness to accept certain minimal limits on executive conduct imposed from the outside and, more fundamentally, a recognition that the wartime powers of the president, while vast, are not plenary—an acceptance that the presidential power to wage war can be enhanced by acknowledging the legislature's role in legitimizing it. Had Bush proceeded thus—as presidents often have in past conflicts—he would have entered his court battles with clear statutory warrant for his positions. Had this happened, I believe the deference he sought from the Supreme Court would have been forthcoming and very nearly absolute.

But Bush did not take this approach. His administration's insistence on what might be termed Article II fundamentalism caused him to take maximalist positions that are genuinely troubling: The president's judgment that a person is an enemy combatant is essentially unreviewable. The courts should defer to the executive, even in the absence of an administrative record to which to defer. Long-term detentions without trials of hundreds of people are entirely outside the purview of the courts. They all amount to the same basic position: Trust us. Trust the executive branch, in a wholly new geopolitical environment, acting with the barest and most general approval from the other political branch, to generate an entirely new legal system with the power of freedom and liberty and life and death over anyone it says belongs in that system. The executive branch learned last spring that exactly one member of the Supreme Court—Clarence Thomas—trusts President Bush that much. The court's skepticism seems to me to have been an entirely foreseeable result that competent counsel advising the president ought to have hedged against. When the history of this period is written, I feel confident that Bush will be deemed exceedingly ill-served by his top legal advisers.

Congressional Abdication

But the president's responsibility, however heavy, is not exclusive. Congress, after all, has its own independent duty to legislate in response to problems that arise in the course of the nation's life. And in a system of separated powers. Congress is not meant to legislate simply for the executive's convenience or at its beck and call. Indeed, if the executive branch sought to shunt the legislature aside in this episode, the legislature certainly proved itself a most willing shuntee. Congress institutionally seemed more than content to sideline itself and let the executive branch and the courts sort out what the law should be.

This abandonment of the field is disturbing on several levels. At the most analytical, America's constitutional design presupposes that each branch of government will assert its powers, that those powers will clash, and that this clash will prevent the accumulation of power in any one branch. This is the famous premise of Federalist 5I: "[T]he great security against a gradual concentration of the several powers in the same department, consists in giving to those who administer each department the necessary constitutional means and personal motives to resist encroachments of the others. The provision for defense must in this, as in all other cases, be made commensurate to the danger of attack. Ambition must be made to counteract ambition." Yet in the war on terrorism. Congress has done very nearly the opposite of countering the executive's ambition. It has run from its own powers on questions on which its assertion of rightful authority would be helpful, and it sloughed the difficult choices onto the two branches of government less capable than itself of designing new systems for novel problems.

The problem of congressional abdication of its responsibilities during wartime is not exactly new. It is most remarked upon in the context of the decision to go to war in the first place, which migrated in the twentieth century almost entirely to the executive branch. John Hart Ely noted, "It is common to style this shift a usurpation, but that oversimplifies to the point of misstatement. It's true our Cold War presidents generally wanted it that way, but Congress (and the courts) ceded the ground without a fight. In fact … the legislative surrender was a self-interested one: Accountability is pretty frightening stuff."[8] Ely's remedy for this problem—treating war powers as presenting jusiticiable questions with which the courts should be actively engaged—presents substantial difficulties on its own terms. Judges, after all, are not foreign policy experts, and decisions concerning war and peace are quintessentially political judgments, not principled legal ones. But even a robustly activist judiciary that was eager to explore such uncharted territories would have difficulty designing an appropriate regime for enemy combatants, because, to put it bluntly, the terms of any debate presented by litigation are destined to be too narrow.

Having no legislative involvement quite simply cuts off policy options. Once you consider the problem of enemy combatant detentions as a set of policy questions, a world of options opens. This world necessarily remains elusive to those who insist on finding in the doctrinal space between *Ex parte Milligan*[9] and *Ex parte Quirin* the answer to the question of how a Louisiana-born Saudi picked up in Afghanistan must be treated in a world in which a hegemonic United States has to consider nuclear terrorism a possibility. To cite only one conceivable example, the Constitution allows the civil commitment of mentally ill citizens who pose a danger to themselves or others. For a reasonably imaginative Congress, this might be a far better model for the alleged al Qaeda operative captured domestically than either the traditional laws of war or the criminal justice apparatus. A regime of civil commitment, after all, would recognize the preventive nature of the arrest, and it would coopt the use of a process that American society already tolerates as adequate for indefinite detentions in another context. Surely, al Qaeda operatives pose at least as great a threat to society as do schizophrenics.

One can imagine other models as well. Immigration law tolerates long detentions based almost entirely on executive branch process. Various forms of military tribunals might be attractive as well, as *Hamdi* intimates. The point is that the terms of the debate are today artificially constrained by the unwillingness of the one branch with the capacity to imagine a system from scratch to engage the problem at all. While individual members of Congress have raised the issue,[10] the congressional leadership—perhaps out of an unwillingness to publicly second-guess the Bush administration, perhaps out of sheer laziness, most likely out of a combination of the two—has shown no interest in actually legislating. Congress, in short, has concurred in the executive's unilateralism, offering neither legal support for its positions nor redirection of them. By the consent of both political branches, in other words, the design of the detention regime is being determined in a dialogue between the president and the courts.

Perhaps the most peculiar aspect of this decision is that it sparked so little controversy. The fact that few observers even comment upon Congress's absence from the discussion says a great deal about how Americans have come intuitively to weigh the responsibilities and contributions of the three branches of government. To be sure, many critics of the administration complain of the absence of specific congressional authority for detentions or military commissions by way of arguing against the legality of the administration's course. But the critics, by and large, are not urging congressional intervention, much less are they describing what a constructive intervention would look like. They have merely cited its absence as a bar to whatever action the administration proposes. Somehow, everyone seems to agree that the initial crack at writing the rules should be left to common-law jurisprudence.

NGOs for the Defense

This agreement—which remains, frankly, inexplicable to me—has put a considerable premium on the performance of nongovernmental actors: the human rights and civil liberties groups that opposed the military in these litigations. While Padilla, Hamdi, and the Guantanamo plaintiffs all had counsel to argue their cases, these groups greatly magnified the arguments against the administration's course, both in amicus filings and in the broader realm of public debate. Consequently, they became, in some sense, the "other side" of the debate—the organized force whose arguments marked the major alternative to the direction the administration chose. Unfortunately, they did not provide the Court with a useful alternative to the administration's vision, for their arguments were marked at once by failures of pragmatism and weak and selective understanding of doctrine. This is forgivable in the case of defense lawyers, who are obliged to advance the arguments most likely to aid their individual clients. And in the human rights and civil liberties groups, the decision was undoubtedly as much strategic as it was driven by conviction. By staking out a hard line, the groups ensured that they had not conceded key points even before any compromises took place. But the result of their wholesale adoption of the defense arguments was to present the court with a strategy for preserving liberty that was as unembracable as the administration's strategy for ensuring security.

Doctrinally, the ground staked out by the human rights community made fetishes of certain components of the laws of war and American constitutional law, even while ignoring other countervailing components of the same bodies of law. The human rights groups generally elided the importance of *Ex parte Quirin,* for example, which quite unambiguously endorses the premise that the American citizen can be detained by the military as an unlawful combatant.[11] Though their briefs were usually more careful than to make this error, they often seemed to deny in public statements that a detainee could be held as an unlawful combatant at all—a position flatly at odds with long-standing traditions of warfare. They nearly uniformly denied that the congressional authorization for the use of force against al Qaeda and its state sponsors necessarily implied the lesser power to detain combatants.[12] And all regarded it as self-evi-

dent that federal courts should supervise the detentions of non-citizens abroad—something they have never done previously in American history.[13]

One doesn't have to be a raging enthusiast for executive power to worry that these positions, particularly cumulatively, are simply inconsistent with any serious attempt to wage war against al Qaeda—even an attempt that does not partake of the excesses in which the Bush administration so indulged. In the rather fanciful regime the human rights groups appear to contemplate (and I acknowledge here that I am blending different arguments into a melange that might reflect no single group's precise position), the citizen is entitled to criminal process even if caught on a battlefield. The courts are engaged in day-to-day monitoring of executive compliance with the Geneva Conventions—though those treaties are not self-executing and have not historically been enforced through judicial action. Even the unlawful combatant—that is, a combatant not entitled to the status of prisoner of war—is nonetheless entitled to the same criminal procedure, the court-martial, as both the lawful combatant and the American soldier accused of misconduct.

It is a beautiful vision, but it does not happen to be the vision encapsulated in either international law or American law. And it's hard even to imagine fighting a war within its constraints. Should someone like Khalid Sheikh Muhammad be entitled to immediate access to counsel upon capture in Pakistan? Should he be able immediately to file a habeas corpus action alleging deprivations of his constitutional and treaty rights? There is embedded in this vision a very deep discomfort with the premise that the war on terrorism is, legally speaking, a war at all.

The consequence of the human rights groups staking out such unflinching ground was that the courts were faced, in all three cases, with a choice between extremes. Instead of confronting a well-constructed—or even a badly constructed—statutory scheme that sought to balance the competing constitutional values at stake in these detentions, it confronted a choice between total deference to the executive, aided only by the most general support from Congress, or total rejection of its claims, including its legitimate claims. In other words, it faced a choice between throwing the baby out with the bathwater and drinking the bathwater. The unifying theme of the Supreme Court's action in the enemy combatant cases is the refusal to choose—that is, the insistence on splitting the difference, even where prior precedent gave it scant leeway to do so.

Splitting the Baby

The performance of the courts in this endeavor was enormously uneven. Unlike the executive, which ultimately takes a unitary position on virtually all issues, and the Congress, which essentially took no position on the enemy combatant questions, the different courts, not to mention the different judges within individual courts, took several positions. And these ran the gamut in terms of quality and seriousness. For example, the district court that handled Padilla's case in New York produced—notwithstanding its ultimate reversal on the jurisdictional question on which the Supreme Court decided the case—the single most compelling judicial opinion yet written on the due process rights of citizens held as enemy combatants.[14] Chief Judge Michael Mukasey's handling of Padilla's case was a model of the combination of deference and skepticism that judges need to show in the war on terrorism, and it clearly became the model for Justice O'Connor's plurality opinion at the Supreme Court level. Judge Robert Doumar in Virginia, by contrast, was completely out of his depth in *Hamdi*. His rulings served to muddy, not clarify, the issues, as did his petulance toward government counsel.

More particularly for our purposes, in both appellate courts in the domestic cases—in the Fourth Circuit in *Hamdi* and in the Second Circuit in *Padilla*—the majority opinions simply adopted one or the other of the ultimately untenable hard-line positions, either the government's or that of the human rights groups and defense bar. In *Hamdi*, the Fourth Circuit declared the government's submission adequate to consign a citizen to his fate, at least where it is "undisputed" that he was captured in a "zone of active combat operations abroad."[15] To render beyond dispute the question of whether Hamdi was, in fact, captured in a zone of active combat abroad without hearing from Hamdi himself, the court found putative factual concessions in court filings, which the man had never seen or approved and which were written by lawyers with whom he had never been permitted to meet. The Second Circuit, meanwhile, declared Padilla's detention unlawful, buying in its entirety the notion that Congress's authorization to use force had not triggered the traditional war power of detaining the enemy until hostilities were at an end.[16] In both cases, dissenting judges showed considerably more sophistication, taking approaches that approximated the one the high court plurality ultimately adopted.[17] But because these were dissents in both courts of appeals, both *Padilla* and *Hamdi* came before the high court with stark stakes indeed: One court had held that the appropriate process was no process at all, while the other had held that—at least absent a neurotically specific act of Congress—nothing short of full criminal process could satisfy the Constitution.

The Guantanamo case approached the courts with the battle lines drawn similarly sharply, albeit for a different reason. The Supreme Court's own opinion in *Johnson v. Eisentrager* left little room for argument at the lower court level as to the jurisdiction of the federal courts over habeas petitions from the base. The Court wrote baldly at that time that "[w]e are cited to no instance where a court, in this or any other country where the writ [of habeas corpus] is known, has issued it on behalf of an alien enemy who, at no relevant time and in no stage of his captivity, has been within its territorial jurisdiction. Nothing in the text of the Constitution extends such a right, nor does anything in our statutes."[18] Any lower court tempted to assert jurisdiction over the base consequently had a high bar to clear in terms of binding precedent. In the *Rasul* litigation, no judge even attempted it. The district court wrote, "Given that under Eisentrager, writs of habeas corpus are not available to aliens held outside the sovereign territory of the United States, this Court does not have jurisdiction to entertain the claims made by Petitioners."[19] The D.C. Circuit Court of Appeals unanimously affirmed, and not a single judge voted for en banc review.[20] In other words, when the Court considered the petition for certiorari, the justices were facing—as a consequence of the fidelity of the lower courts to what *Eisentrager* plainly said—the prospect of being wholly shut out of the discussion of enemy combatants held abroad. (It should be noted that an attempt was made by the Ninth Circuit to assert jurisdiction over the base, but this was after certiorari had already been granted in *Rasul*.[21] Had the Court declined to consider *Rasul*, it would likely have had to jump to settle the conflict between the two circuits that developed as a result of this decision.)

As can probably be gleaned from the discussion so far, I am far more sympathetic to the high court's handling of *Hamdi* than to its resolution of *Rasul*. But critically, I believe the instinct behind both decisions was a similar one: the desire to split the baby between the claims of liberty and the claims of military necessity.

The plurality opinion in *Hamdi*, with all its vagueness and uncertainty, seems to me a creditable job of balancing constitutional values, and one that gets the big picture just about right. It acknowledges, first, the fact that the war on terrorism is not a metaphorical war like the war on drugs or the war on cancer—that is, it is not a statement of seriousness of purpose on a policy question but an actual state of military hostilities authorized by Congress and triggering traditional presidential war powers. Second, it acknowledges that implicit in Congress's authorization to use force is an authorization to detain those using force on the other side, even if they are American citizens. For different reasons, Justices Stevens, Scalia, Ginsburg, and Souter would have refused to recognize even this basic premise. Finally, the plurality recognizes that a citizen so detained is, by virtue of his citizenship, differently situated from a foreign national and entitled to a fair and impartial hearing should he choose to contest his status. These three basic premises seem to me all correct, whether they ultimately work to the government's advantage or to that of the detainees. In the absence of guidance from the legislature, I do not think American society could have expected more from the high court than finding this middle road and taking it.

Finding a middle course was naturally harder in *Rasul*. For jurisdiction, like pregnancy, is not a gray area; it either exists, or it doesn't exist. In this instance, the legal argument for jurisdiction was exceptionally weak. To get around *Eisentrager*, the Court had to argue that the famous holding had effectively been overruled in 1973—at least on the question of statutory jurisdiction in habeas cases—in a decision that does not even mention *Eisentrager*.[22] As noted above, the Court left unclear whether its assertion of jurisdiction applied only to Guantanamo or whether any detainee anywhere has access to American courts. For anyone with a sense of judicial restraint, *Rasul* should properly induce some embarrassment, for it is as dismissive of the Court's own precedent as it is disrespectful of the executive branch's reliance on that precedent in designing its detention policies. As Justice Antonin Scalia put it for the three dissenting justices.

> This is not only a novel holding; it contradicts a half-century-old precedent on which the military undoubtedly relied. The Court's contention that *Eisentrager* was somehow negated by *Braden v. 30th Judicial Circuit Court of Ky.*—a decision that dealt with a different issue

and did not so much as mention *Eisentrager*—is implausible in the extreme. This is an irresponsible overturning of settled law in a matter of extreme importance to our forces currently in the field. I would leave it to Congress to change [the habeas statute], and dissent from the Court's unprecedented holding [internal citations omitted].

But if *Rasul* is an embarrassment, it is one that illuminates the same baby-splitting instinct as the plurality opinion in *Hamdi*. For while the court could not split the difference between the administration and its critics in this case—the substantive issues not being before it yet—it could preserve its ability to split the difference in the future. The result may be a cheap, cynical opinion, but it is one that keeps the justices in the discussion without promising anything tangible. Its vagueness, I believe, is part of its point—a shot across the executive's bow, warning that if it doesn't get its act together, the Court will force it to do so by divining some cognizable rights, just as it divined its own power to consider the detainees' fates in the first place. If the executive behaves responsibly, by contrast, my guess is that the plaintiffs will find that *Rasul* proves an empty vessel for pushing the military toward greater liberality for detainees. In other words, by finding jurisdiction in *Rasul*, however implausibly, the Court positioned itself to play exactly the role it played in *Hamdi*, though admittedly on what will inevitably prove thinner legal reeds.

The baby-splitting instinct evident in these cases is, I suspect, a vision of the future of the legal war on terrorism in the absence of congressional intervention. The courts have positioned themselves not to impose particular processes but, rather, like figure-skating judges at the Olympics, to hold up signs granting marks to the players as they struggle to carve their own way: This process gets a 5.6; this one is inadequate because it lacks a bit more of this value or has too much of that value at the expense of some other one. Because the court is allergic to simply letting one side win—an instinct which, in and of itself, deserves some sympathy given the exceedingly harsh choices posed by the parties—the result is likely to be ongoing uncertainty, the absence of a legal safe harbor for executive conduct, and a big legal question mark hanging over the fates of all detainees held by the military domestically or abroad.

There is, of course, an alternative: a serious and deliberative legislative process that would design a regime within the confines of the Court's dictates to date—a regime to which the courts could defer in the future and which could define the role they should play going forward. This alternative, however, would require two developments: The administration would have to assume a modicum of humility in its dealings with the other branches of government. The administration s foes, meanwhile, would have to accept that war is a reality, not a metaphor, and that, consequently, not everyone detained in the war on terrorism is going to be rushed in front of a magistrate and encouraged to hire Johnny Cochran or Ramsey Clark to handle an immediate habeas action. At this stage, it's hard to say which necessary precondition for a more constructive approach seems a remoter possibility.

Notes

1. *Rasul v. Bush,* 124 S. Ct. 2686 (2004).
2. *Hamdi v. Rumsfeld,* 124, S. Ct. 2633 (2004).
3. *Rumsfeld v. Padilla,* 124 S. Ct. 2711 (2004).
4. Padilla's habeas case was refiled in South Carolina in light of the Supreme Court's ruling and was argued in federal district court there early in 2005. U.S. District Judge Henry F. Floyd, on February 18, 2005, found in favor of Padilla and issued a writ of habeas corpus. The government immediately announced plans to appeal. Even as the habeas case has progressed, however, there has been some indication that Padilla is now a cooperating witness in a case unrelated to the circumstances of his arrest, a status that implies that a plea may be in the works. See Dan Christensen and Vanessa Blum, "Padilla Implicated in Florida Terror Case," *Legal Times* (September 20, 2004).
5. See e.g., *U.S. v. Verdugo-Urquidez,* 494 U.S. 2 5 9 (1990), and *Johnson v. Eisentrager,* 339 U.S. 7 6 3 at 784 (1950). While the latter decision has been called into question by *Rasul,* the former has not. And there still exists no authority for the proposition that the Bill of Rights limits government action against aliens operating in foreign theaters of warfare. The Court, however, has applied the Bill of Rights to some degree in American territories overseas. So, in the wake of *Rasul,* the Court will have to decide whether Guantanamo is truly foreign territory or whether it is analogous to such overseas possessions.
6. In the wake of *Rasul,* this premise has come into considerable doubt. In *Hamdan v. Rumsfeld* (D.D.C. 04-CV1519, November 8, 2004), U.S. District Judge James Robertson held that the Third Geneva Convention was self-executing: "Because the Geneva Conventions were written to protect individuals, because the Executive Branch of our government implemented the Geneva Conventions for fifty years without questioning the absence of implementing legislation, because Congress clearly understood that the Conventions did not require implementing legislation except in a few specific areas, and because nothing in the Third Geneva Convention itself manifests the contracting parties' intention that it become effective as domestic law without the enactment of implementing legislation, I conclude that, insofar as it is pertinent here, the Third Geneva Convention is a self-executing treaty." The opinion, under appeal as of this writing, can be found at http://www.dcd.uscourts.gov/o4-1 5 1 9.pdf. See also *In re Guantanamo Detainee Cases* (D.D.G. 02-CV-02.99, January 31, 2005), which can be found at http://www.dcd. uscourts.gov/02299b.pdf.
7. The first of the rash of detainee suits to follow *Rasul* played out in exactly this fashion at the district court level. In *Khalid v. Bush* (D.D.C. CV 04-1142, January 19, 2005), U.S. District Judge Richard Leon held that notwithstanding *Rasul,* "no viable legal theory exists by which [a federal court] could issue a writ of habeas corpus under these circumstances." The decision can be found at http://www.dcd.uscourts.gov/o4-1142.pdf. On the other hand, less than two weeks later, Senior Judge Joyce Hens Green of the same court handed down *In re Guantanamo Detainee Cases,* in which she held precisely the opposite: The Fifth Amendment applies in Guantanamo and confers due process rights that are violated by the government's review procedures, and the Geneva Conventions are self-executing and confer individual litigable rights as well.
8. John Hart Ely, *War and Responsibility: Constitutional Lessons of Vietnam and Its Aftermath* (Princeton University Press, 1993), ix.
9. *Ex parte Milligan,* 71 U.S. 2 (1866).

10. See, e.g., H.R. 1029, the Detention of Enemy Combatants Act, introduced by Rep. Adam Schiff on February 23, 2003.

11. The briefs in *Hamdi* can be found at http://www.jenner.com/news/news_item.asp?id=12551224. Those in *Padilla* can be found at http://www.jenner.com/news/news_item.asp?id=12539624. The amicus filings of the American Civil Liberties Union, the Center for National Security Studies, Human Rights First, and other human rights and civil liberties groups, for example, all deny that current law authorizes enemy combatant detentions in at least one of the two cases, even if the detainee is granted a meaningful ability to contest his designation.

12. See, again, the amicus filings in both *Hamdi* and *Padilla*. Interestingly, the brief of the libertarian Cato Institute presents a notable exception.

13. The briefs in *Rasul* can be found at http://www.jenner.com/news/news_item.asp?id=12520724. The range of institutional support for the assertion of jurisdiction is dramatic.

14. *Padilla v. Rumsfeld,* 233 F. Supp. 2d 564 (2002).

15. *Hamdi v. Rumsfeld,* 316 F, 3d 450 (2003).

16. *Padilla v. Rumsfeld, 352 F. 3d 695 (2003).*

17. See Judge Motz's dissent from denial of rehearing en banc in *Hamdi*, reported at 337 F. 3d 335, 368 (2003). See also judge Wesley's dissent in *Padilla*. reported at 352 F. 3d 695, 726 (2003).

18. *Johnson v. Eisentrager,* 339 U.S. (1950).

19. *Rasul v. Bush,* 215 F. Supp. 2d 55 (2002).

20. *Al Odah v. United States,* 321 F. 3d 1134 (2003). The decision denying rehearing en banc is reported as *Al Odah v. United States,* 2003 U.S. App. LEXIS 11166.

21. *Gherebi v. Bush,* 374 F. 3d 727 (2003).

22. Justice Stevens's discussion in *Rasul* concerning *Braden v. 30th Judicial Circuit Court of Ky.,* 410 U.S. 484.

BENJAMIN WITTES is an editorial writer for the Washington Post specializing in legal affairs, and the author of *Starr: A Reassessment* (Yale University Press, 2002). This essay is also forthcoming in Peter Berkowitz, ed., *Terrorism, the Laws of War, and the Constitution* (Hoover Institution Press, 2005).

UNIT 5

The Foreign Policy Making Process

Unit Selections

Key Points to Consider

- Construct an ideal foreign policy-making process. How close does the United States come to this ideal? Is it possible for the United States to act in the ideal manner? If not, is the failing due to individuals who make foreign policy or to the institutions in which they work? Explain.

- What is the single largest failing of the foreign policy-making process? How can it be corrected? What is the single largest strength of the foreign policy-making process?

- What changes, if any, are necessary in the U.S. foreign policy-making process if the United States is to act effectively with other countries in multilateral efforts?

- What advice would you give to the president who is considering undertaking military action?

- How would you run a meeting that was organized to respond to a terrorist act? Whom would you invite? What would you expect of those you invited? How much dissent would you permit?

Student Web Site
www.mhcls.com/online

Internet References
Further information regarding these Web sites may be found in this book's preface or online.

Belfer Center for Science and International Affairs (BCSIA)
   http://ksgwww.harvard.edu/csia/
The Heritage Foundation
   http://www.heritage.org
National Archives and Records Administration (NARA)
   http://www.archives.gov/index.html
U.S. Department of State: The Network of Terrorism
   http://usinfo.state.gov/products/pubs/

We easily slip into the habit of assuming that an underlying rationality is at work in the conduct of foreign policy. A situation is identified as unacceptable or needing change. Goals are established, policy options are listed, the implications of competing courses of action are assessed, a conscious choice is made as to which policy to adopt, and then the policy is implemented correctly. This assumption is comforting because it implies that policymakers are in control of events and that solutions do exist. Moreover, it allows us to assign responsibility for policy decisions and hold policymakers accountable for the success or failure of their actions.

Comforting as this assumption is, it is also false. Driven by domestic, international, and institutional forces, as well as by chance and accident, perfect rationality is an elusive quality. This is true regardless of whether the decision is made in a small group setting or by large bureaucracies. Small groups are created when the scope of the foreign policy problem appears to lie beyond the expertise of any single individual. This is frequently the case in crisis situations. The essence of the decision-making problem here lies in the overriding desire of group members to get along. Determined to be a productive member of the team and not to rock the boat, individual group members suppress personal doubts about the wisdom of what is being considered and become less critical of the information before them—than they would be if they alone were responsible for the decision. They may stereotype the enemy, assume that the policy cannot fail, or believe that all members of the group are in agreement on what must be done.

The absence of rationality in decision making by large bureaucracies stems from their dual nature. On the one hand, bureaucracies are politically neutral institutions that exist to serve the president and other senior officials by providing them with information and implementing their policies. On the other hand, they have goals and interests of their own that may not only conflict with the positions taken by other bureaucracies but may be inconsistent with the official position taken by policymakers. Because not every bureaucracy sees a foreign policy problem in the same way, policies must be negotiated into existence, and implementation becomes anything but automatic. While essential for building a foreign policy consensus, this exercise in bureaucratic politics robs the policy process of much of the rationality that we look for in government decision making.

The problem of trying to organize the policy process to conduct a war against terrorism is an especially daunting task. In part this is because the enormity of the terrorist attacks and the language of war embraced by the Bush administration lead to expectations of an equally stunning countermove. Rationality is also strained by the offsetting pressures for secrecy and the need for a speedy response on the one hand and the need to harmonize large numbers of competing interests on the other. Finally, no matter how many resources are directed at the war against terrorism, there will continue to be the need to balance resources and goals. Priorities will need to be established and trade-offs accepted as is evidenced by the debate over the legality and value of domestic spying programs in support of the war

on terrorism. There is no neutral equation or formula by which this can be accomplished. It will be made through a political process of bargaining and consensus building in which political rationality rather than any type of substantive rationality will triumph.

The readings in this unit provide insight into the process by which foreign policy decisions are made by highlighting activity at several different points in the policy process. The first essay, "Law, Liberty, and War," presents a debate between Anne-Marie Slaughter and Jeremy Rabkin over the proper constitutional balance between Congress and the president in conducting foreign policy in the war against terrorism and the Iraq War. The second essay, "Words vs. Deeds," looks at the central place which public opinion polling now holds in foreign policy decision making. The final essay by John Prados, "The Pros from Dover," casts a critical eye on decision making processes and structures put into place by the George W. Bush administration. He asserts that either the system did not work or it worked to keep terrorism off of the foreign policy agenda in its first months in office.

Law, Liberty and War

Has the Bush Administration run roughshod over American civil liberties and distorted Constitutional balances during the Global War on Terror? *You bet it has*, argues Anne-Marie Slaughter. *No way*, says Jeremy Rabkin.

Originalist Sin

ANNE-MARIE SLAUGHTER

How historical periods are defined depends on the purposes of the definer. Geologists look to rock structure, demarking eras such as the Cretaceous, Jurassic, Triassic, Mesozoic and Paleozoic. Economists look to the primary source of wealth: the Iron Age, the Bronze Age, the Industrial Age and now the Information Age. Chroniclers of foreign affairs look to catastrophes: While their business is war *and* peace, their timelines are chiefly defined by wars. Consider how we talk and write about the 20th century: World War I, the interwar period, World War II, the Cold War. After the Cold War came the post-Cold War period, until 9/11, which marked the beginning of the War on Terror. The military is currently planning for "The Long War" against terrorism—and, if there is such a long war, it is a good bet that decades hence historians and political analysts will still be defining time in the cadences of war.

But why not focus instead on naming periods of peace? John Lewis Gaddis has written about "the long peace", describing how United States and the Soviet Union managed to get through over four decades of the Cold War without fighting one another directly. Yet proclaiming peace has not caught on, notwithstanding occasional references to Pax Americana, Pax Britannia and Pax Romana. The reason is not hard to find: Telling citizens that they live in wartime is good for boosting defense budgets. It is also good for expanding presidential power. "War makes the state", wrote celebrated sociologist Charles Tilly, "and the state makes war."

Such ruminations make a worthy backdrop for reading and assessing John Yoo's provocative book, *Powers of War and Peace: The Constitution and Foreign Affairs After 9/11*. Yoo writes to rectify an awkward legal contradiction for political conservatives. Ardent advocates of originalism—a school of Constitutional interpretation that prizes the intent of the Framers and literal reading of the text of our founding document—have heretofore found themselves arguing against the seemingly clear Constitutional text granting Congress the power to declare war. And they must explain away contemporaneous accounts in the *Federalist Papers* making clear that the Framers wanted to give the Executive authority to make war, but only once Congress had decided to go to war in the first place. As Thomas Jefferson put it, "We have ... given ... one effectual check to the Dog of war by transferring the power of letting him loose from the Executive to the Legislative body, from those who are to spend to those who are to pay." In foreign affairs debates, therefore, liberal constitutionalists like Louis Henkin and Harold Koh have been able to claim the originalist high ground, while conservatives have instead made sweeping claims about how the evolving nature of war and new threats to American national security require that the Constitution be interpreted in light of two centuries of practice—the very argument anathema to them in, say, constitutional debates over abortion or the death penalty.

No longer. Yoo offers an originalist understanding of a vast Executive foreign affairs power, checked not by the Constitution itself but only by Congress' ability to push back. The Framers, according to Yoo, designed "a flexible system for making foreign policy in which the political branches could opt to cooperate or compete." In this system, the roles of Congress and the courts are narrowly confined to the specific powers granted them in Articles I and III, respectively. Article II, on the other hand, which defines the Executive's powers, "effectively grants to the president any unenumerated foreign affairs powers not given elsewhere to the other branches."

Yoo's book reads as a long footnote to a Supreme Court brief.

The Powers of War and Peace offers the theoretical grounding for this expansive view of Executive power based on evidence from practice in early U.S. history, the intent of the Framers, and the text and structure of the Constitution. The book reads as a long footnote to a Supreme Court brief upholding the Bush Administration's controversial claims to lawfully detain U.S. citizens as enemy combatants or disregard treaties that have become inconvenient. With Yoo in hand, the Bush Administration need not argue to the courts that it must push out the boundaries of our Constitution in this national emergency. Giving such enormous power to the president in foreign affairs was what the Framers intended in the first place: Congress could fend for itself, Yoo writes, "[s]imply by refusing to do anything, by not affirmatively acting to vote funds or to enact legislation. … [T]he appropriations power and the power to raise the military gives Congress a sufficient check on presidential warmaking."

The key point, of course, is that the Framers wrote in a time of no standing armies, no established political parties and relatively little difficulty in demarcating the line between foreign and domestic affairs. Without standing armies, the Congressional power of the purse was necessary to put soldiers in the field, a very real check on executive war-mongering. But with 1.4 million men and women on active duty in the military today and another 860,000 in the reserves, the Executive branch tends to shoot first and ask Congress to fund later, when our young men and women in uniform are already on the front lines. The political calculus, as any modern president well knows, overwhelmingly favors lining up behind the troops once they are in the field—a decision, according to Yoo, that is entirely up to the president.

Without entrenched partisan politics, it was possible to imagine members of Congress serving as a genuine voice of the people in opposition to the Executive. But with the most partisan system the nation has seen in a century, the President's party votes with him, and it is the opposition alone that must face accusations of starving the troops in the field.

Without shrinking oceans, instant communications and a global economy it was at least possible to limit even a broad Executive foreign affairs power to distinctively and definably "foreign" affairs. But in an age of terrorism practiced by non-state groups both within the territory of the United States and without, by aliens and citizens alike, through a complex system of financing and support that travels through a tangled trail of domestic and foreign transactions, what a president can do abroad—wiretapping, for instance—he can also presume to do at home.

Yoo's history is, to say the least, highly selective. Despite his central claim that the Framers clearly intended a unified executive, Yoo's historical chapter about the writing of the Constitution opens with an admission of the Framers' "silence" about the separation of powers in foreign affairs. Manfully, Yoo tries to explain away messy historical facts—such as the Constitutional Convention's rejection of amendments that would have added to the Constitution explicit language setting out Yoo's own unconventional understanding of the treaty and war powers. (Though these amendments failed, Yoo take pains to note that at least some of the Framers agreed with him.)

But by filling pages with every shred of evidence from the Founding period that might support a unified executive in foreign affairs, Yoo misses the real story. The Framers' animating purpose in abandoning the loose Articles of Confederation for our Constitution was not to resurrect the British monarchy's tradition of a dominant executive. Rather, the Framers were far more concerned about creating a strong central government to harmonize the dissonant foreign policies of the states, which had left the infant United States vulnerable in the 18th-century world of marauding mercantilist great powers. To the extent that the Framers sought what Alexander Hamilton called "energy in the executive", as Stanford's Pulitzer Prize-winning historian Jack Rakove writes in "Making Foreign Policy: The View from 1787", the constitutional provisions "that laid the strongest foundation for a major executive role in foreign policy are more safely explained as a cautious reaction against the defects of exclusive senatorial control of foreign relations than as a bold attempt to convert the noble office of a republican presidency into a vigorous national leader in world affairs."

In light of George Washington's difficulties with a war run by committee during the Revolution, the Framers explicitly chose not to give Congress the power to "make war", that is, to actually conduct it. But they equally explicitly gave Congress the power to "declare war", that is, to start it. Indeed, at the Constitutional Convention, when Pierce Butler of South Carolina formally proposed giving the president the power on his own to start war, Elbridge Gerry of Massachusetts said he "never expected to hear in a republic a motion to empower the executive to declare war." The Constitutional Convention quickly rejected Butler's motion.

Yoo's version of the Constitution is both disingenuous and dangerous.

Moreover, the practice of early presidents confirms this understanding. In 1801, facing depredations by the Barbary pirates, President Jefferson took certain defensive actions but went before the Congress to explain himself. He told the Congress that anything beyond defensive action was for them to authorize. Four years later, during a dispute with Spain, Jefferson put the matter as plainly as possible: "Congress alone is constitutionally vested with the power of changing our situation from peace to war."

By contrast, Yoo's version of the Constitution is both disingenuous and dangerous. Take the striking inconsistency between Yoo's understanding of "flexibility" in the Constitution's treatment of the War Powers and Treaty powers. Yoo argues that "[t]he Constitution did not intend to institute a fixed, legalistic process" in foreign affairs, and goes to great lengths to explain why Articles I and II do not actually restrict the president's war powers in the way historians and legal scholars have long understood. But, flexibility for Yoo does not extend to the treaty power, even though treaties are clearly instruments of foreign affairs. Instead, Yoo insists that treaties must not only satisfy the requirements of Article II, but that they also be subject to additional rigid legal requirements to have the force of law. Yoo infers such "fixed, legalistic process" for implementing treaties in the United States even though no specific language in the Constitution sets out such requirements. This conveniently allows the president to dispose of a host of inconvenient treaties that might restrain his power if their terms had the force of domestic law. And despite Yoo's own history describing the Framers' concern with the states ignoring treaties, he even questions how much the Federal government today can require the states to follow U.S. treaty obligations. Such conclusions leave the reader wondering how much of this book is pure Constitutional interpretation, and how much a manual for the Bush Administration's vision of American unilateralism.

Yoo's most sweeping and dangerous claim is hidden as a legal technicality.

Given Yoo's recent service in an intensely ideological administration, his partisanship here is hardly surprising and easy to spot. Yoo's most sweeping—and most dangerous—claim is hidden as a legal technicality. "Article II", he writes, "effectively grants to the president any unenumerated foreign affairs powers not given elsewhere to the other branches." In other words, whatever is not explicitly granted ("enumerated") to Congress or the courts belongs to the Executive. All that is necessary is to identify a particular power as a "foreign affairs power."

The danger of this view is that the president can claim any new threat to American national security—and those appear all the time—as one he alone is empowered to address. Take the war on terror. The Bush Administration has claimed that the president has the power to declare any American citizen an "enemy combatant", to keep such combatants in jail indefinitely without bringing criminal charges, and to try them through a separate court system without the core protections of the Bill of Rights. Even judges in President Bush's conservative camp are unwilling to trust a president that much. In 2003 the Supreme Court—in an opinion joined by Antonin Scalia—rejected Bush's claim that the president's war powers meant that enemy combatants could not challenge their detention in court. And this past December, a conservative appellate judge once on Bush's Supreme Court short-list (Michael Luttig of the Fourth Circuit) wrote a biting opinion holding that the Bush Administration could not move a U.S. citizen in and out of the protections of the criminal justice system simply by invoking the shibboleth of terrorism and national security.

Yoo's position not only threatens our civil liberties; it is equally dangerous to our national security. He is right about the profound changes America faces in the world and the resulting need for a flexible framework governing foreign affairs powers—a push and pull between the Executive and Congress, with periodic intervention by the courts. But rather than expanding Executive power while pretending that Congress can cut funding to stop U.S. troops already deployed on foreign soil, the solution is to draw clear Constitutional boundaries around the Executive's power, enforceable by the courts if necessary, and to find ways to force, commit or lure Congress to do the job it is supposed to do.

Leslie Gelb and I recently suggested ("Declare War", *The Atlantic Monthly,* November 2005) one approach to this: a new law that would restore the Framers' intent by restoring the declaration of war, and requiring Congress actually to declare war in advance of any commitment of troops that promises sustained combat. The president would be required to present Congress with critical information about war aims and plans; and Congress would in turn hold hearings to scrutinize for itself the intelligence justifying the recourse to war, the costs of fighting, and the administration's plans for the war's aftermath. A full floor debate and vote would follow. The lack of a Congressional declaration would automatically deny funds to that military operation. In Jefferson's words, "Congress must be called on to take it, the right of reprisal being expressly lodged with them by the Constitution, and not with the Executive." Congress must be called on, or must pre-commit itself, to take the same responsibility with respect to how we treat enemy prisoners and fight other critical fronts in the War on Terror.

Congressional participation in foreign affairs, however, is not an end in itself. The Framers' genius was to recognize the practical benefits of American democracy in conducting foreign affairs. In a world of shadowy and immeasurable threats, the real danger of getting war powers wrong is not simply the abuse of power by any one branch of government, but also the use of power without sufficient information, deliberation and imagination to succeed. As any global business recognizes, success today requires managing change and risk under conditions of uncertainty. So too with government. In this effort, many minds are better than one—to sift through and assess the quality of our information, to question and improve our strategies, and to brainstorm and troubleshoot so that tactics too narrowly conceived will not lead us astray.

The intelligence failures that enabled the attacks on September 11 and the rush to war in Iraq (leaving aside the accuracy of the limited intelligence presented to Congress) underscore the danger of leaving critical questions of war solely in the hands of the Executive. Congress' job is not simply to fund or not to fund. It is to question, to probe, to deliberate and to decide, together with the President, on behalf of the people whose sons and daughters will be sent to war and whose tax dollars will be spent. That is the originalist understanding of the Constitution, and the ensuing centuries have only strengthened the case for this interpretation of its text.

ANNE-MARIE SLAUGHTER is dean of the Woodrow Wilson School of Public and International Affairs and the Bert G. Kerstetter University Professor of Politics and International Affairs at Princeton University.

War Stories

JEREMY RABKIN

In the immediate aftermath of 9/11, most Americans wanted to fight the terrorists and the regimes that aided them. Even before that year ended, however, some voices warned that the impulsive, reckless policies of the Bush Administration would ultimately pose more of a danger to Americans and their way of life than the terrorists and their allies: We were, according to such critics, falling into the trap that clever terrorists always set, conspiring unwittingly in our own undoing. That opinion has gained ground as the shock of the initial terror attacks has receded. It is an opinion that owes far less to actual incursions on domestic liberties, however, than to insinuations and second thoughts about whether we need to be "at war" at all.

It is certainly possible to endorse a war while criticizing its conduct abroad and its policy repercussions at home. Such distinctions are not inherently illogical. But almost invariably, the loudest protests against wartime abuses come from those who reject the war in the first place. The fiercest critics of President Lincoln's war measures were the Copperheads, who opposed from the outset the effort to coerce the South by force of arms. The most outspoken critics of Cold War measures were those who dismissed the notion that communists or communism could threaten American security. And so it is with the War on Terror.

The current war has stimulated some measures that might be questioned in peacetime. They look altogether intolerable to those who reject the need for war. On the other hand, those who accept a "war" policy in current circumstances often hesitate to criticize particular security measures lest such criticism undermine general support for the war. It is hard in this setting to sort out competing claims about domestic security measures of the Bush Administration. The debate almost immediately shifts from actual experience to generalized claims about the Administration's posture in the world. After years of debate about the supposed excesses of the Patriot Act, for example, critics in Congress acquiesced earlier this year to its re-enactment with only minor changes. The Patriot Act seems to have been not so much a source of dispute in itself as a symbol of some wider, more amorphous complaint.

Several points about this larger debate do seem reasonably clear, however. The first is that, compared with our experience in past wars, the current war has been quite mild in its impact on domestic civil liberties. In World War II, the Federal government incarcerated more than 120,000 Japanese-Americans, including women, children and old people—all of them long-standing residents and most of them either citizens or immediate relatives of citizens. These unfortunates were held behind barbed wire in excess of two years, and the Supreme Court endorsed the practice essentially on the say-so of the President.

After 9/11 fewer than five thousand people were rounded up. All of them were aliens, almost all recent arrivals and unmarried males of suitable age for combat or terror operations. They were all released within a few weeks. Today's true legal counterpart of *Korematsu,* the 1943 case endorsing the mass detention of Japanese-Americans without any sort of due process, is the case of José Padilla—one person, who is now to be tried before an ordinary civilian court (though admittedly after years of military detention without trial or formal charges).

The same pattern holds regarding freedom of speech. In the Civil War, President Lincoln authorized military trials for anti-war agitators. He deployed the army to shut down an antiwar newspaper in New York and to suppress anti-conscription riots there. There was comprehensive official censorship during World War I and a Federal program to coach state universities on proper wartime curricula. The Cold War saw American Communist Party leaders prosecuted for conspiring to incite unspecified acts of disloyalty in unspecified future circumstances. The House Un-American Activities Committees hounded left-wing screenwriters. Some were ultimately sentenced to prison terms for refusing to testify about possible decades-old communist affiliations of associates in the movie industry. Yet the angriest charge against the Bush Administration is that it has used rhetoric that puts its critics on the defensive, as by ostensibly improper allusions to the 9/11 victims.

Today's legal counterpart to *Korematsu* is the case of José Padilla—*one person*.

So, too, with surveillance. There was a great uproar when it was revealed at the end of 2005 that the Bush Administration had, without proper judicial warrants, monitored phone calls between al-Qaeda suspects overseas and individuals in the United States. Yet President Roosevelt invoked national security to authorize wiretaps on domestic phone calls of suspicious individuals more than a year before the United States entered World War II. The practice continued during the Cold War. It was not until the late 1970s, amid revelations of abusive FBI surveillance activities, that Congress even attempted to regulate such practice with the Foreign Intelligence Surveillance Act.

In the recent dispute about when FISA procedures apply, a second point stands out: Even though the government is acting with greater restraint than in past wars, the clamor about threats to civil liberties is louder today because we now hold the government to higher standards. What critics now regard as outrageous was once regarded as more or less standard practice.

There are often good reasons for moving the goal posts in such ways. Past abuses prompt greater cautions in succeeding generations. No one wants to repeat Cold War abuses. J. Edgar Hoover himself cautioned during World War II against repeating the excesses committed by the Wilson Administration in World War I. Sometimes new technology raises new issues, as with the NSA surveillance systems that today allow immensely powerful computers to monitor vast volumes of telephone and Internet communication without direct human "listening."

Still, in an era in which so much constitutional debate proceeds on the basis of evolving standards, this particular debate has become disorienting. Those most indignant about threats to the Constitution tend to appeal not to traditional standards but to those that are recent or even heretofore unheard of. Over the past few years, for example, some of America's most distinguished law faculties have endorsed the claim that law schools have a First Amendment right to exclude military recruiters from their job fairs without forfeiting Federal funds, as current law requires. When the Supreme Court rejected this argument earlier this year, not a single justice offered so much as a sympathetic nod to this strange new constitutional theory. The harshest critics of constitutional abuses tend to be those who, in other contexts, champion the theory of a "living Constitution", one whose provisions are never quite settled. It is hard *not* to violate a "constitution" that keeps expanding in this way.

A third point follows from the second: Debates about civil liberties in wartime have now expanded to embrace standards regarded as global in scope, supposedly binding on America because they are "international law." Thus has a vast amount of debate centered on the treatment of captured terrorists at Guantánamo: Are they treated in accord with the Geneva Convention? Are they being interrogated in ways prohibited by the UN Convention Against Torture? Is the Bush Administration's disdain for these accepted international standards a threat to America's global leadership? Does the Administration's stance threaten Americans at home who rely on the protections of law?

No U.S. court has ever before presumed to judge military compliance with the Geneva standards.

The last question, though insistently posed by many critics, has scarcely anything to do with the others. The five hundred or so detainees in Guantánamo were taken to that naval base in the Caribbean precisely because it is not, technically, American soil. No American court had ever presumed to question U.S. military actions outside the United States. The Supreme Court had specifically repudiated such interference in a 1950 case about war prisoners held by the U.S. military in occupied Germany. The Court's exceedingly narrow, divided ruling in *Rasul v. Bush* in 2004 has left most questions about the status of Guantánamo detainees open, but assures that domestic courts will now, for the first time, have some role in monitoring external military actions. Some justices have indicated both in concurring opinions and in off-the-bench speeches that U.S. courts should indeed consider whether international standards have been properly applied in these settings. That would be another great novelty: No U.S. court has ever before presumed to judge military compliance with the Geneva standards. But many legal

advocates now insist that the Court reassure foreign skeptics and domestic critics that even overseas the U.S. military will follow what judges can certify as proper legal standards.

One can certainly argue that extreme brutality, even toward foreign prisoners in wartime, has a corrosive effect on military discipline, and that it may ultimately have poisonous moral consequences for any society that sponsors or tolerates such practices. But surely a lot depends on context. Stephen Ambrose's book about a company of paratroopers in World War II, *Band of Brothers,* reports that patrols were sent out behind enemy lines to capture low-ranking German soldiers whom American interrogators would then shoot or threaten to shoot to make others reveal information about enemy positions. It did not occur to Ambrose, author of many works on American military history, to denounce this tactic or to depict it as aberrant. Nor did the producers of the HBO mini-series based on the book feel obliged to suppress this unpleasant fact of history. Neither Ambrose nor his Hollywood adaptors even bothered to incorporate an acknowledgement that such tactics were in violation of the Hague Conventions and the applicable Geneva Convention at the time.

If one takes the idea of war seriously enough, one risks excusing almost anything in the interest of victory. That is the charge hurled most insistently at John Yoo, a professor of law at Berkeley who served as a top advisor in the Department of Justice in George W. Bush's first term. Yoo's internal memos, subsequently leaked by an Administration once thought to be strongly averse to leaks, have been denounced as authorizing torture and encouraging disregard of law.

Most past presidents have tacitly agreed with Yoo's constitutional constructions.

Now Yoo has published an academic study, *Powers of War and Peace: The Constitution and Foreign Affairs Since 9/11.* The book, however, says almost nothing about the convention against torture or the detentions at Guantánamo, and even less about domestic civil liberties. Instead, Yoo pursues seemingly legalistic questions about the separation of powers: Who decides when and whether the United States is at war? Who decides when and whether the United States is still bound by international treaties? Yoo argues that the Founders saw decisions about the resort to war just as they saw decisions about repudiating treaties as inherently an Executive branch prerogative. The power given to Congress to "declare" war simply entails the authority to announce a formality rather than control the strategic decision. Congress retains ultimate authority because it can finally deny funds to any presidential initiative, but the president retains broad powers of initiative in foreign affairs.

Conventional legal scholarship has run strongly in the other direction since the Vietnam War. But Yoo makes a very strong case for his interpretations based on the British practice familiar to the Framers, on what defenders of the Constitution said in ratification debates, and on what their opponents did not say. An honest reading of American history suggests that most past presidents have tacitly assumed the correctness of Yoo's constitutional constructions.

Still, the ultimate point at issue is not historical but philosophical. If one thinks that Congress is supposed to have the first word about the resort to war as well as the last, then one thinks that war must be, generally speaking, a legislative decision that we can adopt or reject like a tax cut. To think that, one must suppose that the world is fundamentally peaceful or at least that the United States is fundamentally at peace with the world, with conflict a rare and discretionary exception. Such a supposition makes it easy to embrace the notion of an international legal system that covers even the conduct of war in its smallest details. One can then suppose that such standards have great authority, even if some of the combatants in a conflict ignore them altogether, because the world remains in some way governed by a fine mesh of legal standards. Many advocates certainly want to live in a world of this kind. It happens, however, not to be the world in which we actually live.

L egal standards have value to the extent that they can be sustained. It does not promote law to ground it on merely wishful or fanciful premises. A proposal for law on such premises is offered in *Before the Next Attack: Preserving Civil Liberties in an Age of Terrorism,* a recent book by Yale law professor Bruce Ackerman. Ackerman acknowledges that terror attacks may indeed require emergency measures. He thinks, however, the responses of the Bush Administration were "disasters" for law and civil liberties because they have not been checked by adequate constraints. So Ackerman advocates a new scheme under which Congress could authorize suspensions of civil liberties for brief periods after an attack, but could only renew such emergency provisions contingent on successively higher majorities within Congress. Nothing in the Constitution warrants requiring Congress to abide by supermajority requirements in this way, but Ackerman argues that the courts could

nonetheless enforce something of the kind if Congress accepted the basic scheme.

Those who are familiar with Ackerman's work will not be surprised by this suggestion. He is best known for arguing that the Constitution can be amended not only by the formal process set out in Article V, but also by an informal political "process": When a contested new approach to the Constitution is defended by a political party or administration and the voters return them to office, that provides endorsement for the new approach. Ackerman's favorite example is, of course, the New Deal. He may now expect that his own constitutional doctrines will be ratified by voters in future elections. Ackerman is the quintessential cheerleader for a "living Constitution", stimulated by growth hormones slipped to it by attentive law professors.

Several times in *Before the Next Attack* Ackerman insists that we do not now face an "existential threat" comparable to that posed by Germany and Japan in the 1940s, and so we cannot now justify such significant abridgement of civil liberties in response. But was Germany really going to land an army in New England, or the Japanese in California? Was a German victory parade in Washington ever more likely than a mass-casualty terror attack today on an American city? No matter: If one wants to advance uniquely high standards of protectiveness toward supposed threats to civil liberties, it is easier to pretend that World War II was a unique exception and that the current war is more like the Cold War, when law professors could insist that the enemy was a figment of the imagination of McCarthyite demagogues.

I concede that war is always a potential threat to civil liberties. But so is defeat in war. Forced to choose between the risk of domestic abuses and the risk of defeat in war, most Americans will not harp on domestic legal standards. It is reasonable to worry about government excesses. It is escapist to pretend, at a time when terrorists plot new assaults on American cities, that our own government is the greatest threat to our security.

***

JEREMY RABKIN is a professor of government at Cornell University and serves on the board of directors of the Center for Individual Rights.

Words vs. Deeds: President George W. Bush and Polling

Kathryn Dunn Tenpas

President George W. Bush pledged repeatedly throughout his presidential campaign that his administration would have no use for polls and focus groups: "I really don't care what polls and focus groups say. What I care about is doing what I think is right." Shackled by that promise, President Bush and his staff have shrouded his polling apparatus, minimizing the relevance of polls and denying their impact. But public records available from the Federal Election Commission, documents from presidential libraries, and interviews with key players paint a fairly clear picture of the Bush polling operation. The picture, which turns out to be a familiar one, calls into question the administration's purported "anti-polling" ethos and shows an administration closely in keeping with historical precedent.

President Bush in Historical Context

Every president since Richard Nixon has hired professional pollsters to take, periodically, the pulse of the electorate. Earlier presidents clearly had relationships with pollsters, who obligingly tacked questions onto their existing polls for the benefit of the administration. But polling was not under White House control. Nixon's use of pollsters marked a turning point in the history of presidential polling because it signaled the birth of White House-commissioned polls. No longer tethered to the timetables and agendas of pollsters like Lou Harris and George Gallup, presidents began to direct both the timing and the substance of their polls. Nor were polls limited to the campaign season; presidents and their staff could test the popularity of various programs and policy initiatives on their own schedule. Scholars, noting that the transfer of campaign tactics to governing was blurring the distinction between the two, began describing the result as the "permanent campaign."

Rapid advances in technology played a big part in the new ways presidents used polling. By the time Nixon took office, computers, though costly, had become sophisticated enough to process vast quantities of data. Not only were telephones ubiquitous enough to make their use in polling methodologically feasible, but the advent of random digit dialing increased the efficiency and validity of telephone polling. In short, the "sci-ence" of polling became more mature, enabling presidents not only to learn about their past performance but to gain "prospective" intelligence. Today, testing key phrases in a speech or catchphrases designed to sell a policy or program has become so commonplace that presidential speeches and public pronouncements endure many rounds of focus group testing before being judged ready for primetime. Innovative techniques like the mall intercept (interviewing shoppers at a mall storefront), tracking polls, overnight polling, dial meters, and focus groups are part of any professional pollster's repertoire. And new Internet focus groups are being used, by the Bush pollsters among others, as a more timely, less expensive way to conduct focus groups. Though still in its nascent stages, Internet polling is thought to be the next generation of survey research, significantly lowering costs while increasing the speed with which polls can be conducted.

The names of many past presidential pollsters are familiar, if not exactly household names. Robert Teeter did polling for Presidents Nixon, Ford, and George H.W. Bush; Patrick Caddell for President Carter; Richard Wirthlin for President Reagan; and Stanley Greenberg (1993-94) and Mark Penn (1995-2000) for President Clinton. Most began as pollsters for the campaign and were "promoted" to presidential pollsters, taking on a higher profile in the process. Indeed, the unprecedented visibility and perceived influence of Clinton's pollsters created much advance interest in President George W. Bush's prospective pollsters. But Bush's determination to be the "anti-Clinton" and his repeated campaign promises to give polls and focus groups no role in his administration led him to relegate his pollsters to near anonymity. Still, their low profile, particularly compared with that of Clinton's pollsters, has not kept them from performing essential polling for the White House.

By the Numbers

The Republican and Democratic National Committees subsidize presidential political expenses such as polling and political travel and routinely report those expenses to the Federal Election Commission. Table 1 sets out polling expenditures only for designated presidential pollsters during the first two years of the

Reagan, Bush I, Clinton, and Bush II administrations. The pollsters for the second Bush administration come in well behind those of Presidents Reagan and Clinton and only slightly ahead of the first Bush administration. Though the parties spent extraordinary amounts on both Reagan and Clinton, Reagan's administration was popularly perceived as being driven by deeply rooted philosophical principles while Clinton's was seen as merely pandering—suggesting that polling does not always taint a president's reputation.

When the party of the president is in power, the national committee becomes a veritable White House annex staffed with loyalists eager to secure the president's reelection. Toward that end, no amount of polling is too much, particularly when the polling can also inform broader party strategy and statewide campaigns. A look at Republican National Committee spending on polling more generally (not just designated presidential pollsters) reveals that it spent roughly $3.1 million during the first two years of the current Bush administration. And even that figure understates the polling available to the White House because it does not include polling conducted on behalf of the National Republican Senatorial Committee and the National Republican Congressional Committee, which totals some $6.5 million—more than double what the RNC spent on polling. Though neither of those organizations is responsible for subsidizing White House polling, Bush's presidential pollsters, Jan van Lohuizen (Voter/Consumer Research) and Fred Steeper (Market Strategies), have done work for these committees totaling more than $800,000—a sum that if added to presidential polling would bump up the Bush total to $2.5 million, more than $1 million more than Bush I. And Karl Rove's extraordinary sway makes it unlikely that any request by him for statewide polls that might be of interest to the president would be denied either by the president's pollsters or by any pollsters doing work for the RNC. In addition, the RNC spent $2.7 million on "political consulting." And although the FEC reports do not detail the various projects, the reports include work by former White House adviser Karen Hughes and a broad range of Republican consulting firms.

National Party Presidential Polling Expenditures
(In 2002 dollars)

ADMINISTRATION	FIRST YEAR	SECOND YEAR	TOTAL
Reagan –			
Richard Wirthlin	1,635,000	2,531,000	4.1 million
Bush I –			
Robert Teeter	831,683	470,811	1.3 million
Clinton –			
Stanley Greenberg	2,433,000	2,415,000	4.8 million
Bush II –			
Jan van Lohuizen			
and Fred Steeper	715,771	947,422	1.7 million

*Data for the current administration obtained on-line from fec.gov with the assistance of Elizabeth Redman and Larissa Davis of the Brookings Institution, April 2003. All other data obtained by author from the Federal Election Commission.

As interesting as the total amount of RNC spending on polling is its timing (figure 1). Rather than being more or less consistent monthly, spending peaks in ways that seem hard to explain. Though noteworthy events—the September 11 attacks and the midterm elections—may account for two of the peaks, Matthew Dowd, senior adviser at the RNC, has indicated that events do not necessarily drive polling. And while pollsters may be interested in gauging the impact of unexpected events or new developments, their billing is not systematic in a way that could support the event-driven explanation. Nevertheless, a statistical regression analysis reveals a general trend upward, roughly an average increase of $4,000 a month, suggesting that, over time, there are forces driving the RNC to spend more money on polling. Short of obtaining White House-commissioned polls, it is impossible to define the precise role that events play in polling. Regardless, the variation in spending reflects the idiosyncratic usage of polling within the Bush administration.

Why Poll?

Presidential documents and interviews with White House staff and pollsters from past administrations suggest that presidents use polling for two primary reasons. The first is tactical. Given the limited resources available to them, new presidents must determine the best way to sell their agenda, minimizing costs and maximizing their influence. Campaign professionals, armed with state-of-the-art public opinion technology and an "outside the Beltway" perspective on pressing issues and problems, provide a service that the modern White House is unequipped to offer. The second reason, rooted in democratic theory, is a president's desire to represent his constituents by acting in consonance with a majority of the public. Although the Bush administration is willing to admit it uses polls to help package and sell its policies to the public, it regards as heresy any suggestion that it follows the polls (even the Clinton administration denied that it used polls for this purpose).

Regardless, presidential pollsters from all administrations since Nixon's have been known to poll on foreign and domestic issues alike. Nixon polled about Vietnam and about admitting China to the United Nations. Carter surveyed American attitudes toward Israel and the Iran hostage crisis. Reagan tracked polls on the Iran-Contra affair and the Marine barracks bombing in Lebanon. During President George H.W. Bush's administration, pollsters Robert Teeter and Fred Steeper conducted polls and focus groups both before and during the Gulf War. Examples of polling on domestic policy—busing, agriculture, government regulation, bilingual education, health care policy, energy, and the budget—abound. Presidential pollsters provide additional data before midterm elections and become pivotal during the president's reelection campaign. Typically, the fourth year of the president's term generates the highest spending on polling. Speech content is another area where pollsters can provide useful advice. Finally, all presidential pollsters need to collect national tracking polls on a regular basis to provide an internal baseline to compare against other polls. In short, presidential polling is a staple of the modern presidency.

Republican National Committee Polling Costs, 2001–2002

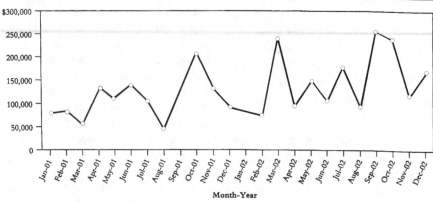

*Data obtained from fec.gov with the assistance of Larissa Davis and Elizabeth Redman of the Brookings Institution, April 2003.

Consumer of Polls: The Bush Political Machine

The way one political insider explained President Bush's attitude toward polling reinforced the president's campaign mantra: "One of the worst arguments a White House adviser can make to the president is to say that 'the polls show X.'" But despite the president's disdain for public opinion polls, he has created a formidable White House political operation that focuses closely on them. The Office of Strategic Initiatives monitors and analyzes the results of numerous public surveys by major networks and news organizations as well as the findings of privately commissioned polls. And access to state surveys and other polls conducted by GOP pollsters informs their analyses. Why does the nature of the White House political operation matter? Because no amount of polling is worthwhile unless it is properly analyzed and incorporated into White House policy and political discussions.

President Bush's chief political confidant, Karl Rove, is considered by Republicans and Democrats alike to be an extraordinarily shrewd presidential adviser. On entering the White House in 2001, Bush established the first White House Office of Strategic Initiatives and appointed Rove its director—giving him a perch from which to survey the political landscape with the aim of expanding the president's electoral coalition in 2004. Unlike Bush's father, who placed his chief political adviser, Lee Atwater, at the helm of the RNC, George W. Bush understands the importance of proximity. Though the president deliberately distances himself from pollster Jan van Lohuizen (political insiders claim the two rarely meet), his close relationship with Rove virtually ensures a key role for polling in presidential policymaking.

Assisting Rove as chief political adviser is Matthew Dowd, the RNC senior adviser who coordinates the pollsters and analyzes the political pulse with the help of van Lohuizen, who conducts focus groups as well as national surveys. And Fred Steeper, 1992 campaign pollster for Bush's father, is assigned a variety of special projects that address specific research ques-

tions, some of which involve focus groups. Combining the less "scientific" focus groups with polling enables the political shop to determine what people are thinking and then test those attitudes rigorously through national surveys. Unlike survey research, the focus group allows researchers to present text from a speech or a segment of a television ad and gauge the intensity of emotions, observe body language, and probe more deeply on key issues. The focus group alone may not be especially helpful, but combined with survey research, it can create a more refined questionnaire that zeroes in on previously tested issues and preferences. Similarly, the focus group technique can be applied after a national survey to probe specific questions and issues. The Steeper-van Lohuizen team clearly enhances the value of survey research while the Rove–Dowd–van Lohuizen/Steeper chain of command ensures that the pollsters stay well outside the political circle—and away from the eyes of the White House press corps.

The final part of this well-oiled political machine is the White House Office of Political Affairs director and recipient of polling data, Ken Mehlman. Since the Reagan administration, this office has become a standard component of all White House political operations, but its influence depends largely on the president and his chief aides. The first President Bush downplayed the office, and it experienced high turnover during the first term of the Clinton administration. But in today's White House, Ken Mehlman's job is deemed an important one—though unlike Karl Rove's macropolitical strategy, Mehlman tends to the care and feeding of state and local partisans in hopes of paving the way for victory in 2004.

White House Polling in Perspective: Perception is Everything

President Bush's use of polling is by no means pathbreaking, nor is the amount of polling particularly astounding. What is unusual about the Bush team's polling operation is the chasm between its words and actions. Never before has a White House engaged in such anti-polling rhetoric or built up such a buffer between the pollsters and the president. The placement of long-time Bush loyalist Dowd at the RNC to coordinate the polling means that the pollsters do not have contact with the White House. Such unusual behavior reflects a broader tension between a determined attempt to avoid the mistakes of Bush the elder—especially the failure after the Persian Gulf War to consider the implications of a stagnant economy for the 1992 reelection campaign—and a continuous effort to shed the vestiges of the Clinton administration. The Bush team fully understands the value of polling, but the perceived overuse of polling within the Clinton administration has led to serious overcompensation, which in turn has bred secrecy and denial. All presidents are subjected to the pressures of the "permanent campaign." Information is integral to any successful presidency. Polling is part of a broader game of politics and policymaking. No one can dictate how presidents use polls, but denying the role of polls in the policy process is fruitless.

KATHRYN DUNN TENPAS, a guest scholar in the Brookings Governance Studies program, is associate director of the University of Pennsylvania's Washington Semester Program.

The Pros From Dover

President Bush surrounded himself with what should have been a crack team of national security experts. So what went wrong? Did their system just not work, or did they have the wrong agenda?

JOHN PRADOS

There is a hilarious scene in the movie *M*A*S*H* where two young doctors from a field hospital at the front in the Korean War travel to Japan and proceed to have their way with local commanders and the military bureaucracy. Arriving to carry out the heart operation for which they have been summoned, the doctors call themselves the "pros from Dover."

In the way life has of imitating art, the national security process of the Bush administration has been the province of its own fresh set of professionals. The result has not been hilarity but something else. With the Bush people having gotten the United States enmeshed in situations of grave concern throughout the globe, it is important to ask whether the American government is up to handling the job, not in terms of capabilities but of policy process.

In the American system of government, the top executive authority, the president, is assisted in areas of foreign affairs and military matters by the National Security Council (NSC). The council consists of the president, vice president, secretary of state, and defense secretary. The national security adviser to the president does not have a statutory role but is typically made a senior member of the council. The director of central intelligence and chairman of the Joint Chiefs of Staff sit as advisers to the group. The president is the king of policy hill, of course, and may arrange the NSC and its work at his whim, organizing and reorganizing whenever it suits him. NSC staff members under the national security adviser directly serve the president by coordinating the issues and providing the chief executive with their understanding of the options, pros, and cons.

Three years into the Bush administration, in spite of a host of developments in the national security realm, there has yet to be any serious inquiry into its methods of policymaking and their impact on American security. That inquiry is overdue.

The Players

George W. Bush has certainly benefited from a dream team of senior advisers on his National Security Council. Bush chose carefully among people of conservative cast of mind to match

his own, and while one may deplore the ideology of the crew, the president's right to be served by the officials he wants is unquestioned. Ideology notwithstanding, the Bush people have the right stuff—the credentials to actually be the pros from Dover—from the top people on the NSC to the second tier at the agencies and staff. On January 21, 2001, an observer could have said this administration was primed for success.

In terms of organization of the policy process, the Bush administration also started out on familiar ground. Presidents create their own policy machinery, and different presidents have approached the national security process in a variety of ways.[1]

The Carter administration designed a two-committee structure that has become almost the standard NSC organization for subsequent presidencies, including that of George W. Bush. In the current scheme, the president meeting with his senior advisers constitutes the National Security Council. Without the president, the rump NSC meets as the Principals Committee, chaired by the vice president or national security adviser. These groups focus on decisions. Below them is the Deputies Committee, a group chaired by the deputy national security adviser, which concentrates on implementing the president's decisions. Staff assistants attend as required. Teleconferencing and secure video links between various U.S. government centers have enabled greater flexibility in participation, but the essence of the system remains the same.

The most remarkable aspect of Bush's national security organization is the role of the vice president. Historically, vice presidents have had a relatively minor impact on national security decision making. Walter Mondale and Al Gore were more active under presidents Carter and Clinton, and Bush's father, George H. W. Bush, had an enhanced role under Ronald Reagan. In the current administration, however, Dick Cheney is of critical importance in virtually all aspects of national security policy. From the first moments of George W. Bush's presidency, Cheney functioned as the power behind the throne, privately advocating policies, then coming out in public with discourse designed to build constituencies for those same policies. He also became the official whom Bush tapped for the tough jobs—and the president's hatchet man. Cheney emerged as an assistant with an agenda more ample than that of his master. His role encouraging Bush to make war on Iraq has been so widely remarked it has virtually eclipsed his work early in the administration heading a presidential commission on energy policy, his views on military transformation, and the task force on federal-local antiterrorism cooperation that Bush appointed him to chair four months before the 9/11 attacks.

To match his policy role, the vice president has crafted a sort of mini-NSC staff among his White House retinue. Where Al Gore as vice president employed Leon Fuerth as his national security adviser (plus a couple of staff aides), and Bush's father, as vice president under Reagan, had a security staff of two professionals (plus aides), Cheney employs a national security staff of 15. The importance Cheney gives that staff is indicated by the fact that his own overall chief of staff, I. Lewis ("Scooter") Libby, serves simultaneously as the vice president's national security adviser. Early last year, at a key moment in the run-up to the Iraq war, Cheney's deputy national security adviser Eric Edelman was appointed U.S. ambassador to Turkey, another indication of the standing of the Cheney national security staff. Edelman was succeeded by Aaron Friedberg, a China expert and former director of policy planning on the Cheney staff. That the staff even had a policy-planning component demonstrates the quantum advance of the Cheney operation over the staff resources available to previous vice presidents.

Cheney himself is no stranger to national security issues, or to government for that matter. In his current incarnation he is mostly known for his role as chief executive of the Halliburton Corporation during the 1990s, but less noted is the extent to which Halliburton worked with and for the U.S. military. More to the point, Cheney was defense secretary—the job Donald Rumsfeld now has—during the first Bush administration, including the first Gulf War. Before that, Cheney served as White House chief of staff to President Gerald R. Ford from 1975 to early 1977 and deputy chief of staff 1974-1975. At the time, he was deputy to Donald Rumsfeld, whom President Ford subsequently sent to the Pentagon. In the Ford White House, Cheney worked on a number of national security issues, most notably advising Ford on how to handle the intelligence scandals of 1975. Cheney was an architect of the presidential commission on intelligence (the Rockefeller Commission) created by Ford in an effort to head off what became the Church and Pike Committee investigations. While the attempt proved unsuccessful, Cheney gained experience he put to work later as a member of Congress and then in his own Pentagon job.

Next to the vice president, the person closest to the Oval Office is the national security adviser. For George Bush this is Condoleezza Rice. Like Cheney—like a number of the pros from Dover—Rice is no stranger to the issues, or even to the national security staff. Retired Air Force Gen. Brent Scowcroft (who held the post of national security adviser for Gerald Ford, alongside Cheney and Rumsfeld) discovered Rice during the 1980s at the Aspen Institute. She was then a recently minted academic with a doctorate in international relations from the University of Denver. Her dissertation was on Soviet political control of the Czechoslovak armed forces. She taught at Stan-

ford University. When Scowcroft did a second tour as national security adviser in the administration of President George H. W. Bush, he brought in "Condi," as she is familiarly known, as director for Soviet affairs. Rice was active on the NSC staff during the passing of the Cold War, when the Soviet Union collapsed, Germany reunified, and the old Yugoslavia disintegrated, leaving in its wake the Bosnian civil war.

Among the stories told about Rice that show her willingness to do whatever was necessary is one from the beginning of the first Gulf War, when the NSC staff person responsible for the Iraq-Kuwait region was Richard Haass. When the first President Bush needed a set of talking points for his initial public comment on the Iraqi invasion of Kuwait, Haass could not respond quickly enough because, unfamiliar with computers, he had to hunt and peck at the keyboard. Rice took over and typed out the paper even though Middle East matters were far from her own bailiwick. In 1991 Rice returned to Stanford as a teacher—but not for long. A month after receiving tenure in 1993 she was appointed provost of the university and held that key management position during difficult years. She quickly rallied to the presidential campaign of George W. Bush, however, and was its foreign policy director from early 1999. Rice not only coordinated Bush's issues papers but kept in line the "Vulcans"—the brain trust of national security experts who periodically assembled to give Bush the benefit of their accumulated wisdom. All the Vulcans (Richard Armitage, Robert Blackwill, Stephen J. Hadley, Richard Perle, Paul Wolfowitz, Dov Zakheim, Robert Zoellick) went on to important jobs or advisory posts in the Bush administration, and it was hardly surprising that Rice landed as national security adviser.

Stephen J. Hadley became Rice's deputy. The only other of the Vulcans to make the leap to work directly within the president's official family, Hadley regarded himself as a detail man. He too had a national security past, having served as assistant secretary of defense for policy under Dick Cheney in the first Bush administration. For those who worried about the influence of Cheney in the White House, Hadley's presence suggested that the vice president, in addition to having his own mini-NSC staff, simultaneously had a front man who was deputy director of the Rice staff itself.

As for the seniors, the members of the actual council of the NSC, they were pros from Dover, too. Donald Rumsfeld has already been mentioned. He is the only person to serve twice as defense secretary—in two different administrations, separated by more than two decades. Colin Powell, retired four-star army general, had been chairman of the Joint Chiefs of Staff during the first Gulf War, a deputy national security adviser to Ronald Reagan, and military assistant to Defense Secretary Caspar Weinberger. CIA Director George Tenet was held over from the Clinton administration and had worked on the Hill, at the White House, or at the CIA since the late 1980s. Their seconds, people like Wolfowitz and Armitage, had similar credentials.

The System

President George W. Bush enhanced the role of his national security adviser by endowing her with cabinet rank. But formal organization of the system remained in limbo until mid-February 2001, when Bush issued his National Security Presidential Directive (NSPD) 1. That document ended speculation as to Vice President Cheney's role—a number of observers had anticipated that Cheney's deep interest in these matters would be reflected by his being made chairman of the Principals Committee.[2] This did not happen. Instead Rice, as national security adviser, would chair the group. What did happen was more significant: By avoiding the chairmanship of the Principals Committee, Cheney left himself free to be an advocate at national security meetings rather than having any responsibility to ensure that all views be aired.

The other significant thing about NSPD 1 was its lateness in the cycle. Most new administrations enter office determined to hit the ground running and typically put out their directives on NSC machinery their first day in office. Bush did not get around to this business for almost a month. By then there had already been two meetings of the Principals Committee. Even the appointments of Condi Rice and the top NSC staffers date from January 22, not the day after the inauguration. The implication is that, at least at the outset, Bush did not consider the national security agenda his top priority.

In terms of size and depth, the Rice NSC staff diminished from the standard under the Clinton administration, but this had more to do with notions of streamlining than with some idea of reducing the importance of national security. Rice cut the staff as a whole by about a third while reducing the number of professional staff from 70 to about 60. She eliminated the legislative affairs and communications offices, limited the staff to a single speechwriter and press spokesperson, and recast some functions. Most importantly, the Russian office merged into a single new desk that included all of Europe, the Balkans, and the former Soviet republics. The Asian affairs office reabsorbed Southeast Asia, which had been assigned to another regional unit in the Clinton White House. North Africa and the Middle East were combined as well. Africa and the Western Hemisphere completed the list of regional offices on the NSC staff. There were also functional specializations, including offices for defense policy and arms control and for intelligence.

Clinton had had an NSC staff unit to supervise nonproliferation and export controls. Under Rice this was reconceptualized as "Nonproliferation Strategy, Counterproliferation, and Homeland Defense." This is instructive for it served as a device to take the ballistic missile defense issue out of the defense policy basket and put it in the much more ideological framework of "homeland defense." That in turn became awkward after the September 11, 2001, attacks, when an Office of Homeland Defense was created at the White House as a parallel to the NSC staff, but in which "homeland defense" held a very different meaning.

The Clinton NSC staff also had a unit covering "transnational threats" and put terrorism at the top of that list. Clinton appointed Richard Clarke, a hard-headed advocate for proactive measures against those threats, to head the unit. Clarke stayed over into the Bush presidency even though, as a press account put it several weeks into the new era, what to do with the transnational threats office was "still up in the air."[3] It is here that the real story begins.

Bush and Terrorism

Bill Clinton's last national security adviser, Samuel ("Sandy") Berger, held a number of briefings for Condoleezza Rice and the incoming national security staff as part of the transition from the Clinton to Bush presidencies. Every NSC staff office had been directed to compile a report and present its view of America's strengths and weaknesses to the new crowd. According to an account that has been disputed, the only one of these sessions Sandy Berger personally attended was that which concerned terrorism (Rice has said through a spokesperson that she recalls no briefing at which Berger was present).[4] Berger had left by the time Richard Clarke made the main presentation, but there can be no doubt that the briefing highlighted the need to act on terrorism.

Berger clearly had terrorism on his plate. The question is, did Rice? Berger would tell the joint House-Senate committee investigating the September 11, 2001, attacks that he had convened the Principals Committee every day for a month in an effort to stave off terrorist attacks timed around the millennium celebrations.[5] He quoted himself as telling Rice, "You're going to spend more time during your four years on terrorism generally and Al Qaeda specifically than any [other] issue."[6] For her part, Rice had numerous questions for Clarke, who was asked to prepare a paper on steps against Al Qaeda. Clarke not only had the paper on Stephen J. Hadley's desk within days of the inauguration, he saw the opportunity to get the new president to sign on to an action plan against terrorism, and his paper amounted to an outline. So far, so good. But Clarke's plan then sat gathering dust for weeks.

In speeches, articles, and conversations during the 2000 campaign, Rice had written and spoken of the need in national security to separate the marginal issues from what was truly important.

What Rice and the Bush team made centrally important in the weeks and months after entering office was not terrorism but changing the U.S.-European relationship. The troubles with "Old Europe" that seem so intractable in the wake of the Iraqi war did not just happen coincidentally in 2002-2003. They were prefigured in the very stuff of the NSC staff reorganization, when the Russian and Western European offices were consolidated. Publicly the Bush administration sought to end any notion of a special relationship with Russia, the former Soviet Union, cutting back funding for special cooperative programs designed to help secure Russian nuclear weapons and expertise, abrogating the Anti-Ballistic Missile (ABM) Treaty, and in a variety of other ways. The move on the ABM Treaty also came as a shock to Old Europe, as did Bush's rejection of the Kyoto protocols on environmental action, and the equally sudden U.S. coyness on formation of an international criminal court. When President Bush made his first visit to Europe in June 2001, these issues were the main stuff of American diplomacy.

On the overarching front of defense policy, the maneuver on the ABM Treaty is itself indicative of the Bush administration's goals. Defense Secretary Rumsfeld used the word "transformation" so many times that it became enshrined as the descriptive term for Bush defense policy. Ballistic missile defenses were a key component, and indeed President Bush chose to deploy a technically immature defense system just to ensure that the United States had committed itself to this program. Rumsfeld's talk about space platforms, his predilection for air force programs, and his fight with the army over its future were the stuff of the transformation.

While circumstances dictated that an action plan on terrorism needed to move to the top of policy hill, the government was preoccupied with anything but that issue. It was only after Bush intervened that anything happened at all. One spring morning, following the departure of CIA briefers who had just given him news in the President's Daily Brief (PDB) of a manhunt for one particular terrorist, Bush complained to Rice: "I'm tired of swatting at flies. . . . I want to play offense, I want to take the fight to the terrorists," Bush said.[7] Rice took the implication that President Bush wanted a plan to attack the terrorists. When she asked the NSC staff how they could put something together, Richard Clarke had his original plan ready.

By late April 2001 the NSC was ready for a policy review on terrorism. After, we are told, six weeks of preliminary sessions, the Deputies Committee met on April 30 to consider an outline plan that Clarke presented. Stephen J. Hadley chaired the meeting, which included Scooter Libby (for Cheney), Richard Armitage (for Powell), Paul Wolfowitz (for Rumsfeld), and John McLaughlin (for Tenet). Here was a case in which the State Department favored going ahead but the CIA proved more cautious. Rather than initiating action, the Deputies Committee called for not one but three policy reviews, one on Al Qaeda, a second on Pakistani internal politics, and a third on the India-Pakistan problem.[8] According to Deputy National Security Adviser Hadley, "the goal was to move beyond the policy of containment, criminal prosecution, and limited retaliation for specific attacks, toward attempting to 'roll back' Al Qaeda."[9] The device of adding extra policy reviews inevitably slowed action, however. As Hadley noted in his response to 9/11 congressional investigators quoted above, between May and July there would be four successive meetings of the NSC Deputies Committee "directly related to the regional issues that had to be resolved in order to adopt a more aggressive strategy."[10] The last one of these sessions discussed the text of a draft presidential directive on July 16.

Meanwhile, on May 8 President Bush created a new unit to focus on terrorism within the Federal Emergency Management Agency, and a new interagency board to consider terrorism issues. He put Cheney in charge of that operation. This was the only actual action President Bush took before September 11, 2001, and it was not about rollback. Cheney's mandate was merely to study preparedness for homeland defense and make recommendations by October.

A second group, the Counterterrorism Security Group (CSG), part of the NSC interagency machinery, was chaired by Richard Clarke. It would be the CSG, not the vice president, that acted, or more properly, reacted. Beginning in March, U.S. intelligence and military sources received a series of reports indicating possible terrorist attacks. First came a report that Al Qaeda operatives in Canada might attack the United States in April.

In April, one source made a rather suggestive speculation that Osama bin Laden was interested in commercial aircraft pilots as terrorists for "spectacular and traumatic" attacks. In May came a report that Al Qaeda supporters were planning to enter the United States to carry out some operation using high explosives. There was also a Pentagon report that seven key suspected terrorists had begun moving toward Canada, the United States, and Britain. Between May and July, the National Security Agency intercepted no fewer than 33 communications suggesting an attack, including one evaluated at the time as an order to execute the plan. In June, the CIA Counterterrorism Center received information that key operatives were disappearing from view. At the end of June, Clarke convened the CSG, and by July 5 there were sufficient alarms to warrant a meeting among Rice, Clarke, and presidential chief of staff Andrew Card.

By then the intelligence scene had shifted and threats seemed centered on the American embassies in Rome, Paris, or Ankara. The CSG met again on July 6, and from then through the end of August, Clarke kept up meetings two or three times a week.[11]

In short, numerous disturbing intelligence reports came in over a period of months *after* President Bush had declared he wanted to go after terrorists, a period of time during which nothing happened with the U.S. government's planning for a rollback of Al Qaeda. Such Bush administration actions that occurred consisted entirely of putting certain selected military forces on precautionary (and defensive) alerts, or issuing warnings to the airlines.

Bush left for Crawford, Texas, and summer vacation on August 4. Two days later, he was given a fresh intelligence report—the PDB again mentioned terrorist attack. As characterized by national security adviser Rice, this PDB "was an analytic report that talked about [Osama bin Laden's] methods of operation, talked about what he had done historically in 1997, in 1998. It mentioned hijacking, but hijacking in the traditional sense, and in a sense said that the most important and most likely thing was that he would take over an airliner holding passengers [and then make demands]."[12]

Much has been speculated about what Bush knew about the Al Qaeda terrorist threat, especially after the leak of the existence of the August 6, 2001 PDB and the report that it had mentioned aircraft hijacking. But the most important thing about the intelligence reports is something we already know: Neither the August 6 PDB, any of the other reports, nor the daily flurry of NSC staff activity on terrorist warnings moved Bush to demand the action plan he had supposedly called for in the spring, to ask that its preparation be accelerated, or to take any other action whatsoever. There is also no indication that Rice, whose job it was to be aware of these alarming reports, made any move to remind the president of his interest in the matter.

Absent presidential initiative, in fact, the plan to roll back Al Qaeda sat dormant six full weeks after mid-July 2001. The draft National Security Presidential Directive was finally considered by the NSC Principals Committee on September 4, and the group recommended that President Bush approve it. When

Rice, or others, claim that an approved directive was on Bush's desk on 9/11, they exaggerate. The president had approved nothing. He had received a recommendation to sign a directive that had finally worked its way up through the bureaucracy.

The response of the Bush administration after 9/11 was rather different. When investigators raised questions regarding what Bush had done about intelligence he had received before the attacks, Vice President Cheney mounted a frontal assault on the 9/11 investigators, alleging they were responsible for the appearance in the press of reports of National Security Agency intercepts regarding the attacks, intercepts that White House spokesmen had themselves mentioned in press briefings in the days immediately after 9/11. Cheney demanded and got an FBI investigation of the investigators.

Ever since the 9/11 attacks the Bush White House has taken pains to avoid the revelation of any of the intelligence material provided to the president. The White House denied this material to the joint congressional committee investigating 9/11. It has also stonewalled the national commission inquiring into the attacks. The official rationale has been that no one should ever see the reports provided to a president.

That is not a legitimate declassification policy. A number of PDBs have been declassified and are in the public domain, including ones sent to President John F. Kennedy during the Cuban Missile Crisis and to President Lyndon Johnson during the Vietnam war. Excerpts of PDBs have been leaked on other occasions, not only the one to Bush for August 6, 2001, but one to his father before the Gulf War of 1990-1991. Our democracy has not been shaken by these revelations. And declassification is an ultimate step; the issue here is whether official inquiries operating under full security safeguards are entitled to view documents that are material to their investigations. The real reason to shield them is political: They would reveal the extent of warnings to George W. Bush in the face of which he stood immobile.

The November 2003 Bush compromise with the National Commission on Terrorist Attacks Upon the United States is designed to protect the president while appearing to cooperate. Under the arrangement, the White House will provide edited texts of some PDBs to a team of four (out of ten) commissioners, who will be permitted to take notes that can then be edited by the White House. Two commissioners will be permitted to review all the PDBs and ask that the White House make available additional ones. This formula will be cumbersome in practice and will not ensure public confidence in the 9/11 investigation.

Fast Forward

The truth about 9/11 is one of two things. Either Rice's NSC machinery did not work, or else it worked perfectly to ensure that what Bush and his cohorts considered a marginal issue like terrorism did not clutter up the schedule of a president intent on another agenda—transforming America's relationships with traditional allies and former enemies. Either of these conclusions is disturbing. Once the Iraq war is factored into the equation the outlook is even more troubling. Again the NSC

machinery operated in a fashion to prevent important objections or alternative policies from coming to the fore. U.S. policy going into the Iraq war was indifferent to alliance politics, to failures to attain needed U.N. approval, to U.S. military objections that the war plan was inadequate, to intelligence warnings that war would be succeeded by guerrilla resistance, to global public opinion, to international disarmament monitors who failed to turn up evidence supporting the Bush rationale for war, and more.[13] Dick Cheney served as an important driver of the policy that would be implemented. Condoleezza Rice became one of its most prominent public advocates; indeed Rice has served far more frequently as a public proponent than any of her national security adviser predecessors. Even Stephen J. Hadley, in the infamous manipulation of speech texts now encapsulated as the "Sixteen Words" controversy, made key contributions to a course of action that became an international and domestic political disaster.

The gang who produced all this were pros from Dover, using a tried and tested organizational structure for national security machinery. How could it be? Hubris, wishful thinking, incorrect assessment of the major issue facing the United States, wrongheaded notions of imposing change on the world—each played a role. Yet no heads have rolled. President George W. Bush promised to bring a new standard of accountability to Washington. In *that* he has succeeded. The picture is not a pretty one.

Notes

1. An overview of presidents' practices is in John Prados, *Keepers of the Keys: A History of the National Security Council from Truman to Bush* (New York: William Morrow, 1991). The Bush in the title is, however, George H. W. Bush, the current president's father. There is no good study of the NSC during the Clinton years.

2. Jane Perlez, "Directive Says Rice, Bush Aide, Won't Be Upstaged by Cheney," *New York Times*, Feb. 16, 2001, p. A10.

3. Karen DeYoung and Steven Mufson, "A Leaner and Less Visible NSC," *Washington Post*, Feb. 10, 2001, p. A6.

4. Massimo Calabresi et al., "They Had a Plan: Special Report: The Secret History," *Time*, August 12, 2002, p. 30. Clinton-era NSC staffer Daniel Benjamin, who worked with Richard Clarke in the transnational threats office, confirms both the briefing session itself and the presence of Berger. See Daniel Benjamin and Steven Simon, *The Age of Sacred Terror* (New York: Random House, 2002), p. 328.

5. Samuel R. Berger, "Joint Intelligence Committee Testimony," prepared text (copy in author's possession), September 19, 2002, pp. 4-5.

6. Daniel Benjamin and Steven Simon, *The Age of Sacred Terror*, p. 328.

7. Barton Gellman, "A Strategy's Cautious Evolution: Before September 11 the Bush Anti-Terror Effort Was Mostly Ambition," *Washington Post*, Jan. 20, 2002, p. A1.

8. The main sources for this account are the Barton Gellman story cited in note 7 and the study by a large team of *Time* correspondents cited in note 4.

9. United States Congress (107th Congress, 2nd Session). Senate Select Committee on Intelligence and House Permanent Select Committee on Intelligence, *Report: Joint Inquiry Into Intelli-*

*gence Community Activities Before and After the Terrorist At-
tacks of September 11, 2001,* hereafter cited as 9/11
Congressional Report (Washington: Government Printing Office,
2003), p. 235. White House sources deny that Richard Clarke's
original January memorandum had featured an actual "plan," Calabresi et al. (cited in footnote 4) note that Slide 14 of Clarke's
presidential transition briefing on dealing with Al Qaeda included
the words "rollback" and "breakup." Although dated December
2002, disputes with the Bush White House over secrecy of material on some of the very subjects under discussion here delayed
the actual appearance of this report for many months, into the fall
of 2003.

10. Ibid.

11. The data on intelligence indications is from the 9/11 Congressional Report, pp. 201-205; the material on Counterterrorism Se-

curity Group activities is from Condoleezza Rice at her news
conference of May 16, 2002 as cited in "Excerpt From National
Security Adviser's Statement," *New York Times,* May 17, 2002,
p. A22.

12. Rice news conference, May 16, 2002.

13. This subject cannot be treated at length here, but see John Prados,
Hoodwinked (forthcoming).

JOHN PRADOS is an analyst with the National Security Archive in
Washington, D.C. His current books are *Hoodwinked* (forthcoming),
on America headed into the Iraq war, and *White House Tapes* (2003),
a selection of recordings that show American presidents at work on key
issues of their times.

UNIT 6

U.S. International Economic Strategy

Unit Selections

25. **America's Sticky Power**, Walter Russell Mead
26. **The New Axis of Oil**, Flynt Leverett and Pierre Noël

Key Points to Consider

- Which type of international system, global free trade or regional trading blocs, is in America's national interest? Explain.

- Which country is the more important trading partner for the United States—Japan, Europe, or Mexico? Defend your answer.

- Select a country in need of debt relief or foreign aid. What type of foreign aid strategy should the United States pursue toward it? How does this compare with current U.S. foreign aid programs?

- Design an economic strategy for ensuring that the United States has an adequate supply of oil and other natural resources in the future.

- Put together an eight-person delegation to the next round of WTO trade talks. Defend your selections. What negotiating instructions would you give them?

- What measures would you use to create a ranking of how powerful a country's economy is? How high would the United States rank?

Student Web Site

www.mhcls.com/online

Internet References

Further information regarding these Web sites may be found in this book's preface or online.

International Monetary Fund (IMF)
http://www.imf.org

United States Agency for International Development
http://www.usaid.gov/

United States Trade Representative
http://www.ustr.gov

World Bank
http://www.worldbank.org

As in so many areas of American foreign policy, the selection of U.S. international economic strategies during the cold war seems to have been a rather straightforward process and the accompanying policy debates fairly minor compared to the situation that exists today. At the most fundamental level, it was taken for granted that the American economy would best be served by the existence of a global free trade system. To that end, international organizations were set up whose collective task it was to oversee the operation of the postwar international economic order. Foremost among them were the General Agreement on Tariffs and Trade (GATT), the International Monetary Fund (IMF), and the International Bank for Reconstruction and Development (the World Bank). It was also widely accepted that many states would not be able to resist pressure from the Soviet Union or from domestic communist parties, due to the weak state of their economies and military establishments. Thus, containing communism would require foreign aid programs designed to transfer American economic and military expertise, goods and services, and financial resources to key states.

Events of the 1960s and 1970s shook the international economic system at its political and economic foundations. There followed a period of more than 20 years in which the international economic system was managed through a series of ad hoc responses to crises and the continued inability of foreign aid programs to produce real growth in the less developed world. U.S. international economic policy during this period was often characterized as one of "benign neglect."

The adequacy of this response is questioned today. Policy makers and citizens today see the international economic order as highly volatile and perhaps even threatening. The focal point of their concern is with the process of globalization. The IMF de-

fines globalization as the growing economic interdependence of countries through the increasing volume and variety of border transactions in goods, services, and capital flows. Most fundamentally, globalization is change-inducing because of its ability to link activities around the world. From a policy perspective the most significant aspect of globalization is that the international economic activity has become so large, rapid, and dense that it has outstripped the ability of governments and international organizations to manage it. Susan Strange described the situation as one of "casino capitalism" because, just as in a casino, a large element of luck determines the success or failure of international economic policies.

It is against this very changed backdrop of globalization that American international economic policy is now made and carried out. We can identify at least three major dimensions to American international economic foreign policy. They are trade, monetary policy, and foreign aid. Subsumed within them are a host of challenging issues and trade-offs such as economic growth, worker's rights, environmental protection, and global equity. The articles in this section highlight important issues encompassing questions in these areas.

The first reading, "America's Sticky Power," identifies economic power as a unique instrument of foreign policy having advantages that neither soft power nor military power possess. It attracts others to the U.S. voluntarily and then entraps them in a web of relations from which they cannot escape easily or without great cost. "The New Axis of Oil" examines how structural changes in the international oil market will impact on American economic prosperity and national security. The two key players in this new marketplace of buyers and sellers are Russia and China.

America's Sticky Power

U.S. military force and cultural appeal have kept the United States at the top of the global order. But the hegemon cannot live on guns and Hollywood alone. U.S. economic policies and institutions act as "sticky power," attracting other countries to the U.S. system and then trapping them in it. Sticky power can help stabilize Iraq, bring rule of law to Russia, and prevent armed conflict between the United States and China.

WALTER RUSSELL MEAD

Since its earliest years, the United States has behaved as a global power. Not always capable of dispatching great fleets and mighty armies to every corner of the planet, the United States has nonetheless invariably kept one eye on the evolution of the global system, and the U.S. military has long served internationally. The United States has not always boasted the world's largest or most influential economy, but the country has always regarded trade in global terms, generally nudging the world toward economic integration. U.S. ideological impulses have also been global. The poet Ralph Waldo Emerson wrote of the first shot fired in the American Revolution as "the shot heard 'round the world," and Americans have always thought that their religious and political values should prevail around the globe.

Historically, security threats and trade interests compelled Americans to think globally. The British sailed across the Atlantic to burn Washington, D.C.; the Japanese flew from carriers in the Pacific to bomb Pearl Harbor. Trade with Asia and Europe, as well as within the Western Hemisphere, has always been vital to U.S. prosperity. U.S. President Thomas Jefferson sent the Navy to the Mediterranean to fight against the Barbary pirates to safeguard U.S. trade in 1801. Commodore Matthew Perry opened up Japan in the 1850s partly to assure decent treatment for survivors of sunken U.S. whaling ships that washed up on Japanese shores. And the last shots in the U.S. Civil War were fired from a Confederate commerce raider attacking Union shipping in the remote waters of the Arctic Ocean.

The rise of the United States to superpower status followed from this global outlook. In the 20th century, as the British system of empire and commerce weakened and fell, U.S. foreign-policymakers faced three possible choices: prop up the British Empire, ignore the problem and let the rest of the world go about its business, or replace Britain and take on the dirty job of enforcing a world order. Between the onset of World War I and the beginning of the Cold War, the United States tried all three, ultimately taking Britain's place as the gyroscope of world order.

However, the Americans were replacing the British at a moment when the rules of the game were changing forever. The United States could not become just another empire or great power playing the old games of dominance with rivals and allies. Such competition led to war, and war between great powers was no longer an acceptable part of the international system. No, the United States was going to have to attempt something that no other nation had ever accomplished, something that many theorists of international relations would swear was impossible. The United States needed to build a system that could end thousands of years of great power conflicts, constructing a framework of power that would bring enduring peace to the whole world—repeating globally what ancient Egypt, China, and Rome had each accomplished on a regional basis.

To complicate the task a bit more, the new hegemon would not be able to use some of the methods available to the Romans and others. Reducing the world's countries and civilizations to tributary provinces was beyond any military power the United States could or would bring to bear. The United States would have to develop a new way for sovereign states to coexist in a world of weapons of mass destruction and of prickly rivalries among religions, races, cultures, and states.

In his 2002 book, *The Paradox of American Power: Why the World's Only Superpower Can't Go It Alone*, Harvard University political scientist Joseph S. Nye Jr. discusses the varieties of power that the United States can deploy as it builds its world order. Nye focuses on two types of power: hard and soft. In his analysis, hard power is military or economic force that coerces others to follow a particular course of action. By contrast, soft power—cultural power, the power of example, the power of ideas and ideals—works more subtly; it makes others want what you want. Soft power upholds the U.S. world order because it influences others to like the U.S. system and support it of their own free will [see sidebar: A Sticky History Lesson].

Nye's insights on soft power have attracted significant attention and will continue to have an important role in U.S. policy debates. But the distinction Nye suggests between two types of hard power—military and economic power—has received less consideration than it deserves. Traditional military power can usefully be called sharp power; those resisting it will feel bayonets pushing and prodding them in the direction they must go. This power is the foundation of the U.S. system.

Economic power can be thought of as sticky power, which comprises a set of economic institutions and policies that attracts others toward U.S. influence and then traps them in it. Together with soft power (the values, ideas, habits, and politics inherent in the system), sharp and sticky power sustain U.S. hegemony and make something as artificial and historically arbitrary as the U.S.-led global system appear desirable, inevitable, and permanent.

Sharp Power

Sharp power is a very practical and unsentimental thing. U.S. military policy follows rules that would have been understandable to the Hittites or the Roman Empire. Indeed, the U.S. military is the institution whose command structure is most like that of Old World monarchies—the president, after consultation with the Joint Chiefs, issues orders, which the military, in turn, obeys.

Like Samson in the temple of the Philistines, a collapsing U.S. economy would inflict enormous, unacceptable damage on the rest of the world.

Of course, security starts at home, and since the 1823 proclamation of the Monroe Doctrine, the cardinal principle of U.S. security policy has been to keep European and Asian powers out of the Western Hemisphere. There would be no intriguing great powers, no intercontinental alliances, and, as the United States became stronger, no European or Asian military bases from Point Barrow, Alaska, to the tip of Cape Horn, Chile.

The makers of U.S. security policy also have focused on the world's sea and air lanes. During peacetime, such lanes are vital to the prosperity of the United States and its allies; in wartime, the United States must control the sea and air lanes to support U.S. allies and supply military forces on other continents. Britain was almost defeated by Germany's U-boats in World War I and II; in today's world of integrated markets, any interruption of trade flows through such lanes would be catastrophic.

Finally (and fatefully), the United States considers the Middle East an area of vital concern. From a U.S. perspective, two potential dangers lurk in the Middle East. First, some outside power, such as the Soviet Union during the Cold War, can try to control Middle Eastern oil or at least interfere with secure supplies for the United States and its allies. Second, one country in the Middle East could take over the region and try to do the same thing. Egypt, Iran, and, most recently, Iraq have all tried and thanks largely to U.S. policy—have all failed. For all its novel dangers, today's efforts by al Qaeda leader Osama bin Laden and his followers to create a theocratic power in the region that could control oil resources and extend dictatorial power throughout the Islamic world resembles other threats that the United States has faced in this region during the last 60 years.

As part of its sharp-power strategy to address these priorities, the United States maintains a system of alliances and bases in-tended to promote stability in Asia, Europe, and the Middle East. Overall, as of the end of September 2003, the United States had just over 250,000 uniformed military members stationed outside its frontiers (not counting those involved in Operation Iraqi Freedom); around 43 percent were stationed on NATO territory and approximately 32 percent in Japan and South Korea. Additionally, the United States has the ability to transport significant forces to these theaters and to the Middle East should tensions rise, and it preserves the ability to control the sea lanes and air corridors necessary to the security of its forward bases. Moreover, the United States maintains the world's largest intelligence and electronic surveillance organizations. Estimated to exceed $30 billion in 2003, the U.S. intelligence budget is larger than the individual military budgets of Saudi Arabia, Syria, and North Korea.

Over time, U.S. strategic thinking has shifted toward overwhelming military superiority as the surest foundation for national security. That is partly for the obvious reasons of greater security, but it is partly also because supremacy can be an important deterrent. Establishing an overwhelming military supremacy might not only deter potential enemies from military attack; it might also discourage other powers from trying to match the U.S. buildup. In the long run, advocates maintain, this strategy could be cheaper and safer than staying just a nose in front of the pack.

Sticky Power

Economic, or sticky, power is different from both sharp and soft power—it is based neither on military compulsion nor on simple coincidence of wills. Consider the carnivorous sundew plant, which attracts its prey with a kind of soft power, a pleasing scent that lures insects toward its sap. But once the victim has touched the sap, it is stuck; it can't get away. That is sticky power; that is how economic power works.

Sticky power has a long history. Both Britain and the United States built global economic systems that attracted other countries. Britain's attracted the United States into participating in the British system of trade and investment during the 19th century. The London financial markets provided investment capital that enabled U.S. industries to grow, while Americans benefited from trading freely throughout the British Empire. Yet, U.S. global trade was in some sense hostage to the British Navy—the United States could trade with the world as long as it had Britain's friendship, but an interruption in that friendship would mean financial collapse. Therefore, a strong lobby against war with Britain always existed in the United States. Trade-dependent New England almost seceded from the United States during the War of 1812, and at every crisis in Anglo-American relations for the next century, England could count on a strong lobby of merchants and bankers who would be ruined by war between the two English-speaking powers.

The world economy that the United States set out to lead after World War II had fallen far from the peak of integration reached under British leadership. The two world wars and the Depression ripped the delicate webs that had sustained the earlier system. In the Cold War years, as it struggled to rebuild and

A Sticky History Lesson

Germany's experience in World War I shows how "sticky power"—the power of one nation's economic institutions and policies—can act as a weapon. During the long years of peace before the war, Germany was drawn into the British-led world trading system, and its economy became more and more trade-dependent. Local industries depended on imported raw materials. German manufacturers depended on foreign markets. Germany imported wheat and beef from the Americas, where the vast and fertile plains of the United States and the pampas of South America produced food much more cheaply than German agriculture could do at home. By 1910, such economic interdependence was so great that many, including Norman Angell, author of *The Great Illusion,* thought that wars had become so ruinously expensive that the age of warfare was over.

Not quite. Sticky power failed to keep World War I from breaking out, but it was vital to Britain's victory. Once the war started, Britain cut off the world trade Germany had grown to depend upon, while, thanks to Britain's Royal Navy, the British and their allies continued to enjoy access to the rest of the world's goods. Shortages of basic materials and foods dogged Germany all during the war. By the winter of 1916-17, the Germans were seriously hungry. Meanwhile, hoping to even the odds, Germany tried to cut the Allies off from world markets with the U-boat campaigns in the North Atlantic. That move brought the United States into the war at a time when nothing else could have saved the Allied cause.

Finally, in the fall of 1918, morale in the German armed forces and among civilians collapsed, fueled in part by the shortages. These conditions, not military defeat, forced the German leadership to ask for an armistice. Sticky power was Britain's greatest weapon in World War I. It may very well be the United States' greatest weapon in the 21st century.

—*W.R.M.*

improve upon the Old World system, the United States had to change both the monetary base and the legal and political framework of the world's economic system.

The United States built its sticky power on two foundations: an international monetary system and free trade. The Bretton Woods agreements of 1944 made the U.S. dollar the world's central currency, and while the dollar was still linked to gold at least in theory for another generation, the U.S. Federal Reserve could increase the supply of dollars in response to economic needs. The result for almost 30 years was the magic combination of an expanding monetary base with price stability. These conditions helped produce the economic miracle that transformed living standards in the advanced West and in Japan. The collapse of the Bretton Woods system in 1973 ushered in a global economic crisis, but, by the 1980s, the system was functioning almost as well as ever with a new regime of floating exchange rates in which the U.S. dollar remained critical.

The progress toward free trade and economic integration represents one of the great unheralded triumphs of U.S. foreign policy in the 20th century. Legal and economic experts, largely from the United States or educated in U.S. universities, helped poor countries build the institutions that could reassure foreign investors, even as developing countries increasingly relied on state-directed planning and investment to jump-start their economies. Instead of gunboats, international financial institutions sent bankers and consultants around the world.

Behind all this activity was the United States' willingness to open its markets—even on a nonreciprocal basis—to exports from Europe, Japan, and poor nations. This policy, part of the overall strategy of containing communism, helped consolidate support around the world for the U.S. system. The role of the dollar as a global reserve currency, along with the expansionary bias of U.S. fiscal and monetary authorities, facilitated what became known as the "locomotive of the global economy" and the "consumer of last resort." U.S. trade deficits stimulated production and consumption in the rest of the world, increasing the prosperity of other countries and their willingness to participate in the U.S.-led global economy.

Opening domestic markets to foreign competitors remained (and remains) one of the most controversial elements in U.S. foreign policy during the Cold War. U.S. workers and industries facing foreign competition bitterly opposed such openings. Others worried about the long-term consequences of the trade deficits that transformed the United States into a net international debtor during the 1980s. Since the Eisenhower administration, predictions of imminent crises (in the value of the dollar, domestic interest rates, or both) have surfaced whenever U.S. reliance on foreign lending has grown, but those negative consequences have yet to materialize. The result has been more like a repetition on a global scale of the conversion of financial debt to political strength pioneered by the founders of the Bank of England in 1694 and repeated a century later when the United States assumed the debt of the 13 colonies.

In both of those cases, the stock of debt was purchased by the rich and the powerful, who then acquired an interest in the stability of the government that guaranteed the value of the debt. Wealthy Englishmen opposed the restoration of the Stuarts to the throne because they feared it would undermine the value of their holdings in the Bank of England. Likewise, the propertied elites of the 13 colonies came to support the stability and strength of the new U.S. Constitution because the value of their bonds rose and fell with the strength of the national government.

Similarly, in the last 60 years, as foreigners have acquired a greater value in the United States—government and private bonds, direct and portfolio private investments—more and more of them have acquired an interest in maintaining the strength of the U.S.-led system. A collapse of the U.S. economy and the ruin of the dollar would do more than dent the prosperity of the United States. Without their best customer, countries including China and Japan would fall into depressions. The financial strength of every country would be severely shaken should the United States collapse. Under those circumstances, debt becomes a strength, not a weakness, and other countries fear to break with the United States because they need its market and own its securities. Of course, pressed too far, a large national debt can turn from a source of strength to a crippling liability, and the United States must continue to justify other countries' faith by maintaining its long-term record of meeting its financial obligations. But, like Samson in the temple of the Philistines, a collapsing U.S. economy would inflict enormous, unacceptable damage on the rest of the world. That is sticky power with a vengeance.

The Sum of all Powers?

The United States' global economic might is therefore not simply, to use Nye's formulations, hard power that compels others or soft power that attracts the rest of the world. Certainly, the U.S. economic system provides the United States with the prosperity needed to underwrite its security strategy, but it also encourages other countries to accept U.S. leadership. U.S. economic might is sticky power.

How will sticky power help the United States address today's challenges? One pressing need is to ensure that Iraq's economic reconstruction integrates the nation more firmly in the global economy. Countries with open economies develop powerful trade-oriented businesses; the leaders of these businesses can promote economic policies that respect property rights, democracy, and the rule of law. Such leaders also lobby governments to avoid the isolation that characterized Iraq and Libya under economic sanctions. And looking beyond Iraq, the allure of access to Western capital and global markets is one of the few forces protecting the rule of law from even further erosion in Russia.

China's rise to global prominence will offer a key test case for sticky power. As China develops economically, it should gain wealth that could support a military rivaling that of the United States; China is also gaining political influence in the world. Some analysts in both China and the United States believe that the laws of history mean that Chinese power will someday clash with the reigning U.S. power.

Sticky power offers a way out. China benefits from participating in the U.S. economic system and integrating itself into the global economy. Between 1970 and 2003, China's gross domestic product grew from an estimated $106 billion to more than $1.3 trillion. By 2003, an estimated $450 billion of foreign money had flowed into the Chinese economy. Moreover, China is becoming increasingly dependent on both imports and exports to keep its economy (and its military machine) going. Hostilities between the United States and China would cripple China's industry, and cut off supplies of oil and other key commodities.

Sticky power works both ways, though. If China cannot afford war with the United States, the United States will have an increasingly hard time breaking off commercial relations with China. In an era of weapons of mass destruction, this mutual dependence is probably good for both sides. Sticky power did not prevent World War I, but economic interdependence runs deeper now; as a result, the "inevitable" U.S.-Chinese conflict is less likely to occur.

Sticky power, then, is important to U.S. hegemony for two reasons: It helps prevent war, and, if war comes, it helps the United States win. But to exercise power in the real world, the pieces must go back together. Sharp, sticky, and soft power work together to sustain U.S. hegemony. Today, even as the United States' sharp and sticky power reach unprecedented levels, the rise of anti-Americanism reflects a crisis in U.S. soft power that challenges fundamental assumptions and relationships in the U.S. system. Resolving the tension so that the different forms of power reinforce one another is one of the principal challenges facing U.S. foreign policy in 2004 and beyond.

WALTER RUSSELL MEAD is the Henry A. Kissinger senior fellow in U.S. foreign policy at the Council on Foreign Relations. This essay is adapted from his forthcoming book, *Power, Terror, Peace, and War: America's Grand Strategy in a World at Risk* (New York: Knopf, 2004).

The New Axis of Oil

FLYNT LEVERETT AND PIERRE NOËL

While Washington is preoccupied with curbing the proliferation of weapons of mass destruction, avoiding policy failure in Iraq and cheering the "forward march of freedom", the political consequences of recent structural shifts in global energy markets are posing the most profound challenge to American hegemony since the end of the Cold War. The increasing control that state-owned companies exercise over the world's reserves of crude oil and natural gas is, under current market conditions, enabling some energy exporters to act with escalating boldness against U.S. interests and policies. Perhaps the most immediate example is Venezuela's efforts to undermine U.S. influence in Latin America. The most strategically significant manifestation, though, is Russia's willingness to use its newfound external leverage to counteract what Moscow considers an unacceptable level of U.S. infringement on its interests. At the same time, rising Asian states, especially China, are seeking to address their perceived energy vulnerability through state-orchestrated strategies to "secure" access to hydrocarbon resources around the world. In the Chinese case, a statist approach to managing external energy relationships is increasingly pitting China against the United States in a competition for influence in the Middle East, Central Asia and oil-producing parts of Africa.

We describe these political consequences of recent structural shifts in global energy markets by the shorthand "petropolitics." While each of these developments is challenging to U.S. interests, the various threads of petropolitics are now coming together in an emerging "axis of oil" that is acting as a counterweight to American hegemony on a widening range of issues.[1] At the center of this undeclared but increasingly assertive axis is a growing geopolitical partnership between Russia (a major energy producer) and China (the paradigmatic rising consumer) against what both perceive as excessive U.S. unilateralism. The impact of this axis on U.S. interests has already been felt in the largely successful Sino–Russian effort to rollback U.S. influence in Central Asia. But the real significance is being seen in the ongoing frustration of U.S. objectives on the Iranian nuclear issue. This will likely be a milestone in redefining the post-Cold War international order—not merely because Iran is likely to end up with at least a nuclear-weapons option, but because of what that will imply about the efficacy of America's global leadership.

Structural Changes

The age of oil has clearly entered a new chapter, as strong demand and a shortage of productive capacity have generated a significantly higher trading range for crude oil than the world has experienced during the last twenty years. The dramatic rise in demand has been fed by high economic growth in emerging markets (where the increments of energy demand associated with specific increments of economic growth are usually greater than in OECD countries), particularly China and India. Overall, surging demand for crude oil from emerging economies has been the most immediate factor exerting upward pressure on prices.

A second element defining the recent structural shift in the international oil market is shrinking surplus productive capacity all along the supply chain. (Global oil supply has increased in recent years, but not as much as demand.) The degree that oil producers around the world expand their productive capacity is likely to be the most important factor affecting oil prices in the future. Not surprisingly, one finds a range of views about the possibilities for relieving the current supply "crunch."

There is significant evidence that there is, in fact, more oil to be discovered and produced, or recovered from already-producing fields, around the world—at the right price and with appropriate levels in investment. Thus, we do not share the unrelieved pessimism of those who argue we have reached the peak point of global oil supplies. However, we are also not inclined to accept the unrestrained optimism of some economists, who argue that high prices will, as they have in the past, necessarily attract the investment required to expand production relative to demand growth. Our skepticism flows primarily from the reality that the upstream oil sector—the exploration and production of crude oil—is far from an open and competitive environment. After 25 years of massive investment by multinational oil companies in exploration and development in oil-producing areas outside of OPEC and the former Soviet Union, the cost of replacing reserves in this "competitive fringe" of the oil industry, where the upstream sector has been relatively open, is now rising rapidly. Meanwhile, a high proportion of the remaining areas suitable for comparatively low-cost renewal of reserves, mostly in the Middle East and former Soviet Union, are off-limits to the international oil industry.

The next quarter-century of the oil age will therefore look quite different from the previous quarter-century: The rise in demand and the decline of several non-OPEC countries' production will have to be met by increased supplies of conventional oil from the Middle East and the former Soviet Union, as well as by unconventional oil (oil shale, tar sands and extra-heavy oil) and synthetic liquids (gas-to-liquids, coal-to-liquids and bio-fuels). Prices will likely be much higher on average and more unstable than in the past, with demand continuing to bump up against productive capacity.

There is an explicitly political dimension to these developments. As the "competitive fringe" of the upstream oil sector has been exploited by the multinational oil industry, the percentage of the world's oil reserves held by publicly traded international oil companies (IOCs) has declined, while the percentage held by state-owned national oil companies (NOCs) has increased. Currently, 72 percent of the world's proven oil reserves are held by NOCs. The ten-largest upstream companies in the world, measured by booked reserves (not market capitalization or production), are all NOCs. ExxonMobil—the largest publicly traded IOC in the world and the iconic symbol of "big oil"—is only the twelfth-largest upstream company in the world in terms of booked reserves. This means that NOCs and their parent governments, not IOCs and their shareholders, ultimately control the pace of development of upstream oil and gas resources.

Under current conditions of rising demand and tight supply, this is giving energy-exporting countries a more subtle but also more durable basis for enhancing their influence and generating new strategic options for themselves than that displayed by OPEC during and immediately after the 1973–74 oil embargo. Only now is the world seeing the full extent of the "OPEC revolution" of the early 1970s: Beyond an explicit cartel of oil producers, there is today an implicit cartel of resource-owning governments that control a large share of the world's known reserves of oil and natural gas. The power of this implicit cartel has been dormant for three decades; its actualization is an event of major economic and political significance that is generating critical challenges to America's regional interests and global standing.

Markets and the Russian Agenda

Russia stands as perhaps the leading exemplar of supply-side trends. After several years of uncertainty and contestation, President Vladimir Putin has successfully reasserted a definitive measure of state control over Russia's upstream oil and gas sectors, with NOCs like Gazprom and Rosneft playing increasingly important roles, the country's pipeline network firmly in government hands, Russian private-sector companies operating within parameters established by Moscow, and formidable barriers in place to large-scale foreign investment.

Suggestions just a few years ago that Russia could supplant Saudi Arabia as a swing producer for the global oil market were misplaced. There is no evidence that Putin or other senior leaders aspire to such a status, or that the Russian oil industry could muster what it would take to play such a role. Nevertheless, under Putin's presidency the internal conditions have been established for Russia to derive a significant measure of external leverage from its status as an important energy producer. In this regard, Putin wants to use Russia's presidency of the G-8 this year to transform Russia's international status from that of a mere (albeit major) energy supplier to that of a global supplier of energy security.

Moscow is using its market power to push back against the United States in arenas where it perceives U.S. infringement on its interests. Since the collapse of the Soviet Union, the list of accumulated Russian grievances over U.S. initiatives has grown ever longer: NATO enlargement, abrogation of the Anti-Ballistic Missile Treaty, basing of U.S. forces in Central Asia, the Iraq War and support for the "color revolutions" in states neighboring Russia. Through the late 1990s, Russia's ability to respond to these provocations was negligible. The Russian military was bogged down in Chechnya, and low oil and gas prices contributed to economic weakness—epitomized by Russia's 1998 currency crisis—making Russia dependent on the United States and other international players for assistance. In recent years, however, Russia's autonomy has been reinforced by high energy prices, and Putin and his advisors have decided they can use this market power to "push back" against the United States.

Russia's unfolding strategy for bolstering its influence in the "near abroad" exemplifies this approach. In some cases, as in the recent controversy over Russian gas shipments through Ukraine, the Kremlin's initiatives seem heavy-handed and not particularly productive. But its approach has been quite effective in establishing a new sphere of influence in the Eurasian south.

Much Western commentary on Russian policy in Central Asia has focused on Moscow's recent successes in establishing military bases in Kyrgyzstan and Tajikistan and encouraging Uzbekistan to evict U.S. military personnel from the Karshi-Kanabad air base. The real story, however, is rooted in energy and Russia's rising market power. Since 2003, Moscow has worked assiduously to establish a new sphere of influence in Central Asia, using regional autocrats' interest in resisting U.S. pressure to democratize, and China's interest in avoiding "encirclement" by U.S. forces, to maximize pressure on America. Russia's status as a major energy producer has given it important tools for pursuing Putin's regional strategy: investment capital with which to assume a leading role in the development and marketing of Central Asian energy resources (with NOCs like Gazprom acting as effective agents of Kremlin policy) and control over access to Russia's state-owned pipeline system, which is essential for moving Central Asian oil and gas to markets in Europe.

Less directly, the oil boom of the last few years has fueled much higher rates of growth in the Russian economy, helping to turn the Russian service sector into a provider of jobs for Central Asian expatriates. Remittances from the expatriate workers constitute an increasingly important source of income for several Central Asian states—perhaps as much as 30 percent of GDP in Tajikistan, for example—which gives Moscow another lever of influence over these states.[2]

Russia has also used its energy-based market power to bolster its political influence in other strategically vital regions in ways that could potentially weaken America's international position. Perhaps most notably, Moscow has taken advantage of its market power to reinforce and enhance its otherwise sagging strategic position in East Asia. Although geopolitical legacies and existing transportation infrastructure orient Russian energy exports toward Europe, Moscow has used the prospect of substantial energy exports from eastern Siberia and the Russian Far East to markets in East Asia to make itself a major factor in the foreign policies of both China and Japan, playing on the interests of Beijing and Tokyo in balancing traditional sources of hydrocarbons from the Middle East in their energy profiles.

The Asian Challenge

Of course, the market power of energy suppliers like Russia is an outgrowth of escalating demand-side pressures. As noted earlier, increased demand, especially from emerging Asia, has been one of the most important factors exerting upward pressure on oil prices since 2003: According to the U.S. Department of Energy, 40 percent of oil-demand growth worldwide since 2001 has come from China alone. Despite a slowdown in China's oil-demand growth in 2005, many market forecasts show demand growth in Asia continuing at impressive rates for years to come.

In the current climate, the political impact of these demand-side pressures is exacerbated by consumer countries' increasing reliance on statist strategies to secure access to hydrocarbon resources on privileged bases, rather than relying solely on international markets to meet their energy needs. The best example of this approach is China's. In 2002, around the time that Hu Jintao became general secretary of the Communist Party, China formally adopted a "going out" (*zou chu qu*) policy of encouraging its three major NOCs—the China National Petroleum Corporation (CNPC), the China National Petrochemical Corporation (Sinopec), and the China National Offshore Oil Corporation (CNOOC)—to purchase equity shares in overseas exploration and production projects around the world, and to build pipelines, particularly to Siberia and Central Asia. The goal of the "going out" strategy is to secure effective ownership of energy resources and transportation infrastructure, measures that China perceives as essential to improving the country's energy security. The adoption of the policy was effectively a codification of long-standing practice, as Chinese energy companies had already engaged in these activities since the 1990s.

China has pursued the "going out" strategy in a wide range of oil-producing regions, including the Caucasus, Central Asia, East and South Asia, Africa and Latin America. In the Middle East, China has employed the strategy in various ways with a number of oil-producing states, including Algeria, Egypt, Iran, Libya, Oman, Saudi Arabia, Syria, Sudan and Yemen. Beijing supports the efforts of Chinese energy companies to win deals with regular high-level visits to and from regions in which the companies are seeking access. China also follows up its network of energy deals by increasing exports of manufactured goods and capital to countries where its NOCs are operating. In some cases, the Chinese appear willing to put expensive packages of side investments on the table in order to secure energy deals, as was recently the case in Angola and Nigeria. Chinese and other Asian NOCs participating in bidding rounds in a number of countries have shown a willingness to pay high prices in order to secure exploration and production contracts, sometimes overbidding IOCs.

However, while increased demand from Asian economies has a very direct effect on global oil prices, the impact of China's statist strategy on the market is probably not as dramatic as some assessments would suggest. It seems doubtful that Chinese NOCs' fledgling efforts to lock up petroleum resources will succeed in keeping a critical mass of oil reserves off an increasingly integrated and fluid global oil market. There is also no reason to anticipate that China's willingness to pay market premiums for privileged access to oil resources in various parts of the world will bolster upward pressure on prices generated naturally by rising demand. The opposite is more likely: The flow of "cheap" Chinese capital into global exploration and production is increasing competition among oil companies to access reserves and forcing IOCs to increase spending and take more risks. Other things being equal, this should bring *more* oil, not less, to market.

Arguably, the Chinese strategy of competing for access to hydrocarbon resources challenges the rules-based international order for trade and investment in energy that the United States has long championed. At a minimum, statist initiatives to secure effective ownership over hydrocarbon resources in foreign countries—with an attendant willingness toward corruption, offering soft loans, and making investments in unrelated sectors and infrastructure projects as part of these initiatives—undercut OECD standards for export financing and other good-governance criteria. And there is a risk that the Chinese approach will be taken as a model by others. This is already happening to some extent with India's Oil & Natural Gas Corporation (ONGC), which is pursuing equity oil deals in many of the same places as the Chinese NOCs—in some cases, as in Iran and Sudan, in consortium with them. Last year, for example, China and India announced an "agreement" aimed at preventing competition over hydrocarbon assets between Chinese NOCs and ONGC from driving up the prices of those assets, as happened in the contest to buy Canada-based PetroKazakhstan. There is also a resurgent debate in Japan as to whether it should take a more statist approach to external energy policy to meet the Chinese challenge. But we are still far from a turning point of massive defections from the market by major consumers and suppliers.

Nevertheless, while the market impact of statist strategies like China's may be minimal, Beijng's "going out" strategy is rapidly becoming a source of geopolitical tensions between China and the United States, with potentially significant implications for the development of the world's most important bilateral relationship during the first quarter of the 21st century. China's search for oil is making it a new competitor to the United States for influence, especially in the Middle East, Central Asia and Africa. China's energy-driven engagement in the Middle East is creating new foreign policy as well as commercial options for energy exporting states, including those at odds with U.S. foreign policy goals, like Iran, Sudan and Syria. (With regard to Sudan, Beijing went so far as to use its status as a permanent member of the Security Council to block the imposition of sanctions on Khartoum over the Darfur genocide.)

In Central Asia, China's interest in diversifying its external sources of energy to mitigate its reliance on the Persian Gulf has motivated Beijing's leading role in the Shanghai Cooperation Organization's campaign to undercut U.S. influence in Central Asia. In oil-producing African countries, Chinese and other Asian NOCs make available to host governments a supply of exploration and production capital that is free from any good-governance and transparency conditions. This, combined with high oil prices, is weakening the leverage that Western governments and international financial institutions can use to improve management of the oil sector and reduce corruption in these countries.

Additionally, Beijing's statist approach to energy security is raising geopolitical tensions with Japan, with prospectively a negative impact on the development of a regional political framework to anchor growing trade and financial interdependence in the world's most dynamic economic zone. Competition between Beijing and Tokyo for specific energy deals in a variety of settings, a bilateral dispute about sovereignty over possible natural gas reserves in the East China Sea, and jockeying over the ultimate destination of a projected Russian eastern oil pipeline have all contributed to the ongoing deterioration of Sino–Japanese relations. Unless these tensions can be ameliorated, it will be increasingly difficult for the United States to manage China's rise on the East Asian scene in a way that ensures long-term regional stability.

Over time, Russian oil and gas could be a major factor buttressing closer Sino–Russian strategic collaboration. Putin's recent meeting with Hu in Beijing, during which the two leaders concluded an agreement for Russia to begin exporting natural gas to China by 2012, was the fifth such meeting in the last year. In theory, a successful commercially grounded oil and gas relationship between Russia and China could be positive for at least some U.S. interests by mitigating China's sense of energy insecurity through reduced dependence on the Middle East (and U.S.-secured Asian maritime routes for their transport). But Moscow is clearly playing on Beijing's sense of energy insecurity to foster a closer geopolitical partnership.

The Axis of Oil and Iran

The implications of the new petropolitics and an emerging axis of oil for America's international influence are illustrated by the way these forces are frustrating U.S. objectives on the Iranian nuclear issue. The policies of key players on this issue are conditioned far more by calculations about the economics and geopolitics of energy than was the case during the run-up to the Iraq War. As the Western powers consider what sort of action against Iran they might collectively support, it is clear that their options in the Security Council are severely limited by Russian and Chinese resistance to the imposition of sanctions or other strongly punitive measures.

With growing market power increasing Russia's capacity for strategic initiative, its calculus of interests regarding the Iranian nuclear issue has become more complex than most Western analysts and policymakers understand. Moscow's policy agenda toward Iran has expanded significantly. Russia continues to have important economic interests in Iran. Moscow anticipates a substantial increase in high-technology exports (for example, civil nuclear technology) to Iran over the next decade. The Iranian market is also potentially lucrative for Russian exporters of conventional weaponry, one of Russia's main sources of foreign-exchange earnings alongside hydrocarbon exports. But over the last three years, Russia has also come to see Iran as an important geopolitical partner in its efforts to rollback U.S. influence, not only in Central Asia but in the Caucasus as well. Moscow's recent proposal to resolve the impasse between the Islamic Republic and the West over Iran's nuclear activities by establishing Iranian–Russian joint-venture entities for uranium enrichment was calculated to serve all of these interests. Such a scheme would allow Moscow to maintain and even expand an Iranian market for its nuclear technology, while also nurturing its developing strategic partnership with Tehran.

It is also increasingly evident that the current leadership in Moscow views the Iranian nuclear issue as an opportunity to frustrate the Bush Administration's unilateralist inclinations. Russian Foreign Minister Sergei Lavrov—formerly Russia's permanent representative to the UN for ten years and a master of Security Council politics and procedure—and his colleagues anticipate that, in the end, the United States may take unilateral military action against Iran, including the Russian-built reactor at Bushehr. They do not expect to be able to block such action anymore than they could block the invasion of Iraq, but they are working prospectively to impose serious costs on the United States for a military strike against Iran by ensuring that Washington lacks international legitimacy for its actions.

For its part, China's approach to the Iranian nuclear issue is directly linked to its assessment of its requirements for energy security. Beijing has already put down a marker, in the form of its opposition to UN sanctions against Sudan, that it will oppose the imposition of multilateral sanctions on an energy-producing state in which Chinese companies operate. In private conversations, senior Chinese diplomats and party officials describe Beijing's policy on the Iranian nuclear issue as seeking to balance a range of interests: a secure supply of oil, nonproliferation and regional stability, the defense of important international norms (including the peaceful resolution of disputes and the sovereign right of states to develop civil nuclear capabilities), securing China's northwest border (meaning Xinjiang province, where there is a significant Muslim population), the development of Chinese–Iranian relations, the development of U.S.–Chinese relations, and the positions of the European Union and Russia. It seems increasingly clear that, in their efforts to balance this set of interests, Chinese officials will remain deeply resistant to the imposition of sanctions on Iran. And as long as Russian opposition provides China with political cover, Chinese officials seem to calculate that they will not have to choose between relations with Iran and relations with the United States.

China's willingness to protect Iran from international pressure would also complicate Western efforts to impose meaningful sanctions on Iran through a "coalition of the willing." Without Chinese participation, a voluntary ban on investment in Iran's energy sector by Western powers would, at this point, be little more than a symbolic gesture, as U.S. companies are already barred from doing business in Iran by U.S. law, and most European IOCs have put potential projects on hold because of the political uncertainties. In recent years, though, Chinese NOCs have committed themselves, at least in principle, to substantial investments in Iran's energy sector, thereby mitigating the impact of restrictions on Western investment.

With the Bush Administration having ruled out direct and broad-based strategic discussions with Iran aimed at a "grand bargain" that would include a resolution of the nuclear issue, the United States and its European partners are headed down an ultimately futile path in the Security Council. The Security Council's failure to deal effectively with the Iranian nuclear issue will confront the United States, during the last two years or so of the Bush Administration's tenure, with the choice of doing nothing as Iran continues to develop its nuclear capabilities or taking unilateral military action in the hope of slowing down that development. Each of these choices is likely to damage American leadership in the world: Doing nothing will highlight U.S. fecklessness, while unilateral action without international legitimacy will further strain America's international standing (and probably not meaningfully impede Iran's nuclear development).

Beyond speculating whether Iran might cut off oil exports in response to sanctions or military action, commentators tend to overlook the implications of the current controversy's outcome for the geopolitics of global energy. How the nuclear issue plays out will largely determine Iran's future as an oil and gas supplier. Iranian oil production relies heavily on a small number of old, "super-giant" fields, where output has plateaued and could soon start to decline. These old fields need massive infusions of investment and technology to increase their recovery rates. Iran is not Saudi Arabia and cannot make the investments itself. Since reopening its upstream oil sector in 1994, Iran has actually taken in only around $10 billion of foreign investment in oil exploration and production, due to a lack of political consensus on the country's oil policy, a difficult and opaque negotiating process, and unattractive contractual terms. Similarly, Iran needs large-scale investment and technology transfers to develop its gas-exporting potential. If the nuclear controversy leads to Iran's further isolation from Western IOCs, there would be a powerful incentive for Tehran to turn to Chinese and other Asian NOCs, supplement their investment capital with expertise from more technologically advanced Russian companies, and rely on government-to-government marketing deals. This would significantly reinforce the economic and political logic behind the axis of oil.

Possible Policies

One step Washington needs to take is to facilitate broader and deeper cooperation between the International Energy Agency (IEA) and China and India. Because these states are not members of the OECD, they are not formally eligible for membership in the IEA, and they have not yet built up the minimum levels of stockpiled oil and petroleum products defined by the IEA for its members. Notwithstanding these barriers, it is clearly in the interests of the United States and its Western partners to establish much closer coordination between emerging Asian economies and the IEA, especially to persuade these states to rely more on international markets and less on exclusive supply deals to meet their energy needs.

At the same time, the United States needs to change its approach to promoting expansion of global energy supplies. It will take more than exhortations about market logic to change elite attitudes and government policies regarding upstream resource development in key energy-producing states. These elites have, by and large, determined that values other than pure market efficiency have priority in their calculations about resource development. Traditional American advocacy of liberalization and internationalization of upstream oil and gas sectors needs to shift decisively toward encouraging NOCs in key producing states to increase investment in productive capacity.

The larger reality is that U.S. foreign policy is ill suited to cope with the challenges to American leadership flowing from the new petropolitics. Current policy does not take energy security seriously as a foreign policy issue or prioritize energy security in relation to other foreign policy goals.

The United States cannot change the course of Moscow's energy policy or foreign policy, but American diplomacy can mitigate Russian policymakers' threat perceptions in exchange for more cooperative Russian behavior. This would require the United States to reach a set of strategic understandings with Moscow encouraging mutual respect for each side's critical interests—and also to make clear privately that Washington and its Western partners will not recognize Russia as a provider of energy security as long as it plays geopolitically on the energy security of others. Vice President Cheney's recent public denunciation of Moscow, coupled with the Bush Administration's refusal to reconsider its strategic approach to Russia, is hardly likely to achieve positive results.

To deal more effectively with China, Washington must recognize that, despite some acknowledgement in Beijing that the "going out" strategy may prove a poor energy security policy, there is still a widely held perception within the Chinese establishment that the international oil market is a foreign (primarily American) construction, operated by Western IOCs in accordance with their interests, and that China cannot bet its energy security on that construction. U.S. policy should encourage Chinese and other Asian NOCs to move along their own paths of internationalization. In this regard, the U.S. Congress's resistance to CNOOC's potential acquisition of Unocal last year sent precisely the wrong message to China.

More broadly, U.S. policymakers need to remember that, even for a global hegemon, to govern is to choose. Washington cannot continue to disregard the impact of its foreign policy choices on the interests of key energy-producing states like Russia if it expects these states not to use their market power in ways that run counter to U.S. preferences. And, similarly, Washington cannot ignore the energy security interests and perceptions of rising consumer countries like China and avoid consequences reflected in these countries' foreign policy choices.

Notes

1. The term "axis of oil" is not new and has been used by various commentators to describe a number of oil-focused relationships, such as the U.S.–Saudi strategic partnership or a possible coordination between India and China in their quest to secure external energy resources. We use the term, in a manner similar to Irwin Stelzer, to describe a shifting coalition of both energy exporting and energy importing states centered in ongoing Sino–Russian collaboration.

2. The authors are grateful to their colleague Fiona Hill for this point.

FLYNT LEVERETT is senior fellow at the Brookings Institution's Saban Center for Middle East Policy and has been appointed visiting professor of political science at the Massachusetts Institute of Technology. **PIERRE NOEL** is research fellow at the French Institute of International Relations (IFRI) in Paris. He will join the Electricity Policy Research Group at Cambridge University's Judge Business School in September.

UNIT 7
U.S. Military Strategy

Unit Selections

Key Points to Consider

- Is military power an effective instrument of foreign policy today? What problems is it best and least capable of solving?

- Does arms control have a future? Can it make the United States more secure, or does it weaken U.S. security?

- How should we think about nuclear weapons today? What is their purpose? Who should they be targeted against? What dangers must we guard against?

- How great is the terrorist threat to the United States? What steps should the United States take to protect itself from terrorist attacks?

- Develop a list of "do's and don'ts" to guide American troops when they are called upon to act as occupation forces.

- Under what conditions should the United States engage in peacekeeping activities?

- Can nuclear proliferation be stopped? What strategy would you recommend?

Student Web Site
www.mhcls.com/online

Internet References
Further information regarding these Web sites may be found in this book's preface or online.

Arms Control and Disarmament Agency (ACDA)
http://dosfan.lib.uic.edu/acda/

Counterterrorism Page
http://counterterrorism.com

DefenseLINK
http://www.defenselink.mil/news/

Federation of American Scientists (FAS)
http://www.fas.org

Human Rights Web
http://www.hrweb.org

FALLOUT SHELTER

During the height of the cold war, American defense planners often thought in terms of needing a two-and-a-half war capacity: the simultaneous ability to fight major wars in Europe and Asia plus a smaller conflict elsewhere. The principal protagonists in this drama were well known: the Soviet Union and China. The stakes were also clear. Communism represented a global threat to American political democracy and economic prosperity. It was a conflict in which both sides publicly proclaimed that there could be but one winner. The means for deterring and fighting such challenges included strategic, tactical, and battlefield nuclear weapons; large numbers of conventional forces; alliance systems; arms transfers; and the development of a guerrilla war capability.

Until September 11, 2001, the political-military landscape of the post-cold war world lacked any comparable enemy or military threat. Instead, the principal challenges to American foreign policy makers were ones of deciding what humanitarian interventions to undertake and how deeply to become involved. Kosovo, East Timor, Somalia, Bosnia, Rwanda, and Haiti each produced its own answer, which presented American policymakers with a new type of military challenge in the form of humanitarian interventions. The challenge of formulating an effective military policy to deal with situations where domestic order has unraveled due to ethnic conflict and bottled-up political pressures for reform remains. However, they are no longer viewed as first-order security problems in the post-cold war era.

With the terrorist attacks on the World Trade Center and the Pentagon, a more clearly defined enemy has emerged. Formulating a military strategy to defeat this enemy promises to be no easy task. President George W. Bush acknowledged as much in defining his war against terrorism as a new type of warfare and one that would not end quickly. To date, the war against terrorism has led to two wars, one that brought down the Taliban government in Afghanistan and one that brought down Saddam Hussein in Iraq. It also brought forward a new national security strategy centered on preemption in place of deterrence. And, most unexpectedly from the point of view of the Bush administration, it has placed the American military squarely in the business of nation building and face-to-face with the problem of fighting counterinsurgencies.

The first set of essays in this unit is by Andrew Bacevich. In "Requiem for the Bush Doctrine" he argues that the Iraq War demonstrated that the United States cannot implement a policy of preventive war. Bacevich outlines the requirements for such a strategy to work and finds that the U.S. military is not up to the task. The second essay, "Base Politics," looks at the interaction between the strategic need for military bases abroad to fight the war against terrorism and the desire for promoting democratization worldwide. The author finds the two are in conflict. Uzbekistan is used as a case study. The third essay asks the question "is the United States winning the war on terrorism?" A poll of experts conducted by the editors of *Foreign Policy* finds most do not believe it is. Their views are compared with that of the public at large more of whom tend to believe the war on terrorism is being won. The final essay in this section, "A Nuclear Posture for Today" raises the question of what type of nuclear strategy should the United States pursue. John Deutch, a former head of the CIA, argues against abolishing the U.S. nuclear force and calls for one capable of preventing a nuclear attack on the U.S. and responding to lesser contingencies.

With changes in the nature of the military threats confronting the United States has come a change in the arms control agenda. The old arms control agenda was dominated by a concern for reducing the size of U.S. and Soviet nuclear inventories. A much broader agenda exists today and it is one with many more players at its core; is the problem of dealing with weapons of mass destruction and the question of whether a national ballistic missile system is an important part of the solution to the problem. The final two essays examine this new agenda. Brent Scowcroft, national security advisor to Presidents George H.W. Bush and Gerald Ford, argues against a particularistic approach to arms control such as the one now in place toward India and Iran. He calls for creating a new fuel-cycle regime that applies to all countries. David Albright takes up the question of "When Could Iran Get the Bomb?" Scenarios suggest it will take at least three years and he calls for renewed international efforts to slow or stop movement in this direction.

Requiem for the Bush Doctrine

"The Iraq War has revealed that the armed forces possess nothing like the depth required to implement a policy of preventive war on a sustained basis."

ANDREW J. BACEVICH

The claim that 9-11 "changed everything" is demonstrably false. What did change as a consequence of that awful day was basic US policy regarding the use of force. Having now been tested and found wanting, that new policy—known as the Bush Doctrine—may already be on its way to the ash heap of history.

Before September 11, 2001, American presidents routinely insisted that when the United States went to war it did so only defensively and as a last resort. Although not always supported by the facts related to the nation's rise to the status of sole superpower, this sentiment accorded nicely with America's self-image as a peaceful nation.

According to President George W. Bush, the events of 9-11 rendered those views obsolete, if not dangerous. In the face of violent Islamic radicals for whom no act, however barbarous, was beyond the pale, the administration concluded that cold war-style deterrence could no longer be counted on to work. Convinced that the prospect of these radicals gaining possession of weapons of mass destruction was not only real but becoming more acute by the day, Bush and his lieutenants determined that the United States could not afford to let the other side fire the first shot. Waging war against the unprecedented menace posed by global terror now obliged the United States to go permanently on the offensive.

Henceforth, the United States needed to shoot first even if that meant acting on fragmentary evidence. In a post–9-11 world, the Bush administration insisted, the risks of delay outweighed the risks of precipitate action. As then-national security adviser Condoleezza Rice famously remarked with regard to Iraq, "We don't want the smoking gun to be a mushroom cloud." The new imperative was to eliminate threats before they could mature.

President Bush unveiled this new doctrine in a speech to graduating cadets at West Point delivered on June 1, 2002. "The gravest danger to freedom," he declared, was to be found at "the perilous crossroads of radicalism and technology." Old conceptions of deterrence meant "nothing against shadowy terrorist networks with no nation or citizens to defend." Rather than passively allowing this enemy to seize the initiative, Bush told the cadets that "we must take the battle to the enemy, disrupt his plans, and confront the worst threats before they emerge. In the

world we have entered, the only path to safety is the path of action. And this nation will act."

The president went on to explain that the United States would "be ready for preemptive action when necessary." But the substance of his remarks indicated clearly that he was referring not to preemption, but to preventive war. The distinction is crucial. Preemption implies launching a war when facing the clear prospect of imminent attack—as, for example, the state of Israel did in June 1967. Preventive war implies initiating hostilities to eliminate the possibility that an adversary might pose a future threat, again as Israel did in its 1981 attack on the partially assembled Iraqi nuclear reactor at Osirak. Effective June 2002, the United States embraced the concept of preventive war. This is the essence of the Bush Doctrine.

Assuming Power

Formidable moral and legal objections have been raised against the doctrine of preventive war. Critics have charged that the Bush Doctrine violates the Charter of the United Nations, and that it opens a Pandora's box, inviting any number of other nations to cite the US precedent as a pretext for their own preventive wars. According to the doctrine's logic, Israel could easily find justification for attacking Iran—and Iran could justifiably attack Israel.

But even leaving such objections aside, a doctrine of preventive war makes sense only if it works—that is, if its implementation yields enhanced security at a reasonable cost. In the American case, the Bush administration's belief in the efficacy of preventive war stemmed from its confidence in American military power. In his introduction to the *National Security Strategy* that the White House issued in September 2002, President Bush wrote that "today the United States enjoys a position of unparalleled military strength." The assumption underlying the Bush Doctrine, never made explicit, was that the unparalleled quality and capabilities of America's armed services made preventive war plausible.

In March 2003, the president implemented the Bush Doctrine, ordering the invasion of Iraq. In doing so, he also put to the test his administration's assumptions about American military power. That test has now continued long enough for us to draw some preliminary conclusions.

The most important of these conclusions is the following: as measured by the effectiveness and capacity of American arms, the quality of American generalship, and the adherence of American soldiers to professional norms, this administration has badly misread what the US military can and cannot do. The sword of American military power is neither sharp enough nor hard enough to meet the demands of preventive war.

At the very top, US military leadership has been at best mediocre if not altogether unsatisfactory.

Stalemate in Iraq

The Bush Doctrine requires military forces able, in the words of the *National Security Strategy*, to "conduct rapid and precise operations to achieve decisive results." Preventive war demands a quick kill. Victory gained swiftly and economically is not only a value in itself. It also conveys an exemplary message to others: resistance is pointless. Such a victory can serve to overawe other would-be adversaries, thereby limiting the occasions requiring the actual use of force.

In Iraq, decisive results have proved elusive. Although the initial march on Baghdad provided ample opportunity for US forces to demonstrate speed and impressive precision, successfully toppling the regime of Saddam Hussein produced not an end to war, but a wider conflict. As is so often the case in war, the enemy has refused to follow our script.

Whether this wider war resulted from carefully laid enemy plans or emerged spontaneously out of the chaos created by Hussein's overthrow hardly matters. The fact is that over two and a half years after launching Operation Iraqi Freedom with high hopes and great fanfare, the United States finds itself mired in a conflict that in a strictly military sense may be unwinnable. The armed forces that innumerable commentators have proclaimed the most advanced and most sophisticated that the world has ever seen have been stymied by 10,000 to 20,000 insurgents equipped with an arsenal of weapons dating from the 1940s and 1950s.

The enterprise launched with expectations of pocketing a quick military success has now evolved into a project that even administration officials concede may drag on for a decade or more. Although President Bush continues to insist that his aim in Iraq is "victory," senior military officers have been signaling just as clearly that extricating the United States from Iraq will require a political solution, which implies something less than vanquishing the enemy. "This insurgency is not going to be settled ... through military options or military operations," Brigadier General Donald Alston, the chief US military spokesman in Baghdad, acknowledged this summer. "It's going to be settled in the political process."

In Iraq, the American way of war devised in the 1980s and refined during the 1990s has come up short. In the heady after-

math of Operation Desert Storm, the Pentagon had grandly announced that this novel approach to warfare, with its emphasis on advanced technology and air power, was providing US forces with what it called "full spectrum dominance." According to its proponents, the new model of waging war promised to banish "fog" and "friction," the terms coined by Karl von Clausewitz to describe the qualities that had throughout history made combat such an arduous, perplexing, and chancy proposition. But in Iraq fog blankets the battlefield: after more than two years of fighting, the enemy remains a cipher. And friction, which, according to Clausewitz "makes even the simplest thing difficult" on the battlefield, has been omnipresent.

The significance of this military failure—and by the standards of preventive war, the Iraq War cannot be otherwise categorized—extends beyond the conflict immediately at hand. As the astute commentator Owen Harries has noted, the conflict in Iraq has shattered the "mystique" of US forces. All the world now knows that an army once thought to be unstoppable can be fought to a standstill. Thirty years after its defeat in Vietnam, it turns out that the United States still does not know how to counter a determined guerrilla force. Far from overawing other would-be opponents, the Iraq War has provided them with a template for how to fight the world's most powerful military to a stalemate—a lesson that other potential adversaries from Pyongyang to Tehran have no doubt taken to heart.

According to an ancient principle of statecraft, the reputation of power is itself power. By deflating the reputation of US forces, the Iraq War has considerably diminished the power of the United States and by extension has called into question the continued utility of the Bush Doctrine.

Empty Boots

The Bush Doctrine assumed not only that the United States had devised methods that endowed coercion with unprecedented effectiveness, but also that US forces possessed the wherewithal to employ these methods anywhere in the world. America's global leadership rests, in this view, on a capacity for global power projection. Yet the Iraq War has revealed that the armed forces possess nothing like the depth required to implement a policy of preventive war on a sustained basis. Our actual staying power has turned out to be far more limited than expected.

In *Imperial Grunts*, his just published tribute to militarized global empire, the author Robert Kaplan writes that "by the turn of the twenty-first century, the United States military had already appropriated the entire earth, and was ready to flood the most obscure areas of it with troops at a moment's notice." While an effective policy of preventive war may well require an ability to flood obscure areas with troops, recent events have demonstrated conclusively that the United States does not possess that ability. A commitment of approximately 140,000 troops to Iraq along with a far smaller contingent in Afghanistan has just about exhausted the resources of the US Army and Marine Corps.

Some of those most critical of the Bush administration's handling of the Iraq War argue that the key to breaking the stalemate

The Strange Triumph Of Unilateralism

G. John Ikenberry

Over the past few years almost all of the world's global and regional governance institutions have weakened. Indeed, it is possible to observe a systematic erosion of the authority and capacities of international institutions and regimes in the security, economic, and political realms. In the 1970s, Samuel Huntington, Michel Crozier, and Joji Watanuki wrote about the "crisis of governability" in the advanced democratic world, in which governments were losing the ability and public confidence to confront fundamental problems of managing domestic economies and addressing crime and welfare. Today, it appears as if the governance crisis has gone global.

- *The United Nations.* At a September summit, member states failed to agree on "grand bargain" reforms of the Security Council. The UN is still vital in peacekeeping and supervising elections, but efforts to make it a central vehicle for global security cooperation and collective decision-making on the use of force have failed. UN management is under a cloud, and efforts to implement reforms have been frustrated.
- *The European Union.* Voters this spring rejected the EU constitution, and Europeans are in the midst of a continent-wide rethinking about what comes next. This is a setback for those who would like Europe to play a more active global role in providing leadership and public goods. The federal vision of Europe is dead. In its place is European political drift.
- *NATO.* The Atlantic alliance still exists, but it has declined as a vehicle for serious strategic cooperation between the United States and Europe. Washington is drawing down its troop deployments in Germany, and the idea of an Atlantic security community increasingly has a ring of nostalgia about it.
- *The G-8 Summit.* Aside from the Bonn summit of 1978, the Group of Eight has always been a disappointment as a mechanism for summoning collective action.
- *World Trade Organization.* The WTO is perhaps the strongest link in the global system of rule-based cooperation. But efforts to reach agreement on agriculture subsidies and other tough issues so far have failed. In the meantime, narrow bilateral or regional trade agreements are proliferating. Some argue that the age of big, multilateral trade agreements is over.
- *The nuclear nonproliferation regime.* Most people outside of Washington think the nuclear Non-Proliferation Treaty is in crisis. The bargains have broken down. Washington has ignored NPT obligations; the Bush administration did not even send the secretary of state to this year's five-year review meeting. Overall, treaty-based arms control is going nowhere, and the United States has pulled back from or resisted a wide range of global security treaties.
- *The American provision of governance.* It is often remarked that the United States itself is a "private" provider of governance through enlightened—if self-interested—rule making and institution building. This "liberal hegemonic" logic of international order, which informed American foreign policy in the past, has been partially replaced by a conservative nationalist logic that questions the whole idea of global governance and rule-based order.

More Demand, Less Supply

It is not unfair to ask: where are the vibrant and growing global and regional institutions to help us collectively tackle the great problems of our age? If the United States is not providing "private" global governance, and if the postwar institutions and functional regimes run by the United States and the other "stake holders" of the international system are in decline or disrepair, where is this taking us? Are we in an era when the demand for cooperative mechanisms and institutionalized collective action is growing but the supply is dwindling? It sure looks like it.

There are several possible explanations for this observed crisis of governance. First, it is possible that the basic observation is wrong—governance is not in decline. Realists would say: certainly there is a crisis in global governance, but it is a 500-year crisis, if not longer. The under-provision of cooperation is inherent in world politics. Things are neither worse nor better than at earlier moments. We should be thankful for the long pause in great-power war and the failure of other major states to balance against the United States.

Second, much of the crisis may have to do with shifts in US policy. This is the hegemonic stability argument—namely, that the supply of rules and institutions ultimately hinges on the logic of behavior that informs the most powerful state in the system. Today, the United States does not have an inclination to sponsor, support, fund, and enforce global rules and institutions.

Third, the crisis may be driven by an inability to infuse international regimes and institutions with democratic accountability and legitimacy. The failure of the European constitution may be the most direct casualty of this sort of constraint. But it may be a more general problem of building and pooling authority above the level of states.

Fourth, more cooperation may be taking place, but just not in the old-style global treaty-based institutional way. Princeton's Anne-Marie Slaughter argues that an entire world of intergovernmental networks is flourishing below the political radar screen. They tend to be informal, practical, and executive-based. They escape the problem of democratic accountability largely because they operate unnoticed. The implication of this view is that there is really not a crisis of governance, merely a shift in the forms of governance.

Finally, there is a view that the crisis is real but is driven by deep shifts in the nature of the challenges that states face. In the economic realm, for example, multilateral trade rules and cooperation were possible during the long postwar era when tariff barriers were the most important impediments to open trade. Tariff reduction lent itself to multilateral exercises. Today, the blockages are built into domestic legislation—blockages that are more difficult to negotiate in global multilateral settings. Likewise, some observers argue that the new security threats—weapons of mass destruction in the hands of illegitimate, unstable, or untrustworthy states—cannot be handled by treaty-based arms control regimes that emerged in the decades of US-Soviet bipolar nuclear summitry. The crisis of governance in this view is driven by a mismatch between the nature of the problems confronting states and the traditional ways in which collective action has been organized.

Continued on next page

Made in Washington

So which is it? As descriptions of the current landscape, these are not all competing or mutually exclusive. New forms of informal cooperation are evident. Still, it is clear something is very wrong with the current system of governance. Looking into the future—with the growing complexities and dangers associated with continued globalization of economies, societies, and cultures and the privatization of technologies of violence—it is obvious that the world will need more, not less, institutionalized cooperation. If we are in an age of declining institutionalized cooperation, well, ergo—we do have a growing problem or, yes, crisis.

In my view, the crisis is generated primarily from choices made by the United States. Washington does not appear to be doing as much today as in the past to sponsor and operate within a system of consensual rule-based governance. Why America is less willing to do so is actually a complex issue. Some of it is very specifically about the Bush administration, and thus about biases and viewpoints that eventually will pass from the scene as President Bush and his team leave office.

But there are also deeper structural shifts in the United States and the global system that make Washington less interested in rule and governance provision. American unipolarity seems to have created problems in how the United States thinks about the provision of international rules, institutions, and public goods. In the past, America provided global "services"—such as security protection and support for open markets—that made other states willing to work with rather than resist US preeminence. The public goods provision tended to make it worthwhile for these states to endure the day-to-day irritations of American foreign policy. But the trade-off seems to be shifting. Today, the United States appears to be providing fewer global public goods while at the same time the irritations associated with US dominance seem to be growing.

It might be useful to think of the dynamic this way: the United States is unique in that it is simultaneously both a provider of global governance and a great power that pursues its own national interest. When America acts as a "liberal hegemon,"championing the WTO, for example, or reaffirming its commitment to cooperative security in Asia and Europe, it is seeking to lead or manage the global system of rules and institutions. When it is acting as a nationalist great power, by protecting its steel and textile industries, for example, it is seeking to respond to domestic interests and its relative power position among nations. And today, these two roles—liberal hegemon and traditional great power—increasingly are in conflict.

G. JOHN IKENBERRY, *a* Current History *contributing editor, is a professor of politics and international affairs at Princeton University. A version of this commentary originally appeared in "America Abroad" at TPMCafe.com.*

---

in Iraq is to send more American troops. In fact, the soldiers needed to do so do not exist.

In September 2001, when President Bush committed the United States to an open-ended global war against terror, he chose not to increase the size of America's military establishment. It was the first time in its history that the United States embarked on a major conflict without expanding its armed services, the president and his advisers tacitly assuming that the existing active duty force of 1.4 million backed up by reserves would suffice for whatever tasks lay ahead. Rather than summoning his fellow citizens to the colors, President Bush famously urged them to go on vacation to rescue the ailing airline industry.

The president's belief that the existing military was large enough turned out to be deeply flawed. Four years after 9-11, the reserves are close to breaking—both recruiting and reenlistment are in free-fall. As for active duty forces, in fiscal year 2005 the heavily burdened US Army experienced its worst recruiting year in over a quarter-century. Whether or not sufficient numbers of volunteers can be found to maintain even the existing force has emerged as a pressing question, despite the fact that at present only 0.5 percent of the American population is in uniform.

Without question, the Pentagon's arsenal contains a sufficient number of bombers, missiles, and attack aircraft carriers to launch strikes against Syria or Iran or North Korea, as some supporters of the Bush Doctrine might advocate. But if the requirement goes beyond inflicting punishment—if it includes putting "boots on the ground"—then the men and women to fill those boots are in increasingly scarce supply.

The Bush Doctrine has brought into sharp relief a mismatch between the administration's declared ambitions and the military resources available to pursue those ambitions. Yet, having decided after 9-11 not to mobilize the country, President Bush cannot now ask Americans to cancel their vacations and instead report to their local recruiter.

Habits of the Highly Ineffective

A doctrine of preventive war also assumes the availability of military leaders who can effectively translate into action the directives of their political masters. It is one thing to order a preventive war; it is another thing to win it.

Ever since the armed services recovered from the debacle of Vietnam, quality leadership has been a hallmark of the American military establishment. Members of the officer corps take their profession seriously. Nothing in the tactical performance of US forces in Iraq or Afghanistan ought to raise second thoughts on that score. The lieutenants, captains, and colonels know their business. They are smart, seasoned, and tough. Whether military leaders at the topmost echelon of command understand the operational and strategic imperatives of preventive war may be another matter, however.

In all of the controversy that the Iraq War has generated, the performance of the most senior US officers—the three- and four-star commanders— has attracted surprisingly little attention. Yet a strong argument can be made that at the very top, US military leadership has been at best mediocre if not altogether unsatisfactory. Two examples will suffice to make the point: General Tommy Franks and Lieutenant General Ricardo Sanchez.

As commanding general of US Central Command, Franks planned and directed the invasions of Afghanistan and Iraq. In Afghanistan, the forces commanded by Franks handily toppled the Taliban regime and scattered, but did not destroy, the Al Qaeda cadres that had used Afghanistan as a safe haven. Osama bin Laden, Al Qaeda's supreme leader and the chief architect of the 9-11 attacks, eluded capture and remains at large. Although ousted from power, the Taliban refused to submit to the new American-installed political order. The effort to pacify Afghanistan continues, a low-level war that may become virtually perpetual. The decision gained by Franks in Afghanistan qualifies at best as partial and incomplete.

By comparison with Iraq, however, Afghanistan looks like a triumph. When it came to planning Operation Iraqi Freedom, General Franks counted on "shock and awe" to paralyze the Iraqi army and facilitate a lightning advance on the Iraqi capital, seen as the centerpiece of Baathist legitimacy. For Franks, Baghdad in 2003 became like Berlin in 1945: capturing it, he believed, meant endgame.

The sword of American military power is neither sharp enough nor hard enough to meet the demands of preventive war.

Even before the war began, dissenting voices warned otherwise. Studies undertaken by the State Department and the US Army War College forecast major challenges *after* Hussein and his henchmen had been removed. Most famously, General Eric Shinseki, then the army chief of staff, suggested that the occupation of Iraq was likely to require "several hundred thousand" soldiers.

These warnings turned out to be prescient. Franks failed to appreciate the political forces that Hussein's removal from power would unleash. His planning for "Phase IV"—the occupation of Iraq—verged on the non-existent. As a consequence, the disorder produced by the overthrow of Hussein caught Franks and his subordinates flat-footed. Out of that disorder there emerged an intense struggle to determine the future of Iraq, a struggle that soon became an insurgency that aimed to oust the "occupying" Americans.

Hardly had the outlines of that insurgency begun to emerge than Franks departed the scene, retiring to write his best-selling memoirs (in which he dismisses Shinseki as an ill-informed meddler). The man inheriting the mess that Franks left in his wake was General Sanchez, who served as senior US ground commander in Iraq for the insurgency's first full year. His mission was clear: snuff out the insurgency. Instead, Sanchez fueled it.

Historians of the Iraq War will likely remember Sanchez as this conflict's William C. Westmoreland—the senior commander who, in failing to grasp the political-military nature of the problem he faced, set US forces on an erroneous course from which recovery became all but impossible.

General Westmoreland, of course, was the senior US commander in South Vietnam from 1964 to 1968. Working within the very narrow constraints imposed on him by the Johnson administration, he concluded that the best way to defend South Vietnam was to capitalize on superior US firepower and mobility to crush the North Vietnamese communists. Westmoreland committed the United States to a protracted war of attrition, confident that his forces could inflict casualties at a rate that the enemy could not sustain. He miscalculated and the ultimate result was American defeat.

Similarly, Sanchez in 2003 judged the correlation of forces in Iraq to be in his favor and decided that a tough, aggressive strategy would disarm the insurgency before it could gain momentum. He too miscalculated, as badly as Westmoreland had. Rather than intimidating the insurgents, his kick-down-the-door tactics emboldened them and alienated ordinary Iraqis who came to see the Americans not as liberators but as an alien occupying force. Over the course of Sanchez's tenure in Baghdad, the insurgency grew in scope and sophistication. His successors have been struggling ever since to regain the upper hand. Today, the conflict drags on, eroding American popular support for the war and sapping the strength of the forces engaged. A doctrine of preventive war requires that the forces engaged accomplish their mission swiftly, economically, and without leaving loose ends. The generals employed to implement the Bush Doctrine have not demonstrated an ability to deliver those results.

The Tarnished Military

Especially in a democracy, a doctrine of preventive war also requires soldiers who manifest a consistently high level of professionalism. To maintain public support for what is, stripped to its essentials, a policy of aggression, the military forces committed to the enterprise must acquit themselves with honor, thereby making it easier to suppress questions about the war's moral justification. As long as US soldiers in Iraq behave like liberators, for example, it becomes easier for President Bush to maintain the position that America's true purpose is to spread the blessings of freedom and democracy.

Sadly, in the dirty war that Iraq has become, a number of American soldiers have behaved in ways that have undermined the administration's liberation narrative. This is a story in which the facts are as yet only partially known. But this much we can say for sure: after the revelations from Abu Ghraib prison and the credible allegations lodged recently by Captain Ian Fishback regarding widespread detainee abuse in the 82d Airborne Division, and with other accounts of misconduct steadily accumulating from week to week, it is no longer possible to pass off soldierly misbehavior as the late-night shenanigans of a few low-ranking sadists lacking adequate supervision. Unprofessional behavior in the ranks of the American military may not have reached epidemic proportions, but it is far from rare.

More sadly still, the chain of command seems determined to turn a blind eye to this growing problem. The courageous Fishback labored for 18 months to interest his superiors in the problem that he had witnessed in Iraq. Only when he brought his concerns to the attention of Human Rights Watch and the US Congress did anyone take notice. A year and a half after the Abu

Ghraib scandal broke, the only senior officer to have been held accountable is a female reservist, Brigadier General Janis Karpinski, who was demoted and forced to retire. Karpinski's complaint of an old boy's club using her as a convenient scapegoat is self-serving, but it may well contain an element of truth. The American officer corps once professed to hold sacrosanct the principle of command responsibility. No more. At the very least it no longer applies to those occupying the executive suites in Baghdad and Washington.

The US military may well be teetering on the brink of a profound moral crisis. Another conflict like Iraq could easily prove the tipping point. That prospect alone ought to temper the Bush administration's enthusiasm for any further experiments with preventive war. At its conception, the Bush Doctrine represented a radical departure from the best traditions of American statecraft. Efforts to implement the doctrine have cost the nation and especially its military dearly without appreciably enhancing American security. It is too much to expect that this administration, committed to the proposition that it must never acknowledge error, will officially abrogate the Bush Doctrine. But the administration ignores reality at its peril. As it contemplates the wreckage caused by its preventive war in Iraq, the White House may well come to see the wisdom of allowing the Bush Doctrine to die a quiet and unlamented death.

ANDREW J. BACEVICH is a professor of international relations at Boston University. His most recent book is *The New American Militarism: How Americans Are Seduced by War* (Oxford University Press, 2005).

Reprinted from *Current History*, December 2005, pp. 411-417. Copyright © 2005 by Current History, Inc. Reprinted with permission.

Base Politics

ALEXANDER COOLEY

Redeploying U.S. Troops

This past July, the government of Uzbekistan evicted U.S. personnel from the Karshi–Khanabad air base, which Washington had used as a staging ground for combat, reconnaissance, and humanitarian missions in Afghanistan since late 2001. The government in Tashkent gave no official reason for the expulsion, but the order was issued soon after the UN airlifted 439 Uzbek refugees from Kyrgyzstan to Romania—a move that Washington supported and Tashkent opposed. (The Uzbek government wanted the refugees to return home, but the international community did not, fearing that they would be detained and tortured by Uzbek security personnel.) The showdown was the latest in a series of confrontations since a much-criticized crackdown on antigovernment demonstrators in the eastern city of Andijon last May.

These events illustrate the enduring problem that U.S. defense officials face as they try to promote democratic values abroad while maintaining U.S. military bases in nondemocratic countries. Although some in Washington acknowledge this tension, they generally argue that the strategic benefits of having U.S. bases close to important theaters such as Afghanistan outweigh the political costs of supporting unsavory host regimes. With the Pentagon now redefining the role of the U.S. military in the twenty-first century, moreover, its officials insist even more on the importance of developing a vast network of U.S. bases to confront cross-border terrorism and other regional threats. Some of them also turn the objections of pro-democracy critics around. They claim that a U.S. military presence in repressive countries gives Washington additional leverage to press them to liberalize. And, they argue, relying on democratic hosts for military cooperation can present problems of its own—such as the 2003 parliamentary vote in Turkey that denied the United States the chance to launch its invasion of Iraq from there.

Such arguments have merit, but they do not tell the whole story. For one thing, the political complications sometimes associated with dealing with democracies are ephemeral. For another, setting up bases in nondemocratic states brings mostly short-term benefits, rarely helps promote liberalization, and sometimes even endangers U.S. security. Engaging authoritarian leaders by striking basing deals with them has done little for democratization in those states because these leaders know that, at bottom, U.S. military planners care more about the bases' utility than about local political trends. The practice can also imperil U.S. strategic interests. Even as authoritarian leaders

flout U.S. calls for liberalization, they often manipulate basing agreements to strengthen their personal standing at home. And when one of these autocrats is eventually ousted, the democratic successor sometimes challenges the validity of the deals the former regime had struck.

Basing agreements made with mature democracies involve far fewer risks. Such deals come at no cost to U.S. legitimacy, and they tend to be more reliable since security commitments approved and validated by democratic institutions are made to last. As U.S. military planners design a global network of smaller, more versatile military facilities abroad, they would do well to reconsider whether the limited benefits of establishing bases in nondemocratic countries are worth the costs those arrangements inevitably generate.

Deals with Devils

Historically, the United States has had little success leveraging its foreign bases to promote democratic values in host countries. After World War II, Washington established bases in both democracies and those nondemocratic states that resisted Soviet influence. U.S. officials consistently defended their deals with nondemocratic countries by claiming that engagement could gradually lead to their democratization. In fact, the United States accomplished little by engaging dictators in this way—except to tarnish its reputation by virtue of the association.

Consider three basing agreements—with Spain, Portugal, and the Philippines—struck in different decades and by U.S. administrations of different ideological leanings. In 1953, the Eisenhower administration signed a bilateral defense agreement with Spain, then under the rule of the dictator General Francisco Franco. The agreement granted the United States the use of a network of air bases, naval stations, pipelines, and communications facilities in Spain in exchange for a $226 million package of military and economic assistance. It was immediately criticized within the United States and by U.S. allies in Europe for giving Franco legitimacy and material support just as other states were trying to exclude his regime from international institutions such as the UN and NATO. U.S. officials long insisted that the U.S. military presence in Spain did not imply official support for his regime. But the Spanish politicians who succeeded Franco after his death in 1975 accused Washington of having tacitly condoned his repressive policies and his secrecy.

In the 1960s, even the idealistic Kennedy administration was quick to temper its calls for decolonization throughout Africa once the prime minister of Portugal, António de Oliveira Salazar, threatened to curtail U.S. access to important bases in the Azores (Portuguese islands in the mid-Atlantic). Lisbon was concerned about calls for self-determination in its African colonies, including Angola and Mozambique. Salazar considered the counterinsurgency in Angola a matter of domestic politics, and he was incensed when in 1961 Washington backed a UN Security Council resolution calling for reform and a UN inquiry. Under mounting pressure from the Pentagon, which did not want to lose the mid-Atlantic facilities, the White House changed its position in early 1962. But the Portuguese government kept the bases' status in abeyance throughout the 1960s to keep its leverage over Washington.

This pattern repeated itself elsewhere in the 1970s and the early 1980s, perhaps most visibly in the Philippines under strongman Ferdinand Marcos. The presence of two major U.S. military installations in the Philippines, Clark Air Base and the Subic Bay naval station, kept U.S. criticism of Marcos in check. Even the Carter administration, despite its determination to promote human rights abroad, softened its stance when the time came to renew a base agreement in 1979. As Marcos asked for ever more U.S. economic and military assistance, Washington complied, effectively helping to prop up the dictator and his cronies until their ouster in 1986.

In all these cases, U.S. engagement did little to promote genuine political reform because the host governments correctly calculated that Washington cared more about its bases than about political liberalization. At the same time, by repeatedly ignoring violations of democratic principles in order to preserve its outposts, the United States exposed itself to charges of opportunism and hypocrisy. Throughout the Cold War, pragmatists in the White House might have answered the accusations by pointing to an overriding strategic purpose: defeating the Soviet Union. But now that the war on terrorism has replaced the war on communism, the costs of such a bargain are much greater.

Insecurity System

If the first problem with establishing bases in nondemocratic states is that doing so can interfere with local democratization, the second—and less appreciated—problem is that it has serious strategic costs for the United States.

First, U.S. support for authoritarian governments can breed just the kind of opposition or radicalism that U.S. bases are indirectly designed to stem. Basing agreements offer propaganda opportunities for both legitimate opposition groups and extremists. And the presence of a U.S. base in an nondemocratic state can generate more extremists than it stops. Take, for example, the case of Saudi Arabia. The 1996 terrorist attack on the Khobar Towers, where U.S. troops were housed, emboldened Islamic extremists to call for the complete withdrawal of U.S. forces from the Arabian Peninsula. The attack raised security concerns for Washington but also suggested to the Saudi government that the U.S. military presence was a domestic political threat. Ultimately, in 2003, Washington was compelled to withdraw 5,000 troops from Saudi Arabia.

Second, nondemocratic regimes are inherently unreliable hosts. It is sometimes assumed that entering into agreements with dictators guarantees the deals' longevity because such regimes are less vulnerable than democracies to shifts in public opinion. But many political scientists now believe that operating without the restrictions of a constitution, an independent judiciary, and an elected legislature actually makes it easier for authoritarian regimes to violate treaties such as military basing agreements. Agreements with an authoritarian state last only as long as the ruling regime does—if even that long—because the status of such treaties is subject to the regime's fortunes rather than to a lasting institutional framework. In the past, the United States has been expelled when its autocratic allies have been toppled from within: Washington lost access to Wheelus Air Base in Libya in 1969 when Colonel Muammar al-Qaddafi took power, as it did to electronic listening posts in northern Iran when Mohammad Reza Pahlavi's regime collapsed in 1979. Even when authoritarian governments do honor basing agreements, they can revise the terms of the deals unilaterally, on a whim, to better serve their domestic purposes or extract material concessions from Washington.

Third, when democratic governments eventually take over in authoritarian countries, U.S. bases there are vulnerable to various forms of backlash. In post-authoritarian elections in Thailand (in 1975), Greece (in 1981), and South Korea (in 1997 and 2002), for example, opposition leaders won office by campaigning against the U.S. military presence, explicitly linking U.S. bases to Washington's support for previous nondemocratic regimes. Sometimes, too, civic groups and media outlets in a state undergoing a democratic transition denounce basing agreements signed with the authoritarian government as symbols of the previous regime's abuses. Worse, in some cases, new democratic governments challenge the validity of preexisting basing agreements, precipitating a severe curtailment of U.S. rights, sometimes leading to expulsion. In the late 1980s, the Spanish Socialist Party (known as the PSOE) refused to extend a basing agreement with the United States for access to the Torrejón air base, near Madrid. And in 1991, the newly empowered post-Marcos Philippine Senate rejected a plan to extend the lease of Subic Bay, terminating the long-standing U.S. military presence there. In these and other cases, the domestic backlash against the U.S. basing presence inflicted considerable operational costs on the U.S. military.

These types of strategic costs all relate to the political difficulties that arise from concluding agreements with nondemocratic regimes. Although U.S. officials have often believed that the United States was unfairly accused of supporting its authoritarian hosts, such perceptions became commonplace in countries where it maintained a military presence. From a practical perspective, separating operational military needs from the local political context has proved difficult.

In consolidated democracies, on the other hand, governments continue to honor their commitments to basing agreements because those deals are guaranteed by an established legal order. Even though the government of Prime Minister

José Luis Rodríguez Zapatero withdrew Spanish troops from Iraq shortly after he was elected in March 2004, it continued to honor a preexisting agreement, which effectively allowed the United States unhindered use of its naval station at Rota and its air base in Morón in support of the Iraq campaign. The same is true of other base-hosting democratic allies, such as Germany and Greece, which also opposed the invasion of Iraq and yet allowed operations connected to the war to take place on their soil.

Some have argued that Turkey's refusal to let U.S. troops use its territory to launch an offensive in northern Iraq in 2003 is proof that democracies can be fickle partners. In fact, however, the episode revealed the institutional weaknesses that characterize democratizing states or young democracies. Although Prime Minister Recep Tayyip Erdogan called the Turkish parliament's close vote against granting the United States access into Iraq a victory for democracy, it was largely the product of his party's relative inexperience at managing its new parliamentary majority and its antagonistic relationship with the country's influential military. (Erdogan was in favor of granting access, and the military reportedly wanted to see his party embarrassed.) The Turkish vote mirrored the uncertainty that characterized Turkish domestic politics at the time. But as democracies become increasingly consolidated and institutionalized, they are able to commit more credibly to their external agreements. Over the long term, democracies make for more predictable and stable base hosts than authoritarian states.

Installation Art

The question of how the United States can best use military bases abroad to ensure its security has resurfaced since the Defense Department started rethinking the overseas deployment of U.S. troops after the attacks of September 11, 2001. To support Operation Enduring Freedom in Afghanistan, the United States established air bases in Kyrgyzstan, Pakistan, and Uzbekistan and signed agreements for refueling rights and airspace access throughout Central Asia. In 2003, to compensate for the loss of access to Turkey, the United States used airfields and ports in Bulgaria and Romania to support its military campaign in Iraq. And over the next few years, the Pentagon will implement the 2004 Global Defense Posture Review (GDPR), which outlined plans for the most fundamental change in U.S. basing strategy since World War II.

The GDPR calls for increasing the number of overseas U.S. facilities by replacing and supplementing large Cold War–era bases in Germany, Japan, and South Korea with smaller facilities known as forward operating sites, or FOSs (small installations that can be rapidly built up), and cooperative security locations, or CSLs (host-nation facilities with little U.S. personnel but with equipment and logistical capabilities), both of which can be activated when necessary. These FOSs and CSLs will be used against sources of regional instability, covering areas where the United States has traditionally been absent. They are likely to be established in eastern Europe (Bulgaria, Poland, and Romania) and Africa (Algeria, Djibouti, Gabon, Ghana, Kenya, Mali, São Tomé and Príncipe, Senegal, and

Uganda), although the exact location of these facilities is still under negotiation. The U.S. expansion in Africa is especially noteworthy, as it is accompanied by increased military-to-military cooperation, such as the Pan Sahel Initiative, under which the U.S. military is assisting Chad, Niger, Mali, and Mauritania in efforts to stem local terrorism. These FOSs and CSLs will be designed to have maximal operational flexibility with minimal political downsides and few limitations on U.S. access. The hope is that by maintaining a lighter footprint, Washington will avoid some of the problems that have periodically arisen in connection with the large U.S. deployments in South Korea and Okinawa, Japan, such as traffic accidents and crimes involving U.S. military personnel.

The GDPR's reforms have already been criticized, especially for their cost, their impracticality, and the dampening effect they could have on traditional U.S. alliances. Yet few critics have pointed out that a considerable number of new facilities are planned in countries with weak or nondemocratic political systems. Washington planners envision that even a small U.S. military presence will help guard against terrorist threats, secure important U.S. economic and energy interests, stabilize the countries hosting bases, and normalize regional politics. More likely, however, the governments of these countries will label both extreme and democratic opposition groups as regional security threats and embroil the United States in domestic political disputes and low-intensity clashes in which it has no compelling interest. Before it sets up more bases in authoritarian countries, the Defense Department would do well to consider some of its recent experiences.

The K2 Problem

Since the September 11 attacks, Washington seems to be repeating some of its old mistakes. When, in October 2001, it set up the Karshi–Khanabad air base (also known as K2) in southern Uzbekistan to launch operations into Afghanistan, it was hardly concerned by its host's democratic deficit. In March 2002, President Bush and Uzbek President Islam Karimov signed a broader strategic cooperation agreement, calling for a partnership in the war on terrorism and establishing ties between U.S. and Uzbek military and security services. In addition to paying $15 million for use of the airfield, as a tacit quid pro quo, in 2002 the United States provided $120 million in military hardware and surveillance equipment to the Uzbek army, $82 million to the country's security services, and $55 million in credits from the U.S. Export-Import Bank. The Uzbek government, for its part, pledged to speed up democratization, improve its human rights record, and promote greater press freedoms. With the exception of some human rights organizations, few in the West criticized the agreement; it was widely hailed as a necessary step in the Afghan campaign.

While operations in Afghanistan continued throughout 2002 and 2003, U.S. officials largely ignored the Uzbek government's failure to fulfill its commitments. In January 2002, Karimov arbitrarily extended his term until 2007, but U.S. authorities held back from denouncing him and praised the new cooperative relationship. They turned a blind eye to the steady increase in political jailings that Uzbek security services were conducting in the name of counterterrorism. And as part of the Bush administration's practice of "extraordinary rendition," they ordered dozens of terrorist suspects shipped to Uzbekistan knowing that law enforcement officials there routinely employ torture.

Signs of open discomfort within the U.S. policy community began to surface in the summer of 2004. In July of that year, the State Department rescinded $18 million in aid to Uzbekistan because of human rights violations. But a month later, during a visit to Tashkent by General Richard Meyers, then chairman of the Joint Chiefs of Staff, the Department of Defense awarded Uzbekistan $21 million in weapons transfers and military assistance.

Matters came to a head with the Andijon crackdown of last May, which highlighted the political compromises Washington was making to maintain access to K2. Uzbek security forces attacked thousands of demonstrators, led by armed militants, who were protesting the conviction of 23 Uzbek businessmen accused of being Muslim extremists. Uzbek government officials claimed that the militants led a prison break, captured a local police station and a military barracks, and took several hostages. But human rights organizations have reported that the demonstration comprised mostly unarmed citizens protesting local political and economic policies. According to witnesses, Uzbek security forces fired indiscriminately into the crowd, mowing down waves of civilians as they tried to flee the scene. International nongovernmental organizations such as the International Crisis Group and Human Rights Watch have estimated the death toll at 700 to 800, well above the official figure of 180, and have accused the Uzbek government of covering up details of the incident by intimidating journalists and witnesses.

Still, fearful of losing access to U.S. bases, some U.S. officials were reluctant to criticize the Uzbek government. The Bush administration initially balked at any condemnation; U.S. defense officials at NATO opposed the alliance's issuing a joint communiqué calling for an international probe. Soon after, however, Secretary of State Condoleezza Rice publicly backed an international inquiry, and a bipartisan group of U.S. senators launched an investigation to determine whether any of the Uzbek security troops involved in the crackdown had received U.S. training or equipment. In response to the scrutiny, Uzbek authorities began to limit nighttime and cargo flights to and from K2 and to complain about payment issues and environmental damage relating to use of the base.

Last July, the relationship finally soured for good. After the United States backed the UN effort to airlift Uzbek refugees from neighboring Kyrgyzstan to Romania against the wishes of the Uzbek government, Tashkent activated a termination clause in the K2 base agreement that required the U.S. military to close the facility within 180 days—dispelling any lingering illusion that the Uzbek regime was a reliable security partner. By ordering the shutdown, Karimov subordinated his commitment to the United States to other geopolitical and domestic goals: expelling the United States ingratiated him with Moscow and Beijing and may have given him a chance to consolidate public support in the face of U.S. meddling in local affairs.

Setting up military bases in nondemocratic states undermines both U.S. security and Washington's commitment to democratization.

Washington's decision to establish a base in Kyrgyzstan in support of Operation Enduring Freedom has proved similarly complicated. U.S. officials have faced tricky political tradeoffs related to the operation of Ganci Air Base, established in 2001 with the consent of then President Askar Akayev. Prior to the basing agreement, Akayev had increasingly entrenched his rule and let democratization efforts backslide. The basing agreement gave Akayev's regime new international credibility by distracting Western attention from his political abuses and anointing him as a partner in the U.S.-led war on terrorism. The small Kyrgyz economy also significantly benefited from the fees and business generated by the air base, which account for five to ten percent of Kyrgyzstan's GDP. Meanwhile, Kyrgyz security services, who obtained military hardware and surveillance equipment as a result of the deal, began emphasizing—and exaggerating—the threat of Islamic extremism to secure continued U.S. assistance. In November 2003, they claimed to have uncovered a plot to bomb Ganci Air Base and allegedly caught three members of a radical Islamic organization with explosives and blueprints of the base. But U.S. officials and Kyrgyz political observers are skeptical about the details of the plot and the circumstances of the arrests.

Now that the Akayev regime has fallen, Washington may face difficulties with his successors. After Akayev was swept out of power in March 2005 by public demonstrations following disputed parliamentary elections, the question of the U.S. military presence was suddenly thrust onto the political agenda of the new Kyrgyz government. In a joint statement issued on July 5, 2005, the Shanghai Cooperation Organization, which consists of China, Kazakhstan, Kyrgyzstan, Russia, Tajikistan, and Uzbekistan, declared that the U.S. military bases in Central Asia had outlived their purpose of supporting the Afghan campaign and should be closed. In his first press conference, a week later, President Kurmanbek Bakiyev announced that the Kyrgyz government would press Washington about the necessity of keeping the base; later, he pledged that he would pursue an "independent" foreign policy. Questions about the orientation of the new regime in Kyrgyzstan remain, but it is already clear that the loss of K2 in Uzbekistan has made Ganci Air Base all the more important to U.S. planners.

In addition to possibly relocating some activities from K2 to Kyrgyzstan, U.S. officials are exploring other options in Kazakhstan, Tajikistan, and Turkmenistan, where the United States has occasionally used airfields for refueling stops. A visit by Secretary of Defense Donald Rumsfeld to Azerbaijan in August 2005 increased speculation that Washington may be considering establishing a military presence there, too. In its determination to maintain a strategic foothold in Central Asia, the United States is once again considering striking deals with nondemocratic regimes—thus giving material support and legitimacy to autocrats and exposing its operational presence to local politics.

Fanning Out

While Washington struggles with political difficulties in Central Asia, its future presence in the Black Sea region—negotiations are under way for bases in Bulgaria and Romania—promises to be more stable politically. Bulgaria and Romania offer a number of attractive large-scale facilities, such as ports on the Black Sea, airfields, and training ranges. Future bases in these countries would not only help safeguard U.S. security interests in the Black Sea region but also serve as important staging grounds for operations in the Middle East and Central Asia.

The recent democratic consolidations of Bulgaria and Romania and the countries' integration into Western international institutions are also likely to create a favorable operating environment for years to come. Both countries supported the U.S.-led campaign in Iraq over the objections of some other European states (confirming their allegiance to Washington) and then in 2004 became NATO members (formalizing their strategic alignment with the West). To secure NATO membership, Sofia and Bucharest had to implement important domestic institutional reforms: they strengthened civilian control over their militaries, downsized and modernized their armed forces, and improved transparency in defense-related matters. Although some political parties in both countries, including the recently elected Socialist Party in Bulgaria, have promised to take a tougher line with the United States, no party with a significant share of the vote actually opposes the idea of a U.S. presence. The Bulgarian and Romanian publics appear to back strongly the prospect of U.S. bases, and many people view these bases as an important political counterweight to the EU's influence.

Any negative reaction that may arise in Bulgaria or Romania to the U.S. bases is most likely to result from unfulfilled expectations about the benefits of the United States' presence there. Consistent with the Defense Department's new basing posture, permanent U.S. deployments will likely be relatively small—no more than 1,000 troops per country—and so the overall economic impact of future bases may not meet the lofty expectations that now prevail. Although both countries' political systems are consolidated, moreover, their media are relatively new and fiercely competitive. Base-related incidents and scandals involving U.S. personnel are sure to draw media attention, as well as public scrutiny over criminal procedures and other legal aspects governing U.S. bases. Nevertheless, given their advanced state of democratization and their integration into the West, Bulgaria and Romania are unlikely to generate the type of internal political pressures that have threatened the U.S. presence elsewhere.

With so much of the United States' international legitimacy now tied to how well it promotes democracy abroad, resolving the tension between its commitment to democratic values and its need for overseas bases must become a priority for Washington. Some U.S. officials have tried to characterize the expulsion from K2 in Uzbekistan as proof of Washington's commitment to democracy, but it was too little too late: the ouster followed several years of apparent unconcern about the abuses of Karimov's regime, and the damage to U.S. credibility had already been done. Additional Uzbekistan-type imbroglios related to basing rights would only hurt Washington more. If the Defense Department is serious about best preparing the United States for a new type of war by redeploying its troops, it would do well to pick stable and democratic places to root.

Planners might object that a threat's location often forces the United States to establish a presence in areas where it otherwise would not choose to go. Even in such extreme cases, however, there is a difference between establishing a base out of necessity and maintaining it after major combat operations are over. Take the case of Uzbekistan. Although the U.S. military has insisted since the fall of 2001 that K2 is vital to U.S. operations in Central Asia, the base's strategic value has considerably diminished over the past several years. Yet at no point between 2001 and the first talk of ousting the United States from K2 this summer did the Pentagon publicly reexamine the base's purpose. The Pentagon's failure to distinguish the strategic justification for establishing a base from the organizational reasons for maintaining one is another impediment to assessing the real costs of various U.S. basing strategies.

Full-on operations such as the war in Afghanistan are less likely in the future, and so as the United States sets out to establish a vaster but lighter presence in various regions, it has more freedom about where exactly to set up its bases. In deciding where to redeploy troops, Pentagon officials should seriously consider the political implications of their choices. They must recognize that by setting up military bases abroad, Washington will inevitably become enmeshed in the domestic politics of its hosts, even if it intends to keep a low profile and a light footprint. Setting up bases in nondemocratic states can be accomplished relatively quickly and easily, but in the long term it undermines Washington's commitment to democratization abroad and its strategic interests. Setting up bases in democracies may generate some media scrutiny, political debate, and public criticism at first, but democracies invariably turn out to be more reliable hosts in the end. Understanding these tradeoffs is essential, especially now that even within strategically important regions the Pentagon has real choices about where to establish its outposts.

The Terrorism Index

Is the United States winning the war on terror? Not according to more than 100 of America's top foreign-policy hands. They see a national security apparatus in disrepair and a government that is failing to protect the public from the next attack.

Following the terrorist attacks of Sept. 11, 2001, Americans understandably rallied around the flag. Having just suffered the deadliest attack ever on U.S. soil, huge percentages believed another attack was imminent. But Americans also had enormous faith that the Global War on Terror would help keep them safe. Just one month after 9/11, for instance, 94 percent of Americans told an ABC News/*Washington Post* poll that they approved of how the fight against terrorism was being handled. The United States then quickly went to war in Afghanistan, closing down a terrorist sanctuary and capturing or killing a number of high-level al Qaeda operatives in the process.

Since 2001, terrorists have found their targets on almost every continent, with bombings in Bali, London, Madrid, and elsewhere. Five years on, however, America has yet to experience another attack. But Americans appear less convinced that their country is winning the war on terror. In the face of persisting threats, including a growing number of terrorist attacks around the world, numerous reports show that Americans are losing faith in their government's ability to wage the war successfully and to protect them from the terrorists' next volley. Barely half of Americans today approve of the way in which the war on terror is being handled, and more than one third believe the United States is less safe today than it was before 9/11.

These pessimistic public perceptions could easily be attributed to the high cost, in both treasure and lives, of counterterrorism efforts. After all, Americans are constantly being told by their elected leaders that their pessimism is wrong, that the war is being won. But they're also told that another attack is inevitable. Which is it? To find out, FOREIGN POLICY and the Center for American Progress teamed up to survey more than 100 of America's top foreign-policy experts—Republicans and Democrats alike. The FOREIGN POLICY/Center for American Progress Terrorism Index is the first comprehensive effort to mine the highest echelons of America's foreign-policy establishment for their assessment of how the United States is fighting the Global War on Terror. Our aim was to draw some definitive conclusions about the war's priorities, policies, and progress from the very people who have run America's national security apparatus over the past half century. Participants include people who have served as secretary of state, national security advisor, retired top commanders from the U.S. military,

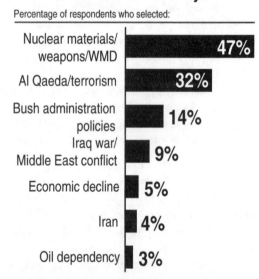

Thinking about the present situation, would you say that the world is becoming safer or more dangerous for the United States and the American people?

Much or somewhat safer **10%**
Much or somewhat more dangerous **86%**

In your view, what is the single greatest threat to U.S. national security?

Percentage of respondents who selected:

Nuclear materials/weapons/WMD	47%
Al Qaeda/terrorism	32%
Bush administration policies	14%
Iraq war/Middle East conflict	9%
Economic decline	5%
Iran	4%
Oil dependency	3%

President Bush has stated that the United States is winning the war on terror. How do you feel about that statement?

Political Affiliation	Percentage of respondents who selected:	
	Agree	Disagree
Total	13	84
Conservative	23	71
Moderate	8	90
Liberal	9	89

With Friends Like These

Wars have a way of making unlikely bedfellows, and the Global War on Terror is apparently no different.

Asked to name the country that has produced the largest number of global terrorists, the index's foreign-policy experts pointed to Saudi Arabia, Egypt, and Pakistan—three of America's marquee allies in the Muslim world. Nearly two thirds (62 percent) identified Saudi Arabia as the leading culprit. Thirteen percent pointed to Egypt, and 11 percent said Pakistan produces the most terrorists. "The jihadist movement," says index participant and Sarah Lawrence College Professor Fawaz Gerges, "was born in Egypt in the late 1960s. After September 11, however, Saudi Arabia has emerged as the leading theater of jihadist-Salafist thought and action."

Although these three states may be widely believed to be incubating terrorists, the cooperation they have offered the United States in fighting terrorism presents a more mixed picture. Approximately two thirds of the experts say that U.S. cooperation with Egypt and Pakistan has been effective. The experts are more divided as to whether Saudi Arabia is doing what it can to counter the terrorist threat.

These perceptions cut to the heart of some of the dilemmas facing the United States. Egypt, for instance, has received more than $50 billion in U.S. military and economic assistance since 1979, yet it resisted recent U.S. efforts to promote political reform. America designated Pakistan a major non-NATO ally in 2004, despite allegations that it has not done enough to capture bin Laden. Saudi Arabia has helped crack down on financial support flowing to terrorist groups, but Saudi leaders have been slow to move against radical elements within their own population. Is the United States doing a poor job of choosing its friends? Maybe. Then again, it may just be keeping its friends close, and its enemies closer.

Which single country has produced the largest number of global terrorists?

Percentage of respondents who selected:	
Saudi Arabia	**62**
Egypt	13
Pakistan	11
Palestine	1
Yemen	1
Iraq	1
Lebanon	1
Afghanistan	1
Iran	1

The Popular Front

Foreign-policy experts may know the issues, but they can sometimes be guilty of groupthink, and the public has a mind of its own. Here's a look at where the index's experts and the American public agree—and part ways.

America is winning the war on terror.

	Agree	Disagree
Experts	13%	**84%**
Public	**56%**	41%

How likely is a major terrorist attack in America this year?

	Likely	Unlikely
Experts	35%	**62%**
Public	**66%**	33%

Has the war in Iraq had a positive or negative impact on the war on terror?

	Positive	Negative	No Impact
Experts	10%	**87%**	3%
Public	38%	**44%**	8%

The United States should close down the detention facility at Guantánamo Bay.

	Agree	Disagree
Experts	**66%**	27%
Public	36%	**58%**

Becoming less dependent on foreign sources of energy will strengthen national security.

	Agree	Disagree
Experts	**82%**	11%
Public	**90%**	8%

SOURCES: CNN/*USA Today*/Gallup Poll, Jan. 20–22, 2006; Harris Poll, Feb. 7–14, 2006; Pew Research Center for the People and the Press, March 16, 2006; CNN/*USA Today*/Gallup Poll, June 16–19, 2005; Public Agenda Confidence In U.S. Foreign Policy Index, January 2006

seasoned members of the intelligence community, and distinguished academics and journalists. Nearly 80 percent of the index participants have worked in the U.S. government—of these more than half were in the executive branch, one third in the military, and 17 percent in the intelligence community.

Despite today's highly politicized national security environment, the index results show striking consensus across political party lines. A bipartisan majority (84 percent) of the index's experts say the United States is not winning the war on terror. Eighty-six percent of the index's experts see a world today that is growing more dangerous for Americans. Overall, they agree that the U.S. government is falling short in its homeland security efforts. More than 8 in 10 expect an attack on the scale of 9/11 within a decade. These dark conclusions appear to stem from the experts' belief that the U.S. national security apparatus is in serious disrepair. "Foreign-policy experts have never been in so much agreement about an administration's performance abroad," says Leslie Gelb, president emeritus of the Council on Foreign Relations and an index participant. "The reason is that it's clear to nearly all that Bush and his team have had a totally unrealistic view of what they can accomplish with military force and threats of force."

Respondents sharply criticized U.S. efforts in a number of key areas of national security, including public diplomacy, intelligence, and homeland security. Nearly all of the departments and agencies responsible for fighting the war on terror received poor marks. The experts also said that recent reforms of the national security apparatus have done little to make Americans safer. Asked about recent efforts to reform America's intelligence community, for instance, more than half of the index's experts said that creating the Office of the Director of National Intelligence has had no positive impact in the war against terror. "Intelligence reform so far has been largely limited to structural reorganization that in most cases produced new levels of bureaucracy in an already overly bureaucratic system," says index participant Bill Gertz, a journalist who has covered the intelligence community for more than 20 years.

The Next Attack

Americans are consistently told that the next terrorist attack on U.S. soil is a question of when, not if. The index's results overwhelmingly agree that the next attack is just a matter of time.

Eighty-four percent of the experts said they believe a terrorist attack on the scale of Sept. 11, 2001, is likely or certain to happen in the next five years. More than a quarter said a 9/11-scale attack is certain to occur in America within the next decade. Asked about the likelihood of a smaller strike akin to the July 2005 London bombings, 91 percent agreed that such an attack is likely or certain by 2016; more than half said that such an attack could happen this year.

But how will the terrorists strike? Roughly two thirds of the experts said that some part of America's infrastructure—a port, train station, or major landmark—will be targeted. That is no surprise, given that terrorists have repeatedly struck these locales in the past. But it may be more alarming that almost the same percentage predict that the next attack will come in the form of a suicide bombing. These results, says index participant Bruce Hoffman, a terrorism expert at the Rand Corp., "reflect a recognition of how easy terrorism has become." Such attacks, he says, "are cheap, unpredictable, and difficult to prevent. All that is required is the will to kill and the will to die, neither of which seems in short supply today."

Americans have never feared a suicide bombing the way the people of Amman or Jerusalem have. But there may be reason to think that will soon change. A recent study by Rand found that 81 percent of all suicide attacks in the past 30 or so years have occurred since Sept. 11, 2001, and the primary motivation for each of these attacks was a military intervention or occupation such as the ongoing operations in Iraq. The odds that America can continue to elude the world's most popular form of terrorism may be fading fast.

What is the likelihood of a terrorist attack on the scale of 9/11 occurring again in the United States in the following time frames?

Percentage of respondents who selected:	No chance or unlikely	Likely or certain
By the end of 2006	65	35
By the end of 2011	21	79
By the end of 2016	16	84

Now consider an attack on the scale of those that took place in London and Madrid ...

Percentage of respondents who selected:	No chance or unlikely	Likely or certain
By the end of 2006	43	57
By the end of 2011	16	84
By the end of 2016	9	91

Regardless of what you think about the timing of an attack, what two methods are most likely to be used in America by global terrorists?

Percentage of respondents who selected:	
Suicide bombing attack	67
Attack on major infrastructure	66
Attack using radiological weapon	20
Cyberattack	12
Attack on chemical or nuclear plants	11
Chemical weapon attack	10
Biological weapon attack	9
Nuclear weapon attack	6

Energy's Highest Price

If you could make something a higher priority in fighting the war on terror, what would it be? A little more than one third of the index's experts said killing or capturing terrorist leaders such as Osama bin Laden. About the same number favored promoting democracy in the Muslim world. More than two thirds said stopping the proliferation of nuclear weapons to rogue states. But devising a more aggressive energy policy?

It may surprise, but the index's experts said that ending America's dependence on foreign oil may be the U.S. government's single most pressing priority in winning the war on terror. Eighty-two percent of the experts said that policymakers should make ending America's dependence on foreign oil a higher priority. And nearly two thirds said that current U.S. energy policies are actually making matters worse, not better. "We borrow a billion dollars every working day to import oil, an increasing share of it coming from the Middle East," says index participant and former CIA director James Woolsey. "[F]or example in Saudi Arabia, billions are transferred to the Wahhabis and like-minded groups who then indoctrinate young people to hate Shiites, Sufis, Jews, Christians, and democracy, and to oppress women horribly."

If U.S. policymakers don't take this vulnerability seriously, terrorists do. Ayman al-Zawahiri, al Qaeda's No. 2, has labeled the global energy infrastructure a key strategic target for terrorists. In February, Saudi Arabia's government foiled an al Qaeda plot to attack the Abqaiq oil facility, the country's largest. Some 30,000 security forces are now guarding the country's oil fields. Global oil markets are so tight that even the threat of a supply disruption can cause a spike in price. These tight markets are partially responsible for the higher prices Americans will pay at the pump this summer. But the index suggests that there may be a greater price for our energy policy: losing the war on terror.

Please rate the impact of these actions or policies on protecting the American people from global terrorist networks.

Percentage of respondents who selected:	Positive impact	Negative impact
War in Iraq	10	87
Guantanamo	16	81
Energy policy	3	**64**
Iran policy	12	60
Public diplomacy	5	58
North Korea policy	1	49
War in Afghanistan	93	4

Please indicate whether each of the actions listed below should be given a higher or lower priority in the war on terror.

Percentage of respondents who selected:	Higher priority	Lower priority
Reduce foreign oil use	**82**	11
Improve intelligence	76	1
Stop loose nukes	68	12
Strengthen the U.N.	68	12
Strengthen DHS	65	9
Kill terrorist leaders	37	16
Increase military	30	36

The index's experts were similarly critical of most of the policy initiatives put forward by the U.S. Congress and President George W. Bush since September 11. Eighty-one percent, for instance, believe the detention of suspected terrorists at Guantánamo Bay, Cuba, negatively affects the war on terror. The index's experts also disapprove of how America is handling its relations with European allies, how it is confronting threatening regimes in North Korea and Iran, how it is controlling the spread of weapons of mass destruction, and its dealings with failing states, to name just a few. "We are losing the war on terror because we are treating the symptoms and not the cause," says index participant Anne-Marie Slaughter, dean of Princeton University's Woodrow Wilson School of Public and International Affairs. "[O]ur insistence that Islamic fundamentalist ideology has replaced communist ideology as the chief enemy of our time ... feeds al Qaeda's vision of the world."

These conclusions about the United States' performance in the war thus far are all the more troubling considering that, although

Americans appear to be growing tired of the war on terror, the index's experts appear to believe that the battle has just begun. Accordingly, a majority agrees that the war requires more emphasis on a victory of ideas, not just guns. That is hardly surprising, considering that nearly 80 percent believe a widespread rejection of radical ideologies in the Islamic world is a critical element to victory. To win the battle of ideas, the experts say, America must place a much higher emphasis on its nonmilitary tools. More than two thirds say that U.S. policymakers must strengthen the United Nations and other multilateral institutions. At the same time, the experts indicate that the U.S. government must think more creatively about threats. Asked what presents the single greatest danger to U.S. national security, nearly half said loose nukes and other weapons of mass destruction, while just one third said al Qaeda and terrorism, and a mere 4 percent said Iran. Five years after the attacks of September 11, it's a reminder that the greatest challenges may still lie ahead.

Grading the Government

A room full of foreign-policy experts can be a tough crowd. So it's hardly surprising that the index experts were highly critical of how the various branches of the U.S. government are fighting the war on terror. Only the National Security Agency received an above-average score of 5.2, on a 0 to 10 scale, where 0 represents the worst possible job of guarding the United States. Every other agency received below-average marks.

Experts gave the Department of Homeland Security (DHS) the worst grade. Its average score was just 2.9. In fact, 36 percent of the experts indicated that the newly created DHS has had a negative impact on America's national security, and nearly 1 in 5 thought the department's funding should be slashed. The U.S. State Department received relatively high marks. Surprisingly, this opinion was not limited to the liberal internationalist wing of foreign-policy elites. Even conservative experts, who have sometimes taken a dimmer view of the State Department's diplomatic efforts, believed that the department's budget is a good investment and that it should be moderately or substantially increased. Overall, 87 percent of the index's experts believe that Foggy Bottom requires more funding, including 72 percent of conservatives.

The index's experts also have a strong opinion of how that money should be spent. Nearly 80 percent agree that a widespread rejection of extremist ideologies around the globe is critical to "winning" the war on terror. Yet the experts simultaneously rated America's public diplomacy efforts the lowest of

any policy initiative, with a median score of just 1.8. Clearly, few believe that the United States is doing its best to win friends and influence people.

Rate each agency's effectiveness at protecting the American people on a scale of 0 to 10.

	Mean score
Dept. of Homeland Security	2.9
Dept. of Defense	4.4
Dept. of State	**4.8**
Dir. of National Intelligence	3.9

Indicate whether agencies should receive an increase or decrease in funding.

Percentage of respondents selecting:	Decrease	Increase
Dept. of Homeland Security	19	43
Dept. of Defense	52	15
Dept. of State	7	**87**
Dir. of National Intelligence	13	39

A Nuclear Posture for Today

JOHN DEUTCH

A Threat Transformed

The collapse of the Soviet Union was a dramatic geopolitical shift that should have led to major changes in the nuclear posture of the United States. The policy reviews undertaken by the Clinton administration in 1994 and the Bush administration in 2002, however, led to only minor alterations. As a result, the United States lacks a convincing rationale for its current nuclear force structure and for the policies that guide the management of its nuclear weapons enterprise.

The end of the Cold War did not mean that the United States could eliminate nuclear weapons altogether. Their existence is a reality, and the knowledge required to make them is widespread. But over the last decade, the nature of the nuclear threat has fundamentally changed, from large-scale attack to the use of one or a few devices by a rogue nation or subnational group against the United States or one of its allies. Countering the proliferation of nuclear weapons—by slowing the spread of nuclear capabilities among states, assuring that nuclear devices do not get into the hands of terrorist groups, and protecting existing stockpiles—has thus become as high a priority as deterring major nuclear attacks.

Unfortunately, the current U.S. nuclear posture does not reflect this shift. Washington still maintains a large nuclear arsenal designed for the Cold War, and it fails to take into account the current impact of its nuclear policies on those of other governments. In fact, with its overwhelming conventional military advantage, the United States does not need nuclear weapons for either war fighting or for deterring conventional war. It should therefore scale back its nuclear activity significantly. Policymakers should sharply decrease the number of warheads deployed with active military forces and make U.S. stockpile activities (of active and retired warheads and nuclear material) more transparent, setting a security standard for other nations. The United States should not, however, abandon effective nuclear forces, and it should even leave open the possibility of certain limited kinds of nuclear tests. A new U.S. nuclear posture, in short, should encourage international nonproliferation efforts without sacrificing the United States' ability to maintain a nuclear posture that deters attack.

Dual Purpose

In the past, U.S. policymakers have considered many potential roles for nuclear weapons: massive retaliation, damage limitation in nuclear exchanges, or controlling escalation in more limited scenarios. Still, they have always understood that the purpose of nuclear weapons is to deter war, not to fight it. For deterrence to work, however, the threat of preemptive or retaliatory use must be credible. It follows that, regardless of the number or the mix of weapons in the nuclear arsenal, they must be maintained ready for use, not kept as "wooden cannon."

During the Cold War, a range of nuclear scenarios defined strategic deterrence of the Soviet Union. The number of weapons in the Single Integrated Operation Plan (SIOP), the nuclear-attack strategy drawn up by the military and approved by the president, depended on the number of attack options, the number of targets (military as well as urban and industrial), and the desired "expected damage" to each target. "Expected damage" depended on the "hardness" of the target, the probability of a weapon's reaching it, and the explosive yield and accuracy of the programmed weapon. It does not require much imagination to appreciate that such a calculation could justify acquiring several thousand strategic weapons, as was indeed the case. In the 1970s and 1980s, the United States and the Soviet Union also accumulated several thousand tactical nuclear weapons, smaller devices intended for regional or battlefield use.

Although the nature of today's threats calls into question the usefulness of the United States' large nuclear arsenal, nuclear weapons continue to play a key role in U.S. security. After all, there is no guarantee that geopolitical circumstances will not change dramatically, and the emergence of a more militant China or Russia's return to totalitarianism might compel the United States to place greater reliance on its nuclear forces. Moreover, Washington's commanding nuclear posture still works to limit the nuclear ambitions of other countries. U.S. allies, most notably Germany and Japan, have forsworn establishing their own nuclear programs in exchange for protection under the U.S. security umbrella. Were the United States to give up its arsenal, other countries might be tempted to develop their own.

The possession of weapons by current nuclear powers does not directly influence the ambitions of states or terrorist groups that already want their own. They believe, rightly or wrongly, that acquiring a nuclear weapon will improve their security situation. A change in the U.S. nuclear posture would certainly not have dissuaded any of the newest members of the nuclear club—Israel, India, and Pakistan from seeking the bomb. North Korea and Iran, meanwhile, are vastly more concerned by the United States' conventional power than they are by its nuclear forces. They would probably seek nuclear weapons even if the United States had none, perhaps even with greater determination.

At the same time, the United States relies on the cooperation of many nations to achieve its nonproliferation objectives, and in this regard the U.S. nuclear posture has important consequences. An effective nonproliferation effort requires restricting the transfer of nuclear materials and technology, encouraging effective inspection by the International Atomic Energy Agency, and strengthening standards for the protection of nuclear materials and facilities. Cooperation is also essential for establishing an international norm that forbids the nuclear ambitions of non-nuclear states. (This goal, in fact, raises a basic hypocrisy on the part of nuclear powers: they retain their own arsenals while denying others the same right. This contradiction prompted Washington unwisely to commit under Article 6 of the Nonproliferation Treaty [NPT] "to pursue good-faith negotiations" toward complete disarmament, a goal it has no intention of pursuing.)

Ultimately, Washington must strike a balance between conflicting goals: maintaining a modern nuclear weapons posture, on the one hand, and curbing the spread of nuclear weapons, on the other. The Bush administration has not struck this balance well. Some officials have made unfortunate policy statements about pre-emption, implying that the U.S. government might even consider a first nuclear strike. The administration's 2002 nuclear posture review unwisely treats non-nuclear and nuclear strike capabilities as part of a single retaliatory continuum. Policymakers have invoked technical and geopolitical uncertainty as an argument for modernizing the weapons complex and maintaining robust testing and production capabilities. Most unfortunately, the Bush administration has proposed work on a new warhead—a low-yield "robust nuclear earth-penetrator." Although it could have argued that some conceptual work on generic warheads is needed to preserve the competence of weapons designers, the administration has instead justified this weapon on the basis of its military utility, hinting at the possibility of development and production in the future. The tone of this proposal ignores the indirect effect that new U.S. warhead research programs have on international attitudes toward non-proliferation.

How Low Can You Go?

Today, the U.S. nuclear arsenal should be managed with two purposes in mind: to deter a nuclear attack against the United States or its allies by retaining an overwhelming nuclear force with high "survivability," and to respond flexibly and precisely to a broad range of contingencies, including chemical or biological attack. The goal is to force any nation or subnational group that contemplates use of a weapon of mass destruction for an act of catastrophic terrorism to consider the possibility of U.S. nuclear retaliation and the complete destruction of its interests or sanctuary.

These purposes are not so different from those of the past, but the new nature of the threat means that many fewer weapons are needed to achieve them. In May 2001, President George W.

Bush said at the National Defense University, "I am committed to achieving a credible deterrent with the lowest-possible number of nuclear weapons consistent with our national security needs, including our obligations to our allies." But just what is the "lowest possible number"?

The answer cannot be calculated using the classic SIOP method: there are no suitable target lists analogous to those drawn during the Cold War. But even a crude estimate of numerical requirements gives a sense of how much smaller the U.S. nuclear arsenal could be.

A fleet of nine Trident ballistic-missile-equipped nuclear submarines—half the size of the current fleet of 18 boats, which is capable of carrying about 3,000 warheads—would constitute a retaliatory force with sufficient survivability. Three partially loaded submarines would be on continuous station, each carrying 16 D-5 missiles with 8 nuclear warheads (a combination of the w76 and the w88), for a total of 384 warheads on alert. Another three would be in transit (carrying an additional 384 warheads in strategic reserve), and still another three would be in overhaul (and thus unarmed) at any given time. (Because each Trident can carry 24 missiles, such a deployment would add up to 1,728 accountable warheads under the counting rules of the Strategic Arms Reduction Treaty, suggesting that these rules may no longer be relevant to either the United States or Russia.) Another 200 operational nuclear warheads would complement the fleet, providing for flexible response. These would be placed on other delivery systems, such as land-based intercontinental ballistic missiles and cruise missiles on sea and air platforms that permit easier command and control.

Such a deployment—less than 1,000 warheads in total—would be smaller than the reduced target proposed by Bush as part of the Strategic Offensive Reductions Treaty: between 1,700 and 2,200 deployed strategic warheads by 2012. But for the sake of deterrence and response, this smaller nuclear force would be enough. China, the nation most likely to try to match the U.S. nuclear capability, is thought to have a total inventory of 400 nuclear weapons, including a small but growing ballistic missile force capable of reaching the United States.

In the past, all nuclear force reductions took place within U.S.-Russian arms control agreements. Given today's geopolitical realities, it is not necessary to wait for formal agreements before moving toward lower numbers. To be sure, the pace of reduction should consider Russian force levels as well as political developments there. But Washington's concern with Moscow's nuclear stockpile has as much, if not more, to do with security and the threat of "loose nukes" than with the threat of Russian attack.

Alarm over the security of nuclear stockpiles also points to the need to change the way nuclear warheads are counted. In the past, Washington counted only operational military warheads and delivery vehicles, the weapons that posed the most immediate threat. Now, however, preventing proliferation requires focusing not only on a country's deployed nuclear capability, but also on the security of its nuclear material and the intentions of those who control it. Accordingly, all nuclear weapons and material—including deployed warheads, warheads undergoing maintenance or modification, decommissioned warheads, and all weapons-grade highly enriched uranium and separated plutonium—should be counted as part of a nation's nuclear inventory.

This revised accounting scheme would do away with the anachronistic distinction between long-range strategic and short-range tactical weapons; today, all nuclear weapons are of equal concern. It would also drive home the importance of securing a country's entire nuclear inventory, including decommissioned warheads and nuclear-related materials (such as spent fuel and low-enriched uranium). Removing a warhead from the active force would shift it to a different accounting category, not drop it from the inventory altogether, because the device and its nuclear material would still require secure supervision.

Meanwhile, the United States should make its own total nuclear inventory known to the public, reporting the number of warheads and the amount of material in each category as an example to other governments. During the Cold War, there was good reason to keep this information secret. Now, however, greater transparency, consistent with proliferation concerns, would enhance U.S. security by giving allies comfort and prospective proliferators pause. Nations resisting disclosure would be inviting increased international scrutiny of their capabilities and intentions.

Low-Profile Management

Responsibility for managing the United States' nuclear weapons complex falls to the National Nuclear Security Administration (NNSA) of the Department of Energy (DOE). The NNSA's budget request for fiscal year 2005 was $6.6 billion, and this is expected to grow to $7.5 billion by 2009. The agency, which has some 35,000 employees, faces significant obstacles, including assuring the competence of its staff. The generation of scientists and engineers that developed, built, and tested nuclear weapons has long since retired. The current work force at the three main weapons laboratories—at Los Alamos, New Mexico; Livermore, California; and Sandia, New Mexico—has little direct experience designing or testing weapons. And the DOE's stringent response to recent unfortunate security lapses has hurt morale and clouded the atmosphere in the laboratories.

In 1992, the Exon-Hatfield-Mitchell amendment barred nuclear tests except those motivated by concern about the safety and reliability of weapons already in the stockpile. Since then there has been general agreement that there is no such need (affirmed by annual Defense Department reviews of nuclear safety and reliability), and the United States has observed a testing moratorium.

In the absence of a test program, the DOE has established a "stockpile stewardship program" designed to preserve the knowledge and technology required to extend the life of existing warheads. Advanced computing technology—bolstered by the DOE's impressive Accelerated Strategic Computing Initiative—has allowed modeling and simulations that can partially substitute for instrumented laboratory tests. The program also includes nuclear-weapons-related subcritical laboratory experimentation, conducted, for example, in the x-ray radiographic test facility at Los Alamos and the laser ignition facility at Livermore.

The premise behind the stockpile stewardship program is that computer simulation of the nuclear explosion sequence (beginning with chemical explosive detonation in the primary and ending with fission and thermonuclear burn in the secondary), confirmed with data from experimental facilities, can give technicians confidence in new or modified weapons. Scientists disagree, however, about whether this premise is correct. Some argue that the current program is enough to confirm the safety and reliability of existing weapons. The only way to prove the effectiveness of the strategy, however, is to demonstrate that computer codes can in fact predict the results of a nuclear explosion, as the program assumes. This suggests the need for a "scientific confirmation test," meant not to ensure stockpile security or to develop new weapons but to prove that the practical physics underpinning the nuclear program still holds. Accordingly, scientific confirmation should be added as an acceptable rationale for testing, in addition to the verification of the correction of a safety or reliability problem that cannot be verified by other means. Indeed, in the past, confidence in the stockpile came largely from development tests, rather than from tests specifically designed to confirm weapons reliability.

The NNSA program also includes several large and costly facilities intended to modernize the production infrastructure. These include a new tritium extraction facility at Los Alamos, a pit disassembly and conversion facility at the Savannah River Laboratory in South Carolina, and plans for a modern pit facility. Each individual project may be justified, but the quantity, size, and timing of such developments contribute to an impression that the U.S. weapons complex is growing and that the United States is not, in fact, reducing the role of nuclear weapons.

A more realistic U.S. nuclear posture would require a smaller but still high-quality weapons research and engineering program and a consolidated production complex. The existing stockpile stewardship program's approach is reasonable, but confirmation that physics knowledge remains adequate may require (and, from a technical point of view, ideally would require) occasional "scientific confirmation tests." Careful timing and management of such tests could mitigate the adverse international reaction they would inevitably cause. Meanwhile, conceptual work on the design of new warheads should not be precluded per se, but if it is proposed and performed there must be no ambiguity about future development. Greater transparency with regard to the activities of the NNSA would also help convince domestic and international audiences that Washington is striking the right balance in managing its nuclear weapons.

Rethinking Arms Control

A new U.S. nuclear posture should include consideration of several current and prospective arms control measures. The most controversial is the Comprehensive Test Ban Treaty (CTBT), which would permanently ban all future nuclear tests, with no provision for withdrawal. The United States has not ratified the CTBT (nor have India, Iran, Israel, North Korea, and Pakistan), but 109 nations (including the United Kingdom, France, Russia, and China) have.

Proponents of the CTBT see its potential for strengthening international norms against nuclear weapons as vital to nonproliferation efforts. They argue that it is especially worthwhile because, with the stockpile stewardship program in place, the United States does not need testing to confirm stockpile safety or reliability. Opponents respond that the CTBT has verification problems, that testing has no direct effect on either the pace or the likelihood of success by determined proliferators such as North Korea and Iran, and that, given the uncertainty of future requirements for new weapons, forgoing forever the possibility of new tests is a mistake.

Both sides in this debate have strengths and weaknesses. Opponents of the CTBT are correct that testing should be allowed if the assurance of stockpile safety or reliability requires it. However, they exaggerate the treaty's verification problems: only very low-yield tests (or tests that insulate the explosion from the surrounding earth) have much of a chance of escaping detection. CTBT advocates, meanwhile, are correct that the treaty would bolster international nonproliferation norms, even if their assertion that no test will ever again be necessary to assure stockpile safety is dubious. (In fact, some CTBT advocates may oppose testing precisely because they believe that confidence in the reliability of nuclear weapons will erode without it—to the point that nuclear weapons will lose their deterrent value and become irrelevant.) Those who attempt to sidestep the issue by claiming that a future president could invoke the supreme national interest to renounce the treaty are implying that it is better to accept a treaty despite major reservations than to work to craft one that resolves difficult issues.

There is, fortunately, a sensible middle ground in this dispute: a CTBT of limited term. Former national security officials Brent Scowcroft and Arnold Kanter have proposed entering into the CTBT for a five-year term (since all agree that U.S. nuclear tests will not be necessary anytime soon), with possible five-year extensions, after ratification by the Senate. Such a compromise would have the advantage of strengthening nonproliferation efforts and thus be preferable to having no CTBT—while leaving open the possibility of not extending the treaty if geopolitical circumstances or stockpile considerations change. A similar approach worked with the NPT, which was ratified in 1969 for a 25-year period, with review conferences every five years, and then made permanent in 1995. Opponents argue that it would be difficult or impossible at this stage to change the terms of the internationally negotiated CTBT. But the CTBT does not enter into force until 44 countries, including the United States, have ratified it, so the choice is whether the United States prefers a renewable five-year CTBT to no CTBT at all.

The U.S. nuclear posture must change to meet a transformed nuclear threat.

A second still-unratified arms control treaty is the fissile material production cutoff treaty, originally proposed by President Bill Clinton at the United Nations in 1993; it would prohibit new production of separated plutonium or highly enriched uranium. This is an attractive measure, because the United States and other nuclear states have ample amounts of weapons-usable material. The ban would prohibit any state from undertaking new production, thus serving basic nonproliferation objectives, and would limit the total amount of material that must be kept secure.

The UN Conference on Disarmament has been deliberating the cutoff treaty for several years. On August 4, 2004, the U.S. ambassador to the UN, John Danforth, announced that the Bush administration, although supportive of the ban, does not believe that effective verification is feasible. This and earlier statements by the Bush administration imply that alleged verification shortcomings will be a barrier to an agreement. But with a new nuclear posture, opposition to this treaty would be inexplicable. No arms control treaty is perfectly verifiable; there is always a risk that a violation will go undetected. Verification could be enhanced if signatory countries agreed to inspections. Traditionally, the United States and other nuclear weapons states have not accepted such inspections, but there is now little reason for the United States to resist them. Here again, transparency is in the interest of the United States. A signatory violating the treaty would be stigmatized as a proliferator before the international community. And a state that refused to sign the treaty would be signaling its interest in acquiring material suitable for making a bomb.

Arms control advocates have proposed two other major changes to U.S. nuclear policy: pledging "no first use" and de-alerting nuclear forces. Even with a changed nuclear posture, however, the arguments for such reforms are not convincing.

Since 1978, Washington has committed to not using nuclear weapons against non-nuclear states that are signatories to the NPT, unless they attack the United States with the backing of a nuclear state. Successive U.S. administrations, however, have also maintained a policy of "strategic ambiguity," refusing to rule out a nuclear response to a biological or chemical attack. Supporters of a stronger no-first-use policy argue that strategic ambiguity sends the wrong signal to other governments: even the United States, with its overwhelming conventional military advantage, sees value in leaving open the possibility of first use. And this impression, they argue, undermines nonproliferation. They underestimate, however, just how much strategic ambiguity aids deterrence by keeping potential adversaries uncertain about a U.S. response.

De-alerting nuclear forces would mean increasing the amount of time between the decision to launch a nuclear weapon and its actual launch, in order to prevent accidental or unauthorized attacks, avoid misunderstanding, and add time to negotiate in a crisis. During the Cold War, a prompt launch capability was necessary to assure the survivability of land-based forces. Those who support de-alerting U.S. nuclear forces correctly argue that such a concern is no longer relevant. But they underestimate the practical obstacles to de-alerting submarine-launched warheads. If warheads were removed from the submarines, maintaining a continuous sea-based deployment would not be possible; the ships would need to be kept close to port, near the warheads, where they would be more vulnerable. Alternatively, communications to submarines on station could be managed to lengthen the time to launch, but it is hard to see how this could serve as a verifiable confidence-building measure. Such a step would be easily reversible anyway, making its usefulness quite limited.

Finally, the United States should make clear that any reduction is not a first step toward the abolition of the U.S. nuclear force. The U.S. nuclear posture should be consistent with foreseeable U.S. security interests. In the distant future, depending on the state of the world, a move to even lower—or potentially back to higher—levels might make sense.

Even with the Cold War over, nuclear weapons remain far more than empty symbols; they cannot simply be eliminated, despite the hopes of some arms-control advocates and the stated goals of the NPT. Nonetheless, the U.S. nuclear posture must change to meet a transformed nuclear threat. The U.S. nuclear force must be strong enough to deter and to survive attack even as it serves, as much as possible, to advance Washington's nonproliferation goals. Instead of treating nonproliferation and the maintenance of a nuclear deterrent as mutually exclusive, the United States must shape and manage its nuclear force in a way that does both.

JOHN DEUTCH is Institute Professor at the Massachusetts Institute of Technology. He served as Deputy Secretary of Defense, Chairman of the Nuclear Weapons Council, and Director of Central Intelligence during the Clinton administration and as Undersecretary of Energy during the Carter administration.

Apocalypse Soon

Robert McNamara is worried. He knows how close we've come. His counsel helped the Kennedy administration avert nuclear catastrophe during the Cuban Missile Crisis. Today, he believes the United States must no longer rely on nuclear weapons as a foreign-policy tool. To do so is immoral, illegal, and dreadfully dangerous.

ROBERT S. MCNAMARA

I t is time—well past time, in my view—for the United States to cease its Cold War-style reliance on nuclear weapons as a foreign policy tool. At the risk of appearing simplistic and provocative, I would characterize current U.S. nuclear weapons policy as immoral, illegal, militarily unnecessary, and dreadfully dangerous. The risk of an accidental or inadvertent nuclear launch is unacceptably high. Far from reducing these risks, the Bush administration has signaled that it is committed to keeping the U.S. nuclear arsenal as a mainstay of its military power—a commitment that is simultaneously eroding the international norms that have limited the spread of nuclear weapons and fissile materials for 50 years. Much of the current U.S. nuclear policy has been in place since before I was secretary of defense, and it has only grown more dangerous and diplomatically destructive in the intervening years.

Today, the United States has deployed approximately 4,500 strategic, offensive nuclear warheads. Russia has roughly 3,800. The strategic forces of Britain, France, and China are considerably smaller, with 200-400 nuclear weapons in each state's arsenal. The new nuclear states of Pakistan and India have fewer than 100 weapons each. North Korea now claims to have developed nuclear weapons, and U.S. intelligence agencies estimate that Pyongyang has enough fissile material for 2-8 bombs.

How destructive are these weapons? The average U.S. warhead has a destructive power 20 times that of the Hiroshima bomb. Of the 8,000 active or operational U.S. warheads, 2,000 are on hair-trigger alert, ready to be launched on 15 minutes' warning. How are these weapons to be used? The United States has never endorsed the policy of "no first use," not during my seven years as secretary or since. We have been and remain prepared to initiate the use of nuclear weapons—by the decision of one person, the president—against either a nuclear or nonnuclear enemy whenever we believe it is in our interest to do so. For decades, U.S. nuclear forces have been sufficiently strong to absorb a first strike and then inflict "unacceptable" damage on an opponent. This has been and (so long as we face a nuclear-armed, potential adversary) must continue to be the foundation of our nuclear deterrent.

In my time as secretary of defense, the commander of the U.S. Strategic Air Command (SAC) carried with him a secure telephone, no matter where he went, 24 hours a day, seven days a week, 365 days a year. The telephone of the commander, whose headquarters were in Omaha, Nebraska, was linked to the underground command post of the North American Defense Command, deep inside Cheyenne Mountain, in Colorado, and to the U.S. president, wherever he happened to be. The president always had at hand nuclear release codes in the so-called football, a briefcase carried for the president at all times by a U.S. military officer.

What is shocking is that today, more than a decade after the end of the Cold War, the basic U.S. nuclear policy is unchanged.

The SAC commander's orders were to answer the telephone by no later than the end of the third ring. If it rang, and he was informed that a nuclear attack of enemy ballistic missiles appeared to be under way, he was allowed 2 to 3 minutes to decide whether the warning was valid (over the years, the United States has received many false warnings), and if so, how the United States should respond. He was then given approximately 10 minutes to determine what to recommend, to locate and advise the president, permit the president to discuss the situation with two or three close advisors (presumably the secretary of defense and the chairman of the Joint Chiefs of Staff), and to receive the president's decision and pass it immediately, along with the codes, to the launch sites. The president essentially had two options: He could decide to ride out the attack and defer until later any decision to launch a retaliatory strike. Or, he could order an immediate retaliatory strike, from a menu of options, thereby launching U.S. weapons that were targeted on the opponent's military-industrial assets. Our opponents in Moscow presumably had and have similar arrangements.

The whole situation seems so bizarre as to be beyond belief. On any given day, as we go about our business, the president is prepared to make a decision within 20 minutes that could launch one of the most devastating weapons in the world. To declare war requires an act of congress, but to launch a nuclear holocaust requires 20 minutes' deliberation by the president and his advisors. But that is what we have lived with for 40 years. With very few changes, this system remains largely intact, including the "football," the president's constant companion.

I was able to change some of these dangerous policies and procedures. My colleagues and I started arms control talks; we installed safeguards to reduce the risk of unauthorized launches; we added options to the nuclear war plans so that the president did not have to choose between an all-or-nothing response, and we eliminated the vulnerable and provocative nuclear missiles in Turkey. I wish I had done more, but we were in the midst of the Cold War, and our options were limited.

The United States and our NATO allies faced a strong Soviet and Warsaw Pact conventional threat. Many of the allies (and some in Washington as well) felt strongly that preserving the U.S. option of launching a first strike was necessary for the sake of keeping the Soviets at bay. What is shocking is that today, more than a decade after the end of the Cold War, the basic U.S. nuclear policy is unchanged. It has not adapted to the collapse of the Soviet Union. Plans and procedures have not been revised to make the United States or other countries less likely to push the button. At a minimum, we should remove all strategic nuclear weapons from "hair-trigger" alert, as others have recommended, including Gen. George Lee Butler, the last commander of SAC. That simple change would greatly reduce the risk of an accidental nuclear launch. It would also signal to other states that the United States is taking steps to end its reliance on nuclear weapons.

We pledged to work in good faith toward the eventual elimination of nuclear arsenals when we negotiated the Nuclear Non-Proliferation Treaty (NPT) in 1968. In May, diplomats from more than 180 nations are meeting in New York City to review the NPT and assess whether members are living up to the agreement. The United States is focused, for understandable reasons, on persuading North Korea to rejoin the treaty and on negotiating deeper constraints on Iran's nuclear ambitions. Those states must be convinced to keep the promises they made when they originally signed the NPT—that they would not build nuclear weapons in return for access to peaceful uses of nuclear energy. But the attention of many nations, including some potential new nuclear weapons states, is also on the United States. Keeping such large numbers of weapons, and maintaining them on hair-trigger alert, are potent signs that the United States is not seriously working toward the elimination of its arsenal and raises troubling questions as to why any other state should restrain its nuclear ambitions.

A Preview of the Apocalypse

The destructive power of nuclear weapons is well known, but given the United States' continued reliance on them, it's worth remembering the danger they present. A 2000 report by the International Physicians for the Prevention of Nuclear War describes the likely effects of a single 1 megaton weapon—dozens of which are contained in the Russian and U.S. inventories. At ground zero, the explosion creates a crater 300 feet deep and 1,200 feet in diameter. Within one second, the atmosphere itself ignites into a fireball more than a half-mile in diameter. The surface of the fireball radiates nearly three times the light and heat of a comparable area of the surface of the sun, extinguishing in seconds all life below and radiating outward at the speed of light, causing instantaneous severe burns to people within one to three miles. A blast wave of compressed air reaches a distance of three miles in about 12 seconds, flattening factories and commercial buildings. Debris carried by winds of 250 mph inflicts lethal injuries throughout the area. At least 50 percent of people in the area die immediately, prior to any injuries from radiation or the developing firestorm.

Of course, our knowledge of these effects is not entirely hypothetical. Nuclear weapons, with roughly one seventieth of the power of the 1 megaton bomb just described, were twice used by the United States in August 1945. One atomic bomb was dropped on Hiroshima. Around 80,000 people died immediately; approximately 200,000 died eventually. Later, a similar size bomb was dropped on Nagasaki. On Nov. 7, 1995, the mayor of Nagasaki recalled his memory of the attack in testimony to the International Court of Justice:

> Nagasaki became a city of death where not even the sound of insects could be heard. After a while, countless men, women and children began to gather for a drink of water at the banks of nearby Urakami River, their hair and clothing scorched and their burnt skin hanging off in sheets like rags. Begging for help they died one after another in the water or in heaps on the banks.... Four months after the atomic bombing, 74,000 people were dead, and 75,000 had suffered injuries, that is, two-thirds of the city population had fallen victim to this calamity that came upon Nagasaki like a preview of the Apocalypse.

Why did so many civilians have to die? Because the civilians, who made up nearly 100 percent of the victims of Hiroshima and Nagasaki, were unfortunately "co-located" with Japanese military and industrial targets. Their annihilation, though not the objective of those dropping the bombs, was an inevitable result of the choice of those targets. It is worth noting that during the Cold War, the United States reportedly had dozens of nuclear warheads targeted on Moscow alone, because it contained so many military targets and so much "industrial capacity." Presumably, the Soviets similarly targeted many U.S. cities. The statement that our nuclear weapons do not target populations per se was and remains totally misleading in the sense that the so-called collateral damage of large nuclear strikes would include tens of millions of innocent civilian dead.

This in a nutshell is what nuclear weapons do: They indiscriminately blast, burn, and irradiate with a speed and finality that are almost incomprehensible. This is exactly what countries like the United States and Russia, with nuclear weapons on hairtrigger alert, continue to threaten every minute of every day in this new 21st century.

No Way to Win

I have worked on issues relating to U.S. and NATO nuclear strategy and war plans for more than 40 years. During that time, I have never seen a piece of paper that outlined a plan for the United States or NATO to initiate the use of nuclear weapons with any benefit for the United States or NATO. I have made this statement in front of audiences, including NATO defense ministers and senior military leaders, many times. No one has ever refuted it. To launch weapons against a nuclear-equipped opponent would be suicidal. To do so against a nonnuclear enemy would be militarily unnecessary, morally repugnant, and politically indefensible.

I reached these conclusions very soon after becoming secretary of defense. Although I believe Presidents John F. Kennedy and Lyndon Johnson shared my view, it was impossible for any of us to make such statements publicly because they were totally contrary to established NATO policy. After leaving the Defense Department, I became president of the World Bank. During my 13-year tenure, from 1968 to 1981, I was prohibited, as an employee of an international institution, from commenting publicly on issues of U.S. national security. After my retirement from the bank, I began to reflect on how I, with seven years' experience as secretary of defense, might contribute to an understanding of the issues with which I began my public service career.

> **To launch weapons against a nuclear power would be suicide. To do so against a nonnuclear enemy would be militarily unnecessary, morally repugnant, and politically indefensible.**

At that time, much was being said and written regarding how the United States could, and why it should, be able to fight and win a nuclear war with the Soviets. This view implied, of course, that nuclear weapons did have military utility; that they could be used in battle with ultimate gain to whoever had the largest force or used them with the greatest acumen. Having studied these views, I decided to go public with some information that I knew would be controversial, but that I felt was needed to inject reality into these increasingly unreal discussions about the military utility of nuclear weapons. In articles and speeches, I criticized the fundamentally flawed assumption that nuclear weapons could be used in some limited way. There is no way to effectively contain a nuclear strike—to keep it from inflicting enormous destruction on civilian life and property, and there is no guarantee against unlimited escalation once the first nuclear strike occurs. We cannot avoid the serious and unacceptable risk of nuclear war until we recognize these facts and base our military plans and policies upon this recognition. I hold these views even more strongly today than I did when I first

spoke out against the nuclear dangers our policies were creating. I know from direct experience that U.S. nuclear policy today creates unacceptable risks to other nations and to our own.

What Castro Taught Us

Among the costs of maintaining nuclear weapons is the risk—to me an unacceptable risk—of use of the weapons either by accident or as a result of misjudgment or miscalculation in times of crisis. The Cuban Missile Crisis demonstrated that the United States and the Soviet Union—and indeed the rest of the world—came within a hair's breadth of nuclear disaster in October 1962. Indeed, according to former Soviet military leaders, at the height of the crisis, Soviet forces in Cuba possessed 162 nuclear warheads, including at least 90 tactical warheads. At about the same time, Cuban President Fidel Castro asked the Soviet ambassador to Cuba to send a cable to Soviet Premier Nikita Khrushchev stating that Castro urged him to counter a U.S. attack with a nuclear response. Clearly, there was a high risk that in the face of a U.S. attack, which many in the U.S. government were prepared to recommend to President Kennedy, the Soviet forces in Cuba would have decided to use their nuclear weapons rather than lose them. Only a few years ago did we learn that the four Soviet submarines trailing the U.S. Naval vessels near Cuba each carried torpedoes with nuclear warheads. Each of the sub commanders had the authority to launch his torpedoes. The situation was even more frightening because, as the lead commander recounted to me, the subs were out of communication with their Soviet bases, and they continued their patrols for four days after Khrushchev announced the withdrawal of the missiles from Cuba.

The lesson, if it had not been clear before, was made so at a conference on the crisis held in Havana in 1992, when we first began to learn from former Soviet officials about their preparations for nuclear war in the event of a U.S. invasion. Near the end of that meeting, I asked Castro whether he would have recommended that Khrushchev use the weapons in the face of a U.S. invasion, and if so, how he thought the United States would respond. "We started from the assumption that if there was an invasion of Cuba, nuclear war would erupt," Castro replied. "We were certain of that…. [W]e would be forced to pay the price that we would disappear." He continued, "Would I have been ready to use nuclear weapons? Yes, I would have agreed to the use of nuclear weapons." And he added, "If Mr. McNamara or Mr. Kennedy had been in our place, and had their country been invaded, or their country was going to be occupied … I believe they would have used tactical nuclear weapons."

> **We must move promptly toward the elimination—or near elimination—of all nuclear weapons.**

I hope that President Kennedy and I would not have behaved as Castro suggested we would have. His decision would have destroyed his country. Had we responded in a similar way the damage to the United States would have been unthinkable. But human beings are fallible. In conventional war, mistakes cost lives, sometimes thousands of lives. However, if mistakes were to affect decisions relating to the use of nuclear forces, there would be no learning curve. They would result in the destruction of nations. The indefinite combination of human fallibility and nuclear weapons carries a very high risk of nuclear catastrophe. There is no way to reduce the risk to acceptable levels, other than to first eliminate the hair-trigger alert policy and later to eliminate or nearly eliminate nuclear weapons. The United States should move immediately to institute these actions, in cooperation with Russia. That is the lesson of the Cuban Missile Crisis.

A Dangerous Obsession

On Nov. 13, 2001, President George W. Bush announced that he had told Russian President Vladimir Putin that the United States would reduce "operationally deployed nuclear warheads" from approximately 5,300 to a level between 1,700 and 2,200 over the next decade. This scaling back would approach the 1,500 to 2,200 range that Putin had proposed for Russia. However, the Bush administration's Nuclear Posture Review, mandated by the U.S. Congress and issued in January 2002, presents quite a different story. It assumes that strategic offensive nuclear weapons in much larger numbers than 1,700 to 2,200 will be part of U.S. military forces for the next several decades. Although the number of deployed warheads will be reduced to 3,800 in 2007 and to between 1,700 and 2,200 by 2012, the warheads and many of the launch vehicles taken off deployment will be maintained in a "responsive" reserve from which they could be moved back to the operationally deployed force. The Nuclear Posture Review received little attention from the media. But its emphasis on strategic offensive nuclear weapons deserves vigorous public scrutiny. Although any proposed reduction is welcome, it is doubtful that survivors—if there were any—of an exchange of 3,200 warheads (the U.S. and Russian numbers projected for 2012), with a destructive power approximately 65,000 times that of the Hiroshima bomb, could detect a difference between the effects of such an exchange and one that would result from the launch of the current U.S. and Russian forces totaling about 12,000 warheads.

In addition to projecting the deployment of large numbers of strategic nuclear weapons far into the future, the Bush administration is planning an extensive and expensive series of programs to sustain and modernize the existing nuclear force and to begin studies for new launch vehicles, as well as new warheads for all of the launch platforms. Some members of the administration have called for new nuclear weapons that could be used as bunker busters against underground shelters (such as the shelters Saddam Hussein used in Baghdad). New production facilities for fissile materials would need to be built to support the expanded force. The plans provide for integrating a national ballistic missile defense into the new triad of offensive weapons to enhance the nation's ability to use its "power projection

forces" by improving our ability to counterattack an enemy. The Bush administration also announced that it has no intention to ask congress to ratify the Comprehensive Test Ban Treaty (CTBT), and, though no decision to test has been made, the administration has ordered the national laboratories to begin research on new nuclear weapons designs and to prepare the underground test sites in Nevada for nuclear tests if necessary in the future. Clearly, the Bush administration assumes that nuclear weapons will be part of U.S. military forces for at least the next several decades.

Good faith participation in international negotiation on nuclear disarmament—including participation in the CTBT—is a legal and political obligation of all parties to the NPT that entered into force in 1970 and was extended indefinitely in 1995. The Bush administration's nuclear program, alongside its refusal to ratify the CTBT, will be viewed, with reason, by many nations as equivalent to a U.S. break from the treaty. It says to the nonnuclear weapons nations, "We, with the strongest conventional military force in the world, require nuclear weapons in perpetuity, but you, facing potentially well-armed opponents, are never to be allowed even one nuclear weapon."

If the United States continues its current nuclear stance, over time, substantial proliferation of nuclear weapons will almost surely follow. Some, or all, of such nations as Egypt, Japan, Saudi Arabia, Syria, and Taiwan will very likely initiate nuclear weapons programs, increasing both the risk of use of the weapons and the diversion of weapons and fissile materials into the hands of rogue states or terrorists. Diplomats and intelligence agencies believe Osama bin Laden has made several attempts to acquire nuclear weapons or fissile materials. It has been widely reported that Sultan Bashiruddin Mahmood, former director of Pakistan's nuclear reactor complex, met with bin Laden several times. Were al Qaeda to acquire fissile materials, especially enriched uranium, its ability to produce nuclear weapons would be great. The knowledge of how to construct a simple gun-type nuclear device, like the one we dropped on Hiroshima, is now widespread. Experts have little doubt that terrorists could construct such a primitive device if they acquired the requisite enriched uranium material. Indeed, just last summer, at a meeting of the National Academy of Sciences, former Secretary of Defense William J. Perry said, "I have never been more fearful of a nuclear detonation than now…. There is a greater than 50 percent probability of a nuclear strike on U.S. targets within a decade." I share his fears.

A Moment of Decision

We are at a critical moment in human history—perhaps not as dramatic as that of the Cuban Missile Crisis, but a moment no less crucial. Neither the Bush administration, the congress, the American people, nor the people of other nations have debated the merits of alternative, long-range nuclear weapons policies for their countries or the world. They have not examined the military utility of the weapons; the risk of inadvertent or accidental use; the moral and legal considerations relating to the use or threat of use of the weapons; or the impact of current policies on proliferation. Such debates are long overdue. If they are held, I believe they will conclude, as have I and an increasing number of senior military leaders, politicians, and civilian security experts: We must move promptly toward the elimination—or near elimination—of all nuclear weapons. For many, there is a strong temptation to cling to the strategies of the past 40 years.

But to do so would be a serious mistake leading to unacceptable risks for all nations.

ROBERT S. MCNAMARA was U.S. secretary of defense from 1961 to 1968 and president of the World Bank from 1968 to 1981.

From *Foreign Policy*, May/June 2005, pp. 29-35. Copyright © 2005 by the Carnegie Endowment for International Peace. Reprinted with permission. www.foreignpolicy.com

When Could Iran Get the Bomb?

What we know and what we don't know about Iran's nuclear program.

DAVID ALBRIGHT

Though hardly transparent, Director of National Intelligence John Negroponte's testimony on Iran before the Senate Intelligence Committee on February 2 was clearly cautious. The U.S. intelligence community judges that Iran probably has neither a nuclear weapon nor the necessary fissile material for a weapon, he stated. If Iran continues on its current path, it "will likely have the capability to produce a nuclear weapon within the next decade," he added. The basis for this estimate remains classified, although Iran's lack of knowledge and experience in building and running large numbers of centrifuges for uranium enrichment was reportedly an important consideration. When pressed, U.S. officials have said that they interpret Negroponte's remark to mean that Iran will need roughly 5–10 years before it possesses nuclear weapons.

Despite this caution, a handful of U.S. officials have since attempted to overstate Iran's nuclear progress, contradicting even this latest estimate. It appears that in the ongoing crisis between Iran and the United States, the crucial struggle for public perception of the Iranian nuclear threat is well under way.

Following an International Atomic Energy Agency (IAEA) briefing of U.N. Security Council permanent members and Germany in mid-March about a group of 164 centrifuges at Iran's Natanz uranium enrichment site, U.S. officials began to distort what the IAEA had said. Under the cloak of anonymity, these officials told journalists that Iran's actions represented a significant acceleration of its enrichment program. The IAEA was "shocked," "astonished," and "blown away" by Iran's progress on gas centrifuges, according to these U.S. officials, leading the United States to revise its own timeline for when Iran will get the bomb. In reality, IAEA officials said they were not surprised by Iran's actions. These U.S. statements, a senior IAEA official told the Associated Press, came "from people who are seeking a crisis, not a solution."[1]

Some outside experts and officials, including Defense Secretary Donald Rumsfeld, may be trying to undermine U.S. intelligence assessments on Iran's timeline to the bomb by highlighting the intelligence community's failure to correctly assess Iraq's weapons of mass destruction efforts.[2] Although the intelligence community deserves strong criticism for its analysis of Iraq's

weapons programs, the more recent Iranian analysis has been subject to more thorough review and is more consensual than the Iraqi assessments. For example, centrifuge experts at Oak Ridge National Laboratory, who challenged faulty CIA conclusions that Iraqi aluminum tubes were for a reconstituted nuclear weapons program long before the war, have been central in assessing Iran's gas centrifuge program for the intelligence community, according to a U.S. intelligence official.

Iran is indeed on the verge of mastering a critical step in building and operating a gas centrifuge plant that would be able to produce enriched uranium for either peaceful or military purposes. However, it can be expected to face serious technical hurdles before it can reliably produce large quantities of enriched uranium.

Many details about Iran's technical nuclear capabilities and plans are unknown, and the IAEA has neither been able to verify that Iran has declared its nuclear activities in full nor to establish conclusively that Iran does not have hidden nuclear enrichment sites. Western governments view with skepticism Iranian denials of intentions to produce highly enriched uranium (HEU) or to build nuclear weapons. Yet there is no evidence of an Iranian decision to build a nuclear arsenal, let alone any knowledge of an official Iranian schedule for acquiring nuclear weapons.

During the past three years of IAEA inspections, the international community has learned a great deal of information about the Iranian program that can be used to estimate the minimum amount of time Iran would need to produce enough HEU for a nuclear bomb. According to several possible scenarios, Iran appears to need at least three years before it could have enough HEU to make a nuclear weapon. Given the technical difficulty of the task, it could take Iran much longer.

With political rhetoric likely to intensify during the coming months, it is essential to have as clear an evaluation as possible of Iranian nuclear capabilities. It is also essential to avoid repeating the mistakes that were made prior to the Iraq War, when senior Bush administration officials and their allies outside government hyped the Iraqi nuclear threat to gain support in confronting Iraq.

Out of the Gate

Iran's recent actions appear aimed at rapidly installing and running gas centrifuges, which can be used to separate uranium 235 from uranium 238—the process known as enrichment. In early January 2006, Iran removed 52 IAEA seals that verified the suspension of Iran's P-1 centrifuge uranium enrichment program that had been in effect since October 2003. (The P-1 centrifuge is a design that Iran developed from plans acquired through the nuclear smuggling network of Pakistani scientist A. Q. Khan.) The seals were located at the Natanz, Pars Trash, and Farayand Technique sites, Iran's main centrifuge facilities. On February 11, Iran started to enrich uranium in a small number of centrifuges at Natanz.

After removing the seals, Iran also started to substantially renovate key portions of its main centrifuge research and development facility, the Pilot Fuel Enrichment Plant at Natanz. Iran secretly began construction on the pilot plant in 2001, and it installed about 200 centrifuges in 2002 and 2003. The pilot plant is designed to hold six 164-machine cascades, groups of centrifuges connected by pipes that work together to enrich greater amounts of uranium to higher enrichment levels than a group of individual centrifuges. The plant has space for additional, smaller test cascades, for a total of about 1,000 centrifuges.

At Natanz and Farayand Technique, Iran quickly restarted testing and checking centrifuge components to determine if they were manufactured precisely enough to use in a centrifuge. By early March, Iran had restarted enriching uranium at the pilot plant in 10- and 20-centrifuge cascades.

Iran also moved processing tanks and an autoclave—used to heat centrifuge feed material known as uranium hexafluoride into a gas prior to insertion into a centrifuge cascade—into its main production facility, the underground Fuel Enrichment Plant (FEP) at Natanz. This plant is designed to eventually hold 50,000–60,000 centrifuges. Iran told the IAEA that it intends to start installing the first 3,000 P-1 centrifuges at the FEP in the fourth quarter of 2006. A key outstanding question is whether Iran has procured from abroad or domestically manufactured all the equipment and materials it needs to finish the first module of 3,000 centrifuges.

Iran's Uranium Conversion Facility at Isfahan, which converts natural uranium into uranium hexafluoride, has continued to operate since restarting in August 2005, following the beginning of the breakdown in the suspension. By May 2006, Iran had produced 110 metric tons of uranium hexafluoride.[3] Assuming that roughly 5 metric tons of uranium hexafluoride are needed to make enough HEU for a nuclear weapon, this stock represents enough natural uranium hexafluoride for more than 20 nuclear weapons. Although this uranium hexafluoride contains impurities that can interfere with the operation of centrifuges and reduce their output or cause them to fail, most IAEA experts believe that Iran can overcome this problem and that the issue of hexafluoride impurity has been overblown in the media. Iran is known to be working to improve the purity of its uranium hexafluoride. If necessary, Iran could use its existing stock of impure material, either further purifying this uranium hexafluoride or settling for reduced output and a higher centrifuge failure rate.

Centrifuge Know-How

A key part of the development of Iran's gas centrifuge program is the operation of the 164-machine test cascades at the Natanz pilot plant, which will be the workhorses of any future centrifuge plant. Iran finished installing its first test cascade in the fall of 2003, but the cascade never operated with uranium hexafluoride prior to the October 2003 suspension. On April 13, 2006, Iran announced that it had produced low-enriched uranium (LEU) in its 164-machine cascade. Soon afterward, it announced that it had enriched uranium up to a level of almost 5 percent.

Restarting the cascade took several months because Iran had to repair damaged centrifuges. According to IAEA reports, many centrifuges crashed or broke when the cascade was shut down at the start of the suspension in 2003. Before introducing uranium hexafluoride, Iran had to reconnect all the pipes, establish a vacuum inside the cascade, and prepare the cascade for operation with uranium hexafluoride.

> Beyond the technical unknowns, ANSWERING THE QUESTION OF HOW SOON IRAN COULD PRODUCE ENOUGH HEU for a nuclear weapon is complicated and fraught with uncertainty.

The initial performance of the P-1 centrifuges in this cascade has been lower than expected. Based on the April 12 statements of Gholam Reza Aghazadeh, head of the Atomic Energy Organization of Iran, the average annualized output of the centrifuges in this cascade is relatively low.[4] In the same interview, Aghazadeh implied that he expects the average output of each P-1 centrifuge to almost double in the main plant.

In addition, Iran has not yet run this cascade continuously to produce enriched uranium. According to a Vienna diplomat, the cascade operated with uranium hexafluoride only about half of its first month of operation, although it continued to operate under vacuum the rest of the time. During this period, according to a May 19 Agence France Presse report, the cascade produced only "dozens of grams" of enriched uranium, far below the more than 2,000 grams Aghazadeh predicted the cascade would produce running continuously for that length of time. The Iranian centrifuge operators do not yet have sufficient understanding of cascade operation and must conduct a series of longer tests to develop a deeper understanding.

The IAEA reported in April that Iran is building the second and third cascades at the pilot plant. A senior diplomat in Vienna said in a late-April interview that the second and third cascades could start by early summer. This schedule would allow Iran to test multiple cascades running in parallel, a necessary step before building a centrifuge plant composed of such cascades. The diplomat speculated that Iran could continue with this pattern, installing the fourth and fifth in July and August, respectively. The space for the sixth cascade is currently occupied by the 10- and 20-machine cascades, he said.

Iran would likely want to run its cascades individually and in parallel for several months to ensure that no significant problems develop and to gain confidence that it can reliably enrich uranium in the cascades. Problems could include excessive vibration of the centrifuges, motor or power failures, pressure and temperature instabilities, or breakdown of the vacuum. Iran may also want to test any emergency systems designed to shut down the cascade without losing many centrifuges in the event of a major failure. Absent major problems, Iran is expected to need until the fall or later to demonstrate successful operation of its cascades and their associated emergency and control systems.

Once Iran overcomes the technical hurdle of operating its demonstration cascades, it can duplicate them and even create larger cascades. Iran would then be ready to build a centrifuge plant able to produce significant amounts of enriched uranium either for peaceful purposes or for nuclear weapons.

The Underground Path

Answering the question of how soon Iran could produce enough HEU for a nuclear weapon is complicated and fraught with uncertainty. Beyond the technical uncertainties, several other important factors are unknown. Will Iran develop an enrichment capability but produce only LEU for use in nuclear power reactors and not any HEU for use in a nuclear weapon? Will Iran withdraw from the Nuclear Non-Proliferation Treaty (NPT), expel IAEA inspectors, and concentrate on building secret nuclear facilities? How does the Iranian regime perceive the political risks of a particular action, such as trying to make HEU in the pilot plant? What resources will Iran apply to finishing its uranium enrichment facilities? Will there be preemptive military strikes against Iranian nuclear sites?

For the purposes of these estimates, a crude fission nuclear weapon is estimated to require 15–20 kilograms of weapon-grade uranium (HEU containing more than 90 percent uranium 235).[5] Iran's most direct path to obtaining HEU for nuclear weapons is to build a relatively small gas centrifuge plant that can make weapon-grade uranium directly.[6] If Iran built such a plant openly, it would be an acknowledgement that it seeks nuclear weapons and would invite a harsh response from the West and the IAEA.

As a result, Iran would likely pursue such a path in utmost secrecy, without declaring to the IAEA the facility and any associated uranium hexafluoride production facilities. Because Iran announced earlier this year that it was ending its implementation of the Additional Protocol—an advanced safeguards agreement created in the 1990s to fix traditional safeguards' inability to provide adequate assurance that a country does not have undeclared nuclear facilities or materials—the IAEA would face a difficult challenge discovering such a clandestine facility. The IAEA has already reported that it can no longer effectively monitor centrifuge components, unless they are at Natanz and within areas subject to IAEA containment and surveillance.

A centrifuge plant containing about 1,500–1,800 P-1 centrifuges is sufficient to make more than enough HEU for one nuclear weapon per year. (Each P-1 centrifuge is assumed to have an output of about 2.5–3 separative work units [swu] per year.[7]

With a capacity of 4,500 swu per year, this facility could produce as much as 28 kilograms of weapon-grade uranium a year.[8])

Iran has enough components to build up to 5,000 centrifuges, according to some senior diplomats in Vienna. Other senior diplomats, however, have said that Iran may not have 5,000 of all components, and that many components are not expected to pass quality control. In total, Iran is estimated to have in hand enough decent components for at least 1,000 to 2,000 centrifuges, in addition to the roughly 800 centrifuges already slated for the pilot plant. Iran could also build new centrifuge components, and, in fact, may have already started to do so.

Worst-Case Scenarios

If Iran decides to obtain highly enriched uranium (HEU) for use in a nuclear weapon, its two most likely paths would be to develop a clandestine or a "breakout" centrifuge enrichment capability. In either worst-case estimate, the earliest Iran would have enough HEU for a nuclear weapon would be in 2009.

Beginning of 2006–End of 2007

If the construction of a secret plant with 1,500–1,800 centrifuges had begun in early 2006, its completion would not be likely before the end of 2007.

Beginning of 2008–End of 2008

It would take approximately one year for this plant to produce enough HEU for a nuclear weapon.

Beginning of 2009–Months later

Converting the HEU into weapon components would take a few months, meaning the earliest Iran could have a nuclear weapon would be sometime in 2009.

Late 2006–2009 or 2010

Iran has said it will begin installing 3,000 centrifuges in its production-scale plant in late 2006. If there are no major delays, this module could be complete in 2009 or 2010.

Months later

Centrifuges in the production-scale plant could be reconfigured relatively easily to make HEU and could produce enough material for a weapon in as little as a few months. Converting the HEU into weapon components would take an additional few months.

If Iran had started to build a clandestine plant with 1,500–1,800 centrifuges in early 2006, it could assemble enough additional usable machines in about 15–18 months, or by about mid-2007. It would need to assemble centrifuges at the upper limit of its past rate, about 70–100 centrifuges per month, to accomplish this goal. In the meantime, Iran would need to identify a new facility where it could install the centrifuge cascades, since it is unlikely to choose Natanz as the location of a secret plant. It would also need to install control and emergency equipment, feed and withdrawal systems, and other peripheral equipment. It would then need to integrate all of these systems, test them, and commission the plant. Iran could start immediately to accomplish these steps, even before the final testing of the 164-machine cascades at Natanz, but final completion of a clandestine plant would be highly unlikely before the end of 2007.

Given another year to make enough HEU for a nuclear weapon, and a few more months to convert the uranium into weapon components, Iran could have its first nuclear weapon in 2009. By this time, Iran could have had sufficient time to prepare the other components of a nuclear weapon, although the weapon may not be small enough to be deliverable by a ballistic missile.

This result reflects a worst-case assessment for arms control. Iran can be expected to take longer, as it is likely to encounter technical difficulties that would delay bringing a centrifuge plant into operation. Factors causing delay could include difficulty assembling and installing so many centrifuges in such a short time period, inability to achieve the relatively high separative work output used in these estimates, difficulty acquiring sufficient dual-use equipment overseas, taking longer than expected to overcome difficulties in operating the cascades as a single production unit, or a holdup in commissioning the secret centrifuge plant.

Iranian officials have recently announced that they are also working on developing the more advanced P-2 centrifuge, the designs for which were also obtained from the Khan network. Iran's progress on this centrifuge appears to lag behind that of the P-1 centrifuge, as evidenced by a lack of procurement records for P-2 parts. The IAEA has been unable to determine the exact status of the P-2 program, but what is known appears to exclude the existence of undeclared P-2 facilities sufficiently advanced to significantly shift projections of the amount of time Iran would need to produce nuclear weapons.

Readying a "Breakout"

Another way that Iran could produce HEU for nuclear weapons would be to use its Natanz production facility, even though the centrifuge module is being designed to produce LEU for use in nuclear reactors. Iran has said it intends to start installing its first module of 3,000 centrifuges in the production facility's underground halls in late 2006, though it doesn't presently have enough centrifuge parts to complete the module. Since the pilot plant would likely have already produced a relatively large amount of LEU, the time to produce enough HEU for a nuclear weapon in this facility could be dramatically shortened.

At the above rates of centrifuge assembly, and assuming that it has, can produce, or acquire abroad enough P-1 centrifuges and associated equipment, Iran could finish assembling the module's 3,000 centrifuges sometime in 2008. Although Iran would likely build and operate some cascades before all the centrifuges are assembled, it will probably need at least another year to finish this module, placing the completion date in 2009

or 2010. Unexpected complications could delay the commissioning date. Alternatively, Iran could accelerate the pace by manufacturing, assembling, and installing centrifuges more quickly. Given all the difficult tasks that must be accomplished, however, Iran is unlikely to commission this module much before the start of 2009.

If Iran decided to make HEU in this module, it would have several alternatives. Because of the small throughput and great operational flexibility of centrifuges, HEU for nuclear weapons could be produced by reconfiguring the cascades in the module or by batch recycling, which entails feeding the cascade product back into the same cascade for subsequent cycles of enrichment.

Reconfiguration could be as straightforward as connecting separate cascades in series and carefully selecting the places where new pipes interconnect the cascades. Iran's 3,000-centrifuge module is slated to be composed of almost 20 164-centrifuge cascades, operating together under one common control system. With such a setup, reconfiguration would not require the disassembly of the individual cascades and could be accomplished within days. Such a setup could lessen by 10 percent the enrichment output, and the HEU's final enrichment level may reach only 80 percent, which is still sufficient for use in an existing implosion design, albeit with a lower explosive yield.

With a reconfigured plant, and starting with natural uranium, 20 kilograms of HEU could be produced within four to six months. If Iran waited until it had produced a stock of LEU before reconfiguring and then used this stock as the initial feedstock in the reconfigured plant, it could produce 20 kilograms of HEU in about one to two months.

Batch recycling would entail putting the cascade product back through the cascade several times, without changing the cascade's basic setup. Starting with natural uranium, cascades of the type expected at Natanz could produce weapon-grade uranium after four to five recycles. Twenty kilograms of weapon-grade uranium could be produced in about six to twelve months. If the batch operation started with an existing stock of LEU, the time to produce 20 kilograms of weapon-grade uranium would drop to about one to two months.

Whether using batch recycling or reconfiguration, Iran would likely operate the module to make LEU so that any production of HEU would be expected to happen quickly. Still, using either of these breakout approaches, Iran is not likely to have enough HEU for a nuclear weapon until 2009, and technical obstacles may further delay the operation of the module in the production facility.

Looking at a timeline of at least three years before Iran could have a nuclear weapons capability means that there is still time to pursue aggressive diplomatic options and time for measures such as sanctions to have an effect, if they become necessary.

In the short term, it is imperative for the international community to intensify its efforts to disrupt or slow Iran's ongoing overseas acquisition of dual-use items for its centrifuge program. Iran has encountered greater difficulty acquiring these items because of the increased scrutiny by key supplier states and companies, forcing Iranian smugglers to look elsewhere. As Iran applies more devious methods or seeks these items in other countries, greater efforts will be required to thwart it from succeeding.

It is vital to continue to understand what Iran has accomplished, what it still has to learn, and when it will reach a point when a plan to pursue nuclear weapons covertly or openly could succeed more quickly than the international community can react. Although these estimates include significant uncertainties, they reinforce the view that Iran must foreswear any deployed enrichment capability and accept adequate inspections. Otherwise, we risk a seismic shift in the balance of power in the region.

Notes

1. George Jahn, "U.N. to Inspect Iran Enrichment Program," Associated Press, March 25, 2006.
2. In an April 18, 2006 interview on the *Laura Ingraham Show*, Rumsfeld said he was "not confident" that the U.S. intelligence community's estimate of Iran's nuclear timeline was accurate (transcript available at www.defenselink.mil/transcripts/2006/tr20060418-12862.html). At a May 9, 2006 press conference, he said that the "wrong" intelligence used to justify the U.S. invasion of Iraq should "give one pause" when evaluating the credibility of intelligence regarding Iran ("Rumsfeld: Iraq Errors Affect Assessment of Iran," CNN, May 9, 2006).
3. This quantity refers to the amount of uranium mass in the uranium hexafluoride.
4. The annualized average output of each centrifuge was about 1.4 separative work units (swu) per machine per year, based on Aghazadeh's statement of a maximum feed rate of 70 grams per hour and the production of 7 grams per hour of 3.5 percent enriched uranium. The feed and product rates imply a tails assay (the fraction of fissionable uranium 235 in the waste stream) of 0.4 percent. This relatively low output could mean that the aluminum centrifuge rotors are spinning at a lower speed than possible. For the main plant, Aghazadeh said that 48,000 centrifuges would produce 30 metric tons of low-enriched uranium per year. Assuming a tails assay of 0.4 percent and a product of 3.5 percent enriched uranium, the estimated average output of each machine would be about 2.3 swu/year. With an assumed tails assay of 0.3 percent, the estimated output rises to 2.7 swu/year, high for a Pakistani P-1 design but possible if the centrifuge is further optimized.
5. Iran could be expected to initially build a crude, implosion-type fission weapon similar to known designs. In 1990, Iraq initially planned to use 15 kilograms of weapon-grade uranium in its implosion design. An unclassified design using almost 20 kilograms was calculated in a study by the author and Theodore Taylor in about 1990. A larger quantity of HEU is needed than the exact amount placed into the weapon because of inevitable losses during processing, but such losses can be kept to less than 20 percent with care.
6. Alternatively, Iran could secretly build a "topping plant" of about 500 centrifuges and use a stock of low-enriched uranium produced in the pilot plant as feed to produce HEU. However, the estimated timeline for this alternative route is not significantly different from the one outlined in this scenario.
7. These values for separative work are at the high end of the possible output of Iran's P-1 centrifuge. Actual values may be less.
8. This calculation assumes a relatively high tails assay of 0.5 percent. As a centrifuge program matures and grows, it typically reduces the tails assay to conserve uranium supplies.

DAVID ALBRIGHT is president of the Institute for Science and International Security and a member of the *Bulletin's* Editorial Advisory Board.

UNIT 8
The Iraq War and Beyond

Unit Selections

Key Points to Consider

- How important are allies and/or the United Nations in the reconstruction of Iraq?

- How important is Iraq to the security interests of the United States?

- Make a list of dimensions along which you would measure the success or failure of the U.S. foreign policy toward Iraq. How would you rate the situation today along these dimensions?

- How quickly should the United States undertake another "Iraq War?" What words of advice would you give policy makers about to embark on such a war?

- When and under what conditions should the United States leave Iraq?

- What should U.S. foreign policy be toward Iran?

Student Web Site
www.mhcls.com/online

Internet References
Further information regarding these Web sites may be found in this book's preface or online.

White House: Renewal in Iraq
   http://www.whitehouse.gov/infocus/iraq/

The Iraq War, from its planning through its conduct, and post war occupation and reconstruction, has been the single defining feature of the George W. Bush administration's foreign policy. The Iraq War has come to sharply divide the American public. For its supporters, the Iraq War is the second campaign of the first war of the twenty-first century, the war against terrorism. For its detractors, the Iraq War has served to detract the United States from more critical threats emanating from terrorist groups such as al-Qaeda and has isolated the United States from its traditional allies. Conflicts of opinion extend beyond the war to questions about the handling of intelligence and decision making procedures prior to the terrorist attacks of September 11, 2001. Because it is so central to American foreign policy we have organized a separate section around evaluations of the Iraq War and its implications for American foreign policy.

In order to better understand the chain of events that led the authors of these essays to take the positions they did we present a timeline of the Iraq War beginning with President Bush's 2002 State of the Union address. While rumors that the Bush administration was determined to go to war with Iraq after the defeat of the Taliban in Afghanistan were widespread in Washington, they took on a new intensity following this speech.

- **January 29, 2002**: In his State of the Union address Bush identifies Iraq, North Korea, and Iran as an "axis of evil" and promises that the U.S. would not allow "the world's most

dangerous regimes to threaten us with the world's most destructive weapons."
- **September 12, 2002**: Bush addresses the opening session of the United Nations and challenges it to confront the "grave and gathering danger" of Iraq or become irrelevant.
- **September 17, 2002**: The Bush administration releases its national security strategy that replaces deterrence with preemption.
- **October 10, 2002**: Congress authorizes the use of force against Iraq.
- **November 27, 2002**: Weapons inspections resume in Iraq following a unanimous November 8 Security Council resolution calling for tougher arms inspections in Iraq.
- **December 21, 2002**: Bush approves deployment of U.S. forces to the Persian Gulf.
- **February 14, 2003**: UN Weapons Inspector Hans Blix asserts that progress has been made in Iraq.
- **February 24, 2003**: The U.S., Great Britain and Spain introduce a resolution at the Security Council authorizing the use of military force against Iraq. France, Germany and Russia oppose the resolution.
- **March 17, 2003**: Bush presents Saddam Hussein with a 48 hour ultimatum to leave Iraq.
- **March 19, 2003**: Operation Iraq Freedom begins with a decapitation strike aimed at Iraqi leadership targets in Baghdad.

- **March 21, 2003**: Major fighting in Iraq begins.
- **April 9, 2003**: Baghdad falls.
- **May 1, 2003**: President Bush declares an end to major combat operations
- **May 19, 2003**: Thousands in Baghdad peacefully protest U.S. presence.
- **May 23, 2003**: UN Security Council lifts sanctions and gives U.S. and Great Britain authority to control Iraq until an elected government is in place.
- **July 9, 2003**: Secretary of Defense Donald Rumsfeld admits that the cost of the war was underestimated by one-half. He now places it at $3.9 billion/month and acknowledges that far more troops than anticipated will be needed for the occupation.
- **July 17, 2003**: US combat deaths in Iraq reach the level of the Persian Gulf War.
- **December 13, 2003**: Saddam Hussein is captured.
- **April 29, 2004**: Photos aired of torture and mistreatment of Iraqi prisoners by U.S. personnel at the Abu Ghraib prison.
- **June 8, 2004**: UN Security Council passes resolution ending formal occupation and outlining a role for the UN in post-transition Iraq.
- **June 28, 2004**: US transfers power to the new Iraqi government.
- **September 8, 2004**: US casualties reach 1,000 dead. One month later a report estimates Iraqi war-related casualties to be as high as 10,000.
- **October 6, 2004**: US top weapons inspector issues report concluding that Iraq destroyed its illegal weapons months after the 1991 Persian Gulf War.
- **December 1, 2004**: US announces that it plans to expand military presence in Iraq to 150,000 troops.
- **January 30, 2005**: Iraq holds first multiparty election in 50 years.
- **April 28, 2005**: Prime Minister Ibrahim al-Jaafari and his cabinet are approved by the National Assembly,

- **June 16, 2005**: Agreement reached on increasing Sunni participation in drafting of a new constitution.
- **October 15, 2005**: Iraqi's vote on new constitution
- **October 25, 2005**: Number of deaths of U.S. soldiers fighting in Iraq reaches 2,000.
- **December 15, 2005**: Iraq holds parliamentary elections
- **March 15, 2006**: Saddam Hussein testifies for the first time at his trial
- **April 22, 2006**: Nuri al-Maliki of the Shiite Dawa Party is approved as Prime Minister breaking a long political deadlock.
- **June 8, 2006**: Abu Musab al-Zarqari, head of al Qaeda in Iraq, is killed in a U.S. air strike.
- **June 22, 2006**: Republican controlled Senate rejects a Democrat proposal to start a withdrawal of troops from Iraq.

The first reading in this section, "Lifting the Veil," provides findings from recent public opinion polls from the Middle East. The author concludes that defeating terrorism will require defeating the rage that fuels it. The next article examines the lessons the Iraq War holds for building democracy. Written by a senior advisor to the Coalition Provisional Authority in Iraq, "Iraq and Democracy: the Lessons Learned" outlines a strategy for building democracy in post conflict environments. The next three articles take up the question of what should the United States do now in Iraq. In "Centripetal Force: The Case for Staying in Iraq" Lawrence Kaplan characterizes the United States as an honest broker and peacekeeper and argues against withdrawal. William Odom presents the opposing position in "Withdraw Now." He sees the Iraq War as having been a flawed policy from the outset. The third essay, "The Right Way: Seven Steps toward a Last Chance in Iraq" presents a strategy for victory but holds doubts about the American public's willingness to give it time to succeed. The final essay in this section, "Contemplating the Ifs," shifts the focus to Iran and examines the military options open to the United States as well as the possible reactions of others, including China.

Lifting the Veil

Understanding the Roots of Islamic Militancy

HENRY MUNSON

I n the wake of the attacks of September 11, 2001, many intellectuals have argued that Muslim extremists like Osama bin Laden despise the United States primarily because of its foreign policy. Conversely, US President George Bush's administration and its supporters have insisted that extremists loathe the United States simply because they are religious fanatics who "hate our freedoms." These conflicting views of the roots of militant Islamic hostility toward the United States lead to very different policy prescriptions. If US policies have caused much of this hostility, it would make sense to change those policies, if possible, to dilute the rage that fuels Islamic militancy. If, on the other hand, the hostility is the result of religious fanaticism, then the use of brute force to suppress fanaticism would appear to be a sensible course of action.

Groundings for Animosity

Public opinion polls taken in the Islamic world in recent years provide considerable insight into the roots of Muslim hostility toward the United States, indicating that for the most part, this hostility has less to do with cultural or religious differences than with US policies in the Arab world. In February and March 2003, Zogby International conducted a survey on behalf of Professor Shibley Telhami of the University of Maryland involving 2,620 men and women in Egypt, Jordan, Lebanon, Morocco, and Saudi Arabia. Most of those surveyed had "unfavorable attitudes" toward the United States and said that their hostility to the United States was based primarily on US policy rather than on their values. This was true of 67 percent of the Saudis surveyed. In Egypt, however, only 46 percent said their hostility resulted from US policy, while 43 percent attributed their attitudes to their values as Arabs. This is surprising given that the prevailing religious values in Saudi Arabia are more conservative than in Egypt. Be that as it may, a plurality of people in all the countries surveyed said that their hostility toward the United States was primarily based on their opposition to US policy.

The issue that arouses the most hostility in the Middle East toward the United States is the Israeli-Palestinian conflict and what Muslims perceive as US responsibility for the suffering of the Palestinians. A similar Zogby International survey from the summer of 2001 found that more than 80 percent of the respondents in Egypt, Kuwait, Lebanon, and Saudi Arabia ranked the Palestinian issue as one of the three issues of greatest importance to them. A survey of Muslim "opinion leaders" released by the Pew Research Center for the People and the Press in December 2001 also found that the US position on the Israeli-Palestinian conflict was the main source of hostility toward the United States.

It is true that Muslim hostility toward Israel is often expressed in terms of anti-Semitic stereotypes and conspiracy theories—think, for example, of the belief widely-held in the Islamic world that Jews were responsible for the terrorists attacks of September 11, 2001. Muslim governments and educators need to further eliminate anti-Semitic bias in the Islamic world. However, it would be a serious mistake to dismiss Muslim and Arab hostility toward Israel as simply a matter of anti-Semitism. In the context of Jewish history, Israel represents liberation. In the context of Palestinian history, it represents subjugation. There will always be a gap between how the West and how the Muslim societies perceive Israel. There will also always be some Muslims (like Osama bin Laden) who will refuse to accept any solution to the Israeli-Palestinian conflict other than the destruction of the state of Israel. That said, if the United States is serious about winning the so-called "war on terror," then resolution of the Israeli-Palestinian conflict should be among its top priorities in the Middle East.

Eradicating, or at least curbing, Palestinian terrorism entails reducing the humiliation, despair, and rage that drive many Palestinians to support militant Islamic groups like Hamas and Islamic Jihad. When soldiers at an Israeli checkpoint prevented Ahmad Qurei (Abu al Ala), one of the principal negotiators of the Oslo accords and president of the Palestinian Authority's parliament, from traveling from Gaza to his home on the West Bank, he declared, "Soon, I too will join Hamas." Qurei's words reflected his outrage at the subjugation of his people and the humiliation that Palestinians experience every day at the checkpoints that surround their homes. Defeating groups like Hamas requires diluting the rage that fuels them. Relying on force alone tends to increase rather than weaken their appeal. This is demonstrated by some of the unintended consequences of the US-led invasion and occupation of Iraq in the spring of 2003.

On June 3, 2003, the Pew Research Center for the People and the Press released a report entitled *Views of a Changing World June 2003*. This study was primarily based on a survey of nearly 16,000 people in 21 countries (including the Palestinian Authority) from April 28 to May 15, 2003, shortly after the fall of Saddam Hussein's regime. The survey results were supplemented by data from earlier polls, especially a survey of 38,000 people in 44 countries in 2002. The study found a marked increase in Muslim hostility toward the United States from 2002 to 2003. In the summer of 2002, 61 percent of Indonesians held a favorable view of the United States. By May of 2003, only 15 percent did. During the same period of time, the decline in Turkey was from 30 percent to 15 percent, and in Jordan it was from 25 percent to one percent.

Indeed, the Bush administration's war on terror has been a major reason for the increased hostility toward the United States. The Pew Center's 2003 survey found that few Muslims support this war. Only 23 percent of Indonesians did so in May of 2003, down from 31 percent in the summer of 2002. In Turkey, support dropped from 30 percent to 22 percent. In Pakistan, support dropped from 30 percent to 16 percent, and in Jordan from 13 percent to two percent. These decreases reflect overwhelming Muslim opposition to the war in Iraq, which most Muslims saw as yet another act of imperial subjugation of Muslims by the West.

The 2003 Zogby International poll found that most Arabs believe that the United States attacked Iraq to gain control of Iraqi oil and to help Israel. Over three-fourths of all those surveyed felt that oil was a major reason for the war. More than three-fourths of the Saudis and Jordanians said that helping Israel was a major reason, as did 72 percent of the Moroccans and over 50 percent of the Egyptians and Lebanese. Most Arabs clearly do not believe that the United States overthrew Saddam Hussein out of humanitarian motives. Even in Iraq itself, where there was considerable support for the war, most people attribute the war to the US desire to gain control of Iraqi oil and help Israel.

Not only has the Bush administration failed to win much Muslim support for its war on terrorism, its conduct of the war has generated a dangerous backlash. Most Muslims see the US fight against terror as a war against the Islamic world. The 2003 Pew survey found that over 70 percent of Indonesians, Pakistanis, and Turks were either somewhat or very worried about a potential US threat to their countries, as were over half of Jordanians and Kuwaitis.

This sense of a US threat is linked to the 2003 Pew report's finding of widespread support for Osama bin Laden. The survey of April and May 2003 found that over half those surveyed in Indonesia, Jordan, and the Palestinian Authority, and almost half those surveyed in Morocco and Pakistan, listed bin Laden as one of the three world figures in whom they had the most confidence "to do the right thing." For most US citizens, this admiration for the man responsible for the attacks of September 11, 2001, is incomprehensible. But no matter how outrageous this widespread belief may be, it is vitally important to understand its origins. If one does not understand why people think the way they do, one cannot induce them to think differently.

Similarly, if one does not understand why people act as they do, one cannot hope to induce them to act differently.

The Appeal of Osama bin Laden

Osama bin Laden first engaged in violence because of the occupation of a Muslim country by an "infidel" superpower. He did not fight the Russians in Afghanistan because he hated their values or their freedoms, but because they had occupied a Muslim land. He participated in and supported the Afghan resistance to the Soviet occupation from 1979 to 1989, which ended with the withdrawal of the Russians. Bin Laden saw this war as legitimate resistance to foreign occupation. At the same time, he saw it as a *jihad*, or holy war, on behalf of Muslims oppressed by infidels.

When Saddam Hussein invaded Kuwait in August 1990, bin Laden offered to lead an army to defend Saudi Arabia. The Saudis rejected this offer and instead allowed the United States to establish bases in their kingdom, leading to bin Laden's active opposition to the United States. One can only speculate what bin Laden would have done for the rest of his life if the United States had not stationed hundreds of thousands of US troops in Saudi Arabia in 1990. Conceivably, bin Laden's hostility toward the United States might have remained passive and verbal instead of active and violent. All we can say with certainty is that the presence of US troops in Saudi Arabia did trigger bin Laden's holy war against the United States. It was no accident that the bombing of two US embassies in Africa on August 7, 1998, marked the eighth anniversary of the introduction of US forces into Saudi Arabia as part of Operation Desert Storm.

Part of bin Laden's opposition to the presence of US military presence in Saudi Arabia resulted from the fact that US troops were infidels on or near holy Islamic ground. Non-Muslims are not allowed to enter Mecca and Medina, the two holiest places in Islam, and they are allowed to live in Saudi Arabia only as temporary residents. Bin Laden is a reactionary Wahhabi Muslim who undoubtedly does hate all non-Muslims. But that hatred was not in itself enough to trigger his *jihad* against the United States.

Indeed, bin Laden's opposition to the presence of US troops in Saudi Arabia had a nationalistic and anti-imperialist tone. In 1996, he declared that Saudi Arabia had become an American colony. There is nothing specifically religious or fundamentalist about this assertion. In his book *Chronique d'une Guerre d'Orient*, Gilles Kepel describes a wealthy whiskey-drinking Saudi who left part of his fortune to bin Laden because he alone "was defending the honor of the country, reduced in his eyes to a simple American protectorate."

In 1996, bin Laden issued his first major manifesto, entitled a "Declaration of Jihad against the Americans Occupying the Land of the Two Holy Places." The very title focuses on the presence of US troops in Saudi Arabia, which bin Laden calls an "occupation." But this manifesto also refers to other examples of what bin Laden sees as the oppression of Muslims by infidels. "It is no secret that the people of Islam have suffered from the oppression, injustice, and aggression of the alliance of Jews and Christians and their collaborators to the point that the blood of the Muslims became the cheapest and their wealth was loot in the hands of the enemies," he writes. "Their blood was spilled in Palestine and Iraq."

Bin Laden has referred to the suffering of the Palestinians and the Iraqis (especially with respect to the deaths caused by sanctions) in all of his public statements since at least the mid-1990s. His 1996 "Declaration of Jihad" is no exception. Nonetheless, it primarily focuses on the idea that the Saudi regime has "lost all legitimacy" because it "has permitted the enemies of the Islamic community, the Crusader American forces, to occupy our land for many years." In this 1996 text, bin Laden even contends that the members of the Saudi royal family are apostates because they helped infidels fight the Muslim Iraqis in the Persian Gulf War of 1991.

A number of neo-conservatives have advocated the overthrow of the Saudi regime because of its support for terrorism. It is true that the Saudis have funded militant Islamic movements. It is also true that Saudi textbooks and teachers often encourage hatred of infidels and allow the extremist views of bin Laden to thrive. It is also probably true that members of the Saudi royal family have financially supported terrorist groups. The fact remains, however, that bin Laden and his followers in Al Qaeda have themselves repeatedly called for the overthrow of the Saudi regime, saying that it has turned Saudi Arabia into "an American colony."

If the United States were to send troops to Saudi Arabia once again, this time to overthrow the Saudi regime itself, the main beneficiaries would be bin Laden and those who think like him. On January 27, 2002, a *New York Times* article referenced a Saudi intelligence survey conducted in October 2001 that showed that 95 percent of educated Saudis between the ages of 25 and 41 supported bin Laden. If the United States were to overthrow the Saudi regime, such people would lead a guerrilla war that US forces would inevitably find themselves fighting. This war would attract recruits from all over the Islamic world outraged by the desecration of "the land of the two holy places." Given that US forces are already fighting protracted guerrilla wars in Iraq and Afghanistan, starting a third one in Saudi Arabia would not be the most effective way of eradicating terror in the Middle East.

Those who would advocate the overthrow of the Saudi regime by US troops seem to forget why bin Laden began his holy war against the United States in the first place. They also seem to forget that no one is more committed to the overthrow of the Saudi regime than bin Laden himself. Saudi Arabia is in dire need of reform, but yet another US occupation of a Muslim country is not the way to make it happen.

In December 1998, Palestinian journalist Jamal Abd al Latif Isma'il asked bin Laden, "Who is Osama bin Laden, and what does he want?" After providing a brief history of his life, bin Laden responded to the second part of the question, "We demand that our land be liberated from the enemies, that our land be liberated from the Americans. God almighty, may He be praised, gave all living beings a natural desire to reject external intruders. Take chickens, for example. If an armed soldier enters a chicken's home wanting to attack it, it fights him even though it is just a chicken." For bin Laden and millions of other Muslims, the Afghans, the Chechens, the Iraqis, the Kashmiris, and the Palestinians are all just "chickens" defending their homes against the attacks of foreign soldiers.

In his videotaped message of October 7, 2001, after the attacks of September 11, 2001, bin Laden declared, "What America is tasting now is nothing compared to what we have been tasting for decades. For over 80 years our *umma* has been tasting this humiliation and this degradation. Its sons are killed, its blood is shed, its holy places are violated, and it is ruled by other than that which God has revealed. Yet no one hears. No one responds."

Bin Laden's defiance of the United States and his criticism of Muslim governments who ignore what most Muslims see as the oppression of the Palestinians, Iraqis, Chechens, and others, have made him a hero of Muslims who do not agree with his goal of a strictly Islamic state and society. Even young Arab girls in tight jeans praise bin Laden as an anti-imperialist hero. A young Iraqi woman and her Palestinian friends told Gilles Kepel in the fall of 2001, "He stood up to defend us. He is the only one."

Looking Ahead

Feelings of impotence, humiliation, and rage currently pervade the Islamic world, especially the Muslim Middle East. The invasion and occupation of Iraq has exacerbated Muslim concerns about the United States. In this context, bin Laden is seen as a heroic Osama Maccabeus descending from his mountain cave to fight the infidel oppressors to whom the worldly rulers of the Islamic world bow and scrape.

The violent actions of Osama bin Laden and those who share his views are not simply caused by "hatred of Western freedoms." They result, in part at least, from US policies that have enraged the Muslim world. Certainly, Islamic zealots like bin Laden do despise many aspects of Western culture. They do hate "infidels" in general, and Jews in particular. Muslims do need to seriously examine the existence and perpetuation of such hatred in their societies and cultures. But invading and occupying their countries simply exacerbates the sense of impotence, humiliation, and rage that induce them to support people like bin Laden. Defeating terror entails diluting the rage that fuels it.

HENRY MUNSON is Chair of the Department of Anthropology at the University of Maine.

Iraq and Democracy: The Lessons Learned

"The United States squandered its extraordinary military victory through a series of gross strategic mistakes, acts of ideological blindness, and a breathtaking failure to prepare militarily and politically for the postwar era."

LARRY DIAMOND

Iraq is not yet lost. The December parliamentary elections—with their extraordinary voter turnout and their promise of more inclusive Sunni involvement in government—marked a turning point on the difficult path of stabilizing that tortured country. But Iraq is not yet won either, and it is important to understand why.

Whatever happens in the months and years to come, it is clear that in the two years following the toppling of Saddam Hussein's regime, the United States squandered its extraordinary military victory through a series of gross strategic mistakes, acts of ideological blindness, and a breathtaking failure to prepare militarily and politically for the postwar era. For the benefit of future policy making, it is vital that the United States learn the essential lessons for building democracy after conflicts that Iraq has taught.

Win the Peace

The first lesson of America's experience in Iraq is that the stabilization—not to mention the democratization— of a state that has collapsed or been toppled through violent conflict is an intrinsically difficult and protracted process that requires a huge commitment from both internal and international actors. To generate and sustain this commitment, any effort at administration and reconstruction of the postconflict state must mobilize legitimacy, both internally in the postconflict country as well as internationally. It is therefore ill-advised to go to war against a country for the specific purpose of democratizing it, or without compelling strategic reasons that muster broad international support.

It was also a mistake to have gone to war largely alone. Washington can say that a coalition of some 30 countries joined the effort, but no sustained public opinion polling from any of these countries indicated that their publics supported what their governments were doing with the United States. In terms of international public opinion, the Iraq War was largely an American effort. As we have seen in Iraq, a war that lacks broad international sympathy and support depletes America's stock of "soft power" (and even over time its hard military power), creates a host of special postwar problems, and tends to weaken the international consensus behind democracy promotion as an endeavor.

It was unfortunate that the United States failed to correct its own international weakness and isolation in the postwar administration of Iraq. While it constructed a Coalition Provisional Authority (CPA) with the military and administrative participation of many countries (most prominently Britain), the occupation was in its design and structure overwhelmingly American. The Iraqis knew it. The United Nations—which was ready to work in close partnership with the United States as it had in Afghanistan but was largely spurned—knew it. And America's allies knew it. Clearly, the United States needed to do much more than it did in Iraq to generate legitimacy and trust.

A second and related lesson underscores what Washington knew before it went in, and what the Pentagon leadership ignored to the great misfortune of both Iraqis and the United States: that the United States needs to prepare in advance for a major commitment and resource it adequately. As James Dobbins and his colleagues noted in a 2003 RAND study, *America's Role in Nation-Building: From Germany to Iraq*, the typical successful experience involves an overwhelming commitment of force not so much for winning the war—which the United States could accomplish with the speed and maneuverability of Secretary of Defense Donald Rumsfeld's new military—but for winning the peace and securing it in the immediate aftermath of the war.

From the day that Baghdad fell on April 9, 2003, it was clear that the United States did not have enough troops on the ground.

It never had enough troops. Indeed, it never had enough of any kind of resource needed to secure the postwar era. Nor did it have the right mix of troops. It was missing, for example, enough military police. What it needed— what the world needs—is a sort of muscular *gendarmerie*. These would be well-armed and -trained mobile police that can be deployed in a situation like Baghdad and use non-lethal force to prevent the kind of massive looting of government institutions and public infrastructure that occurred in the war's aftermath. Even without this, senior Army officers had sought several hundred thousand troops—at least twice or even three times the number the United States had on the ground—to invade and then stabilize Iraq after the war. By a greater order of magnitude, the United States needed more military police, more civil-affairs officers, more armored vehicles, more helicopters, more body armor— more of everything.

Not only did the US leadership fail from the beginning to deploy sufficient military resources to secure the country, to deter and face down potential spoilers, and to seal the borders to prevent Al Qaeda and other foreign jihadists from pouring in from Syria and Saudi Arabia—it also did not have in place enough resources for the civilian component of the postinvasion phase, including the capability to move civilians about the country while adequately protecting them. These failures led to a situation in which the United States could not effectively implement either the economic reconstruction plans or the political and civic reconstruction plans that it had for Iraq because it was so dangerous to move around.

Besides the need for sufficient legitimacy and resources, the experience in Iraq yields more specific lessons about building electoral systems that could aid Washington in the promotion of democracy in the next few years in the Arab world. Of course, if the United States were to become more active in this regard, as President Bush has committed it to doing, it will not confront the circumstances of a shattered state and a post-totalitarian landscape in the way it has in Iraq. Still, the American experiment in Iraq offers hands-on experience in several areas.

Buy Time for Politics

Building a level and pluralistic playing field is extremely important. The United States encountered in Iraq the "flattened landscape" that was found in the Soviet Union, Romania, and some of the other postcommunist countries after their ruling regimes fell. These nations had essentially no civil society or pluralistic array of political parties.

In the shadows of severe authoritarianism in the Muslim Middle East, the one type of political group that can mobilize outside the state's gaze and build support tends to involve some degree of radical Islamist ideology. If a country moves from a political vacuum very rapidly to elections, it will not have a level playing field because of the overwhelming advantage of recently surfaced Islamist movements and parties, whose democratic credentials or commitments are at best ambiguous and at worst entirely absent. Moreover, in the absence of established political parties and civil society, the Islamist or authoritarian tendency will have a tremendous head start.

This creates concern about how to buy time and mobilize resources to try to level the political playing field. It is one of the issues that concerned the Coalition Provisional Authority, and it is one of the reasons why the CPA wanted to delay elections in Iraq. Unless there is time for different types of political parties, social movements, and civic organizations to develop—including groups that can project a more moderate, democratic, secular, or, at least, democratic Islamist orientation onto the political and electoral landscape—then the electoral arena will be dominated by a force that is not democratic.

After nearly three years and a bitter cost in lives and treasure, the United States now has a real chance to help Iraq move toward stabilization.

Or it may become polarized, as it did in Iraq, along ethnic and identity lines. The January 2005 election, for all of its deeply moving character and successful elements, was largely an identity referendum. Ninety percent of the Kurds voted for the Kurdish list, more than 70 percent of the Shiites voted for the United Iraqi Alliance (a coalition of Shiite religious parties), and about 70 percent of the Sunnis did not vote.

Grand Ayatollah Ali al-Sistani, the most powerful Shiite leader, had demanded early direct elections for both a constituent assembly and a transitional parliament. Although the reasons why the United States resisted this were understandable, they were not based solely on the need for time to develop the administrative agenda and electoral framework. Washington was worried, frankly, that people who might not be committed to democracy and a liberal agenda would win—and win overwhelmingly. Yet because the American occupation was so badly lacking in legitimacy within Iraq (and internationally), authorities did not have the standing and trust that would have been required to delay elections very long without the Shiite south violently resisting.

As a result of the skillful mediation of the United Nations and its special envoy, Lakhdar Brahimi, a compromise was reached in February 2004 that delayed elections for a transitional national assembly until January 2005. This was about eight months longer than Sistani and the Shiite religious parties wanted to wait, but it was about two years earlier than might have been desirable and achievable if there had been from early in the postwar period a more broad-based, legitimate interim administration, of Iraqis, chosen by Iraqis.

There needs to be a strategy for democratization in the Arab world, and it needs to be serious in terms of having true democratization as the goal. It is not enough to engage in what Georgetown University's Daniel Brumberg and other specialists have called "tactical liberalization"—a game of hide-and-seek, back-and-forth, but never real, sustained movement toward democracy. At the same time, change should be gradual enough to give time for political parties to build their organizations, craft programs, and mobilize political support—points also made by a 2005 Council on Foreign Relations task force report on political change in the Arab world and the US role, *In Support of Arab Democracy*.

Go Local First

In addition to how soon elections are held, it also matters where and in what order they are held. This is another lesson that the Iraqi postwar experience reinforces and sustains. It helps to have local elections first. The CPA was mistaken not to have gone ahead with local elections in many communities— local elections that different Iraqi communities were asking for, that many civilian and military CPA officials wanted to hold, and that Ambassador Paul Bremer and other officials in the CPA headquarters in Baghdad vetoed and prevented from happening.

Of course, critics argued that there was no electoral register, no voting infrastructure, no parties, no electoral law. These were serious obstacles. Yet the United States could have used—and in a few cases local officials did in fact use— the records of household registration for Iraq's food-ration system and other practical means in order to register voters and allow them to cast ballots to choose local leaders. When local elections occur early, new actors emerge who have credibility and legitimacy, and who have roots in their community. This process of pushing forward local leaders, and encouraging them to garner support from within their own communities, tends to soften or deemphasize the major identity cleavages in a country. It could have exercised some brake on the political tendency of elections in a postconflict situation to become an identity referendum or a deeply ideological and symbolic process.

> It is ill-advised to go to war against a country for the specific purpose of democratizing it, or without compelling strategic reasons that muster broad international support.

The United States and its allies should not, of course, apply what has been learned inflexibly and without reflecting on the local situation of a country that is emerging out of conflict or moving, hopefully, into democracy. But the lesson of Iraq regarding early local elections could also apply to a number of Arab nations where political openings are occurring, or where the people are at least appealing for them. Democratization in these countries might be more viable and sustainable if it proceeded with early emphasis on truly democratic and open local-level elections, where less is at stake.

Power can thus be dispersed and a more pluralistic landscape can emerge without people feeling that their vital interests might be threatened. The practice of local political competition, and the need for victorious politicians and parties to deal with practical issues of local and municipal governance, might then generate the pragmatism in governance and the construction of mutual political trust and tolerance that could enable democratization to proceed more fully to higher levels of authority.

This points to yet another lesson of the Iraq experience: the importance of decentralized authority. If local and even mid-level provincial elections are going to be meaningful, power has to be devolved and resources provided to lower levels of government. Arab states historically have been extremely centralized. This was one of the problems of Iraq; it is one of the problems characteristic of virtually all of the world's petro-states. When people conduct politics only in a central political arena, this becomes conducive to the polarization of politics around larger identities. It is not conducive to a just distribution of resources or to a democratic approach to politics. If there is only one political arena at the central national level— and everything is at stake in that arena—then no one can afford to lose.

If, on the other hand, a large number of local elections takes place, then Sunnis in Anbar Province and Kurds in Kurdistan and Shiites in the city of Basra know that whatever happens in the center, they are going to be able to exercise some political power in their province. And if they receive some guaranteed share of the oil wealth to spend in their provinces and their communities, this takes some pressure off national-level politics. (We perhaps are beginning to see that the Sunnis, who have historically been the strongest advocates for a highly centralized fiscal and political system—since they controlled it—are waking up to the fact that decentralization can be useful to them. If the negotiations this summer for a new constitution had not been so rushed, and if they had not adopted such a radical formula for regional power, which could potentially eviscerate the central government, the Sunnis might have gravitated more clearly to this understanding.)

Pick the Right System

The electoral system matters. Yet, partly because it seemed administratively easier to manage in the difficult circumstances of Iraq in late 2004 and January of 2005, the electoral system selected by a United Nations team was inappropriate for Iraq. The Iraqi interim government and the United States had invited in UN officials to help choose, train, and advise a new Iraqi electoral commission. Bremer and the CPA had insisted on having an independent electoral commission, even when many Iraqi political parties involved in the governing council wanted to relentlessly politicize and split up control of this body. This, too, is a lesson from Iraq. The electoral process requires popular confidence, and that comes from a neutral, professional electoral administration that is totally insulated from partisan politics.

But the system chosen for the January elections was proportional representation in a single nationwide district, one that only a few other relatively small countries use (such as the Netherlands and, ironically, Israel). While proportional representation made sense for Iraq, the absence of any district basis for the system did not. No area of the country had any indication of what kind of minimum representation it would have in parliament. Since the Sunni areas had been the site of far greater violence and disruption, Sunnis feared that they would wind up being severely underrepresented in such a system, which accords seats to parties purely on the basis of national vote totals. This was one of the major reasons the Sunni Arab parties boycotted the January 30 elections—a disastrous move for them, and for the country, since it intensified the polarization and violence.

Generally, proportional representation is useful in managing ethnic conflict and ensuring a just, inclusive result. But using only a single nationwide district leaves no possibility for local candidates, local identities, and local initiatives to emerge. And there is nothing that is more conducive to an election's becoming an identity referendum than a single national-list system in which voters hardly even know who the candidates are. They are literally just voting for a party and a symbol. In the case of Iraq, that meant most Shiites were simply voting for Sistani's picture on a poster.

If Iraq had adopted a system of smaller-scale multimember districts based, for example, on the boundaries of the 18 provinces—something many of us who were within the CPA recommended for the first national elections—or even open-list systems under which people could look at the candidates and vote for individual candidates and rank them, that might have allowed local leaders to emerge and develop some constituencies. It could also have required elected officials to be responsible and accountable to local-level constituencies.

Fortunately, the provincial-list proportional representation system is precisely what Iraq adopted for the December 15 elections. This decision, which then assured a minimum number of seats for each province in the new parliament, played a major role in giving Sunni Arab parties confidence to participate vigorously in the elections. Although some Sunnis complained about the allocation of seats to their provinces (based on voter registration figures), their political and religious leaders urged full participation in the election, and even the die-hard Saddamist and Al Qaeda terrorists largely refrained from the kind of violence and intimidation that suppressed the Sunni vote in January. As a result, Sunni voter participation soared on December 15, with ordinary Sunni voters now feeling the same pride and resolve in participating that other Iraqi communities had in January. The election itself was an unprecedented logistical and political success, with some 11 million Iraqis (over two-thirds of those registered) voting at more than 6,000 polling stations, and with only 18 reported attacks against polling sites (compared to about five times that in January). Even in the immediate aftermath of the balloting (as this magazine went to press), it was clear that the widespread and enthusiastic participation would ensure a much more representative parliament, and so at least the possibility of a more inclusive government. In the coming months, however, the stabilization of Iraq will depend to a great extent on whether the different political and sectarian groups are able to share power and fashion a more broadly acceptable constitutional bargain, particularly on federalism and the control of oil and gas resources.

Disarm the Militias

Another lesson made obvious in Iraq is that any effort at post-conflict reconstruction must confront the problem of order. A country cannot build a democratic state unless it first has a state—a set of institutions of political authority that exercise a monopoly over the means of violence in a territory. If a democratic electoral process is to be successful and sustained to allow the emergence of a truly democratic system, attention must therefore be paid to the problem of armed force outside the control of the state. Armed groups controlled by political parties and political movements can use this private force to aggrandize their power, intimidate voters, and create an undemocratic playing field.

The CPA tried over many months to implement in essence a "DDR" plan—disarmament, demobilization, and reintegration of militias into the Iraqi economy and society. But the effort began too late. It lacked the force and legitimacy to be implemented effectively. And it was ultimately derailed by the twin insurgencies of the Falluja-based Sunni resistance and the Shiite fighters under Muqtada al-Sadr that erupted in April 2004, and then by the lack of enthusiasm for the disarmament effort on the part of the Iraqi interim government that took power on June 28.

Iraq thus went into elections in January 2005 facing not only a virulent Sunni-based insurgency, but also increasingly muscular and ambitious Shiite militias on the streets as well. In the north was the country's most powerful Iraqi armed force, the Kurdish peshmerga, which had been extending the power and de facto borders of Kurdistan through force, even as it brought a degree of stability to the far north unknown in the rest of Iraq. The existence of these powerful, non-state militias could not help but affect the electoral environment.

To a degree that will take some time to fully assess, the mobilization of the militias did diminish the freedom and fairness of the December 15 elections. This was particularly so in the southern provinces, where militias associated with the Shiite religious parties of the United Iraqi Alliance intimidated and obstructed opposing political forces, attacked their headquarters, ripped down their campaign banners, and terrorized, assaulted, and assassinated a number of their candidates and campaign workers. The electoral misconduct was particularly brazen in Basra, where many police cars and government buildings displayed the electoral symbol of the Alliance, or the ballot number of its electoral list, 555, and where Iraqi police officers urged people to vote for the 555 list on election day (in open defiance of the electoral rules).

The militia problem is going to get considerably worse in future elections. Moreover, it is not just voting we must worry about. During the past year in particular, the militias of the Shiite Islamist parties and movements have used their high degree of organization and their coercive power to penetrate the police and the military. In the context of the provincial electoral victories that their parties and movements won in January 2005, they also have taken control of local governments and imposed harsh interpretations of sharia, or Islamic law. At the same time they have exacted vigilante vengeance against Sunnis believed involved with the insurgency or Hussein's regime.

A kind of Islamic state is emerging in the Shiite south. Although the Islamist parties—gathered together in the United Iraqi Alliance (still with the implicit blessing of Ayatollah Sistani)—did not do quite as well nationally in the December elections as they had in January, within the southern provinces they remain determined to consolidate their hold on power. For some time to come, there may be little that the United States can do to prevent the drift to Islamic rule in the southern provinces, except try to strengthen moderate and secular groups throughout Iraq, while standing up vigorously for basic principles of human rights and constitutionalism.

Meanwhile, the international community, the United States, the United Nations, the Europeans— everyone with a stake in a peaceful, stable Iraq, including, obviously, the Iraqi state itself—will need to confront the problem of very substantial armed force in the hands of private actors, political parties, and religious and social movements. These groups are bound to use that force in ways that will undermine democratic principles and processes if they are not demobilized.

Unfortunately, demobilizing them has never been more difficult, not only because many of their parties have won political power and legitimacy, but also because they have increasingly merged with the Iraqi state. A major test of Iraq's stability and viability in the coming months will be whether the units of the new Iraqi army and police are loyal to the state as a whole, or to the parties and movements from which they were recruited as militia fighters.

Deal with the Insurgents

Even with the success of the December 15 elections, Iraq will not become a full democracy any time soon. There are simply too many groups on the ground, too powerful and too violent, that do not value or want a truly democratic order. Yet, with the prospect of a more legitimate and inclusive parliament and government, there is a chance for Iraq to turn away from the incremental descent into civil war and toward stabilization—if the insurgency can be significantly diminished.

Although the Iraqi armed forces are considerably larger, and more capable and spirited, than they were a year ago, there is still no prospect of defeating the insurgency through military means alone. Rather, turning the corner on the insurgency requires a political process that divides the more tactical elements of the insurgency—the Sunni tribal, political, and religious forces that have been seeking at least some share of power in the new order, and an end to the American occupation—from the diehard Al Qaeda and Saddamist elements.

In this respect, it is possible to see hopeful signs on the horizon. Despite their concerns and anxieties over the rise of targeted violence and assassinations against Sunnis, the Sunni parties and movements participated massively in the December elections and appear to have won a share of seats in much closer proportion to their share of the population than they did in January, when they boycotted the vote.

In November 2005, the Arab League gathered in Cairo to hold the broadest meeting yet of Iraqi political forces, including members of the transitional government and elements associated with the Sunni-based insurgency. They agreed on the principles of power-sharing and on the need to establish a timetable for American withdrawal. At the same time, the US ambassador in Iraq, Zalmay Khalilzad, has shown a flexibility, deftness, and interest in negotiation with insurgent elements that his predecessors lacked.

There are now three imperatives. First, power-sharing must be made to work so that all groups see that they can better secure their interests through peaceful participation in politics and government than through violence. Second, compromise must be achieved in the forthcoming process to review and amend the constitution adopted in October (over the bitter objections of the Sunni Arab communities, which voted overwhelmingly against it). In particular, the federal system must be revised to clearly establish central government control over future (as well as current) oil and gas production, and to rule out the creation of new governing regions, or at least to limit the number of provinces that can come together into a single region. This would remove one of the most alarming Sunni concerns, a Shiite super-region with control over most of the country's oil resources. And third, comprehensive negotiations are needed between the United States and the insurgents, involving as well the new Iraqi government and the mediation of the United Nations and the Arab League.

Through such negotiations, it may be possible to entrench power-sharing provisions and develop a mutually acceptable plan for American military withdrawal. This would lead many of the Sunni insurgent groups to suspend the violent struggle and to take visible public steps to discourage and delegitimate the continuation of the insurgency. With greater Sunni cooperation, it may also become possible to isolate, capture, kill, or expel the Al Qaeda fighters who have been responsible for the most destructive and destabilizing violence.

After nearly three years and a bitter cost in lives and treasure, the United States now has a real chance to help Iraq move toward stabilization. It will not be quick or easy, and real democracy may be years away. But compared with the tyranny of Hussein or the chaos since the invasion, stabilization would count as considerable progress. It would also improve long-term prospects for democratization efforts elsewhere in the region, if the bitter lessons learned in Iraq are heeded.

LARRY DIAMOND, a *Current History* contributing editor, is a senior fellow at the Hoover Institution at Stanford University and the author of *Squandered Victory: The American Occupation and the Bungled Effort to Bring Democracy to Iraq* (Times Books, 2005). In 2004 he served as a senior adviser to the Coalition Provisional Authority in Baghdad.

Reprinted from *Current History*, January 2006, pp. 34-39. Copyright © 2006 by Current History, Inc. Reprinted with permission.

Centripetal Force:
The Case for Staying in Iraq.

LAWRENCE F. KAPLAN

For a return visitor, Baghdad International Airport offers a fitting portal into the new Iraq. Unlike the military side of the airport, where U.S. transport planes and helicopters operate in an industrious roar, the civilian side, which US-AID renovated in 2003, now languishes in disrepair. Iraqi Airways flights, on which it was possible to light up a cigarette until recently, still come and go. But, in the terminal itself, the rest room floors are smeared with excrement, wires hang from the ceiling, and pay phones have been ripped from the walls. An emblem of war and poverty? Not really. The transportation minister, an ally of Moqtada Al Sadr and his rebellious Mahdi Army, has delegated responsibility for the airport's maintenance to the children of Sadr City, the Shia slum and the Mahdi Army's Baghdad base of support. The 14-year-olds in blue jumpsuits smoke, huddle, and even play tag. What they do not—and cannot—do is maintain an airport.

Not everything the U.S. enterprise touches here turns to gold. But everything it lets go of does seem to turn into dirt. With U.S. reconstruction aid running out, Iraq's infrastructure, never fully restored to begin with, decays by the hour. Iraq's political arena, from which the Americans had no choice but to withdraw, has dissolved into something unrecognizable, carved up for sectarian advantage and without a center to keep its parts from spinning away. In both cases, the United States may have given all it reasonably could be expected to give. But, when it comes to America's withdrawal from Iraq's security arena, a process that accelerates with each passing week, the only explanation can be that the White House, for all of its high-minded rhetoric about standing with Iraq, has decided not to. The insurgency continues to rage. Iraq's security forces still cannot operate on their own. And, as what was once a largely one-sided Sunni campaign of terrorism rapidly approaches something like parity (with the Shia taking up arms in their own defense), the likelihood of a civil war has surged. So, too, contrary to the delusions of war supporters and critics alike, has the importance of the Americans.

As the war takes a sectarian turn, the United States begins to look, even to many Iraqis, like an honest broker, more peacekeeper than belligerent. Sheik Humam Hamoudi, one of Iraq's most powerful Shia and a leader of the Supreme Council for Is-

lamic Revolution in Iraq (SCIRI), knows this better than most. He sits, literally, atop the Iraqi government—in a sprawling office suite above Baghdad's convention center, where Iraqi politicians wheel and deal. As with many Shia politicians, Hamoudi, donning a clerical robe and turban, becomes animated when the subject turns to the U.S. military's campaign against Sunni insurgents. If anything, he believes it has been prosecuted with insufficient vigor. And, although he complains that the Americans have placed undue restraints on the Shia-dominated security forces, he likens the effect of a U.S. withdrawal from Iraq to "a child when he wants to walk and you ask him to play football." Absent the Americans, he says, Baghdad would be transformed into another Beirut.

Hundreds of miles to the west, in an Arabesque villa that rises out of the desert near the Syrian border, Sheik Abdullah Al Yawar—Hamoudi's mirror image in the Sunni community—echoes his concern. Al Yawar wields so much power in this insurgent hotbed that U.S. Army officers say he can turn the violence on and off like a faucet. For the moment, at least, he has turned it off, responding to pleas and aid from his American interlocutors. But he worries that the same Iraqi security forces that Hamoudi claims the United States has muzzled operate with too little American oversight. He claims they have been running amok through his province, beating and arresting his constituents and chanting Shia slogans. "If the Americans leave," he warns, "there will be rivers of blood." In their own way, then, both sheiks see the U.S. military presence for exactly what it has become: a buffer—between Iraq's sects and between relative order and complete mayhem.

Whether you measure Iraq's well-being through its infrastructure, politics, security, or even geography, one thing is clear: Where the Americans do not operate, very little else does. The level of corruption that pervades Iraq's ministerial orbit, for instance, would have made South Vietnam's kleptocrats blush. The problem extends beyond a simple lack of good governance. In a case that has been highly publicized in the Iraqi press, Sunni lawmaker Mishaan Al Juburi was recently charged with embezzling funds meant to pay for the protection of an oil pipeline in Iraq's north. Not all that unusual, but prosecutors suspect he then funneled the money to insurgents who blew up the pipeline.

According to a U.S. Government Accountability Office report published earlier this month, an interagency group of State Department, military, and contracting officials concluded that "critical infrastructure facilities constructed or rehabilitated under U.S. funding have failed, will fail, or will operate in suboptimized conditions following handover to the Iraqis." Absent U.S. oversight, politicians from competing sects have transformed the ministries into personal fiefdoms, where expertise counts for nothing and connections for everything. And, just as the ministries have proved impervious to direction from above, local factories and refineries ignore the ministries.

One of the reasons Baghdad has only a few hours of electrical power each day is that electricity plants in the provinces refuse to provide it—reasoning, as the head of a plant in Iraq's south put it, that Baghdad had enough power under Saddam Hussein. Although partly a consequence of the security situation, corruption has helped drive every public service measure—electricity, potable water, heating oil—down below its prewar norm.

The dysfunction works its way down to the street, too, which becomes apparent on a visit to the home of Bakr (he asked that his last name not be used), an engineering student who lives in the middle-class Waziriya neighborhood. One morning, as he was studying, Bakr explains, he looked out his window and noticed men setting up a mortar in the middle of the street. As the government encourages all Iraqis to do, he called the Interior Ministry's emergency line, 130, to report the insurgents. "They didn't answer," Bakr recounts.

"The next day, my friends warned me not to call, because your telephone number appears and they sell it to the insurgents." He insists we drive his Opel—the Humvee of the Sunni, as Iraqis call it—to an adjacent neighborhood so he can prove the point. There, faded on a wall, hangs the picture of a young man and the announcement of his death. The dead man, Bakr explains, got through to the emergency line.

A nother casualty has been the authority of Prime Minister Ibrahim Jafari, whom the ministries routinely ignore. On the day the preliminary results of December's elections were announced, Jafari invites the election commissioners for dinner. The liberal activist Mustafa Al Kadhimiy wrangles two invitations, and, as we wait at the gate, Jafari's guards radio back and forth on their walkie-talkies—signing off with what, even in Iraq, stands out as religious phrasing: "Yes, believer." A concrete path leads to a footbridge and then across a moat, winding around Jafari's villa until it ends in a heated tent, which, Mustafa notes disapprovingly, is of Iranian vintage. But it is Jafari's relations with Iraq, not Iran, that most concern American officials here. Unlike his predecessor, Iyad Allawi, Jafari has a reputation for being cerebral, detached, and, most of all, weak.

His dinner guests look utterly exhausted. "The Sunni parties attack us," explains chief electoral officer Adil Al Lami. "We receive violence, assassination attempts." One commissioner seems to be on the brink of a nervous collapse. But not Jafari. As the commissioners pick at their kebobs, the prime minister announces that he has completed one of Thomas L. Friedman's books. Have I read *The Lexus and the Olive Tree*? As a television in the corner of the room conveys images of the carnage outside, Jafari admits to being partial to the works of Noam Chomsky. Why won't Chomsky come to Iraq? he asks. The commissioners don't know what to say. And, apart from expressing doubts about a Chomsky visit, neither do I. Later, asked if the prime minister offered this line of conversation for the benefit of a visiting American, a source close to Jafari responds, "No, this is how he talks in public. No one understands what he is talking about. But Iraqis—they like this. If they can't understand him, they think he knows something." Indeed, Jafari has become well-known for delivering inscrutable speeches that wander from Western philosophy to Arab literature and back again, leaving even seasoned translators perplexed. The confusion extends to his deliberations with the Americans. "Today, with our current government," Jafari tells me, "we tell the MNF [multinational forces] when to go. ... The MNF wait for our orders." Yet, when pressed on his relationship with coalition forces, Jafari sounds a more humble—and increasingly familiar—note. "If they leave today," he says, "we would be defeated."

Jafari's weakness notwithstanding, the imperial taint that colored the Coalition Provisional Authority (CPA) and its hand-picked successor, Allawi, made it impossible for either to govern effectively. While Iraqis subsequently voted along sectarian lines, in this hollowed-out state, where tribe and religion remain the basic affiliations, this hardly came as a surprise. Even Mithal Al Alusi, one of a dwindling band of liberals still committed to the dream of a secular Iraq, has come to terms with the pathologies of Iraqi political life. Alusi made the mistake of traveling to Israel in 2004, and, for his sins, insurgents murdered his two sons. Bodyguards ring his house; a gun lies beside him on the couch. "The mistakes here are by the Iraqi side, not the American side," he says. "The Iraqi politicians only believe it is in their interest to push sectarian divisions." Kadhimiy echoes the sentiment. "Iraqi politics, it has moved beyond the Americans, except, you know, on security issues," he says. "There, the Americans, they still control everything."

W ith security having been the exclusive property of the Americans for so long, Iraqis still ask when full ownership of their country will be returned to them. The million-dollar trophy that National Security Adviser Mowaffaq Al Rubaie keeps in his home study suggests the restoration has begun. For many Americans, the memory of Iraqis (supported by U.S. forces off-screen) pulling down Saddam's statue in Al Firdos Square still provides an inspirational bookend to the U.S. invasion. For Iraqis today, the statue—or at least its head—just provides a bookend. As the national security adviser tells it, in the aftermath of the invasion, a senior American officer tried to abscond with Saddam's head. But he only made it as far as Kuwait, where the authorities alerted Rubaie, who subsequently reclaimed the head for Iraq. So here it sits, in the national security adviser's study, where Iraqi elites express their hatred for Saddam by hitting him on the head with the soles of their shoes. "I put it here to remember Saddam is always here," he explains.

Iraqi forces, Rubaie concedes, have not reached the point where they can operate independently of the Americans. As if to prove the point, an American military officer in civilian clothes hovers in the background, answers the national security adviser's phone when a reporter calls, lives and travels with Rubaie, and, his fellow government ministers say, probably does much of the national security adviser's job for him. At the same time, Iraq's security forces have started to emerge from the shadow of their American instructors. Their training has been accelerated, and, in the near future, Rubaie sees "Iraqi security forces taking over, Iraqi forces taking the front line, [and] MNF doing logistical and support [functions]. By the end of 2007," he predicts, "we're very likely to see the last U.S. soldier."

According to the U.S. military, the Iraqi police force currently fields about 121,000 men, close to the number planned for, while the Iraqi armed forces number about 106,000 soldiers, nearly two-thirds of the force estimated for the end of this year. The Iraqi army no longer melts away in combat, nor does it suffer from mass desertions, as it did during its first battles in 2004. Army recruits now undergo a basic training course similar in length to their American counterparts, officers attend service schools, and Iraqis provide much of the instruction. As the security forces grow more competent, they have rapidly expanded the amount of territory under their control, which now includes several neighborhoods in Baghdad and large swaths of western Iraq.

But the professionalism of Iraq's security forces can be overstated, which becomes apparent to me a week later in western Iraq. As a U.S. Army convoy approaches within a few hundred yards of a U.S. outpost at a castle in Tall Afar, gunfire erupts on all sides. The Humvees speed toward the castle gate, where an Abrams tank links up with them, providing the convoy with extra firepower as it winds it way toward a forward operating base outside the city. The shooting, officers back at the base say at first, came from insurgents. Neither I nor the soldiers caught in the middle of it had that impression, and an officer later confirms what we know to be true: The Iraqi police, overwhelmingly Sunni in this area, and the Iraqi army, overwhelmingly Shia and Kurd, were firing on one another.

Sectarian clashes present one problem. The fact that the Army still cannot operate without access to U.S. firepower, logistics, communication, and intelligence presents another. Even conceding the Bush team's fanciful premise that Iraq will have 110 combat battalions operating by the end of the year (compared with three fully effective battalions a year ago and 40 today), American officers dismiss as wishful thinking the official line that Iraqi troops can replace U.S. troops on a one-to-one basis and then operate just as effectively as their American mentors.

As for the Iraqi police, if civil war comes to Iraq, it may be ignited as much by them as by the insurgents. For Iraq's police are, to an extent not fully grasped in Washington, not police at all. As one of his parting acts in June 2004, CPA chief L. Paul Bremer signed Order 91, outlawing militias in Iraq. In response, thousands of Shia militiamen exchanged their street clothes for police uniforms. As they have gotten better at combating Iraq's Sunni guerrillas, the insurgency, at least in Baghdad and its southern outskirts, has weakened, with attacks declining since last fall. The only problem is that brutality is one of the tactics that achieved these results.

The Interior Ministry's extrajudicial antics first came to light last November, when U.S. troops stumbled across a torture chamber in Baghdad operated by Interior police. Every week brings more handcuffed and decomposed bodies discovered in garbage dumps, rivers, and hastily dug pits. "Scores of individuals are regularly detained in the middle of the night and without judicial warrant," a recent report by the U.N Assistance Mission for Iraq says. "The rule of law continues to be challenged by the existence of militias and other groups who continue to act with impunity, confirming an urgent need for the State to assert control over its security forces." But these forces were never the state's to begin with. Unlike the Iraqi army, which operates in tandem with U.S. forces, the police recruit and operate locally, and, until recently, they did so largely free of U.S. supervision.

To rein in the brutality, American commanders have dispatched 4,000 military advisers to work and live alongside police and commando units. SCIRI's Hamoudi, for one, chafes at the interference, claiming the Americans—by condemning abuses at the Interior Ministry and thereby creating a "general feeling that the U.S. and British are biased toward Sunnis"— have strayed too far from the embassy compound. Pointing to comments by American Ambassador Zalmay Khalilzad, Hamoudi says, "When the U.S. or British ambassador intervenes to press against Shia, it is illogical." But there is a logic at work here. Just as the Americans create a buffer for Iraq's Shia by training and equipping their security forces to combat the insurgency, they're also building a buffer for Iraq's Sunnis, who increasingly rely on the U.S. military to keep those same forces in check. In areas like Salman Pak and Tall Afar, the once viscerally anti-American Sunni population has even turned to the Americans for protection.

For a glimpse of what Iraq would look like in the event of a precipitous U.S. withdrawal, one need look no further than Tall Afar, where there *was* a precipitous U.S. withdrawal. Before the Third Armored Cavalry Regiment (3rd ACR) launched its offensive to clear Tall Afar last September, the city, like Falluja before it, had become a horror show. With only 400 soldiers from the 25th Infantry Division patrolling the roughly 10,000-square-mile sector around it, officers say, there simply weren't enough troops to pacify the city. During the Falluja offensive in November 2004, police stations across the province fell to insurgent attacks, and Tall Afar itself fell under guerrilla control. On the western side of the city, tension between Sunni and Shia tribes escalated into open warfare; the remnant of the Shia-dominated police force launched brutal reprisals against the population; and forces loyal to Abu Musab Al Zarqawi moved into the city, mounting their own campaign of atrocities—killing patients in the local hospital, kidnapping and beheading hostages, and forcing children to act as human shields. "I know people at home will roll their eyes," says one American officer, "but Restore Rights [the September 2005 operation to clear Tall Afar] cleansed this place of something genuinely evil."

Police headquarters in Tall Afar is located on the grounds of a centuries-old Ottoman castle, which sits on a large hill in the center of the city. From its parapets, one can usually see the entire city, but it is pouring rain, and even tanks slide in the mud. The castle also houses the mayor of Tall Afar, Najim Abdullah Jabouri, who, until recently, was the city's police chief as well. The mayor still operates as the city's de facto sheriff—a bullet-riddled police vest hangs on the wall of his office. The power has gone out, and it is freezing and nearly pitch-black, but the mayor seems relieved just to be here. Only a few months ago, he says, "Zarqawi was ejecting Shia from the city; and the sky—it was raining mortars. Now, we target the insurgents, not each other." Even today, 3rd ACR has Tall Afar locked down, with tanks on street corners and patrols crisscrossing the city. "The American Army is mediator and judge," the mayor says. "It is a higher authority than any institution in Iraq." So desperate, in fact, is the mayor to block 3rd ACR from leaving that he has penned a letter to President Bush, pleading for the unit to stay. "Our security forces are not well- equipped," he explains. "We are undertrained, nowhere near the situation where we can take care of our own responsibilities."

Still, the violence in Tall Afar has declined sharply. Following Operation Restore Rights, attacks on U.S. forces in Tall Afar dropped from about seven per day to one. At first, the city's Sunni leaders refused to cooperate with U.S. forces, citing the brutality of a Shia commando brigade operating in the area. But 3rd ACR had the brigade pulled back, and it released detainees whom the Sunni sheiks would vouch for. In addition, explains Lieutenant Colonel Christopher Hickey, whose Sabre Squadron operates out of the castle that houses police headquarters, "I knew I needed Sunni police to get information from the population. The Shia police were just inflaming sectarian violence." After pressing local leaders to encourage police recruits, Sunnis began to sign up, eventually swelling an exclusively Shia force of 200 into a majority Sunni force of 1,700. And, as Hickey predicted, intelligence tips began flowing in. The regiment also poured millions of dollars into the city, funding 150 water, electricity, school, and cleanup projects. At the same time, it embedded advisers with Iraqi army and police units. Today, 3rd ACR personnel live among Iraqi platoons and among the population itself, having fanned out across the city and established 29 patrol bases—including directly between the warring Sunni and Shia tribes.

Having melted into a once-hostile population center, the Americans have become an essential part of the landscape here—their own tribe, in effect. Seen from a helicopter roaring above Nineveh province, telephone wires provide the only evidence of modernity among the ancient forts, castles, and clay huts that dot the plain below. In this primitive universe, it's easy to confuse the door gunners, their aviation helmets emblazoned with Superman logos (the "S" actually stands for their unit, Stetson Troop), with actual supermen. Which many Iraqis do: Wedged between tribes of Sunnis Arabs, Turkomen, Shia, and Kurds, a regal and persecuted people—the Yazidis—call Nineveh province home. The Yazidis, who, among other things, don't wear blue, don't eat lettuce, and take a somewhat nuanced view of Satan (their Muslim neighbors have accused them, falsely, of being devil worshippers), initially confused the arrival of the Americans with the Second Coming. An officer at the forward operating base in Sinjar elaborates: "They think that, um, we're Jesus."

The Yazidis aren't the only ones. At a base in central Iraq a few days earlier, two U.S. helicopters taxi to a halt near a C-130. The crew chiefs jump out and guide two rows of detainees, handcuffed and blindfolded, away from the prop blast. A detainee's fate, as I learned last year on stumbling across a similar scene in Baghdad, depends largely on his destination. The idea of prisoners begging to get *into* Abu Ghraib may seem like a stretch, but, more than anything else, they fear being turned over to the Iraqi security forces. They know the Americans probably won't kill them, and that, in all likelihood, they will be released in a few days.

As for the Americans themselves, the soldiers value their roles here just as much as the local population does. Back at regimental headquarters, framed pictures of the fallen line the wall—3rd ACR has lost 42 men during its yearlong tour, and many more have been terribly wounded, including the regiment's command sergeant major. And, yet, contrary to the faux moral posturing of those who claim to speak for the troops back home, when the troops do speak, what they say is invariably some variation of "leave us alone to do our job." The soldiers' confidence in their mission derives in part from a sense of ownership that the Army has about Iraq. While Colin Powell's reported warning on the eve of the invasion— "If you break it, you own it"— applies even as the war grinds toward the end of its third year, for the Army at least, it is equally true that, when you break it, it owns *you*. Having bled so much here, the officer corps cannot entertain the possibility that they did so in vain. Its members truly believe that victory, even at this late date, may be within reach.

In Tall Afar, it genuinely is. To be sure, 3rd ACR, which a Pentagon review of dozens of units in Iraq rated as the most adept at counterinsurgency, hardly counts as a typical unit. There are, to begin with, the officers gathered around the commander, among them a Harvard graduate student wounded here and a Middle East historian who can recite every detail about British operations around Tall Afar in the 1920s. There is the Iraqi-American interpreter who has established himself as a power broker among Nineveh's clans. There is the regiment's self-contained aviation squadron, its gunships baring snarling shark's teeth and its scout choppers having shut down infiltration across the Syrian border. Then there are the soldiers themselves, who benefited from unusual training (devoted largely to counterinsurgency as well as to Iraq's customs and language) and whose professionalism in dealing with Iraqis arguably has yielded more diplomatic triumphs than the combined exertions of every Foreign Service officer in Iraq.

There is, finally, the commander himself. With his raspy voice and shaved head, Colonel H.R. McMaster bears a closer likeness to the brusque officers that Robert Duvall brought to life in *Apocalypse Now* and *The Great Santini* than to the tweedy scholar on the book jacket that made him famous. McMaster's Ph.D. dissertation, which scolded the joint chiefs of staff for not protesting more forcefully Lyndon Johnson's march to war in Vietnam, appeared in 1997 as a book— *Dereliction of Duty*—that became required reading at the Pentagon. A parade of retired generals has wielded *Dereliction of Duty* as a club against today's military leaders, charging them with the same sins that the book accuses their Vietnam-era predecessors of committing. But, if McMaster sees parallels to the civil-military relations of the Vietnam era, he's not saying. When it comes to the operational realm, however, he freely concedes to drawing from the Army's experience in Vietnam. "The important thing that emerges from Vietnam is that the political, economic, and military have to go together," he says. "You have to isolate insurgents from external support. You have to develop security forces. You have to provide security for the population." Which is exactly what he did in Tall Afar, having enshrined the principles of counterinsurgency in his unit's tactics well before the term returned to favor in Washington last year. The press, in turn, has anointed McMaster a latter-day John Paul Vann, and an army of journalists has descended on this remote corner of western Iraq. (A sergeant complains that his soldiers still distract themselves with tantalizing images of Lara Logan, the swimsuit model–cum—"60 Minutes" correspondent, who dropped in from the sky recently.)

In an Army that has spent three years launching big-unit sweeps, relying heavily on firepower and otherwise heeding ground commander Lieutenant General Thomas Metz's admonition not to "put much energy into trying the old saying 'win hearts and minds,'" 3rd ACR has done exactly the reverse. Yet, rather than duplicate the Tall Afar operation in towns and cities across Iraq, the White House's "National Strategy for Victory in Iraq" declares, "Our forces will increasingly move out of the cities ... and conduct fewer patrols and convoy missions." The administration intends to draw down troop levels to 100,000 by the end of the year, with the pullback already well underway as U.S. forces surrender large swaths of the countryside and hunker down in their bases. The plan infuriates many officers,

who can only say privately what noncommissioned officers say openly. "In order to fix the situation here," Sabre Squadron's Sergeant José Chavez says, "we need at least 180,000 troops." Iraq, however, will soon have about half that. An effective counterinsurgency strategy may require time and patience. But the war's architects have run out of both.

Al Yawar, the most powerful Sunni sheik in 3rd ACR's area of operations, cannot grasp this essential truth. So he has invited Colonel Joel Armstrong, the regiment's one-man State Department, to lunch. En route, Armstrong's helicopter and another Black Hawk flying escort wind along creek beds, hugging the desert floor. Eventually, the bleached landscape below yields a surprise: a miniature Versailles. A few hundred yards from the sheik's compound, the choppers set down next to a horse corral. An army of security guards— tribesmen with New York Yankees caps—usher the colonel and his fellow officers inside, where the combination of marble floors, ornate chandeliers, gilded wall trim, and a roaring fireplace casts them all in an orange glow. As for the sheik, despite the robe, headdress, and gold sash tied across his waist, he bears an uncanny resemblance to John Gotti.

He wields a similar power, having, as the colonel points out, "convinced his people not to fight us and be peaceful." The sheik presents Armstrong with a list of detainees he wants released and asks about a paving project the Americans have promised. The local mayor, it seems, has embezzled the funds, and Al Yawar would like the Americans to supervise the project more closely. More than that, he would like assurances the Americans will stay. "The government is not listening to the Sunnis," he explains. The Iraqi army, in particular, incenses him. "They hit and kick people. They are not from this region." By contrast, "The Americans—they are in the middle. They are on neither side. This is why we trust them. But, if the Americans leave, who will I talk to?"

Back at the base after lunch, Armstrong mulls over the meeting. Along with the rest of the regiment, he will head home soon. During his year here, he developed a close relationship with the sheik, and he will clearly miss his Iraqi counterpart. Armstrong shares some of the sheik's concerns, and he shares what could well be the epitaph for the U.S. enterprise in Iraq. "We're only an honest broker," he says, "so long as we're here."

Withdraw Now

"The invasion of Iraq may well turn out to be the greatest strategic disaster in us history. And the longer America stays, the worse it will be."

WILLIAM ODOM

Until Congressman John Murtha's call this fall for a pull-out from Iraq, there was little serious public debate in the United States about whether it makes sense to continue a struggle that had been launched unwisely. Belatedly, that seems to be changing.

The Bush administration responded quickly to the Pennsylvania Democrat's challenge with a speech by the president at the US Naval Academy at the end of November, and with the release of a document entitled *A National Strategy for Victory in Iraq.* Neither the speech nor the strategy document indicated a significant change of course. Both appeared to suggest that President George W. Bush will continue to dig deeper into the hole he has created. The arguments trotted out for "staying the course" are the same ones we have long heard from the White House and the Defense Department.

A subtle reading of the administration's response might lead one to see it as the beginning of the end—a cover for a failed strategy by progressively redefining "victory" in Iraq to such a low standard that withdrawal seems acceptable. At this point, however, the former reading, suggesting intent to dig even deeper, seems the more plausible.

It never made sense to invade Iraq, and the longer US forces stay there, the greater the damage to America's interests. The war was and remains in the interest of Al Qaeda and Iran, both longtime enemies of Saddam Hussein. It has detracted from America's pursuit of Al Qaeda, and it has nearly destroyed the Atlantic alliance. From enjoying incredibly strong worldwide support in the fall of 2001 the United States has sunk to a new low in its standing in the world.

Darkness at the Tunnel's End

Supporters of the current policy offer a long list of justifications, most of which consist of dire predictions about what would transpire if the United States withdraws from Iraq. Yet most of these warnings—of civil conflict, lost US credibility, bolstered terrorists, hampered democracy, inadequate security, regional instability, and the like—already have come true. And others may come to pass no matter how long American forces remain in Iraq. I believe a much stronger case can be made that

an early withdrawal will not make the situation all that much worse, and in some regards will improve it.

Consider the danger of leaving a civil war in the aftermath of an American withdrawal. The Iraqis, in fact, are already fighting Iraqis. Insurgents have killed far more Iraqis than Americans. This is civil war. The United States created a civil war when it invaded; it cannot prevent a civil war by staying. As for American credibility: What will happen to it if the course the administration is pursuing proves a major strategic disaster? Would it not be better for America's long-term standing to withdraw earlier than later in this event?

Proponents of staying the course argue that withdrawal will embolden the insurgency and cripple the move toward democracy. There is no question the insurgents or other anti-American parties will take over the government once the United States leaves. But that will happen no matter how long the United States stays in Iraq. Any government capable of holding power there will be anti-American, because the Iraqi people are increasingly becoming anti-American.

The United States will not leave behind a liberal, constitutional democracy in Iraq no matter how long it stays. Holding elections is easy. It is impossible to make a constitutional democracy in a hurry. President Bush's statements about progress in Iraq are increasingly resembling President Lyndon Johnson's assurances during the Vietnam War. Johnson's comments about the 1968 election are very similar to what Bush said in February 2005 after the election of a provisional parliament. Why should we expect an outcome in Iraq different from what occurred in Vietnam?

Leaving a pro-American liberal regime in place in Iraq is impossible. Postwar Germany and Japan are not models for Iraq. Each had mature—at least one generation old—constitutional orders by the end of the nineteenth century. Their states had both endured as constitutional orders until the 1930s. Thus General Lucius Clay in Germany and General Douglas MacArthur in Japan were merely reversing a decade and a half of totalitarianism—returning to nearly a century of liberal political change in Japan and a much longer period in Germany.

To impose a liberal constitutional order in Iraq would be to accomplish something that has never been done before. Of all the world's political cultures, an Arab-Muslim one may be the most resistant of any to such a change. The administration's supporters cite Turkey as an example of a constitutional order in an Islamic society. But Turkey (which has been known to backslide occasionally) has a decidedly anti-Arab culture.

A Terrorist Training Ground

It is also said that Iraq will become a haven for terrorists without a US military presence. But Iraq is already a training ground for terrorists—having become one since the United States invaded. The CIA has pointed out to the administration and Congress that Iraq is spawning so many terrorists that they are returning home to many other countries to further practice their skills there. The quicker a new dictator wins political power in Iraq and imposes order, the sooner the country will stop producing well-experienced terrorists.

Another argument made is that American training and support are essential to the creation of a viable Iraqi military. As President Bush puts it, "We will stand down as the Iraqis stand up." Yet the insurgents are fighting very effectively without us or European military advisers to train them. Why do the soldiers and police in the service of the present Iraqi government not do their duty as well? Because they are uncertain about committing their lives to this regime. They are being asked to take a political stand, just as the insurgents are. Political consolidation, not military—technical consolidation, is the challenge.

The issue, in other words, is not military training; it is institutional loyalty. The United States trained the Vietnamese military effectively. Its generals took power and proved to be lousy politicians and poor fighters in the final showdown. In many battles over a decade or more, South Vietnamese military units fought very well, defeating Vietcong and North Vietnamese Army units. But South Vietnam's political leaders lost the war.

Even if Washington were able to successfully train an Iraqi military and police force, the likely result, after all that, would be another military dictatorship. Experience around the world teaches us that military dictatorships arise when the military's institutional modernization gets ahead of political consolidation.

The Region at Risk

For those who worry about destabilizing the region, the sensible policy is not to stay the course in Iraq. It is rapid withdrawal, with Washington reestablishing strong relations with its allies in Europe, showing confidence in the UN Security Council, and trying to knit together a large coalition—including Europe's major states, Japan, South Korea, China, and India—to back a strategy for stabilizing the area from the eastern Mediterranean to Afghanistan and Pakistan. Until the United States withdraws from Iraq and admits its strategic error, no such coalition can be formed. Those who fear leaving a mess are actually helping make things worse while preventing a new strategic approach with some promise of success.

Iranian leaders see US policy in Iraq as being so much in Tehran's interests that they have been advising Iraqi Shiite leaders to do exactly what the Americans ask them to do. The

December parliamentary elections have allowed the Shiites to take power legally. Once firmly in charge, they can settle scores with the Baathists and Sunnis. If US policy in Iraq begins to undercut Iran's interests, then Tehran can use its growing influence among Iraqi Shiites to stir up trouble, possibly committing Shiite militias to an insurgency against US forces.

The American invasion has vastly increased Iran's influence in Iraq, not sealed it out, and it is unlikely to shrink as the Shiite majority grasps the reins of government. Would it not be better to pull out now rather than continue America's present course of weakening the Sunnis and Baathists, opening the way for a Shiite dictatorship?

The civil conflict America leaves behind may well draw in Syria, Turkey, and Iran. But today each of those states is already deeply involved in support for or opposition to factions in the ongoing Iraqi Civil war. The very act of invading Iraq almost ensured that violence would involve the larger region. And so it has and will continue, with or without us forces in Iraq.

Yet this does not mean the United States would leave the area. I believe that stabilizing the region from the eastern Mediterranean to Afghanistan is very much an American interest, one it shares with all its allies as well as with several other countries, especially China, Russia, and India.

The Global Balkans

Former national security adviser Zbigniew Brzezinski has called this region the "global Balkans," a name that recalls the role of the European Balkans during the two or three decades leading up to the outbreak of World War I. By themselves the Balkan countries were not that important. Yet several great powers, especially Russia and Austria, were jockeying for strategic advantage there as they anticipated the collapse of the Ottoman Empire and competition for control of the straits leading from the Black Sea into the Mediterranean. Britain and France wanted neither Russia nor Austria to dominate; Germany, although uninterested in the Balkans, was allied to Austria.

From a strategic viewpoint, the assassination of Archduke Ferdinand in Sarajevo in 1914 was unimportant, but it set in motion actions that soon brought all of the major powers in Europe to war. Four empires collapsed, and the doors were opened to the Communists in Russia and the Nazis in Germany as a result.

Many US officers in Iraq know that while they are winning every tactical battle, they are losing strategically.

Brzezinski's point is that the Middle East and Southwest Asia have precisely that kind of potential for catalyzing wars among the major powers of the world today, although nothing in the region objectively merits such wars. (Middle East oil as a "strategic" factor is largely a red herring. Oil producers have always been willing to sell their oil, even to bitter enemies. The Soviet Union sold oil to the "imperialist" West during the height of the cold war.)

Brzezinski calls for the United States to lead the states of Europe plus Russia, Japan, and China in a cooperative approach to stabilizing this region so that it cannot spark conflicts among them. As he rightly argues, the task of stabilization is beyond the power of the United States alone. With allies, however; it can manage the challenge.

After Al Qaeda's attacks in the United States in September 2001, the European members of NATO invoked Article Five of the North Atlantic Treaty, meaning that they considered the attack on America as an attack on them all Article Five had never been invoked before. Moreover, more than 90 countries worldwide joined one or more of five separate coalitions to support the US war against Al Qaeda. Seldom has the United States had so much international support. It was a most propitious time, therefore, for dealing with "the global Balkans" in precisely the way Brzezinski suggested.

Over the next year and a half, however, in the run-up to the invasion of Iraq, many neoconservatives, both inside and outside the administration, disparaged NATO and other US allies as unnecessary for "transforming the Middle East." Because the United States is a superpower, they insisted, it could handle this task alone. Accordingly, we witnessed Secretary of Defense Donald Rumsfeld's team and some officials in the State Department and the White House (especially in the vice president's office) gratuitously and repeatedly insult the Europeans, dismissing them as irrelevant. The climax of this sustained campaign to discard America's allies came in the UN Security Council struggle for a resolution to legitimize the invasion of Iraq in February–March 2003.

From that time on, we have seen most us allies stand aside and engage in schadenfreude over America's painful bog-down in Iraq. Winston Churchill's glib observation that "the only thing worse than having allies is having none" was once again vindicated.

The Wrong Strategy

Two areas of inquiry follow naturally from this background. First, how could the United States induce its allies to join its efforts in Iraq now? Why should they put troops in Iraq and suffer the pain with Americans? Could Washington seriously expect them to do so? Second, is remaining in Iraq the best strategy for a coalition of major states to stabilize the region? Would a large NATO coalition of force plus some from India, Japan, and China enjoy more success?

On the first point, there is no chance that America's allies will join it in Iraq. How could the leaders of Germany; France, and other states in Europe convince their publics to support such a course of action? They could not, and their publics would not be wise to agree if their leaders pleaded for them to do so.

On the second point, Iraq is the worst place to fight a battle for regional stability. Whose interests were best served by the US invasion of Iraq in the first place? It turns out that Iran and Al Qaeda benefited the most, and that continues to be true every day us forces remain there. A serious review of America's regional interests is required. Until that is accomplished and new and compelling aims for managing the region are clarified, continuing the campaign in Iraq makes no sense.

Once these two realities are recognized, it becomes clear that US withdrawal from Iraq is the precondition to America's winning the support of allies and a few others for a joint approach to the region. Until that has been completed, they will not join such a coalition. And until that has happened, America's leaders cannot even think dearly about what constitutes US interests there, much less gain agreement about common interests for a coalition.

By contrast, any argument for "staying the course," or seeking more stability before the United States withdraws—or pointing out tragic consequences that withdrawl would cause—is bound to be wrong, or at least unpersuasive. Putting it bluntly, those who insist on staying in Iraq longer make the consequences of withdrawal more terrible and also make it harder to find an alternative strategy for achieving regional stability.

Once the invasion began in March 2003, all of the ensuing unhappy results became inevitable. The invasion of Iraq may well turn out to be the greatest strategic disaster in US history. And the longer America stays, the worse it will be. Until that is understood, the United States will make no progress with its allies or in devising a promising alternative strategy.

"Staying the course" may make a good sound bite, but it can be disastrous for strategy. Several of Hitler's generals told him that "staying the course" at Stalingrad in 1942 was a strategic mistake, that he should allow the Sixth Army to be withdrawn, saving it to fight defensive actions on reduced frontage against the growing Red Army. He refused, lost the Sixth Army entirely, and left his commanders with fewer forces to defend a wider front. Thus he made the subsequent Soviet offensives westward easier.

To argue, as some do, that the United States cannot leave Iraq because "we broke it and therefore we own it" is to reason precisely the way Hitler did with his commanders. Of course America broke it! But the Middle East is not a pottery store. It is the site of major military conflict with several different forces that the United States is galvanizing into an alliance against America. To hang on to an untenable position is the height of irresponsibility. Beware of anyone, including the president, who insists that this is the "responsible" or "patriotic" thing to do.

The Refuge of Scoundrels

Many US officers in Iraq, especially at company and field grade levels, know that while they are winning every tactical battle, they are losing strategically. And they are beginning to voice complaints about Americans at home bearing none of the pains of the war. One can only guess about the enlisted ranks, but those on a second tour—perhaps the majority today—are probably anxious for an early pullout. It is also noteworthy that US generals in Iraq are not bubbling over with optimistic reports the way they were during the first few years of the Vietnam War.

Their careful statements and caution probably reflect serious doubts that they do not, and should not, express publicly. The more important question is whether repressive and vindictive behavior by the secretary of defense and his deputy against the senior military—especially the Army leadership, which is the critical component in the war—has made it impossible for field commanders to make the political leaders see the facts.

Most officers and probably most troops do not believe that it is unpatriotic and a failure to support the troops to question the strategic wisdom of the war. They are angry at the deficiencies in materiel support they get from the Department of Defense, and especially about the irresponsibly long deployments they must now endure because Rumsfeld and his staff have refused to enlarge the ground forces to provide shorter tours. In the meantime, they know that the defense budget lavishes funds on the maritime forces and programs like the Strategic Defense Initiative while the Pentagon refuses to increase dramatically the size of the Army.

One could justly anticipate that in conditions such as these, the opposition party—the Democrats today—would be advocating a pullout. Yet none were until Congressman Murtha surprised both the White House and his own party by putting things as plainly as I have. Although he has infuriated the administration and terrified some of his fellow Democrats, he seems to have catalyzed a political debate that is long overdue.

Why was it so late in coming? And why are so many Democrats still dodging and weaving on an issue of such dramatic important for the country? Why such an egregious evasion of political responsibility? I can only speculate. The biggest reason is because Democrats were not willing to oppose the war during the 2004 presidential campaign. Former Vermont Governor Howard Dean alone took a clear and consistent stand on Iraq, and the rest of the Democratic Party trashed him for it. Most Democratic leaders in Congress voted for the war and let that vote shackle them later on. Now they are scared to death that the White House will smear them with lack of patriotism if they suggest pulling out.

Aid and Comfort

No one will be able to sustain a strong case for withdrawal in the short run without going back to the fundamental misjudgment of invading Iraq in the first place. Once the enormity of that error is grasped, the case for pulling out becomes easy to see.

The US invasion of Iraq mainly served the interests of three groups. It benefited Osama bin Laden's Al Qaeda, by making Iraq safe for Al Qaeda, by positioning US military personnel in places where jihadist operatives could kill them, by helping to radicalize youth throughout the Arab and Muslim world, by alienating America's most important and strongest allies—the Europeans—and by squandering us military resources that otherwise might be used to finish off Al Qaeda in Pakistan.

The invasion also benefited the Iranians, who had been invaded by Hussein's army and suffered massive casualties in an eight-year war with Iraq. And it benefited extremists in both Palesllnian and Israeli political circles, who do not really want a peace settlement and who probably believe that bogging the United States down in a war in Iraq will give them the time and cover to wipe out the other side. The Iraq War was never in America's interest. It has not become so since the war began.

GENERAL WILLIAM ODOM, a senior fellow at the Hudson Institute, served as director of the National Security Agency under President Ronald Reagan from 1985 to 1988.

The Right Way:

Seven Steps Toward a Last Chance in Iraq

KENNETH M. POLLACK

Iraq hangs in the balance. December's elections once again demonstrated the desire of Iraqis for a prosperous, pluralist, and pacific country. There should be little doubt that the vast majority of the Iraqi people want to see reconstruction succeed. This is the most powerful of the positive factors that could enable a new Iraqi state to overcome sectarian differences and serve as a force for stability in the larger Middle East.

But both the Iraqi people and the American people are growing increasingly frustrated with the persistent failings of reconstruction. They worry that the United States and the new Iraqi government do not have a strategy that can succeed. For this reason, 2006 will likely prove decisive for the future of Iraq: reconstruction efforts must finally begin to show tangible results, or else people in both Iraq and America will lose faith that positive outcomes are even possible. And the brutal reality is that time is running out. A six- to twelve-month window of opportunity may be all that remains before the spiral toward possible chaos and civil war is beyond control.

Iraq is beset by a host of deep-seated problems. In some cases these are masked by superficial aspects of progress. For instance, security has increased somewhat in many parts of Iraq because sectarian militias have taken control there and because looters and petty criminals have been consolidated into organized crime rings. This is not a meaningful improvement, because it carries within it the seeds of its own destruction. While Iraq may seem "safer" for the moment, it is, in fact, less secure for the longer term.

The most damaging reality of all is that the United States created a security vacuum in April of 2003 that it has never properly filled. This has given rise to two related and interlinked phenomena: a full-blown insurgency, largely based in the Sunni tribal community of western Iraq; and a failed state, in which the governmental architecture has essentially collapsed. Thus, Iraq not only faces problems similar to those that the United States confronted in Vietnam—and the British in Northern Ireland, the French in Algeria, and the Russians in Afghanistan—but also many that plagued Lebanon in the 1970s and 1980s, and Yugoslavia in the 1990s. Confronting the problems of Iraq means crafting a strategy that will not only defeat the insurgency but will simultaneously deal with the myriad problems stemming from Iraq as a failed state, one that is at this point held together almost entirely by the American military presence.

The clock may be ticking, but all is not lost; it is possible to imagine a different strategic approach. Over the past several months the Saban Center for Middle East Policy at the Brookings Institution brought together a group of experts on Iraq, military affairs, reconstruction, and democratization to undertake a thorough review of U.S. policy on Iraq. This group, the Iraq Policy Working Group, reflected a wide range of beliefs and politics. It included military and civilian personnel who have served in various governments. Most of them have also had significant on-the-ground experience in Iraq. The group met to try to answer this question: If America can't leave Iraq precipitately, what should we be doing differently to give ourselves the greatest prospect of success? The result is a 70,000-word report on all aspects of Iraq policy, from security to economics to politics.

What follows is a summary of some key points about shifting American strategy to make it more likely that reconstruction will succeed. Solutions to the many problems that the United States faces in Iraq do exist. Indeed, there was not a single problem that the Iraq Working Group addressed—from stamping out the insurgency to reconciling Iraq's warring factions to eradicating the corruption plaguing Iraq's new ministries—for which an effective response cannot be envisaged. The real question facing the United States is not whether there are workable ideas but whether the administration is willing to change its strategy, quickly and decisively—and whether the American people are willing to give these workable ideas the time they need to show results.

1. Make Protecting the Iraqi People and Civilian Infrastructure Our Highest Priority.

There is a large, coherent body of literature on the practice and history of counterinsurgent warfare, and what is most remarkable about it is that it all draws on the same lessons. So does the literature on stability operations—operations that address the problems of failed states. The principal one is that the most important mission of counterinsurgency forces is to provide basic safety for the population against attack, extortion, threat, and simple fear. If the people are afraid to leave their homes—or worse still, if they are afraid even while in their homes—the guerrillas and other forces of chaos have effectively won. The people will not support the government; they will be susceptible to insurgents and extremist militias; they will not go about their normal business; and the economy will suffer, as will the political system. This is precisely what any insurgent seeks to accomplish, and what the Iraqi insurgents largely have done. Consequently, American forces must fundamentally reorient their priorities to make what is called "area security"—protecting Iraqi towns and neighborhoods—their highest concern.

The United States and the Iraqi security forces must focus on making the Iraqi people feel safe in their homes, their streets, and their places of business. This does not mean simply deploying soldiers in defensive positions around Iraqi population centers (although in some cases that can be helpful). It means establishing a constant presence throughout those areas to reassure the population and deter (or defeat) insurgents or militias. Constant patrols (principally on foot); checkpoints; and security personnel deployed at major gathering points—markets, entertainment, religious or political events, and even main intersections or thoroughfares—create that sense of constant presence. Security personnel should conduct searches routinely for any person entering a large facility—a business or apartment complex, a *suq* or shopping mall, a sports arena, etc. Fixed defensive positions, checkpoints, or ambushes can be employed against known routes of attack or infiltration by the insurgents. Key infrastructure must be guarded—with personnel for a single facility; and with sensors, patrols, and quick-reaction teams for pipelines, roads, communications lines, or water/sewage lines.

2. Shift the Strategic Emphasis from Offensive to Defensive Military Operations.

President Bush stated last summer that "the principal task of our military is to find and defeat the terrorists, and that is why we are on the offense." While this is an accurate description of the American military approach, it is, unfortunately, wrong in terms of what is needed. The right formulation would be that "the principal task of our military is to protect the Iraqi people, and that is why we are mainly on the defense." Instead, the approach we are employing in Iraq—concentrating our forces in Iraq's western provinces where the insurgents are thickest and support for reconstruction weakest—means committing the cardinal military sin of reinforcing failure. Such an approach has resulted in failures against guerrilla warfare throughout history. Moreover, it has meant ceding control over much of the populace to the forces of chaos (the militias), which is the cardinal sin of stability operations (the name for operations designed to deal with failed states). Our efforts to "take the fight to the enemy" and mount offensive sweep operations designed to kill insurgents and eliminate their strongholds have failed to work,

and likely will continue to do so, as was the case in Vietnam and other lost guerrilla wars.

Large-scale offensive military operations cannot succeed, and can be counterproductive, against a full-blown insurgency. The guerrilla does not need to stand and fight, but can run or melt back into the population and so avoid crippling losses. If the counterinsurgency forces do not remain and pacify the area for the long term, the guerrillas will be back within weeks, months, or maybe years, but they will be back nonetheless. Meanwhile, the concentration of forces on these sweep operations means a major diversion of effort away from securing the population.

This is precisely what is happening in Iraq. While there needs to be an offensive component to any strategy no matter how defensive in orientation, the offensive component in counterinsurgency campaigns should mostly consist of limited attacks on unequivocally clear and important insurgent strongholds, or immediate counterattacks against guerrilla forces when they are vulnerable after an attack of their own. One of the hardest things for highly effective conventional militaries like ours to understand is that in unconventional warfare, like counterinsurgency and stability operations, the path to victory is to remain on the strategic defensive in the military arena while going on the offensive in the political and economic arenas.

Our efforts to "take the fight to the enemy" have failed to work. Large-scale offensive military operations cannot succeed against a full-blown insurgency. We should concentrate on defense.

The administration's recently adopted "clear, hold, and build" strategy is a step in the right direction, but still falls short of the mark. Of greatest importance, it is being implemented in the wrong part of Iraq (the Sunni Triangle) and so is continuing to draw off forces from where they are most needed, in southern and central Iraq, where the public favors reconstruction but is souring on it because of the persistent state of insecurity. However, even within the Sunni Triangle, the United States is not employing enough troops to meaningfully "hold" areas or enough resources to really "build" there. For instance, during Operation Iron Hammer last September, the U.S. 3rd Armored Cavalry Regiment, boasting nearly 5,000 troops, cleared Tal Afar, but was replaced just a few weeks later by a battalion roughly one-tenth its size. That is simply not enough troops to 'hold' Tal Afar. Similarly, after the Marine reduction of Fallujah, the United States left only a brigade-sized formation there, which has been large enough to prevent the town from reverting back to the control of the insurgents and Sunni militias but not enough to actually preserve security and stability there or make it possible for meaningful economic and political reconstruction to begin.

3. Emphasize Population Security in the South and Center of Iraq.

In a pattern reminiscent of our disastrous early experiences in Vietnam, the American (and Iraqi) military forces have concentrated on trying to capture or kill insurgents and clear out their strongholds in western Iraq, where both the population and support for American reconstruction is thinnest. As noted above, not only is this unlikely to succeed but, in so doing, we have denuded central and southern Iraq of the forces so desperately needed to maintain order, enable the economy to revive, and prevent the militias from taking over. By leaving these areas without adequate protection, the Coalition has left the people there prey not only to insurgent attacks but to crime and lawlessness more generally, which has crippled economic and political revival. It has also left the vast bulk of Iraq's population vulnerable to the militias, which take over wherever there is not a significant Coalition military presence and provide the people the protection, food, and other basic necessities that the Americans and the Iraqi central government have not supplied. In this way, through intimidation or accommodation, the sectarian militias have taken over much of central and southern Iraq, where most of Iraq's population resides.

The security vacuum the United States created after the fall of Saddam Hussein is what made it possible for the militias—which are probably a greater threat than the insurgents—to establish themselves. The only way to reverse this phenomenon is to fill that vacuum.

Not only do the militias distort reconstruction but, along with the Sunni insurgents, they are the force most likely to bring civil war to Iraq. In fact, the militias are probably a greater threat to the future of Iraq than is the insurgency. As President Bush rightly pointed out, the insurgency is itself composed of at least three different primary groups: the Salafi Jihadists like Abu Musab al-Zarqawi's al-Qaeda in Mesopotamia; the last of Saddam Hussein's leading henchmen, who know that the new Iraq has nothing to offer them except the hangman's noose; and a large group of Sunni tribes and others who are much more like the Shiite (and Sunni) militias that now dominate central and southern Iraq than they are like the other two groups. Like the other militias, these groups are fighting because they seek power and control over swaths of Iraq, they fear what the new Iraqi government will mean for them, and they fear the violence of the Shiite militias just as the Shia fear them. Incidents of ethnic cleansing, assassination, and other violence by Shiite militias and Sunni militias/insurgents against one another and against Iraqi civilians are becoming more and more common in Iraq and will provoke a civil war if they are not brought under control.

The security vacuum the United States created after the fall of Saddam Hussein is what made it possible for the militias to establish themselves; the only way to reverse this phenomenon is to fill that vacuum. Very few of the Shiite militias have ever tried to resist Coalition forces when they moved into an area in strength, because they understood that doing so was essentially suicidal. Once the Coalition has concentrated sufficient forces to move back into a population center in central or southern Iraq, it should be able to do so. Then, Iraqi and American forces must remain in strength over time, and in so doing obviate the rationale that drove the locals to support the militia. This is critical, not only to create a basis for defeating the insurgency but to prevent the failed-state aspects from causing the country to spiral out of control.

Once these enclaves are secured, and as additional Iraqi security forces are trained, they should be slowly expanded to include additional communities. This approach, which has been put forward most notably by the military analyst Andrew Krepinevich, is typically referred to either as a "spreading ink spot" or as a "spreading oil stain" because the counterinsurgency forces slowly spread their control over the country, depriving the guerrillas of support piece by piece. The administration has embraced this idea rhetorically, but not operationally.

If implemented properly, a true counterinsurgency approach can succeed in winning back the entire country. However, it means ceding control over some parts at first and taking some time before all of Iraq will be seen as a stable, unified, pluralist state. Nevertheless, it is worth considering that the United States and the Iraqi government currently do not control much of the country, because it is in the hands of insurgent groups or militias. Thus, the strategy is really about *acknowledging* that we can control only part of the country with the forces currently available—and using them to exert our control over the most important parts rather than squandering them playing Whac-A-Mole with insurgents in parts that we cannot control.

The key to this approach is that it "solves" the problem of inadequate force levels, which was one of the original mistakes of the war. The problem here was that we did not have an adequate concentration of forces to secure the country against either the insurgents or the problems of Iraq as a failed state (like organized crime and the militias). The guiding principle of a spreading-oil-stain approach is that it allows the counterinsurgent force to concentrate in part of the country and then slowly pacify the rest, using time to substitute for numbers.

Numbers in warfare are always slippery, but it is impossible to avoid them for planning purposes. For both counterinsurgency operations and stability operations, the canonical figure is that there need to be twenty security personnel (military and police) per 1,000 of the population. The population of Iraq today is roughly 26 million, which would suggest the need for 520,000 security personnel. However, the 4 million or so Kurds who live inside Iraqi Kurdistan enjoy considerable safety because they are protected by approximately 70,000 peshmerga fighters. To secure the remaining 22 million people, then, would require about 440,000 security personnel. This number is the baseline figure for what will be required ultimately to stabilize Iraq. Unfortunately, we are far from that number. At present, the

United States has 135,000 to 160,000 troops in Iraq at any given time. They are joined by roughly 10,000 British and Australian troops, along with a grab bag of other detachments that may withdraw in 2006 and so should not be considered for planning purposes. There are probably some 40,000 to 60,000 Iraqi security personnel in the army, national guard, police force, and other units that are capable of participating in security operations in a meaningful way. This yields a total of 185,000 to 230,000 Coalition security personnel, a force that should be capable of securing a population of 9 million to 11.5 million, or about half of Iraq's population outside Kurdistan.

If the United States and the Iraqi government were to begin with only this baseline of troops and were to employ a traditional counterinsurgency strategy, withdrawing most of their forces from those areas of Iraq most opposed to reconstruction and instead concentrating the troops and resources on areas of high importance and high support for reconstruction, its starting oil stain could encompass Baghdad, all of central Iraq, and a significant portion of southern Iraq, with a smaller "economy of force" presence in northwest Iraq to prevent the situation there from deteriorating. Different strategists might draw the oil stain differently, but that is a very big area to start with and would allow the further pacification of the rest of Iraq within a number of years.

4. Train Iraqi Forces Properly. A Showy "Acceleration" Is Worse Than Useless.

The single greatest problem with all American efforts to train a new Iraqi military has been (and to some extent, continues to be) political pressure to quickly produce more trained Iraqi units in order to "show progress" in Iraq. This has been disastrous. The first training program instituted by Major General Paul Eaton's team was a perfectly reasonable one, and could have achieved its objectives had the Bush administration not demanded that Eaton both speed up the training course and increase the numbers of Iraqis trained. Even today, both the administration and its critics continue to press for *accelerated* training—meaning getting people through the training pipeline in shorter amounts of time—and a more rapid deployment of Iraqi forces to take over for American soldiers.

This is the worst approach we could take. The quality of Iraqi forces is far more important than their quantity if our goal is for the Iraqis to shoulder a greater and greater share of the burden of securing their country. The only way to produce troops sufficiently capable of doing so is to give them the time, in both formal and informal training, to develop such quality.

Like all new military units, Iraqi formations, even after their formal training is completed, need time to further jell. Unit cohesion starts to be formed in training, but it is inevitably tested by the first operations that a formation undertakes and can really emerge only in an operational environment—and only if the unit survives its early experiences. So, too, with the confidence of Iraqi recruits, and with the leadership skills of their officers.

What's more, the process of vetting—weeding out those unsuited for the tasks at hand or those working for the enemy—is a lengthy one, and it is not unusual for soldiers and officers to do well in training but fail once placed in actual combat situations. Therefore, Iraqi troops not only need longer periods of formal training; they desperately need longer periods of informal training in the kind of permissive conditions that will enable them to learn and bond without being thrown into high-intensity combat.

The United States believed, at least twice since the fall of Baghdad, that it had adequately trained and prepared Iraqi security forces only to have them collapse in combat. In April of 2004, roughly half of the security forces in southern and central Iraq melted away when confronted by the revolt of Muqtada al-Sadr's Mahdi Army. Similarly, in November of 2004, coalition personnel believed that the Iraqi security forces around Mosul were doing fine: they had gone through the existing training programs, were deployed in and around the city, and seemed to be doing an excellent job maintaining law and order. However, that month, Sunni insurgents mounted a series of major attacks, and all but one battalion of these Iraqi security forces evaporated.

The nagging question plaguing Iraq's security forces is, how can we be sure that this latest force, which also seems to be fully capable and participating in combat operations, does not fall apart like its predecessors in southern and central Iraq in April of 2004 and around Mosul in November of 2004? The only answer to that question is time. The more time we give Iraqi formations to train, conduct exercises, and operate first in conditions that favor success, the more likely they will be to survive the test of real combat.

5. Create a Unified Command Structure.

This is another well-known lesson that the United States continues to ignore. First, there needs to be a single "campaign chief" heading the entire effort. That person should have complete control over both the civilian and military sides of the American effort. There are arguments as to why that person should be from the military, but equally good ones as to why he or she should be a civilian. The historical evidence is equally mixed, but what it suggests is that the personality and skills of the individual are far more important than where he or she comes from. This campaign chief should have the authority and purview of something like a Roman proconsul, and be capable of making executive decisions on all matters to achieve the goal.

If America does not begin to get things right—and this means making sweeping changes to our approach—within the next few months, we face the prospect of a vicious cycle propelling Iraq toward full-blown civil war.

Beneath that campaign chief and his or her deputy there must be a fully integrated chain of command. Every division, brigade, and battalion must be part of it, as should the personnel of every civilian agency in country. Ideally the United States would create reconstruction committees at every level of the chain of command, and these committees would bring together, at a minimum, the relevant military commander, the relevant State Department officer, a USAID official, and an intelligence officer, and their Iraqi counterparts. At present, American military personnel are often the only Americans in any given town or neighborhood in Iraq. They have neither the skills, the resources, nor the time to spend on aid contracts, political negotiations, engineering projects, and the like. These are jobs that should be handled by civilian agencies, but because those personnel are not present outside the Green Zone, their jobs fall on the shoulders of the military. Military officers have risen admirably to that challenge, but it is one they should not have to bear.

The administration's nascent plan to deploy Provincial Reconstruction Teams to Iraq has some merit, but is by no means enough, because it will not erect an integrated hierarchy reaching from the bottom to the top of Iraqi society. The PRTs in Iraq rely too heavily on military personnel and so are better suited to helping with security-sector than civilian-sector reforms. More important, PRTs are teams that work with local Iraqi officials; they are not a hierarchy that integrates the reconstruction effort both horizontally and vertically, which is what Iraq desperately needs.

6. Decentralize Power and Oil Revenues.

Iraq's central government is now fully constituted but essentially powerless. It lacks the resources and the institutions to tackle any of the challenges facing the country. Iraq's ministries are understaffed and eviscerated by endemic corruption of a kind that compares unfavorably even with Saddam Hussein's regime. Iraq's political leaders are consumed by discussions over power-sharing, and often care little about their constituents. The Iraqi capital is incapable of doing much for the Iraqi people, but quite capable of preventing the rest of the country from providing for itself. In the long run Washington must try to build the capacity of Iraq's central government. But in the short term it is critical to shift authority and outside resources away from Baghdad and toward local governments that might be able to start delivering the basic necessities Iraqis crave. The United States can help with this process by expanding its efforts to provide funds directly to local governments to be spent at their discretion, and by pressing the new Iraqi government to transfer control over the country's various police forces from the Ministry of the Interior to local authorities. Without control over financial or security power, local governments will be irrelevant. Washington also needs to help reduce the role of Iraqi ministries by shifting implementation, contracting, and some elements of regulation to local governments.

Iraq's oil revenues must be used both to build central-government capacity and to decentralize power and authority. That oil can be a blessing or a curse. At present it is mostly a curse, fueling the vicious infighting among political elites looking for a bigger (illegal) cut of Iraq's oil revenue. This revenue must be used instead to create incentives for Iraqi politicians to start caring about their constituents, to promote the decentralization of power beyond Baghdad, and to foster the process of national reconciliation by removing oil as an issue to be fought over.

The only way this will be possible is if Iraq switches to a relatively fixed system of distribution that provides funds to several "baskets." Some money would still have to go to the central government to pay for national defense, government salaries, and other indivisible functions, but this will cost a lot less if decentralization is pursued. Other money should be provided directly to local governments, preferably in two forms: one portion divided up on a fixed basis by population in each province and municipality, and another in which varying amounts would be apportioned to different communities based on the deliberations of the Iraq National Assembly. The purpose of this latter pool would be to force Iraq's parliamentarians—who currently pay little attention to the needs of their constituents—to fight for their communities or risk losing their jobs. Finally, yet another basket should provide some money directly to the people in the form of regular deposits into individual bank accounts, which would help capitalize Iraq's withered banking system. Giving the Iraqi people a direct stake in oil revenues would also galvanize them to oppose both organized crime and the insurgents who steal the oil and its revenues. Finally, putting money into the hands of the people and giving them a choice over how to spend it would allow market forces to help lead Iraq's economic recovery.

7. Bring in the International Community.

Although the topic has largely faded from the op-ed pages, there are important roles to be played by the United Nations and the international community. Now that the December elections have ushered in what is to be Iraq's permanent and fully sovereign new government, it is a fitting moment for the United States to begin handing over some of the burden of guiding Iraq's reconstruction to an international body. This would be helpful because the United States is increasingly wearing out its welcome; shifting to a more international approach would allow us to prolong the process of reconstruction longer than would a go-it-alone approach.

Moreover, it remains the case that the United Nations, through its various agencies, can call upon a vast network of personnel and resources vital to nation-building. One of the greatest problems the United States has faced is that we simply do not have enough people who know how to do all of the things necessary to rebuild the political and economic system of a shattered nation. We have not tried to do such a thing since at least Vietnam—if not since South Korea, Germany, and Japan. The UN has worked with thousands of people with the relevant skills in Cambodia, Bosnia, Kosovo, East Timor, Afghanistan, and elsewhere. The ability to tap into a much bigger network is, in and of itself, a crucial virtue of the United Nations.

Is UN participation possible? Very much so, if the United States is willing to address two key problems: security and political cover. The violence plaguing Iraq has driven out most UN and nongovernmental organization, or NGO, personnel, and they are unlikely to return until the security situation improves. Here the answer, once again, is to implement a spreading-oil-stain approach in accord with traditional counterinsurgency doctrine. It is one of the many reasons why this strategy, and no other, succeeds in situations like the one the United States faces in Iraq. If Washington (and Baghdad) can demonstrate to UN agencies and NGOs that there are parts of Iraq that are largely safe—and that their personnel will remain in those safe zones—there is every reason to believe they would be willing to send more help.

The politics might be a bit more tricky. The problem here is that many UN member states cannot or will not participate in a post-conflict occupation that is not under UN auspices. Likewise, many NGOs do not want to be part of something that they see as an act of American imperialism. Their politics notwithstanding, the obvious solution would be for the United States to accept a UN-authorized high commissioner, as we did in Bosnia—a move that senior American military officers in fact favor, precisely because it would help bring in more international personnel and would reduce some of the need for the United States to prevent the newly empowered Iraqi government from doing anything rash. Instead, that thankless task would largely fall to the high commissioner.

The United States must approach 2006 as a watershed year in Iraq. Either America—and it really is America, because the Iraqis simply do not have the military, political, or economic capacity to solve their own problems yet—really begins to get things right or we face the prospect of a vicious cycle propelling Iraq toward a full-blown civil war. For this reason, the gradual, evolutionary changes that the United States has made to its military, political, and economic approaches to Iraq since April of 2003 will no longer suffice. Within the next year—that is all the time they have—Washington and Baghdad must make sweeping changes to prove that they understand the problems and are putting in place new policies that can solve them.

KENNETH M. POLLACK is the director of research at the Saban Center for Middle East Policy at the Brookings Institution. His most recent book is *The Persian Puzzle* (2004).

Contemplating the Ifs

W. PATRICK LANG AND LARRY C. JOHNSON

The war drums are reverberating while warnings about an Iranian nuclear threat are becoming more frequent and dire. The 2005 National Intelligence Estimate (NIE) concludes that Iran, if left to its own devices, is about a decade away from manufacturing the key ingredient for a nuclear weapon. In making a judgment about the soundness of that estimate, it would be prudent to recall the October 2002 NIE on Iraq's WMD capability. That estimate proved to be altogether wrong in alleging the existence of such programs in Iraq. Should we wager that the estimate on Iran is more accurate?

In contrast to the claims made in the run-up to the war in Iraq, the Bush Administration will prove to be fully justified by the facts in the case of Iran. Iran continues to provide direct operational support both to Al-Qaeda and a congeries of other Islamic terrorist groups. Moreover, the regime has carried out mass-casualty terrorist attacks against the United States. Iran played a direct role in the 1996 attack on the U.S. military base in Dharan, Saudi Arabia, and, regardless of how accurate the NIE is, Iran is seriously pursuing the development of the only real weapon of mass destruction: a nuclear bomb. The extensive reporting in the *New York Times* on the contents of a laptop computer obtained in Iran by U.S. intelligence bears directly on the subject. The computer is reputed to have contained a mass of details pointing to Iranian intentions to produce a miniaturized weapon that could be mated with a guided missile. U.S. intelligence officials believe, according to their own sources, that the ongoing Iranian ballistic missile program has now produced a vehicle that has a 2,000-kilometer range and is geared towards developing a ballistic missile with a 6,000-kilometer range. There is a very real and gathering threat from Iran—but the United States needs a viable policy, not sloganeering or wishful thinking, for dealing with Tehran.

The Bush Administration has warned Iran that it will suffer dire consequences if it fails to cease and desist from its nefarious nuclear activities. But Iran's leaders apparently see our warnings as mostly bark rather than bite—and they are probably correct in doing so. An all-out conventional military assault seems implausible to most people, unless all other measures fail. This is why the media, the blogosphere and the think-tank community are rife with rumors about plans to deal with Iran's nuclear program by using commandos or surgically targeted air strikes.

Friends in the intelligence community tell us that civilian officials at the Department of Defense have been pushing aggressively for almost two years to "do something violent" in Iran. But before we embark on another military operation, we must reckon the costs; we must ensure that we are willing to pay those costs; and we should ensure that neoconservative enthusiasts would not be tempted to say—if venturing into Iran becomes a misadventure—that it was impossible to foresee negative consequences. There are a lot of bad things that could happen if we launch a pre-emptive war with Iran. Before we act, we must thoroughly consider what our viable military options are.

A conventional military invasion is out of the question. The war in Iraq has fully committed and stretched our ground military capability. Even the announced "drawdown" from Iraq would still leave us short of the numbers we would need. We do not have the resources, in terms of troops or airlift, to go it alone in Iran. Iran is almost twice the size of Iraq and slightly larger than Alaska. Iranians number over 68 million. A ground invasion would require at least a half-million troops. The number of troops needed for such an operation would dwarf the numbers that we have seen employed in Afghanistan and Iraq. In order to meet the ever-hungry appetite of our commitments in Afghanistan and Iraq, we are already rotating active Army and Marine Corps troops from far distant continents. Brigade Combat Teams of the divisions in Europe and Korea have already served rotational tours of combat duty. The ability of the National Guard and Marine Reserve to sustain deployments is rapidly being exhausted both institutionally and politically.

Realistically, a conventional invasion would require a large ground force requiring many new brigade-sized units. The administration could try to use leadership cadres from existing forces to command new private soldiers, but obtaining that mass of soldiers would require bringing back the draft. In our opinion, that requirement effectively cancels out the possibility of a ground invasion of Iran. Unless John Bolton, the U.S. ambassador to the United Nations, persuades his Russian and Chinese colleagues at the UN to call for a blue-helmeted invasion or NATO decides to take part, count out the option of a ground operation. Public opinion in Europe, which fails to account for the gathering Iranian threat, would almost certainly preclude military action by NATO.

Commandos and Air Raids

What about the much-discussed commando-attack option? Such an approach might entail simultaneous Army Ranger, Special Forces and airborne troop raids on Iran's nuclear facilities. In addition, Marine units that could be helicoptered in from ships in the Persian Gulf could presumably attack targets close to sea. This would involve perhaps a thousand men and many aircraft.

With such an attack, we should not indulge visions of anything like *The Guns of Navarone* or *Where Eagles Dare*. Iran's nuclear program involves a large complex of facilities scattered over an immense area, deep within a country that would not welcome our men. A commando option might sound good at first glance, ignoring the fact that Iran is a large, hostile country. The recent elections demonstrate convincingly that there are literally millions of people in Iran just waiting for an opportunity to help the "authorities" hunt down a commando force. There is no equivalent of the French Maquis waiting to act as guides and provide shelter.

Moreover, the United States does not possess the assets needed to conduct a true attack by infiltration on these targets, since we have nothing like the needed number of Special Forces soldiers or CIA operatives with the language, regional or cultural training needed to successfully operate behind Iranian lines. We haven't exactly been producing large numbers of commandos with a perfect command of Farsi, and this type of mission is too risky and complicated to be entrusted to hastily recruited bands of Iranian exiles.

Complicating matters is the fact that Iran's many nuclear facilities spread around the country are hardened and defended against attack. Commando and light forces could, conceivably, at least partially destroy those targets, but there is also the looming possibility that the raids would fail to significantly impair Iran's nuclear capability and that we would encounter difficulties in extracting our forces. This is not a suitable target set for special-operations forces. Iran might gain leverage by seizing U.S. troops; moreover, the probability of large numbers of casualties make this an unsuitable mission for Special Forces, Rangers or airborne troops.

A worthwhile air campaign would require a massive Air Force and Navy effort, involving about a thousand aircraft and cruise-missile strike sorties (one trip by one aircraft for the use of one missile), launched from platforms redeployed all over the planet. Air strikes come with the risk of downed pilots. Although combat search and rescue units would be deployed, their ability to operate may be constrained by Iran's defenses. Iran still has an air force and has had more than 15 years to study U.S. air-warfare tactics from its ringside seat on the border of Iraq.

More positively, America's technically oriented intelligence agencies are well suited to draw on existing data to target Iran's nuclear facilities. The United States could attack facilities with nuclear weapons at a fraction of the effort and cost of conventional raids, but the rational among us know that option will not be exercised. In attacking the Iranian nuclear program, we would be seeking to prevent the destabilizing use of nuclear weapons. The last thing we would want to do is use them ourselves and contribute to the destabilization.

The Israeli Mirage

Faced with these questions, some are advocating an Israeli solution to the Iranian threat—that is, to stand aside and let Israel launch air action or commando strikes. Those proposals are hardly viable. The 1981 Israeli air attack against Iraqi nuclear facilities in Osirak involved a target much closer to Israel, one set of above-ground and essentially unguarded buildings, and half a dozen aircraft. The 1976 Israeli commando raid at Entebbe, Uganda, involved one aircraft-load of troops in a very primitive setting. The differences in scale and distance between those operations and what would have to be done in Iran are impressive.

Analysts that propose the Israeli option seem to be envisioning imaginary assets. An Israeli operation might achieve little more than angering the Iranians. Their air force lacks the strength, range, tanker capability and targeting capability to conduct such massive and distant operations. The Iranian nuclear target set would require numerous waves of restrike missions after bomb damage assessments were made.

In addition, the Israelis would have to fly over Jordan, Iraq, the Gulf states and Saudi Arabia. All of these countries would object loudly, and they are all allies of the United States. Would the Shi'arun government of Iraq assent to Israeli overflight for such a mission or allow Israel to use Iraqi air bases? Ignoring the Iraqi government is not an option. After all, the current Iraqi government is the sovereign authority. We made it that way. The government becomes more entrenched in power by the day, thanks in large measure both to strenuous U.S. efforts and Iran's maneuvering.

Iran's Recourse

In this atmosphere of building tension, Iran is not going to sit idly by and wait for America to crush it. Tehran has nearly achieved the installation of a friendly government on its western border. While U.S. bases in Iraq could potentially be used to infiltrate Iran with spies and commandos and, more importantly, to support and launch air strikes, those bases are vulnerable politically, not to mention logistically. The supply lines of food, water, fuel and bullets to U.S. bases run from Kuwait to the north and through the Iraqi Shi'a heartland. Iranian intelligence agencies have given Iraqi Shi'a massive support since the U.S. invasion. The Shi'a are well organized and control the country through which U.S. supplies are moved. Islamic militants loyal to the likes of Ali al-Sistani and Moqtada al-Sadr could easily cut vital supply lines.

Iran can also play the oil card. If Iran were attacked, Iran could half its oil exports and thereby immediately impact the global price. It would be unwise to hope that Iran, as part of its national security plan, is not willing to shut down Persian Gulf oil exports. Iran is well equipped to shower Persian Gulf states and oil fields with missiles, or to shut down exports with a variety of other military, terrorist or political methods. At a minimum, a U.S. military air campaign, even if successful in wrecking the Iranian nuclear program, would severely disrupt oil markets for at least six months. Such a disruption would hurt the world economy, not just that of the United States. In addition, there are countries sympathetic to Iran, such as Venezuela, that have indicated they are more than willing to cut off their oil supply to the United States. The United States could find itself facing a 20–30 percent shortfall in oil imports (and that estimate assumes that the Saudi fields are untouched and that oil imports continue to flow unimpeded).

Finally, Iran can play the global terror card. Unlike Al-Qaeda, groups tied directly to Iran continue to have robust capabilities and could cause a lot of trouble over the short term. Hizballah in particular has a significant presence in South America. U.S. commercial and transportation assets there would certainly be targeted, further inflicting damage to the U.S. economy.

The latter point raises an even more intriguing question— what would the Chinese do? They hold a substantial amount of U.S. debt. What happens if they decide to find some other currency to hold instead of the dollar? This could add an entirely new and dangerous dimension to an attack on Iran. Put simply, the United States spends too much and saves too little, and Asia saves too much and spends too little. The Chinese would view a disruption in the flow of oil out of the Persian Gulf as a damaging blow to the U.S. economy. Although the dollar traditionally has been the currency people seek during a crisis, the growing imbalance with China creates new dynamics that could convince the Chinese that holding dollars no longer made economic sense. Under such a scenario, dumping dollars on the international market would trigger an inflationary spiral in the United States.

The scenario of an inflationary spike triggered by China's dumping of dollars may strike some as fanciful. The point for U.S. planners and policymakers, though, is to recognize that war brings unintended consequences that go well beyond the tactical realities on the ground where the fighting occurs. At a minimum, we should contemplate how a pre-emptive military strike in Iran could harm other U.S. foreign policy interests. A crisis in Iran would not occur in a vacuum.

We wish there were a simple, painless, guaranteed solution for persuading Iran not to go nuclear. Iran, for its part, is going to pursue its national interest, and its leaders believe that Iran is in a stronger position if it has nuclear weapons. Unless the world community comes together to isolate and condemn Iran for pursuing this goal, there is little likelihood that Iran will wilt in the face of sanctions.

China's role in this regard is critical. If China continues to do business as usual with Iran, then Iran is likely to continue its efforts to develop a nuclear weapon capability. If that happens, we will face the stark choice of accepting a nuclear Iran or pursuing a military option.

Nuclear Armed and Dangerous

With nuclear weapons in hand, Iran will become the dominant local power in the Persian Gulf. They will have no pressing need to use these weapons, because their mere possession will ensure that everyone in the region, including Israel, will have to deal with them as a major power. We, too, would probably have to learn to deal with them on this basis.

A nuclear-armed Iran would not pose so large a threat to the region if it lacks dependable, long-range delivery platforms. As an interim strategy, the United States ought to consider stepping up efforts to ensure that North Korean or Chinese missiles do not find their way into Iran's inventory. An Iran equipped with nuclear weapons it could not deliver would pose less of a threat. If Iran acquires weapons that it can deliver via a No Dong missile, for example, then Iran's Middle East neighbors, particularly Saudi Arabia, would face a substantive concern requiring a reassessment of regional power alignments.

The impending crisis of Shi'a nuclear power may have at least one beneficial outcome, in that it may create an opportunity to rebuild bridges to the Sunni Islamic world that were destroyed by our misadventure in Iraq. Iran would love for the dispute over nuclear weapons to be cast as a conflict between the "crusading infidels" and God's faithful. This makes it doubly important that our diplomatic effort to contain Iran would draw on the help of Turkey, Jordan, Saudi Arabia, Pakistan, Afghanistan and Egypt.

An Iran armed with nuclear weapons would bolster both the supply source and morale of jihadi forces. The possession of such power by Iran would greatly undercut the goals of modernism and democracy, which the United States has promoted in the Islamic world. The probability of a major war in the region would be greatly increased.

What would be the posture of the United States if the Iranians gain nuclear weapons? Would we maintain forces in the Persian Gulf and in Iraq? How safe would Europe feel, given the ranges of ballistic missiles Iran is developing, plus those that the Chinese have previously sold to Middle Eastern countries (Saudi Arabia for example)? In the end, it may become necessary to confront Iran militarily over its emergent nuclear power status, but the costs would be so high that all diplomatic resources should be exhausted before such measures are adopted.

W. PATRICK LANG is president of Global Resources Group, Inc., a consulting firm, and former head of Middle East Intelligence at the Defense Intelligence Agency. Larry C. Johnson is managing director of BERG Associates, an international consulting firm specializing in money laundering investigations and counter-terrorism. He served in the Central Intelligence Agency and the State Department.

From *The National Interest*, Spring 2006, pp. 26-30. Copyright © 2006 by National Interest. Reprinted by permission.

Index

Index

Test Your Knowledge Form

We encourage you to photocopy and use this page as a tool to assess how the articles in *Annual Editions* expand on the information in your textbook. By reflecting on the articles you will gain enhanced text information. You can also access this useful form on a product's book support Web site at *http://www.mhcls.com/online/*.

NAME:

DATE:

_____

TITLE AND NUMBER OF ARTICLE:

_____

BRIEFLY STATE THE MAIN IDEA OF THIS ARTICLE:

_____

LIST THREE IMPORTANT FACTS THAT THE AUTHOR USES TO SUPPORT THE MAIN IDEA:

_____

WHAT INFORMATION OR IDEAS DISCUSSED IN THIS ARTICLE ARE ALSO DISCUSSED IN YOUR TEXTBOOK OR OTHER READINGS THAT YOU HAVE DONE? LIST THE TEXTBOOK CHAPTERS AND PAGE NUMBERS:

_____

LIST ANY EXAMPLES OF BIAS OR FAULTY REASONING THAT YOU FOUND IN THE ARTICLE:

_____

LIST ANY NEW TERMS/CONCEPTS THAT WERE DISCUSSED IN THE ARTICLE, AND WRITE A SHORT DEFINITION:

We Want Your Advice

ANNUAL EDITIONS revisions depend on two major opinion sources: one is our Advisory Board, listed in the front of this volume, which works with us in scanning the thousands of articles published in the public press each year; the other is you—the person actually using the book. Please help us and the users of the next edition by completing the prepaid article rating form on this page and returning it to us. Thank you for your help!

ANNUAL EDITIONS: American Foreign Policy 07/08

ARTICLE RATING FORM

Here is an opportunity for you to have direct input into the next revision of this volume.
We would like you to rate each of the articles listed below, using the following scale:

1. **Excellent: should definitely be retained**
2. **Above average: should probably be retained**
3. **Below average: should probably be deleted**
4. **Poor: should definitely be deleted**

Your ratings will play a vital part in the next revision.
Please mail this prepaid form to us as soon as possible.
Thanks for your help!

RATING	ARTICLE
	1. Grand Strategy in the Second Term
	2. Hegemony on the Cheap
	3. The Dilemma of the Last Sovereign
	4. The Eagle Has Crash Landed
	5. Strategic Fatigue
	6. Exploiting Rivalries: Putin's Foreign Policy
	7. The United States and Russia in Central Asia: Uzbekistan, Tajikistan, Afghanistan, Pakistan, and Iran
	8. China's Response to the Bush Doctrine
	9. The Fallout of a Nuclear North Korea
	10. America's New Strategic Partner
	11. The U.S. and Latin America Through the Lens of Empire
	12. Politics on Edge: Managing the U.S.-Mexico Border
	13. China's Africa Strategy
	14. The Author of Liberty: Religion and U.S. Foreign Policy
	15. The Tipping Points
	16. Trade Talk
	17. The Return of the Imperial Presidency?
	18. The Truman Standard
	19. In Defense of Striped Pants
	20. The Need for a Military Draft: Protecting Superpower Status

RATING	ARTICLE
	21. Checks, Balances, and Wartime Detainees
	22. Law, Liberty and War
	23. Words vs. Deeds: President George W. Bush and Polling
	24. The Pros from Dover
	25. America's Sticky Power
	26. The New Axis of Oil
	27. Requiem for the Bush Doctrine
	28. Base Politics
	29. The Terrorism Index
	30. A Nuclear Posture for Today
	31. Apocalypse Soon
	32. When Could Iran Get the Bomb?
	33. Lifting the Veil: Understanding the Roots of Islamic Militancy
	34. Iraq and Democracy: The Lessons Learned
	35. Centripetal Force: The Case for Staying in Iraq
	36. Withdraw Now
	37. The Right Way: Seven Steps Toward a Last Chance in Iraq
	38. Contemplating the Ifs

(Continued on next page)

NO POSTAGE
NECESSARY
IF MAILED
IN THE
UNITED STATES

BUSINESS REPLY MAIL
FIRST CLASS MAIL PERMIT NO. 551 DUBUQUE IA

POSTAGE WILL BE PAID BY ADDRESEE

McGraw-Hill Contemporary Learning Series
2460 KERPER BLVD
DUBUQUE, IA 52001-9902

ABOUT YOU

Name _____   Date _____

Are you a teacher? ☐   A student? ☐
Your school's name
_____

Department
_____

Address _____ City _____ State _____ Zip _____

School telephone # _____

YOUR COMMENTS ARE IMPORTANT TO US!

Please fill in the following information:
For which course did you use this book?
_____

Did you use a text with this ANNUAL EDITION? ☐ yes ☐ no
What was the title of the text?
_____

What are your general reactions to the *Annual Editions* concept?
_____

Have you read any pertinent articles recently that you think should be included in the next edition? Explain.
_____

Are there any articles that you feel should be replaced in the next edition? Why?
_____

Are there any World Wide Web sites that you feel should be included in the next edition? Please annotate.
_____

May we contact you for editorial input? ☐ yes ☐ no
May we quote your comments? ☐ yes ☐ no